The Friary Learning Centre

Sport in the Global... the la ✓ KT-425-397

General Editor: J.A. Mangan

SOCCER, WOMEN, SEXUAL LIBERATION

**Soccer, Women and Sexual
Liberation**

SPORT IN THE GLOBAL SOCIETY

General Editor: J.A. Mangan

The interest in sports studies around the world is growing and will continue to do so. This unique series combines aspects of the expanding study of *sport in the global society*, providing comprehensiveness and comparison under one editorial umbrella. It is particularly timely, with studies in the cultural, economic, ethnographic, geographical, political, social, anthropological, sociological and aesthetic elements of sport proliferating in institutions of higher education.

Eric Hobsbawm once called sport one of the most significant practices of the late nineteenth century. Its significance was even more marked in the late twentieth century and will continue to grow in importance into the new millennium as the world develops into a 'global village' sharing the English language, technology and sport.

SOCCER, WOMEN, SEXUAL LIBERATION

Kicking Off a New Era

Editors

FAN HONG
J.A. MANGAN

De Montfort University (Bedford)

FRANK CASS
LONDON • PORTLAND, OR

First published in 2004 in Great Britain by
FRANK CASS PUBLISHERS
Crown House, 47 Chase Side, Southgate,
London, N14 5BP

and in the United States of America by
FRANK CASS PUBLISHERS
c/o ISBS, 920 NE 58th Avenue, Suite 300
Portland, Oregon 97213-3786

Website: www.frankcass.com

Transferred to Digital Printing 2006

British Library Cataloguing in Publication Data

A catalogue record of their book is available from the British Library

ISBN 0-7146-5509-0 (cloth)
ISBN 0-7146-8408-2 (paper)

Library of Congress Cataloging-in-Publication Data

A catalog record of this book is available from the Library of Congress

This group of studies first appeared as a special issue of *Soccer and Society* (ISSN 1466-0970), Vol.4, Nos.2/3, Summer/Autumn 2003, published by Frank Cass

Printed in Great Britain by Antony Rowe Ltd., Chippenham, Wilts

Contents

List of Illustrations

List of Tables

Series Editor's Foreword

The American Sue Sally Hale disguised herself as a man and played professional polo from 1950 to 1965 at a time when women were banned from playing the game professionally. Her ruse was comic – and effective: she tucked her hair into her helmet, flattened her breasts with tape, wore a baggy shirt and sported a false moustache. She was never found out! To add insult to injury, after games she 'became a woman again' and partied with the players as an impressed female admirer.[1] Her dexterity reinforced her deception on the polo ground: 'She could ride a horse like a Comanche and hit a ball like a Mack truck', a sports commentator later observed when she eventually became the first woman to be allowed to join the US Polo Association.[2]

If many women soccer players of 2003 do not 'have everything' as, allegedly in the view of some, befits the modern woman, many now have a great deal more in many countries than she had in the USA in 1950. Sue Sally Hale lived up to Jacobean playwright Ben Jonson's assertion that 'If women have a will they do it against all the watches of the world.'[3] She is a sportswoman for all sportswomen.

It is hoped that *Soccer, Women, Sexual Liberation* will help their cause at least on soccer pitches. It reveals that many women soccer players of the world have some way to go to 'have something', never mind 'have everything'. If 'the future is feminine', as Sepp Blatter has boldly proclaimed, then FIFA's priority should be to ensure that women everywhere have the fullest opportunity to play soccer – recreationally and occupationally. That is a task well worth undertaking.

A note of caution – Nawal El Moutawakel, the first African, Muslim and Arab woman to win an Olympic gold medal, after watching a Moroccan girls' soccer game on wretched cactus-strewn scrub on the edge of a Berber village in the Atlas mountains, remarked: 'I knew how easy it was for me because of the support of my [middle-class] family. But I know there are millions of little Nawals out there who do not have the courage or the necessary support to go out and jog and feel the beauty of sport.'[4]

She makes the strongest of points, revealed so tellingly in an earlier Sport in the Global Society collection, *Freeing the Female Body: Inspirational Icons*,[5] namely, the advantages middle-class women have in the world of modern sport. Writers on women and sport should never 'be blinded by illusions of sisterly solidarity and so neglect destructive class differences associated with modern sport'.[6]

FIFA could do no finer thing than to set as its *top* priority women's classless access to soccer all over the world.

J. A. MANGAN
Director
International Centre for Socialization, Sport, Society
De Montfort University (Bedford) July 2003

NOTES

1. See her obituary in *The Daily Telegraph*, 3 May 2003, 29.
2. Ibid.
3. Ben Jonson, *Volpone* (Corvino), Act II, Sc.III quoted in Colonel Phillip Hugn Dalbiac, *A Dictionary of Quotations* (London: Nelson, n.d.), p.123.
4. See Tom Knight, 'Foundations Laid for A Better Future', The *Daily Telegraph* (sports section), 20 May 2002, S7.
5. J. A. Mangan and Fan Hong (eds.), *Freeing the Female Body: Inspirational icons* (London: Frank Cass, 2001), passim.
6. See Katherine McCrone, 'Class, Gender and English Women's Sport, c1890-1914', *Journal of Sports History*, Vol.18, No.1 (Spring, 1991), 161.

Managing Monsters

J.A. MANGAN

Women's advance in modern sport has been too frequently characterized by condescension and confrontation, denial and defiance, proscription and persistence, and too often, by necessary forced entry and grudging accommodation. This is strikingly apparent from the evidence set out in *Soccer, Women, Sexual Liberation* by women (and men) who have closely examined Africa, America (North and South), Asia and Europe.

There is more than a grain of truth in the assertion that behind the lengthy history of women's slow advance onto global football fields lies attempts at what has been termed 'Managing Monsters'. Any attempted metamorphosis from allocated feminine role to asserted feminine role has provoked ridicule, anger and anxiety – and not just from men!

Women's historical social role has recently been well described:

> The familiar categories of wife, mother and virgin represent traditional roles for women in patriarchal societies. Within their typically subjugated roles, women found ways to project power and to be exemplars of socially sanctioned ideals of womanhood. By contrast, sexually assertive women, who rejected traditional constraints imposed on women, were viewed as dangerous to society.[1]

This lucid observation, written about women in sixteenth- and seventeenth-century Europe, has more recent world applications.

Marina Warner, in her 1994 Reith Lectures 'Managing Monsters: Six Myths of Our Time', considered the threat of the 'serpentine metamorphosis of the monstrous female'[2] and, allegorically, directed her listeners to some overlooked scientific data about the infamous insect – the female praying mantis:

> Eckehard Liske and W. Jackson Davis of Santa Cruz California ...videotaped the mantises' courtship while the insects thought they were in private and found a pleasant ritual dance in place of cannibalism – and with both partners surviving. The researchers say that until now scientists have distracted the insects by their presence and by watching them under bright lights – and that they didn't give them enough to eat.[3]

Warner remarked, 'This most loved creature in the surrealist bestiary of misogynist folklore famous for devouring her mate alive after mating, has been vindicated. Let them alone, give them enough to eat and look! They fall into peaceful mutual post-coital slumber.'[4]

The pleasing outcome of mutually satisfying intercourse apart, Warner's related point, on a human level, is well made: 'Sovereignty over self – not over others; the right to govern one's own person, not the right to govern others ... emancipation through understanding',[5] and she adds for good measure, 'monsters are made, not given and if monsters are made not given, they can be unmade too'.[6]

The struggles of women footballers across the world has involved the persistent 'unmaking' of laughable pseudo-logic, crude stereotype and malicious myth. Illustrations abound in *Soccer, Women, Sexual Liberation*.

Optimism regarding the future is justified. Nevertheless caution is needed in this optimism. One message to be found in *Soccer, Women, Sexual Liberation* is that in a world economy undergoing revolutionary change in many areas, 'regardless of the country examined and regardless of whether per capita income has increased, stagnated or decreased, women have been over-represented among the losers or under-represented among the winners ... economic transformation has led to fewer gains or greater losses for women. The outcome of economic transformation, therefore, does not appear to be random.'[7] In the countries considered in *Soccer, Women, Sexual Liberation*, this analysis holds true. In China – originally host to the 2003 Women's Football World Cup – economic transformation and associated rapid economic growth, post Mao, have had 'two contradictory consequences for the position of women ...'.[8] On the one hand, increased employment opportunities have strengthened the bargaining power of women; on the other hand, gender discrimination in hiring and firing has reduced the status of women ...'.[9] As *Soccer, Women, Sexual Liberation* reveals, this also holds true for Chinese women *in football* – inside and outside the immediate family. Any solution to pernicious and persistent inequality in society, and in football, will depend on economic growth, government policies and the effectiveness of women's organizations. As in the past so in the future, to a significant extent: 'Only if women organize to voice their needs through labour unions, political office and women's organizations will they be able to become equal players in the transformed world economy of the future'[10] *and* in the transformed world of global football: economic progress, gender influence and 'a level (football) playing field' all go together! Progress will ensue but it will not be easy; gender certainties and uncertainties, commercial conservatism, governmental priorities could all bar the way. Certainly, 'in a dynamic capitalist world the rules keep changing'[11] – but, as yet, neither sufficiently fast nor sufficiently advantageous to adequately benefit women. One reason is clear enough. 'As long as the governing ideology of the sports business is determined by the demands of commercialization, athletic activity at all levels will continue to be more reactionary than progressive, *even as women make gains*'[12] (emphasis added). To commercialization, as already made clear, should be added gender resistance and political inertia.

2

There is, of course, as already stated, some room for optimism. An earlier collection in Sport in the Global Society revealed how some courageous women in recent times, 'through a re-evaluation, reconstruction and rehabilitation of their "*bodies*" and women's bodies in general, have influenced and determined, directly and indirectly and to a lesser or greater extent, the status of many modern women of the modern "global village"'.[13]

Within the narrower framework of women's football, *Soccer, Women, Sexual Liberation* has added other women to this iconic pantheon – and in many cases, their contributions are far from complete.

One crucial issue, incidentally, to be confronted in the future with regard to women's football, to a greater extent beyond Europe and North America than within them, is the role government – national and local – will need to play in the twenty-first century: Both state and public sector organizations have an obligation to ensure essential social services including educational and leisure opportunities for involvement in sport. This obligation should be both proactive and reactive. In the latter case because 'its policies, programmes and services compensate for the shortcomings of the private sector. In the former case because it has a civic responsibility to improve health, well-being and the quality of life of those it caters for – in partnership with commercial concerns or independently in its own right.'[14] *Soccer, Women, Sexual Liberation* reveals disquieting tendencies in both Northern and Southern hemispheres to abrogate these responsibilities – in total and in part. It is equally clear that action to halt this tendency will only be adequately made when women obtain a voice – individually and collectively – on state and public sector decision – and have a presence at local and national levels.[15] This must be a priority for the future.

Finally, the rest of the world, as in so many other things, will follow America in the creation of an increasingly symbiotic relationship between culture, sport and commerce. Women must be to the fore in this process. And American women lead the way – the USA Women's Football World Cup is evidence of this.[16]

The so-called 'consciousness industries', it has been noted, now add to the value – economic *and* cultural – of finished commercial products. Nike Air Jordan shoes furnish a perfect illustration. Their exorbitant price owes much to innovative advertising campaigns that have 'both capitalised on, and indeed, accentuated Michael Jordan's cultural prominence'.[17] With the result that, 'Air Jordan Shoes ... furnished with a symbolic value ... effectively transformed a gaudy concoction of leather, nylon and rubber into a prized cultural commodity'.[18]

The importance of this phenomenon to women's football is obvious and is made abundantly clear in *Soccer, Women, Sexual Liberation*. Absorption into the 'consciousness industries' should be an ambition of modern sportswomen, their agents, promoters and sponsors. This will result in increasing wealth, power and influence. For women it could occur more slowly than in the case of men, but it will occur. At the centre of the now intrinsically linked culture, commerce and

3

sport is the media – and in particular, commercial network television – the entertainment industry's driving force in the early twenty-first century.[19] It should not be overlooked that:

> Since revenue from the sale of advertising space represents network television's principal revenue stream (augmented by sponsorship income and syndication fees), the size and composition of programme audiences assumes critical importance; audiences effectively become commodities sold by media outlets to advertisers. Under this economic system, the boundaries between advertiser and programmer interests have been virtually erased. With scant regard for television's educative and informative potential, commercial television networks routinely originate repetitious and bland menus of entertainment-oriented programming (game shows, situation comedies, docudramas and infotainment), designed solely to secure mass audiences.[20]

The good news for women footballers is that:

> Sport is on the menu too, offering a number of unique qualities: It is relatively inexpensive and easy to produce (certainly compared with equivalent programming lasting upwards of two hours); it is practically the only live television genre involving uncertain outcomes; it has a historically and culturally entrenched popular appeal … So, in purely pecuniary terms (and that is primarily what they are motivated by) live sport coverage is an attractive proposition for the major networks.[21]

Even better news is that so-called late capitalism's 'broadening exploitative reach has brought female, ethnic and grey markets into the televised sport universe'.[22] The twenty-first century will most certainly be an era of a 'seductively consumerist union of commerce, sport and television of benefit to sports women'.[23]

However this could have drawbacks. The Olympics, it has been argued, offer a commercial scenario at once pleasing and unpleasing. The Atlantic Olympics saw an NBC strategy to attract women viewers by shaping the Games into a distinctively 'feminine' televisual spectacle. The strategy was both a ratings and a financial success. This gendered Olympic strategy in the crucial 18–34 female demographic segment, saw improved NBC ratings of 16 per cent on Barcelona and 69 per cent on Seoul![24] So far, so good. However, could it be that, as it has been suggested, 'the political potential of an increased female presence in the Olympic spectacle was neutralised by the demeaning way in which NBC chose to represent and engage women',[25] namely, the orchestration of viewers' emotional investment by constructing simulated narratives seemingly freshly evolving before their eyes'?[26]

Perhaps television's capacity for massaging, reconstructing and repackaging sport for maximum audience appeal is the price women's football will have to pay, and will be willing to pay to advance the sport's security. The plain fact is that the media generate the fund that stabilizes, ensures and expands a sport's future – if sports administrators negotiate cleverly enough.

If football world cups are to be a media celebration of soccer womanhood in the way that the Olympics has become a media celebration of Olympic womanhood, with its emphasis on appropriate sexuality, then there are clear implications for appearance, behaviour and performance in the media's projection of an 'appealing' stereotypic feminine spectacle.

Is the NBC Atlanta Olympic coverage a harbinger of things to come in women's football, bringing a 'tear to the eye and bullion to the coffers'?[27] In such a situation what hope has a marketing strategy beyond the media directed at the wider community – a feature of the American Football World Cup?[28] Clearly the future has prospects and perils: there is nothing new in this. What needs to be new is the greater presence of women footballers in places where decisions are made about their game. Prospects may then see at least some of the perils off!

NOTES

1. Annette Dixon (ed.), *Women Who Ruled: Queens Goddesses, Amazons in Renaissance and Baroque Art* (Michigan: Merrill in association with The University of Michigan Museum of Art, 2002), p.119.
2. Marina Warner, *Managing Monsters: Six Myths of Our Time* (London: Vintage, 1995), p.16.
3. Ibid.
4. Ibid.
5. Ibid.
6. Ibid., p.31.
7. See the Introduction by the editors, 'Women and Economic Transformation', in Nhid Aslanbeiqui, Steven Pressman and Gale Summerfield (eds), *Women in the Age of Economic Transformation* (London: Routledge, 1994), pp.1–2. For a detailed discussion of the general global position of women in an era of tumultuous economic change, see the whole of the Introduction.
8. Ibid., p.4.
9. Ibid., p.6. For a further discussion of contemporary Chinese women's economic position, see Gale Summerfield, 'Chinese Women and the Post-Mao Economic Reforms', in Aslanbeiqui, Pressman and Summerfield (eds.), *Women in the Age of Economic Transformation*, pp.113–28.
10. Ibid.
11. Linda J. Borish and Barbara L. Tischler (Guest Editors), Editorial, *Rethinking History*, 5, 1 (Spring 2001), 6.
12. Ibid.
13. See J.A. Mangan, 'Epilogue: Prospects for the New Millennium: Women, Emancipation and the Body', in J.A. Mangan and Fan Hong (eds) *Freeing the Female Body: Inspirational Icons* (London: Frank Cass, 2001), p.237.
14. For a valuable consideration of this issue, see Lucie Thibault, Lisa M. Kikuhs and Wendy Frisby, 'Partnership between local Government Sport and Leisure Departments and the Commercial Sector: Changes, Complexities and Consequences', in Trevor Slack (ed.), *The Commercialization of Sport* (London: Frank Cass, 2003), pp.19–38.
15. Ibid.
16. See Donna de Varona, 'M's' in Football: Myths, Management, Marketing, Media and Money: A Reprise', Introduction, *Soccer, Women, Sexual Liberation: Kicking Off a New Era* (London: Frank Cass, 2003).
17. David L. Andrews, 'Sport in the Late Capitalist Moment', in Slack (ed.), *The Commercialization of*

     Sport, p.6.
18. Ibid.
19. Ibid.
20. Ibid., p.31.
21. Ibid.
22. Ibid., p.10.
23. Ibid.
24. Ibid., p.22.
25. Ibid.
26. Ibid., p.17.
27. Ibid., p.19.
28. See Varona, 'M's' in Football'.

'M's' in Football: Myths, Management, Marketing, Media and Money. A Reprise

DONNA DE VARONA
1999 World Cup Chairman

In the summer of 1999, shortly before China and the United States held a worldwide television audience captive in the enthralling final match of the Women's World Cup, Sepp Blatter, President of FIFA, asked me to write a paper on the approaches which ensured that the United States World Cup Organizing Committee produced the most successful women's sporting event ever staged in the United States. I am pleased to share my insights as to how our tournament, which met with an enormous amount of pre-event cynicism, was finally accepted with overwhelming enthusiasm.

In this foreword about the evolving history of women in sport – which includes adjustments to the original text, as the passage of time has required – I include five themes: Myths, Management, Marketing, Media and Money. These topics, as they relate to organizing a world-class event, are as pertinent today as they were in 1994 when the United States hosted the Men's World Cup and the 1996 Olympic soccer events during the Atlanta Games.

In reviewing the success of the 1999 Women's World Cup, credit has to be given to Alan Rothenberg, who served as the President and CEO of the 1994 Men's World Cup. Alan Rothenberg not only brought Men's and Women's World Cup Soccer to the United States, he was also instrumental in making the 1999 Women's World Cup a model event for women athletes. It can never again be doubted that women soccer players can attract interest, fill stadiums or earn high television ratings. Taking into consideration the differences in the world's cultures, I sincerely hope my reflections will be helpful to future Women's World Cup Championships.

Progress in women's soccer has indeed been made, but still not enough as the contributors to the book *Soccer, Women, Sexual Liberation: Kicking Off a New Era* make absolutely clear. Here I will describe how Myths, Management, Marketing, Media and Money have influenced the growth, popularity and success of girls and women in sport. My reason for using a United States model is that by sharing our experience, it may serve to help others in adapting the concepts to their programmes within the context of their own cultural experiences and realities.

MYTHS

The United States represents an evolution in women's sports that began in the late 1960s and is just beginning to realize its potential. It is difficult to believe that as late as 1986 there were only approximately 50,000 female soccer players in the United States. Today that number is over seven and a half million. In 1970 only one in 27 American school-age girls were involved in sport, but as of 2003 almost one in two participate in school sport.

Just what are the factors that have contributed to the success of women athletes in the United States? The easy answer would be 'money', but in truth it is not the entire answer. The success of women athletes in America has come as a result of hard fought battles waged in the nation's Capitol, legal system, educational institutions and sports governing bodies.

In attempting to create sports opportunities for women during the 1970s, the most tenacious obstacles women faced were myths about women competing in sports. The following myths have presented, and still, present, tremendous barriers to women in sport:

1. Participating in sport will make women unfeminine.
2. Participating in elite sport will harm women's reproductive organs and will result in the inability to produce children.
3. Women do not need to learn about the lessons of life on the playing fields of sport, but men do.
4. Women will never be accepted as real athletes because they are not as strong, fast and muscular as men are.
5. Women athletes will never be as popular as male athletes; therefore, they will not attract audiences large enough to make women's sport financially profitable and viable.
6. Women are not as interested in sport as men are; therefore, opportunities should not be wasted on them.

In the late 1960s and early 1970s, as a response to race and sex discrimination in the United States, a new leadership emerged which challenged the organizational structures and management of sporting systems throughout the United States. Through the process of individual initiatives and government action, changes began to take place, which resulted in newfound opportunities for women interested in sport.

MANAGEMENT: GOVERNMENT LEGISLATION

During the 1970s, athletes, sports administrators, parents and political leaders began a revolution in women's sport that led to the following initiatives: In 1972 Congress passed Title IX of the Equal Education Amendments Act, which forbade sex discrimination in schools that received federal funding. For the first time in history girls and women were given access to elite sports programmes as well as sports scholarships in colleges and universities. As a result of this legislation, nationwide women's elite school soccer programmes grew from a handful to over 1,000. With the opportunity provided, interest followed, and thus college campuses became the ultimate nurturing ground for maturing athletes. In 1996, as a consequence of the changes initiated in the 1970s, women on the United States Olympic team won gold medals in basketball, fast pitch baseball, soccer, team synchronized swimming and gymnastics, not to mention gold medals in all the athletics and swimming relay events.

MANAGEMENT: OLYMPIC COMMUNITY

Educational institutions were not the only organizations transformed through government initiatives. In 1978 Federal legislation mandated a restructuring of the entire national Olympic sporting community. It also became illegal to discriminate on the basis of sex in programmes offered through both the United States Olympic Committee and its member institutions, such as individual sports federations.

MANAGEMENT: PRIVATE INITIATIVES

In 1974 I worked with the tennis player Billie Jean King, the skier, Suzy Chaffee and others to create an organization dedicated to supporting girls and women in sport. Since its inception, the Women's Sport Foundation has been a powerful force in protecting and supporting the rights of women athletes. In an effort to provide training grants to developing athletes, money-raising campaigns were launched. Research projects were also undertaken to dispel the many myths that had prevented women from benefiting from sport. Eventually, important findings from these research projects were used to convince members of the International Olympic Committee to support the inclusion of a women's marathon in the 1984 Olympic Games. Most recent data from this research was incorporated in commercial messages promoting the 1999 Women's World Cup Soccer Tournament.

MARKETING RESEARCH TO DISPEL MYTHS

The findings of the research on women's participation in sport were as follows:

1. Girls and women who participate in sport are less likely to abuse drugs, suffer from depression, and/or engage in self-destructive behaviour.
2. Girls and women who participate in sport are more likely to complete high school studies and strive for higher education.
3. Women who compete in sport are more likely to lead productive and successful lives.

4. Women who exercise are less likely to suffer from osteoporosis and cancer.

These studies also supported the notion that participating in sport is a powerful tool in teaching girls and young women how to become successful in life after competition.

MARKETING: MAKING SOCCER A POPULAR SPORT IN THE UNITED STATES

In the early 1980s the soccer community, inspired by the progress made in all women's sports, initiated development programmes which treated girls and boys equally. These community-based programmes catered for children of all playing capabilities. Recreational soccer formed the foundation of a nationwide youth soccer pyramid that encouraged fun and placed participation above winning. Community-initiated soccer programmes utilized both state school facilities as well as community parks and recreation soccer fields. Often considered a second-class sport in a nation which gives clear priority to American football, elite level soccer was developed in co-ordination with, but also outside of, school programmes. Unlike American football players who are developed almost entirely through school programmes, elite soccer players are also nurtured through special year-round programmes which are organized and supported separately from state school programmes. In the process, soccer has become a model for the creation of an emerging sport from grassroots level to elite level. American soccer now claims over 20 million participants. Therefore, because of the large number of those actively involved, the grassroots soccer community in the United States is financially self-supporting. It derives revenues from dues as well as local sponsors. However, although soccer attracts a large number of participants, professional soccer for men, and now women, is as yet struggling to become a feasible commercial business.

MARKETING THE 1999 WOMEN'S WORLD CUP

Given the historical context of American women's soccer as well as the status of American women in sport, the next question is: How did our Women's World Cup Organizing Committee come up with a plan to market the 1999 World Cup? The answer is that we first focused our efforts on successful women's schemes that had been developed since the early 1970s. We also appreciated early on that our core fan base was different from that of the men's World Cup and from professional soccer. Both factors proved important.

Our mission statement was essentially, 'To make the 1999 Women's World Cup a breakthrough event before the turn of the century to inspire the next generation'. This assertion emanated from the success of the 1996 Olympics when women's soccer as an event within a larger event broke all attendance records for the women's game. Our target markets included the grassroots soccer community, that is, soccer dads and mums, young girls and boys, and teenage girls and women. We also decided that the Women's World Cup, unlike the 1994 Men's World Cup, basically should cater to America's grassroots soccer community.

We knew that during the US-hosted Men's World Cup, American soccer fans were unhappy that they were unable to buy tickets for major matches because those tickets had been promised to the visiting teams and their sponsors. Another reason for their displeasure was that the tickets were too expensive. In October of 1997, the 1999 Women's World Cup Organizing Committee offered early and exclusive access to affordable World Cup tickets many months before they were made available to the public at large, in order to win back the support and loyalty of the American soccer community. We wanted to ensure America's soccer families felt like partners in this overall effort. By April of 1999 over 300,000 tickets (of the 650,000 which were eventually bought) had been sold.

Prior to the World Cup opening match in June of 1999, an escalating press and media campaign utilized our World Cup and Olympic gold-medal-winning soccer players to publicize and promote the tournament. The World Cup Organizing Committee also established a soccer coalition, which marketed the World Cup to its own federation members. Local clubs were encouraged to attend pre-World Cup matches and events. Speeches and clinics were given nationwide to numerous sports organizations in an effort to enlist their support. Youth soccer clubs were encouraged to schedule tournaments around the dates of the World Cup and if teams could not attend world cup matches, soccer-players were asked to watch the games on television. The Women's Professional Basketball League (WNBA), also co-operated not only by promoting the Women's World Cup during their television broadcasts, but the League, when possible, made sure women's professional basketball games did not conflict with important World Cup soccer matches.

In an outreach programme, we created a Women's World Cup Soccer presence at hundreds of youth soccer tournaments nationwide. An official poster contest was held, 'Watch Me Play' inscribed bracelets (the slogan of the event) were distributed everywhere. An official song was commissioned and performed by the popular teen singing sensation, Billie. Soccer clinics for dads and daughters were offered and luncheons and dinners were arranged with men and women in leadership positions who could help or promote the World Cup.

All avenues of promotion and marketing were explored and when possible utilized. The cornerstone of our marketing effort was put in place with a commitment by the ABC Television Network and its cable partners, ESPN 1 and 2 to broadcast all 32 matches to over 70 countries. This pre-tournament television commitment added credibility to the World Cup marketing campaign, which served to attract other prominent partners. For instance, *Sports Illustrated Magazine, Sport Illustrated for Women* and *Sports Illustrated for Kids*, all joined ABC as sponsors of the World Cup and in so doing helped generate even more interest in the tournament. Personal profiles, promotional videos and humorous

11

commercials which featured national team players were broadcast over many networks and cable outlets. These spots were also aired during men's Major League Soccer games. One of the creative commercial spots, which was orchestrated to the song '*Anything You Can Do I Can Do Better*', featured basketball star Michael Jordan mimicking Mia Hamm through a series of athletic challenges. Finally after a round of free throws in which Mia matches Michael shot for shot the commercial ends with Mia flipping Michael on his back in an unexpected karate move. In another television spot, President Clinton was shown calling the ESPN sports information hot line on his official presidential phone to check up on the status of the women's soccer team.

The prestige of the World Cup was also enhanced when President Clinton attended the quarterfinal as well as the final matches at the Pasadena Rose Bowl. As the tournament made the transition from the sports page to front-page news, even entertainment's most popular late night television talk show host requested interviews with America's inspirational women soccer players.

The active participation of all of the members of the US team in the promotion of the 1999 World Cup was central in building up the profile of the tournament. As the tournament began to take hold, the many matches which had been played in the United States against other teams in 1998 paid huge dividends. More stories were focused on international players from visiting teams simply because members of the sports press had met the game's most talented players before the World Cup commenced. As a former athlete I can appreciate just how stressful it was for the athletes not only to market the World Cup, but to compete in it as well. They were true partners: without their understanding and willingness to work with us, the tournament would not have become the breakthrough success we were counting on.

MONEY

In order to stage the 1999 World Cup, The United States Soccer Foundation (USSF), which was established as a direct result of the profits generated by the financially successful 1994 Men's World Cup, loaned the Women's World Cup Organizing Committee its start-up funding. Fortunately, its own language of incorporation to support women's soccer committed the USSF to underwrite this enterprise. Without the USSF's financial help it would have been very difficult for the United States to host the Women's World Cup.

THE FUTURE

Even with the proven success of the 1999 Women's World Cup, there still remain enormous challenges in staging a world-class women's sporting event. Few sponsors are willing to invest the kind of money that men's sporting events readily command. Additionally, women's world cup organizing committees inherit FIFA's official sponsors, which have no obligation to promote or support the women's game. This was certainly the situation with the 1999 World Cup Organizing Committee, which ended up with many 'deadbeat' sponsor relationships that could not be replaced with committed ones. Therefore our financial success came only as a result of ticket sales.

CONCLUSION

In conclusion, those who have influence over soccer on a global basis have the opportunity to keep the momentum of the 1999 World Cup in motion. This means the staging of additional and significant competitions, awarding prize money for World Cup teams and designating women to leadership, officiating, management and coaching positions. Appointments such as these would serve to insure that, and here I quote FIFA President Sepp Blatter, 'the future of soccer is feminine'.

Many wonder what the future holds for women's soccer. In the United States, the future is here in large part because of the success of the World Cup. During the summer of 1999, front-page news and television coverage elevated the game to a new status and attracted enough sponsors to launch a Women's Professional League. In its third year, the WUSA (Women's United Soccer Association) depends on its star players to continue to market the new league in a sporting marketplace that is burdened with a weakening economy and too much inventory. To survive the challenges ahead the WUSA must continue to enlist new sponsors and create a partnership with a committed and prominent television network. Once again America's veteran soccer players have embraced these challenges. Inspired by the thousands who supported them in the summer of 1999 they refuse to believe what the sceptical espouse, that the 1999 Women's World Cup was just a one-off event. Therefore, it is our collective responsibility not to fulfil this expectation; after all, in the beginning few believed in the potential of a women's world cup. Fortunately, from the very first world cup in 1991, packed stadiums and widely enthusiastic crowds have proved disbelievers wrong. In 1999 our tournament had the advantage of a partnership with television, and at last the women's game was played on a world stage, giving soccer fans what they hunger for: enthusiastic, dynamic players who give all they have while competing for the ultimate prize in the world's most popular game. Now it is up to all of us to help women's soccer stay in the spotlight and keep the early dreams alive. The structure is in place for women's soccer to become a tower of strength in the twenty-first century.

While we all look to the future, with regard to past, present and future, it is very much to the credit of the editors of *Soccer, Women, Sexual Liberation: Kicking Off a New Era*, Fan Hong and J.A. Mangan, that they have ensured that a global record of the evolution of women's soccer in the twentieth and the early twenty-first centuries is now available in a readable and attractive book.

1

Women's Soccer in the United States: Yet Another American 'Exceptionalism'

ANDREI S. MARKOVITS and
STEVEN L. HELLERMAN

It is noteworthy that the earliest and most consistent leading powers of women's soccer – the United States and its two fiercest rivals, Norway and China – represent countries in which the men's game has played a secondary role at best, with overall quality and success far inferior to that in established soccer powers such as Germany, England, Italy, Spain, France and Holland in Europe, and Brazil, Argentina, Colombia, Uruguay and Mexico in Latin America, and – more recently – South Korea in Asia. Indeed, it has only been in recent years that the national women's teams of Brazil and Germany have joined the United States, China and Norway at the pinnacle of women's soccer. And the reason is obvious: women succeeded *precisely* in countries where soccer was not completely occupied by men, and thus did not fully constitute what we have termed (in our previously published studies on sport) 'hegemonic sports culture'.[1] Put differently, the men's game did not dominate in the United States, Norway and China at anywhere near the level it has in the countries where the men's game constitutes the absolute core of hegemonic sports culture.

In writing our study for this important volume on women's soccer, we are reasonably certain that the story of women's soccer in the United States features several items and developments that remain particular to the sport in America. This actually bespeaks soccer's unique status in the sports culture of the United States (a topic amply discussed in our previous work). Thus, we feel sure that with over eight and a half million known female soccer participants, the United States is most certainly near or at the top of a list of countries with such athletes.[2] Moreover, beyond the importance of quantitative figures, it is the quality of this presence that renders the status of women's soccer in the United States so different in comparison to its position in other countries. Nowhere else is women's soccer the cultural equivalent of – or even superior to – the men's game, as it is in the United States. Where else would women players be much better known to the general public than men? After all, July Foudy, Mia Hamm, Brandy Chastain – to mention but three stars – are more widely recognized than their male equivalents in the United States, be they of the Alexi Lalas or the Brandon Donovan generation. Moreover, in no other country would it be possible – or even conceivable – for women players to serve as the expert (that is, 'colour') commentators on national television, explaining the intricacies of the men's game to the viewing public, as occurred with regularity during the men's World Cup in June 2002.

This study is dedicated to an analysis of the reasons, origins and present manifestations of this particular American sports 'exceptionalism'.[3] This includes the history of women's soccer in the United States, particularly the various components of the game and their development in recent years. In this study, we concentrate on the game's recreational manifestations as well as its competitive dimensions, ranging from youth league, high school and college soccer all the way to the professional game as embodied in the Women's United Soccer Association (WUSA) and the American women's national team (usually referred to as Team USA). We end our study with some thoughts regarding the future of women's soccer in the United States, especially pertaining to its inevitable interaction with the men's game, and how – if at all – it might possibly contribute toward making soccer and/or women's sports a significant part of America's sports culture.

Though women's sports in general, and women's soccer in particular, have followed a very different trajectory to that experienced by men's team sports – particularly those that have achieved the status of hegemonic sports culture throughout the world (usually soccer) or in the United States (what we have termed the 'Big Three and One-half' of baseball, [American] football, basketball and ice hockey) – some similarity in their respective evolutionary paths are apparent. The Big Three and One-half in the United States (and men's soccer in most other countries) all underwent a process of 'modernization' – mostly during the crucial period of 1870 to 1930 – on their way to becoming primary occupants of the cultural 'sports space'. First, games for children and youths became the venues of recreation for adults, but initially with participation and camaraderie as the only purpose. Eventually, however, the ethos of casual games for exercise and fellowship ('playing for fun') gave way to organized competition with victory as its predominant, perhaps even sole, reason ('playing for keeps').[4] In the United States, this occurred in nearly every men's team sport at every level (including interscholastic and intercollegiate competition). This development coincided with the creation of formal organization and ongoing 'rationalization', regardless of whether or not a sport ever achieved a following much beyond the actual participants on the field or court.[5] However, the history of women's team sports in general – and soccer in particular – diverges from this timeline, as participatory recreation almost always superseded the drive for competition over a long period, at least until the 1970s. This was the case particularly at those institutions which represent a key facet of American sports (and another 'exceptionalism'), as well as perhaps the most important foci for the development of women's sports and women's soccer in the US: the athletic programmes at the nation's colleges and universities (see below).[6]

Once a competitive team sport has achieved a sufficient level of 'rationalization', it may attract some measure of spectatorship and following from modest numbers of enthusiasts. In the United States, sports like lacrosse and volleyball – played by both men and women at the college, semi-professional, and (more recently) professional levels – have progressed to this point and not much further (though each has its relatively small coterie of supporters at various geographic and institutional locales). But with the men's sports of soccer throughout most of the world and the Big Three and One-half in the US, taking the next step proved decisive: charismatic entrepreneurs succeeded in commodifying and marketing the sport, its games, and its participants while institutionalizing an organized structure for the sport and intrinsically attaching the identification of teams to geographic areas or – in the case of college athletics – institutions. Hence, enter the era of professional players, managers, coaches, owners – the protagonists of modern sport culture. We have noted that for a sport to have successfully penetrated a nation's sports space this process had to be completed by 1930.[7] However, in the case of women's soccer (and women's sports in general) in the United States, the modernization process (somewhat akin to that experienced by the Big Three and One-half of men's sports) did not really commence until the last two decades of the twentieth century, at which point the sport's evolution accelerated quite dramatically.

RECREATIONAL SOCCER

Any analysis regarding the proliferation of women's soccer as either recreational activity or spectator sport requires highlighting two key milestones separated by a full generation in time: first, the institution of Title IX of the 1972 Federal Education Amendments to the Civil Rights Act of 1964 (subsequently strengthened by Congressional legislation in 1988); and second, the success of the 1999 Women's World Cup (held in the United States) in attracting significant numbers of attendees and – more importantly – television viewers, along with the concurrent success of Team USA on the field and in garnering a wide and popular following of fans among the general public, many with little or no previous interest in soccer and/or women's sports. The years between saw the popular proliferation of soccer on college campuses, at high schools and as a recreational activity for boys and girls throughout the United States, particularly among middle-class and upper-middle-class families, mostly through participation in organized youth leagues and scholastic athletic programs.

We have argued that much of this acceptance and popularity for recreational soccer (but not, significantly, soccer as a spectator sport, nor its attendant culture as found in most other nations of the world) was directly attributed to – and perhaps the one lasting legacy of – the ill-fated North American Soccer League (NASL) of 1967 to 1985, a professional venture that featured some of the greatest players of the game (most notably and conspicuously the legendary Pelé) and the closest thing to routinized quality first division soccer Americans had seen up to that point. It was the NASL that provided a sort of legitimation for the sport among the American professional and commercial managerial classes who desired a game for their children that was allegedly nonconfrontational, non-violent, 'multicultural', often coeducational, non-competitive, and different from what many of the upscale and educated viewed as the crass and crude milieu of the Big Three and One-half, precisely the very world represented by soccer in most countries discussed in the essays of this anthology.[8] This proliferation of recreational soccer for children 'from above' placed the foci for play almost entirely in organized leagues under the auspices of national organizations, such as the American Youth Soccer Organization (AYSO), United States Youth Soccer Association (USYSA) and the Soccer Association for Youth (SAY), as well as more recently-formed groups that specifically focus on developing 'elite' soccer talent: the Super Y-League and US Club Soccer. This represents an obvious divergence from the ways in which soccer took root in nations where it does indeed represent hegemonic sports culture: 'from below' as the pastime and passion of the masses, where kids (almost exclusively boys) play the game on their own in the streets, playgrounds and sandlots (as each of the Big Three initially took root in the United States and ice hockey in Canada).

By nearly every measure, soccer's recreational surge in the United States has been truly impressive, indeed meteoric: In 1980, the total combined registration for the three aforementioned youth soccer leagues (AYSO, USYSA and SAY) stood at 888,705; in 2001 it had increased to 3,884,423.[9] A breakdown of these figures according to gender is not available, but an estimation of AYSO registration of six to 18-year-olds for 2001–2002 provides totals of approximately 348,000 registered girls and 317,000 boys.[10] During the last two decades of the twentieth century, soccer became the second favourite participatory team sport in the US, trailing only basketball and surpassing baseball by a wide margin. And though the combined totals for baseball and its 'sibling' softball remain far ahead of soccer when participants of all ages are taken into account, this is not the case regarding both the under-18 and under-12 age groups, where soccer comes out slightly ahead.[11]

In terms of overall participation, the increase in the number of female players has continued, while the overall number of male players in the United States has actually declined. According to the Sporting Goods Manufacturers Association, a trade group, in 1987 there were 9.0 male participants and 5.4 females per 100 people. In 2001 there were 8.6 male and 6.7 female participants per 100 people (a decline of 4.4 per cent and an increase of 24.1 per cent, respectively). The definition of 'participant' includes all those who have played some soccer at least once during the previous year. Among six to 11-year-olds, there are 4.9 million boys (a rate of 38 per cent) and 3.9 million girls (31 per cent) who fit this description. In the 12 to 17-year-old category, the participation rate for males and females is considered statistically even (24.1 and 25.1 per cent, respectively), as there are 3.06 million boys and 3.13 million girls.[12] Most impressive is the increase of over 700 per cent in the number of girls playing organized varsity and junior varsity soccer in high schools over a 20-year period: from 41,119 players in 1980–81 to 292,086 players in 2000–01.[13] The exponential rise in the number of American girls playing organized and competitive soccer in high schools and recreational leagues has provided a solid foundation for women's soccer at both the college and professional levels. This is exemplified by the success of the American team at the inaugural Under-19 Women's World Championship in September 2002 in the Canadian city of Edmonton, Alberta, where the US dominated by winning its first five matches (by scores of 5-1, 4-0, 6-0, 6-0 and 4-1) on the way to eventually defeating the host team in the final, a 1-0 overtime thriller.[14] Perhaps the greatest indicator for the relatively high levels of esteem and status attained by youth and women's soccer in the United States is the appearance of the newly-crowned champion American women's U-19 team on the cover of (and in a full feature article inside) *Soccer America*, the sport's premier magazine in the United States. It is almost impossible and unimaginable that a similar accomplishment by young women would ever garner such prominent exposure and coverage in the comparable publication of any country where soccer (as played by men) has achieved the status of hegemonic sports culture.

THE COLLEGE GAME[15]

The roots of women's soccer at American colleges go back much further than the inclusion of Title IX in federal legislation, though it could be said that the 'modern era' of the game begins with Title IX. Physical education for girls and young women started to gain some measure of acceptance at women's colleges and girls' prep schools towards the end of the nineteenth century, though competitive sports for females was still frowned upon in many places.[16] Women were playing soccer on the campuses of the Seven Sister colleges in the Northeast as part of intramural programs and at the direction of physical education departments in the early 1900s.[17] A book entitled *Field Hockey and Soccer Rules for Women*, published by Frost and Cubberley in 1923, indicates acceptance of both sports into the physical education curriculum for girls at the elementary, middle and high school levels, and for young women in college. Both sports originated in Europe and proliferated as recreation for females in the United States. Yet field hockey was by far the more popular, as the United States Field Hockey Association was founded at Bryn Mawr College in 1922, while women's soccer would establish no such overarching organization until the 1980s. Hence, many proponents of girls' and women's soccer during the first half of the twentieth century viewed it as a 'forerunner for field hockey'. Though soccer was played by women on campus in earlier years, the oldest records denoting the game are from 1924 at Smith College, where the women's athletic program allowed and promoted the formation of regular teams and the playing of competitive matches at the 'interhouse, interclass and intramural' levels, while most women's athletics occurred as a part of the 'play days' featured as a component of a rountinized physical education program.[18] The vast majority of women's athletic and/or physical education departments viewed intercollegiate competition as 'elitist', instead preferring egalitarian participation for the sake of physical fitness and recreation for all over competitiveness (that is, teams composed of only the best players) with victory as the goal. Hence, most women's athletic programs banned intercollegiate matches in all team sports; Smith did so beginning in the 1940s, an exclusion that would last until 1971.

The first known intercollegiate competition involving women's soccer occurred in the 1950s between several Vermont colleges, though it is unclear which of these teams were given the status of varsity (where today funding and administration would originate in a school's athletic department) or were considered clubs (funded through student activities organizations). Regardless, the women playing soccer at Johnson State College, Castleton State College and Lyndon State College (where the players did indeed receive a varsity 'letter', making Lyndon State the first school to do so) represent an evolution from informal recreation for its own sake to competitive contests between organized teams from separate institutions. Additionally, women's soccer teams from the Canadian universities of Bishops, McDonald and McGill also participated in matches against the Vermont schools. The team hosting a match determined the rules, since specific aspects of the game were sometimes in dispute, and the players from both squads usually met for a meal or snacks and beverages in the host school's dining room after the game.[19]

By the late 1960s, the National Association for Girls and Women in Sport (NAGWS) – the organization with the most control over women's athletics in the United States – had changed its philosophy to accept and promote competitive varsity programs for women. (The NAGWS would eventually become the Association for Intercollegiate Athletics for Women [AIAW], itself subsumed by the cartel-like National Collegiate Athletic Association [NCAA] in 1982.) As the ethos of women's sports changed to accept intercollegiate competition, the Seven Sister schools added soccer as a team sport, including competition between schools. However, it was Brown University in 1975 that gained the distinction as the first to bestow varsity status on a team at the beginning of what might be considered the 'modern era' of women's sports. Additionally, schools such as Castleton (which granted varsity status to its team the same year as Brown), Cortland State College in New York, Cornell, Colgate, the University of Rochester and State University of New York-Albany were fielding squads for intercollegiate matches. By 1978, the New England Intercollegiate Women's Soccer Association could count at least 13 teams with varsity status representing universities in the northeast, as well as an additional 16 schools fielding teams designated as 'clubs' (and 11 schools with teams of unknown status). That same year saw the first Ivy League Tournament for women's soccer, while by the end of the decade the sport was being played by squads with club and varsity status throughout the nation. The first intercollegiate national championship

19

tournament for women's soccer, sponsored by the AIAW, was held in 1981. The following year, the NCAA – having expanded its domain to include women's collegiate athletics – sponsored the first National Championship Tournament for Women's Soccer. The proliferation of women's sports on campus further accelerated in 1988 with passage by the US Congress of the Civil Rights Restoration Act that widened the interpretation and enforcement of Title IX, making compliance with gender equity regulations a priority for most college athletic programs. Women's soccer has been a particular beneficiary of Title IX, as the sport can provide a college with the opportunity to include at least 20 female student-athletes on a team with a minimal level of expenses for equipment.

The growth of women's soccer as an intercollegiate sport since the early 1980s has been truly phenomenal. In 1982, a total of 103 colleges – representing 10.2 per cent of NCAA member schools – fielded varsity teams for a total of 2,743 players. In 2001, there were varsity teams from 824 colleges (78.6 per cent of NCAA member schools) for a total of 18,548 players. It is somewhat noteworthy that there were nearly 90 fewer men's varsity soccer programs (732) in 2001.[20] However, men's soccer is somewhat more popular with spectators on campus: Six men's teams from NCAA Division I schools averaged over 2,000 spectators in 2001, while no women's teams did so (though Texas and North Carolina both managed to average at least 1,900); and 16 men's squads topped one thousand in average attendance, compared to 12 for women's teams.[21] And the success of soccer for both genders at the college level should be kept in perspective when compared to intercollegiate football and basketball on the men's side, both significant occupants of the American cultural sports space. Additionally, women's basketball is generally much more popular and draws far more spectators on campus (and television viewers at home) than soccer, while women's intercollegiate volleyball also draws more spectators than soccer. However, women's soccer has quite recently developed both a venue and institution that – at least in 1999 – far surpassed all of the attention ever bestowed on any other women's team sport: the Women's World Cup Championship and the American national team, the latter having been comprised exclusively of women who played soccer at American colleges.

THE UNITED STATES NATIONAL TEAM

With females involved in the game at the recreational, scholastic and college level to a degree unprecedented anywhere else in the world, American women became the very best in a sport in which its men – at least until the 2002 World Cup – have remained marginal at best. The United States women's national team has dominated the sport on the world level as its most consistent and successful performer. Only the national women's team of Norway (World Cup champion in 1995, Olympic champion in 2000) has approached the success of the Americans. Team USA won the first women's World Championship in China in 1991, took third place in the 1995 tournament in Sweden, won the first Olympic gold medal awarded for women's soccer at Atlanta in 1996 as well as the gold at the Goodwill Games of 1998, and won the title at the 1999 Women's World Cup, played in the United States, in what proved far and away the most popular event in the entire history of women's team sports, while garnering the highest television audience ever attained for any soccer game in the US, men's or women's. Above all, the 1999 tournament created a moment when for the very first time the game enjoyed a genuine popular following in the United States, as large numbers of Americans truly cared and followed this event to an extent never before experienced by soccer. It did so again briefly during the Sydney Olympics in 2000, when Team USA lost the gold-medal game to Norway, 3-2, in what arguably was the best-played and most exciting match in the history of women's soccer to date.

Significantly, the success of the US national team has directly led to the establishment of the first venue for routinized professional women's soccer, the Women's United Soccer Association (see below). In retrospect, it can be said that the success of Team USA on the field and the success of the 1999 World Cup in garnering the interest and attention of the American public and media put women's soccer 'on the map', carving out a recognizable niche (though one still quite diminutive in comparison to the Big Three and One-half) in the cultural sports space of the United States. Though not getting anywhere near the media attention devoted to either men's sports or individual women's sports, the American national team had drawn decent numbers of spectators to some matches prior to the 1999 tournament, such as a 1997 match between the United States and England in San Jose, California, that attracted a crowd of over 17,000.[22] But it was the 1999 World Cup that engendered a new-found popularity and respect for women's soccer far beyond the confines of recreational activity or a small number of spectator enthusiasts for the college game.

As noted above, all of the United States national team's players are products of the nation's college soccer world, in marked contrast to what is found on the men's side, where the college game has been an impediment to the development of first-rate American soccer players.[23] That women playing team sports at the professional level now represents an acceptable and positive development for most Americans highlights the progress made in the United States for gender equality, and the differences between the ways in which both the game of soccer and sports played by women are perceived in the United States in comparison to most other nations, particularly where soccer and its (overwhelmingly male) culture dominate the sports space. As Julie Foudy, midfielder for Team USA and the San Diego Spirit of the WUSA (as well as a member of the league's board of directors, and president of the Women's Sports Foundation) said so clearly: 'Everyone plays soccer here [in the United States]. Girls are encouraged. But you travel abroad, and the game is considered a man's world in so many cultures. A girl is considered a freak if she plays. We've been to Spain, and jumped into a men's game and been looked at like we were crazy.'[24]

21

The 1999 World Cup of Women's Soccer represents nothing less than a watershed event in the history of both women's team sports and soccer in the United States in terms of attendance, media attention, television ratings, cultural awareness and potential for the future. Total attendance for the tournament topped 650,000, while games featuring Team USA included 79,972 at the New Jersey Meadowlands, 65,080 in Chicago, 50,484 in Foxboro, Massachusetts, 54,642 in Landover, Maryland, and 73,123 at Palo Alto, California. Matches not including the American team did not fare as well, but still drew respectable numbers of fans; for example, 20,129 fans attended Germany-Mexico at Landover.[25] The games were televised on three networks (ABC on regular broadcast television, ESPN and ESPN 2 on cable), where cumulative ratings were respectable, if not stellar: ESPN averaged a Nielsen rating of 1.45 for all its telecasts of the tournament, including a 3.8 for the US-Brazil semi-final (on a Sunday afternoon), the highest rating soccer had ever achieved on cable television. The ratings increased over the course of the tournament, peaking at the 11.4 national rating and 31 share ABC garnered for the US-China final in which more than 92,000 spectators saw the US win in a shoot-out after the teams had played to a scoreless tie (to date the most-watched soccer game ever in the US, including any men's World Cup contests).[26]

Perhaps most impressive of all, Team USA attracted media coverage – which started slowly and steadily increased toward the crescendo of the final, then gradually subsided over the next two weeks – that could easily rival what is routinely directed at the Big Three, and in one month far surpassed all the cumulative media coverage garnered by the top professional men's soccer organization in the United States, Major League Soccer (MLS), in its entire existence over six seasons. Each night of the tournament, late night television talk-show host David Letterman displayed a photo of the women's national team in which all 20 players appeared to be wearing nothing but Late Show T-shirts, while Letterman himself transformed the term 'soccer moms' into 'soccer mamas', highlighting an aspect of women's team sports heretofore avoided or actually suppressed: An image of femininity and wholesome sexual appeal purveyed as a message 'that women can be both athletic and feminine in an endeavor that, in many countries, still carries the stigma that women who play are somehow unwomanly'. Indeed, a side-angle photo of US defender Brandi Chastain 'crouched behind a soccer ball wearing only her cleats and her rippling muscles', drew the attention of journalists, pundits and reporters, as well as many people with little previous interest in soccer.[27]

The players of Team USA were the cover stories for *Time*, *Newsweek* and *Sports Illustrated* the week after the final, and also graced the cover of *People* magazine (with glowing personal profiles on all 11 starters inside) the following week. Public appearances of the full squad after the tournament – at Disneyland, the Women's National Basketball Association (WNBA) All-Star game, on NBC television's Today Show (and outside the studio), at the White House meeting President

Clinton (who had attended two tournament matches, including the final) – all rated high-profile coverage in both the sports and main news sections of nearly all American daily newspapers and on local television news shows, as well as on the ubiquitous Cable News Network (CNN). All these developments bespoke qualities of culture that go well beyond the confines of the (mostly indifferent) public perception usually accorded to women's team sports, or soccer as a recreational or spectator activity. Indeed, the players of Team USA had achieved – at least for a few weeks – the rarity of 'crossover stardom', a status attained by only a few select athletes of the Big Three and One-half. Perhaps most significantly, the US team's most prominent members – Foudy, Chastain, Mia Hamm (at the time considered the best female player in the world; and still the game's most recognizable woman star more than three years later), Kristine Lilly, Michelle Akers (probably the greatest female player in the sport's history), and Briana Scurry (the goalie, and the only African American member of the starting 11) – became nationally known sports figures and heroes, role models for millions of young American girls who now aspire to be players. (Perhaps not so surprising, the women of Team USA also attracted a following among adolescent soccer-playing boys.) Several have netted lucrative sponsorship and promotional deals; Hamm, in particular, is regularly seen in television commercials and magazine advertisements.

It is not an exaggeration to say that the success of the American women's national team in 1999 and the attention accorded the World Cup tournament that year provided the initial impetus for what could conceivably become a long and fruitful history of women's professional soccer in the US and, perhaps, the world. The exceptional success of the American women's game – in notable contrast to the status of their male counterparts, with the possible exception of the 2002 World Cup – fulfils two key conditions essential to making any sport popular in the United States or, for that matter, in most places: attractiveness for being the very best (that is, quality as a means), and attractiveness for winning and making their fans feel proud for being American in a sport where being American had not been a major source of pride and satisfaction (that is, quality as an end). And though a successful Women's World Cup was not a sufficient condition for the establishment of a women's professional soccer league in the United States, it most definitely constituted a necessary one. Such a league was indeed established, beginning play in the spring of 2001.

THE WOMEN'S UNITED SOCCER ASSOCIATION (WUSA)

Women's soccer may present an opportunity to utilize what we have termed the 'institutionalization of primacy' – along with global excellence – that has been a key requisite for the successful perpetuation of any team sport and major league in the American sports space.[28] To wit: it is a given for Americans (as well as for sports fans in the rest of the world) that Major League Baseball, the National Football League, National Basketball Association and National Hockey League all represent the ultimate of their respective sports. Indeed, athletes in any of the Big Three and One-half from anywhere in the world must by necessity aspire to play in these North American venues if they want to 'reach the top'. Yet, the situation for soccer – specifically, on the men's side – has been exactly the opposite, while soccer itself (again, the men's game) is exceedingly diffuse in terms of its institutionalization. Unlike the aforementioned major leagues of the Big Three and One-half, there is no single pinnacle in soccer, but instead several competitive forums and institutions that could make a legitimate claim for primacy: each of the elite four leagues in Europe, the European championship tournaments (annually), or the World Cup tournament (quadrennially).

But in terms of women's soccer, a venue does indeed now exist that fulfils the requisite of institutional primacy necessary for success in the American sports space: the Women's United Soccer Association, in which not only the best American players compete, but also where the top women soccer players from all over the world may be found (when not playing for their national sides). Hence, in noted contrast to its male counterpart, MLS, the WUSA may quite possibly harness both the forces of nationalism and the requisite of institutional primacy to establish soccer on a permanently firm footing in the American sports space. In doing so, it may also redefine how women's team sports and their participants are perceived and valued by American society (and, perhaps, in other nations), while possibly establishing a new female milieu of sports spectatorship, following and affect, expanding and changing the ways in which women relate to team sports as fans. Indeed, for women's soccer to become a permanent feature of American sports as culture (that is, beyond the activity of the participants and the following of a small or modest number of enthusiasts), we have argued that this would have to occur.[29]

The WUSA was founded in the spring of 2000 by John Hendricks, Chairman and CEO of Discovery Communications, along with other high profile corporate investors such as Cox Communications, Time Warner Cable and Comcast Corporation, with an initial stake of $40 million under a plan that the league would be profitable – or at least self-sufficient – within five years.[30] Like MLS, the WUSA is organized and funded as a 'single entity business structure'. Rather than owning individual franchises linked through confederation (as found in the Big Three and One-half in the US, and most professional sports leagues throughout the world), 'club operators own a financial stake in the league, not just their individual team', while player contracts are owned by the league, not the teams.[31] Prior to reaching an accommodation with MLS executives who had their own plans for a professional women's league, the brand new WUSA signed all 20 players from the champion American national team, designating each a 'founding player' awarded with equity shares in the league.[32] Player salaries in the WUSA are currently set at a yearly minimum of $27,000 and a maximum of $85,000, while the league consists of eight teams located throughout the United States (Atlanta, Boston, Carolina, New York, Philadelphia, San Diego, San Jose and

Washington, DC), each playing a 22 game season from April through August. A four-team playoff culminates in the Founders Cup league championship (won by San Jose in 2001, Carolina in 2002).[33] As noted, the WUSA provides the forum for the best of women's soccer from both the United States and around the world. Hence, no less than nine players from China were on WUSA rosters for 2002, while some of the league's top performers – including Hege Riise (Norway), Marinette Pichon (France; the league's Most Valuable Player for 2002), and Birgit Prinz (Germany) – hailed from outside the United States.[34] So the WUSA has indeed fulfilled the requirements for institutional primacy, while also utilizing the public's identification with the success of American athletes on the world stage.

Those affiliated with the WUSA remain quite optimistic for the future, despite attendance figures and television ratings that declined from the league's first season to its second, as expenses have far exceeded the initial $40 million seed, reportedly by close to double at the end of 2002.[35] To cut costs, the WUSA reduced roster sizes from 20 to 18 players and moved its league offices from New York to Atlanta.[36] Average attendance per match dipped from 8,104 for 2001 to 6,957 for 2002; a total of 585,374 spectators for 84 matches in 2002, with a high of 24,000 at RFK Stadium in Washington, DC, on 7 July to a low of 4,002 at Mitchell Field in New York (Uniondale, Long Island) on 20 July.[37] With the exception of specific World Cup matches in recent years, soccer on television has always been a tough sell to an American audience. So it should be no surprise that the ratings for cable broadcasts of WUSA games have been quite low, though the decline of 75 per cent from the first season (0.4 on Turner Network Television and the now-defunct CNN-Sports Illustrated) to 2002 (0.1 on PAX TV) could be viewed as precipitous.[38] At the end of 2002, the league's solvency remained contingent on the willingness of Hendricks (openly and affectionately called 'St John' by WUSA players) to provide the funds necessary to maintain operations.[39]

Two items allow for our own guarded optimism regarding the WUSA: demographics, and the high profile in the United States for Team USA in international tournaments (specifically the World Cup and, to a lesser extent, the Olympics). The WUSA's own research reveals that 66 per cent of its 'fan base' (those attending at least one game) were female in 2001, 70 per cent in 2002.[40] This qualifies as evidence that the league is indeed creating something of a culture of affect and following among those it must attract and retain in order for it (and women's soccer) to succeed at the 'big time' level and stake out territory in the American sports space. Demographic analysis of the television audience for the 1999 Women's World Cup revealed that prior to the final (when the television audience just about broke even by gender) 'women made up only 34 per cent of the World Cup audience on ESPN and 35 per cent on ESPN 2, compared with 39 per cent for ESPN's WNBA games and 40 per cent for the NCAA women's basketball championship tournament'.[41] (Indeed, these figures for women's basketball reveal something of a weakness in the female fan base for that sport.) As we have argued, a fundamental change in the way most women and girls relate to team sports needs to occur – a change from the activity of recreation and participation to a culture of spectatorship, following, and affect (if not exactly the same as what is found in the hegemonic sports culture that is overwhelmingly male, then some sort of variation involving significant numbers of females) – in order for a women's team sport (soccer in this case) to become a truly significant player in the American sports space. Additional good news from the league's demographic analysis is that nearly 30 per cent of those attending its games are under the age of 15, mostly girls accompanied by older family members (more than 50 per cent of whom have an annual income of at least $80,000).[42]

The other cause for cautious optimism is that the WUSA will continue to benefit from the publicity and popularity of the national team, as well as the presence of stars from the national teams of other nations, highlighted at least every two years in the World Cup and Olympics, respectively. Meantime, new up and coming American stars in the league will vie for places on the national team roster, creating additional 'buzz' with fans. But, again, most of these fans will have to be nurtured and developed from a huge demographic group that previously has not generally been receptive to, or active in, 'sports talk': females. But perhaps (and only time will tell) the germinal for the cultivation and development of a new and potentially prolific sports culture now exists, as represented by the fledgling WUSA and its fans.

CONCLUSION

Taking advantage of soccer's unusual position in America's sports space, it has been the women's game that has attained a unique prominence in the world rather than the men's. Indeed, we argue emphatically that this fascinating 'exceptionalism' was indeed the consequence of another 'exceptionalism', namely the absence of soccer as a major part of America's hegemonic sports culture. Put differently, with American football, baseball, basketball and ice hockey completely covering the male-dominated sports space of the United States, the women succeeded in a niche that remained unoccupied by the men. Both situations are quite unique to the United States and as such are related to the primary of all 'exceptionalisms', namely the absence of a large socialist/social democratic/communist party as the main political representative of the American working class throughout the twentieth century. This basically states that America's modernization process was similar to that of other comparable advanced industrial democracies, but not the same. The United States never became better or superior, as so many of America's current detractors accuse Americans of projecting to the world. It just developed differently. One of those differences has been the phenomenal success of the so-called 'new women's movement' that has reshaped American public life to a degree unthinkable even 20 years ago. While women clearly still have a very long and arduous road in their journey towards complete equality with men, they have indeed attained a

26

presence in America's public life that bespeaks a phenomenal progress. One of these realms has been that of sport. And with sport playing such a crucially defining moment in America's public identity, it is certainly no mean feat that women have become integral parts of this formerly virtually all-male domain.

As this study demonstrates, soccer has furnished a unique venue in which women could affirm their respected arrival in America's public space. There is no doubt that women's soccer is here to stay in this space. The only question remains as to its overall weight in America's larger sports culture. To be sure, at the time of this writing it still occupies a relatively marginal position therein. But this need not remain so for perpetuity. Indeed, why should a world that was created by very particular social forces and their interaction between 1870 and 1930 define hegemonic sports culture forever? Change has already arrived and will certainly increase with the passage of time. Whether women's soccer will emerge victorious at the end of this transformative process nobody can tell with certainty. However, what we can indeed assert at this moment is the fact that women's soccer in the United States was present at this process's creation.

NOTES

1. Andrei S. Markovits and Steven L. Hellerman, *Offside: Soccer and American Exceptionalism* (Princeton, NJ: Princeton University Press, 2001). Also, Andrei S. Markovits and Steven L. Hellerman, 'Soccer in America: A Story of Marginalization', *Entertainment and Sports Law Review*, 13, 1–2 (1995–96), pp.225–55; Andrei S. Markovits and Steven L. Hellerman, 'The "Olympianization" of Soccer in the United States: From Marginalization in America's "Sports Space" to Recognition as a Quadrennial Event in American Mainstream Culture', *American Behavioral Scientist*, 46, 11 (July 2003), pp.1533–49.

   A brief description of 'hegemonic sports culture' and 'sport space' are in order: By hegemonic sports culture we mean a social construct that comprises what people breathe, read, discuss, analyse, compare, and historicize in relation to a particular sport. Above all, it comprises the act of 'following' much more than that of 'doing'. As to sport space, we mean a qualitative and quantitative structure that each country and culture possesses wherein certain sports are more prominent than others. Indeed, it is typically a 'hegemonic sports culture' that comprises a country's sport space.

2. US Soccer Foundation, Chicago, Illinois, 'Soccer in the USA, 2002–2003', p.5. The exact figure for 2001 is 8,862,000. This consists of all females who have played the game at least once during the previous year. The figure for American males is 10,390,000; the combined total for both genders is 19,042,000.

3. See Markovits and Hellerman, *Offside*, pp.7–9; 39–51. A brief description of 'American exceptionalism' might be in order here. First of all, it in no way means that Americans are somehow better or more gifted and talented. It is not a normative term at all, but an empirical one that – if anything – bespeaks a clear Euro-centred starting point.

   Following the German sociologist Werner Sombart's seminal work, published in 1906, in which he posed the question why the United States did not have 'socialism' like Europe did, political scientists, sociologists and other social scientists specializing in European affairs have often been struck by a similar observation. Concretely, what were the reasons that throughout the twentieth century the United States was the only advanced industrial democracy that did not comprise what has come to be called 'socialism'? Or put differently, why did no large social democratic and/or communist party become the major political representative of the American working class?

   In pondering this question throughout his own work on Germany and other European countries in a comparative context, Andrei Markovits then drew the analogy of this 'exceptionalism' to that of sport, soccer in particular.

4. See Warren Goldstein, *Playing for Keeps: A History of Early Baseball* (Ithaca, NY: Cornell University

Press, 1989); and Markovits and Hellerman, *Offside*, pp.13–33.

5. Allen Guttmann, *From Ritual to Record: The Nature of Modern Sports* (New York: Columbia University Press, 1978) and Markovits and Hellerman, *Offside*, pp.23–33.

6. See Markovits and Hellerman, *Offside*, pp.42–4.

7. Ibid., Chap. 2.

8. See Markovits and Hellerman, *Offside*, pp.163–9. Greatly flawed as it was, the NASL spawned a nationwide awareness of the sport not previously attained. There is no way to prove a direct connection, but much greater numbers of American youth began to take up the sport as the NASL saga wound down, and the number of participants – including and particularly girls and young women – continued to increase in subsequent years.

9. US Soccer Foundation, 'Soccer in the USA, 2002–2003', p.17.

10. John Enriquez, Registration Manager for the American Youth Soccer Organization (AYSO), personal communication, 9 Dec. 2002. These figures represent an estimate compiled from a total of AYSO team rosters reported for either 2001 or 2002.

11. US Soccer Foundation, 'Soccer in the USA, 2002-2003', p.15. Total participants for basketball: 38,663,000; soccer: 19,042; softball: 17,679; baseball: 11,405. Soccer participants in the under-18 age group stands at 14,972,000, compared to 6,445,000 for softball and 8,119,000 for baseball (combined: 14,564,000). The number for soccer participants under 12 years of age is 8,775,000, compared to 2,742,000 for softball and 4,731,000 for baseball (combined: 7,473,000).

12. 'The Superstudy of Sports Participation: Soccer', Sporting Goods Manufacturers Association International and American Sports Data, Inc., 2002.

13. US Soccer Foundation, 'Soccer in the USA, 2002–2003', p.16.

14. Scott French, 'Déjà vu', *Soccer America*, 57, 19 (23 Sept. 2002), 8–13.

15. Unless otherwise specified, the information for this section on women's collegiate soccer in the US is derived from: Shawn Ladda, 'The Early Beginnings of Intercollegiate Women's Soccer in the United States', *The Physical Educator*, 57, 2 (Spring 2000), 106–12. Accessed through Lexis-Nexis search, Wilson Web: http://vweb.hwwilsonweb.com/cgi-bin/webcl; and Shawn Ladda, 'The History of Intercollegiate Women's Soccer in the United States', (Doctoral Dissertation, Columbia University, 1995).

16. Women were playing basketball at Vassar and Smith colleges in 1892, barely a year after James Naismith, a YMCA physical education instructor, had invented the game. See Bill Gutman, *The History of NCAA Basketball* (New York: Crescent Books, 1992).

17. The Seven Sister colleges are Vassar, Smith, Wellesley, Bryn Mawr, Mount Holyoke, Barnard, and Radcliffe.

18. The term 'program' has been retained throughout in the original spelling as it is a standard term of American college courses.

19. The post-game socializing with meals and/or beverages is somewhat reminiscent of the milieu for the earliest baseball games between organized clubs of middle-class men in New York (c.1845–55) and the earliest games of what would evolve into American football between students from Harvard and organized clubs in the Boston area and, more importantly, students from Harvard and McGill University (c. late 1860s through the early 1870s). In the case of these nineteenth-century contests, the post-game activities were often considered equal to or even more important than the game itself. See Markovits and Hellerman, *Offside*, pp.55–7, 71–3.

20. 'NCAA Sport-By-Sport Participation and Sponsorship: Women's Sports, 1982–2001', NCAA website: http://www.ncaa.org/index.

21. '2001 Division I Men's Soccer Attendance', and 'Division I Women's Attendance', NCAA website: http://www.ncaa.org/index.

22. US Soccer Federation, *US Soccer Federation Media Guide* (1998), p.12.

23. See Markovits and Hellerman, *Offside*, pp.121–7.

24. Harvey Araton, 'A Pioneer in Her Sport and Beyond', *New York Times*, 28 July 1998, p.C23. The contrast regarding the perception of women's soccer in the US and that found in Europe and Latin America has been striking: Most German, English and Brazilian newspapers ignored the 1999 Women's World Cup or ran articles ridiculing it. In Europe, the occasional serious piece was not included in the sports pages, but in the 'human interest' or 'features' sections. German television broadcast only the second half of the US-China final (commencing at 11 p.m. local time), preferring instead to air its usual late-night Saturday soccer talk show featuring an off-season interview with the coach of a Bundesliga club.

25. John Powers and Shira Springer, 'Profits Starting to Add Up', *Boston Globe*, 10 July 1999, p.G12; 'Soccermania Grips US: It's a Sellout for Women's World Cup Final', *International Herald Tribune*, 10–11 July 1999, p.19; *USA Today* (June 1999), p.26C.
26. Bob Herzog, 'Lovefest Continues for US Women's Team', *Newsday*, 14 July 1999, p.A65; and Steve Zipay, 'Women's TV Numbers Join '99 Finals, '98 Series', *Newsday*, 12 July 1999, p.A43. The Women's World Cup final's rating of 11.4 was not far off from Game One of the 1999 National Basketball Association Finals (11.5) and the first game of the 1998 baseball World Series (12.3).
27. Jere Longman, 'Pride in Their Play, and in Their Bodies', *New York Times*, 8 July 1999, pp.D1, D4. When Chastain threw off her shirt – to reveal a sports bra – after scoring the clincher in the final's shoot-out, some speculated that this was either an act of wanton exhibitionism, an instant of 'momentary insanity' (as Chastain herself claimed), a blow for gender equality (as shirt shedding by male players in celebration of a victorious moment is something of a tradition in soccer), or a shrewd and calculated marketing ploy, since the sports bra in question was a Nike prototype planned for mass production. See Richard Sandomir, 'Was Sports Bra Celebration Spontaneous?', *New York Times*, 8 July 1999, p.S6; and Melanie Welds and Ann Oldenburg, 'Sports Bra's Flash Could Cash In', *USA Today* (13 July 1999), p.2A.
28. See Markovits and Hellerman, *Offside*, pp.159–61. Though another American 'exceptionalism', this aspect of American team sports is mostly an outgrowth of their development in relative geographic isolation in the era we have identified as crucial to the establishment of modern hegemonic sports culture (1870–1930).
29. See Markovits and Hellerman, *Offside*, pp.26–7, 179–80, 270–71.
30. WUSA Communications Department, Atlanta, Georgia, *WUSA 2002 Official Media Guide*, pp.6, 8.
31. Ibid., p.21.
32. See Markovits and Hellerman, *Offside*, pp.180–81; and *WUSA 2002 Official Media Guide*, p.32. Nineteen of the 20 players from the Team USA's 1999 World Cup roster play in the WUSA. Michelle Akers retired soon after the 1999 tournament, but was still awarded a financial stake in the league.
33. Paul Dodson, WUSA Manager of Sports Communications, personal communication (19 Nov. 2002).
34. *WUSA 2002 Official Media Guide*, p.34. 'Best of the Best', *Soccer America*, 57, 18 (9 Sept. 2002), 33.
35. Scott French, WUSA: 'Profitable by 2007? Increased Revenues Spark Hope as Attendance, TV Ratings Decline', *Soccer America*, 57, 18 (9 Sept. 2002), 35. Though WUSA officials say expenses have declined by 28%, league founder John Hendricks said that 'the league will have spent, by the end of 2002, $75 million–$80 million in total. (In addition, $24 million was spent on stadium development.)' According to Hendricks, the balance between revenues and expenses was approximately $20 million and 'That would make for revenues of about $9 million in 2002 and $5.5 million in 2001. Doing the math, WUSA investors have lost about $55 million since the league's formation.'
36. Michelle Smith and Dwight Chapin, 'WUSA is Gearing for Seconds', *San Francisco Chronicle*, 13 April 2002, p.C3.
37. Paul Dodson, WUSA Manager of Sports Communications, personal communication (19 Nov. 2002).
38. French, 'Profitable by 2007? Increased Revenues Spark Hope as Attendance, TV Ratings Decline', 35.
39. George Vecsey, 'WUSA Recognizes Its New Talent Amid Thanks for "St. John"', *New York Times*, 25 Aug. 2002, p.SP8.
40. *WUSA 2002 Official Media Guide*, p.170; and 'The Smart Way to Reach America's Families', WUSA promotional kit, 2002.
41. Richard Sandomir, 'Sale of Cup Merchandise Just Didn't Take Off', *New York Times*, 13 July 1999, p.D4.
42. 'The Smart Way to Reach America's Families'.

2

The Game of Choice:
Girls' and Women's Soccer in Canada

M. ANN HALL

On a late summer afternoon, some 47,000 enthusiastic fans packed into Commonwealth Stadium in Edmonton, Alberta to witness the final of the 2002 FIFA under-19 women's gold-medal soccer game. The stadium was a sea of red and white – Canadian flags waving, faces painted and hair dyed in the nation's colours. Canada was playing the United States, having defeated teams from six other countries to reach the final. Despite the partisan crowd and exuberant 'Ca-na-da!, Ca-na-da!' chants, they lost 1-0 in extra time to a stronger American team. For two amazing weeks, this remarkable group of teenage girls had captivated the city and legions of fans. Canadian team captain Christine Sinclair was the tournament's most valuable player and the highest scorer. Media coverage was astounding with extensive daily coverage in the local and national newspapers and games broadcast live on television. The future, most observers proclaimed, was nothing but bright for women's soccer in Canada.

While Canada is known as a hockey nation, it is not particularly noted for soccer. Yet, among active five to 14-year-olds, soccer is a game of choice, ranking just behind ice hockey for boys and swimming for girls.[1] Far more Canadian girls play soccer (28 per cent) than do ice hockey (6 per cent), and the growth during the 1990s and into the new millennium has been spectacular. Of the total player registration in 2002, the number of females was 307,258 representing 39 per cent of the 789,289 registered players in Canada. For the past several years, females have accounted for over one-third of the new registrations each year. If schools are included, there are probably close to two million soccer players in Canada. Although the vast majority of players, both male and female, are youths (under 18 years), there are over 33,000 adult women in Canada playing the game. Ontario, Quebec, British Columbia and Alberta are the provinces with the largest numbers, although the discrepancy between the numbers of males and females registered is often less in provinces with fewer players.[2]

The 1990s and new millennium have brought some remarkable changes to women's sport, especially in North America. One change is the valorization of team sports for girls and women especially at the participatory level, but also increased opportunities for women to make a living playing sport. Another, certainly connected, is the new marketing of women's sport, especially team sports, and the making of female sport stars into commodities. Soccer, along with basketball, ice hockey, softball and volleyball, have gained unquestioned respect, and its women stars unprecedented celebrity. Most see these changes as good for women's sport. This is the story of one such team sport, now known as 'soccer' to Canadians and Americans, but 'football' to the rest of the world.

EARLY HISTORY

In the fall of 1922, a football team of young English women arrived in Quebec City aboard the SS *Montclare*, all set for a tour of North America. The Dick, Kerr Ladies Football Club was named after their employer, an ammunition factory in Preston. Formed during World War I to raise money for the war effort and charity, they were unbeatable and highly popular, attracting huge crowds such as the 53,000 who came to Goodison Park in Liverpool on Boxing Day 1920. The all-male Football Association resented their popularity, and on the pretence that gate receipts were not going entirely to charity, took action to protect the men's game. In 1921 they banned women from playing on FA affiliated pitches throughout Britain.[3]

Across the Atlantic, the touring Dick, Kerr Ladies expected to play women's teams in both Canada and the United States, although organizers were uncertain who they would play. At the same time, the Dominion Football Association went on record 'as opposed to women playing football and will not permit any clubs affiliated with the DFA to play against the ladies' team which proposes to tour Canada'.[4] Were there any women's soccer teams in Canada at this time to challenge the Dick, Kerr Ladies? References are scattered and not easily documented, but there were a few. In Hillcrest and Blairmore, small mining towns nestled in the Crowsnest Pass of the Rocky Mountains, two teams – the 'married' and 'single' ladies – played exhibition games for the benefit of local residents. 'Amazons stage terrific battle', proclaimed one headline in the *Lethbridge Herald* in the summer of 1922, explaining that it was one of the 'most gruelling and keenest games of football by the rivals' this season.[5] There were probably other teams in southern Alberta, because sportswomen in Calgary were indignant when the Dominion Football Association banned soccer clubs from playing against the touring English team: 'If men allow women to work in factories, if they allow them to go in want at times when unemployed, then surely they should be sportsmanlike enough to allow women to choose and regulate their own sports without interference.'[6] The men of the Dominion Football Association provided little in the way of a rationale preventing women from playing soccer, although one suggested 'a woman was not built to stand the bruises gotten in playing football'. The member from Ontario observed that ladies' football was played in Hamilton, but he regarded it a 'shame' that it be allowed.[7]

Immediately following the war, and throughout the 1920s, was a period of tremendous excitement for Canadian sportswomen and the fans that supported them. Certainly the media, especially daily newspapers, began to take notice. Often called the 'golden age' of women's sport, it was a time when popular team sports like basketball, ice hockey and softball became sufficiently organized to hold provincial and Dominion championships; when the best athletes, especially in track and field, began to compete internationally and eventually at the Olympic Games; when women leaders and administrators took control of women's sport, claiming they knew what was best for girls and women, although the advice of men would still be needed. It was also an era when traditionalists, mostly in the form of the male sports media, but also physical educators of both genders, issued warnings about the intensity of female competition and the wisdom of their participation in international events such as the Olympic Games.

For instance, Dr Arthur S. Lamb, physical education director at McGill University in Montreal, consistently stated that 'highly undesirable forms of competition are doing a great deal of harm, not only to the girls themselves, but to the promotion of safe and sane participation for our women of tomorrow'.[8] In an address to the Ontario Educational Association in 1923, he drew attention to women's international track and field events (he had voted against their participation in the Olympics). As another example, he mentioned the recent tour of the Dick, Kerr Ladies football team throughout the United States, which was played entirely against men's teams. Although a strong advocate of physical education for all, rather than highly specialized programmes for the talented few, male or female, Lamb prescribed special restrictions for women – no over-specialization, excessive competition or exploitation. 'All of the benefits to be secured can be had without these risks through careful supervision and selection of activities. There is no good reason why girls should not play games as much as boys, but there are many reasons why there should be very careful legislation concerning the extent of participation, safeguards against exploitation and special regulations adopted for the rules of play, which in most cases must differ from the rules of play for boys.'[9]

Whereas other team sports, like basketball, baseball (later softball) and ice hockey, were readily taken up by Canadian women in the late nineteenth century, and were reasonably well organized by the 1920s, this was not the case with soccer. Basketball was played and encouraged in schools, whereas softball and certainly ice hockey were started and developed through mainly working-class sports clubs for women, and in the case of hockey also through universities. Soccer was not encouraged in schools, universities or in the women's sports clubs. These were organized and run by women for women, although certainly male coaches were the norm. In other words, softball, basketball and ice hockey were seen as women's sports; clearly soccer was not (even by women).[10]

WOMEN'S SOCCER DISAPPEARS

There are no references to girls or women playing soccer in Canada after these early, isolated instances in the 1920s.[11] The period between the wars (1920–39) is considered the 'golden years' of men's soccer in North America when immigrants from Britain and other European countries poured into Canada and the United States, bringing with them their love of the game. No doubt they also brought their traditional, entrenched attitudes about women playing a men's sport. Although clubs and leagues mushroomed throughout the country, there was no room for women in this masculine preserve. Even for men, things began to change during the Depression with the national association suffering financially, and with it the many clubs and leagues, only to be completely obliterated during World War II, when the Dominion Football Association and all provincial associations were forced to suspend their activities. The war had a devastating effect on soccer in Canada, such that in the post-war period it was forced to begin all over again.[12]

After the war and during the 1950s, men's soccer also had to compete with professional ice hockey and Canadian football for public attention, and certainly in the media. In 1950, for example, there were fewer than 3,000 amateur players and six professionals registered with the Canadian Soccer Football Association, as it was then known.[13] Post-war immigration from Europe again brought skilled and enthusiastic players, but soccer was not embraced as a 'Canadian' game. Schools, for example, opted to teach football instead, making it the traditional fall sport for boys. For girls and women, the immediate post-war period was characterized by a remarkable emphasis on beauty, grace, femininity and, for some athletes, glamour. Gone for the most part were debates about whether or not sport would masculinize women competitors, because the proof was there for all to see that so long as women participated in 'beauty producing' sports like figure skating, synchronized swimming or gymnastics, and as long as they looked feminine on the tennis or badminton courts, golf courses and ski hills, they would not be criticized. But athletes sweating on the basketball courts, softball pitches, ice hockey rinks and on the cinder tracks were suspect, their femininity continually questioned.[14] Women's team sports in Canada had a tough time in the post-war era; it was simply not the time to introduce a new one like soccer.

The only evidence of women's soccer in Canada during the 1950s found so far was in anglophone Montreal. McGill University formed a women's team in 1950, which usually played just one home-and-away series with McDonald College, also in Montreal, as well as a number of exhibition games against teams from Bishop's University and several local high schools. On occasion they also played a team from Johnson's Teacher's College in Vermont.[15] The team was likely formed at the instigation of Dorothy Nichol, a pioneer in developing women's athletics at McGill. Upon graduating from McGill in 1949, she joined the department of women's athletics as an instructor, and lobbied for the development and funding of women's intercollegiate sports, specifically basketball, ice hockey and soccer.[16]

On the men's side, the game was kept alive by the many immigrants from Europe who came to Canada after World War II, but as they established their own

2.1. Young fans at the 2002 FIFA Under-19 Women's World Cup in Edmonton, Canada. (Photograph: Uwe Welz)

2.2. Sonia Denoncourt, accredited by FIFA in 1995, is widely regarded as the finest female soccer referee in the world. She is presently Coordinator of Referee Development for the Canadian Soccer Association. (Photograph: Sonia Denoncourt)

2.3. Charmaine Hooper (centre) is one of several Canadian players competing in the professional Women's United Soccer Association in the United States. On the left is Silvana Burtini, and on the right is referee Sonia Denoncourt in Canada versus the USA, July 2001. (Photograph: Freestyle Photography)

families, they wanted their children to learn and participate in a favourite sport. They switched from playing to coaching and were the driving force behind the next phase in the development of the game in Canada – minor soccer.

REBIRTH IN THE 1970S

By the 1960s, and certainly with the formation of the Canadian Minor Soccer Association in 1969, there was an explosion in the popularity of the game among children and youth. Teams, leagues and school programmes were established initially for boys and male youth, especially those born in Canada, but soon girls made it clear that they too wanted to play. For instance, the district of Lac St Louis on the west island of Montreal, already had some 18 clubs, and many of them began girls' teams as early as the late 1960s. This had the immediate effect of attracting mothers, who developed an interest in the game by becoming team managers and league administrators.[17]

Also typical was Scarborough, a large suburb of Toronto, where in 1972 there were 14 girls' teams, more than double those of the previous year. 'Not only', wrote a reporter for the *Toronto Star*, 'has the sport grown among the minors, it has permeated the distaff side too.'[18] Nonetheless, players were overwhelmingly male. At the 1973 Calgary [Alberta] Invitational Tournament, for example, there were over 100 scheduled games for boys, with only four for girls. Yet by 1976 so many girls wished to play that the Calgary Minor Soccer Association included 60 teams and sponsored the first all-girls tournament in Western Canada, where teams from Calgary and Edmonton in Alberta, Regina and Saskatoon in neighbouring Saskatchewan, as well as several teams from the United States, competed in a two-day event.[19] In 1973, there were three girls' soccer teams in all of British Columbia, but by 1980 there were 317 organized into seven districts competing under the banner of the newly formed B.C. Girls Soccer Association.[20]

Rather than permit girls to play on boys' soccer teams, the norm was to set up soccer leagues specifically for girls primarily in the 7–14 age group. For instance, the Greater Niagara Falls Minor Soccer Association started a girls' league in 1974 because a young female player was removed from her boys' team when it moved into the playoffs at the end of the previous season. Wide publicity was given to her plight in the local media. By the mid-1970s in Canada there were a growing number of legal challenges to girls being forbidden to play on boys' teams, although mostly in baseball and ice hockey. Complaints of this nature were made to provincial human rights bodies, who then decided whether or not to accept the case, and if they did, whether to resolve it informally or proceed formally. Very few cases actually went to litigation, but those that did were landmark decisions and generally helped to confirm girls' right to play with boys.[21]

These cases were also important because they helped focus debate around an issue that split the women's sport community: sex-separated versus sex-integrated sports and organizations. On one side were those who argued that only through separate (but equal) programmes for girls and boys would equality be achieved, and if girls were allowed to integrate on boys' teams, so must boys be allowed to play on girls' teams. This would, in their view, be extremely harmful to girls' and women's sport. The integrationists, on the other hand, argued that ability and not sex (now usually referred to as 'gender') should be the criterion for forming athletic teams. Girls who did not have the opportunity to participate in a particular sport, except through an all-male team or league, should be permitted to play with boys if they have the necessary skills. They also argued that the 'disadvantaged' individual (in this case girls) be allowed to play in boys' leagues; whereas boys, who were considered 'advantaged' should not be allowed to play in girls' leagues. Finally, they maintained that because resources were often not available for a parallel girls' structure, one league would be more efficient and less costly.

For the most part, amateur soccer in Canada managed to stay out of these debates because of its policy of establishing separate (and, it maintained, equal) leagues for girls. However, there were a few complaints that came to light and received media attention. For example, in 1975 two women law students at the University of Toronto were prohibited from playing on their faculty soccer team (there was no women's soccer league) because the director of intramural sports felt they would be exposed to unnecessary risk if allowed to play with the men. The women took their grievance to the Ontario Human Rights Commission arguing for participation on the basis of merit rather than gender.[22] The case was eventually resolved informally and intramural teams at the University of Toronto were opened to both genders.

In 1981, another case involving the prestigious Robbie Tournament – an international boys' tournament organized by the Scarborough Youth Soccer Association and sanctioned by the Canadian Soccer Association (CSA) – made the headlines. Two teams, one from the United States and the other from Denmark, included a girl on their rosters. The American girl, a nine-year old who had played on her team for four years because there wasn't a girls' division in her age group, was allowed to play, but the 16-year-old Danish player was not, simply because she was older and presumably more vulnerable to injury. As a result, two members of the National Action Committee on the Status of Women brought a complaint on her behalf before the Canadian Human Rights Commission. The complainants alleged that the CSA's decision to remove the girl from the team was a denial of access to opportunity on the grounds of gender and age. The case took a ridiculous three years to resolve, and in 1984 a formal tribunal found that the CSA (or any national sports governing body for that matter) did not fall within the jurisdiction of the *Canadian Human Rights Act* despite substantial federal funding, its interprovincial and national activities, its national character, and its incorporation as a federal legal entity.[23] What the case did demonstrate was the weakness of federal human rights legislation in the context of sport-related cases.

Like other Canadian sport associations, soccer did not always welcome females especially if they wanted to play on boys' teams, which many had to do before clubs, community centres, schools and universities began to initiate programmes for girls and women. To be fair, many centres encouraged boys and girls playing together and it was only when a team came under the jurisdiction of a controlling body that problems arose. For example, as late as 1992, the Ontario Soccer Association still believed it could prevent girls from playing with boys. Erin Casselman and Suzanne Ouellet were two Belleville high school students who played on the local boys' team. They had played throughout the year, but when their team reached the quarter finals of the Ontario championship, they were told it would be disqualified if they continued to play because they were girls in a boys' competition. A complaint was laid with the Ontario Human Rights Commission, and after an inquiry, the Ontario Soccer Association was barred from interfering with the right of female players to compete for team positions on the same basis as males.[24]

In a wide-ranging report written for the Canadian Soccer Association, John Pooley, an experienced soccer coach and university physical educator, emphasized the need to develop girls' and women's soccer in Canada: 'Girls and women are playing soccer in many countries although, for the most part, this is a recent innovation. *The Association should promote a program to encourage females to become members of the Association and to affiliate with provincial associations.* Canada will be left behind the rest of the world if this important element is neglected' [italics in original].[25] Subsequently, at its annual meeting in 1977, the Canadian Minor

Soccer Association voted to promote girls' soccer at the interprovincial level and establish regional competitions in four age categories.[26] Comparative participation figures show that at this time girls comprised 10 per cent of the under-18 youth soccer players in Canada (12,342 females to 105,732 males).[27] Also significant was the appointment of a Youth Development Coordinator for the Canadian Soccer Association: Kevan Pipe, a former player, coach and administrator with a strong background in sports administration. By 1978, there were three regional 'club' championships for girls (Atlantic, Eastern and Western Canadian) in three age-categories (under 14, 16 and 18).

An initial foray by Canadian women into international soccer occurred in October 1978 when a team from the Greater Vancouver Women's Soccer League travelled to the Republic of China (Taiwan) to compete in the World Women's Invitational Soccer Tournament. The IODE (Imperial Order of the Daughters of the Empire) Roadrunners had made their first international trip in 1977 – a two-week excursion to Hawaii to compete against club teams and the Hawaii Women's League all-star teams. The team was then invited by the Asian Ladies Football Confederation to participate in the world tournament, providing they could raise sufficient funds to get to Taiwan. They competed not as a representative Canadian team, but under the auspices of their club, beating several of the 13 teams in the tournament.[28]

By the end of the 1970s, soccer was on its way to becoming a very popular sport among Canadian youth. In some areas the game was growing so fast that organizers had trouble finding facilities and qualified people to keep pace. Although not as many girls played as boys, their game was growing just as quickly through clubs and city leagues, and thriving in elementary and secondary schools, thus forming the basis for spectacular growth and change over the next two decades.

TWO DECADES OF REMARKABLE CHANGE

The last two decades of the twentieth century saw extraordinary changes in girls' and women's soccer in Canada. Most notable was the remarkable growth at the grassroots level. In 1980, there were probably no more than 16,000 registered female soccer players in the country, but by 2000, there were a total of 270,145. The ratio of female to male players steadily declined – from an estimated one to eleven in 1980 – to less than one to two by 2000.[29] Soccer was fast becoming the team game of choice for many girls and young women across the country.

As the numbers grew, so did the opportunities to play and compete, at higher and higher levels. There are now opportunities for women to make a living playing soccer, considered impossible a few years ago. Those who played in the late 1970s remember the frustration of not being able to continue competing because there was simply no place to go. Sylvie Béliveau, a very talented player from Québec, is a good example. When she played between 1978 and 1982, there were no provincial teams and only national championships for club teams.

Although she would continue to hone her skills as a varsity player at the Université de Sherbrooke, there was no national women's inter-university championship (not until 1987), and certainly no national women's team to aspire to (one was formed in 1986). At the age of 19, Béliveau launched a coaching career, and women's soccer has benefited from her experience and expertise ever since. She was appointed assistant coach of the national team in 1986 and head coach in 1991, a position she held until 1995. She has attended all of the women's world championships either as an observer, head coach or member of the FIFA technical study group. Since 1998, she has been an international FIFA instructor, and is called upon to give coaching clinics throughout the world. Today she works for the Association Régionale de Soccer de l'Outaouais as Coordonnatrice Sport-Études, a programme enabling young student-athletes to both train and attend school. She is also a Board member of the Canadian Soccer Association specifically responsible for female soccer.[30]

The growing development of talent, along with increasing opportunities to play and compete, also meant that high performance teams became a reality. The first national women's team programme, for example, was established in 1986. In the early years the team laboured in obscurity, and received little support from the Canadian Soccer Association. They did not qualify for the first Women's World Cup in 1991 sanctioned by FIFA, and because they came tenth in the 1995 tournament, they did not qualify for the 1996 Atlanta Olympics, when women's soccer made its debut. Tremendous publicity surrounded the third World Cup, played in seven American cities in the summer of 1999, especially around the team from the United States, led by Mia Hamm. All 32 games were televised live with strong ratings, and spectators filled the stadiums to capacity. The final game played in the Rose Bowl in Pasadena, California, between the United States (who won) and China, attracted some 90,000 fans, the largest crowd ever to watch a women's sporting event. Unfortunately the Canadians were again not in the top eight, and hence they failed to qualify for the 2000 Olympics in Sydney. Although not going to the Olympics was a disappointment, certainly for the players, the experience gained in international competition was invaluable. If it had not been for the pioneering and persistent efforts of Neil Turnbull, head coach of the first women's national team from 1986 to 1991 (also head coach from 1995 to 1999) and Sylvie Béliveau (head coach from 1991 to 1995), the national team programme would not be where it is today.

The women's national team has seen better times in the past couple of years. Since 1999, they have been coached by Even Pellerud, who led Norway to win the World Cup in 1995. He has been instrumental in turning the women's programme around. The team has chalked up victories against both China and the United States, and most importantly they have qualified for the 2003 World Cup in the United States. A priority of the Canadian Soccer Association is the identification and development of young players for the national teams. Their goal is to identify up to 200 of the best young male and female players in Canada, and then provide them with every opportunity to develop and succeed at the international level. For females, there are now three youth development teams – under 16, 17, and 19 – with players from the first two feeding into the Under-19 national team, which in turn feeds into the senior national women's team. The Under-19 national team has a full-time coach – Ian Bridge, who is also assistant to Even Pellerud, coach of the senior national team. All this has certainly revitalized the women's national team programme, but it will be a few years before the impact of the new feeder system will be felt in terms of international success.

Another outstanding player, coach and leader is Tracy David, who also played when there were far fewer competitive opportunities for girls and women. Growing up in a small town in British Columbia, she first played on a boys' team and then finally, when she was 15, on a girls' team. In 1978, she played in the first under-18 Girls Club National Championship for the Edmonton Ajax. As a student at the University of Alberta, she helped organize the university women's soccer club team, which eventually evolved into the Edmonton Angels. David captained this highly successful team for nine years, and it consistently won National club titles. Seeing the need for organized, competitive soccer at university level, she lobbied the University of Alberta Athletics department for a varsity women's soccer team and helped organize competitive women's soccer at university level. She coached the highly successful University of Alberta Pandas for 15 years before moving back to British Columbia as head coach of the University of Victoria Vikes women's soccer team. Today, there are 43 university women's soccer teams spread over four Regional Associations coordinated through Canadian Interuniversity Sport. Tracy David was recently honoured for her pioneer efforts in women's soccer by being the second woman inducted into Canada's Soccer Hall of Fame and Museum.[31]

Carrie Serwetnyk was the first woman inducted into the Soccer Hall of Fame and Museum. She was the first Canadian woman to play soccer professionally and certainly among the first of its 'global' players. As a youngster in the 1970s she played the game in Mississauga, a suburb of Toronto. Skill and talent earned her an athletic scholarship at the University of North Carolina, where she was a top scorer in the mid-1980s and, at the same time, a member of Canada's newly formed national women's team. After college, she played club soccer in France, and in 1992 signed a US$100,000 contract with the Japanese club owned by the Fujita Corporation in the 10-team Japanese women's professional league. She signed with Yomiuri the following year, helping her team win the championship. No doubt Carrie Serwetnyk would love to have played professional soccer in North America but she was just a little ahead of the opportunity. Another top Canadian player, Charmaine Hooper, spent most of the 1990s as a high-scoring forward-for-hire in overseas women's leagues, playing a season in Norway, one in Italy, and then four in Japan, where she won two scoring titles.[32]

The excitement generated in the United States by their team's success in the 1999 World Cup and at the 2000 Olympics contributed to the establishment of a women's professional soccer league. The eight-team Women's United Soccer Association (WUSA) began playing in the spring of 2001 with franchises located in Atlanta, Boston, New York, Philadelphia, Raleigh-Durham, San Diego, the San Francisco Bay Area and Washington DC. The main investors in the league are television and cable companies including Time Warner Cable and Discovery Communications. The WUSA features top players from the United States as well as the best internationals from many different countries. So far, five Canadian players have played in the WUSA: Silvana Burtini had a highly successful season with the Carolina Courage before she retired; Amy Walsh played one season for The Bay Area CyberRays; Charmaine Hooper and Sharolta Nonen have played two seasons for the Atlanta Beat, as has Karina LeBlanc for the Boston Breakers.[33] Many top Canadian players also compete in the W-League (of the United Soccer Leagues), a semi-professional outfit throughout Canada and the United States, which serves as the development league for the WUSA. In 2003, Canada had three teams in the W-League – Ottawa Fury, Toronto Inferno and Vancouver Breakers.

Another trail blazing Canadian in women's soccer is Sonia Denoncourt. Widely regarded as the finest female soccer referee in the world, she has become a role model for other aspiring officials, female and male alike. By the age of 22, Denoncourt had been playing soccer for more than ten years, and officiating for eight, when she decided that doing both well was impossible and she would concentrate on officiating. Ten years later, in 1995, she became an accredited FIFA referee, one of a very select few in the world. By 1997 the FIFA list contained just 56 female referees from 39 countries. In 1996, Denoncourt became the first woman to referee in Olympic soccer, overseeing the German women's 3-2 victory over Japan in the opening game, as well as four other matches. She broke the gender barrier in men's soccer by refereeing, to positive acclaim, matches in first division games in El Salvador and Brazil, and in the North American men's professional league. In addition to her international refereeing duties, she has become a sought after FIFA speaker and clinic conductor, and has recently taken a position with the Canadian Soccer Association as Coordinator of Referee Development.[34] In 1999, another Canadian woman made the FIFA referee list; she is Jill Fedirchuk (now Proctor) from Vancouver. In addition, there are two FIFA women assistant referees in Canada – Kim Chalmers from Alberta and Denise Robinson from Ontario.

Canadian players, coaches and officials have been making their mark on the world soccer stage for some time. In February 1999, FIFA organized the first ever promotional game – the FIFA World Star team against the USA. The result was 2-0 for the world team. Three Canadians stood out: Sonia Denoncourt officiated, Sylvie Béliveau co-coached the world team (along with Gunilla Paijkul from Sweden) and Charmaine Hooper scored both goals for the victorious world team and was named MUP of game.[35]

The growth in women's soccer over the past 20 years has been dramatic, not just in Canada, but elsewhere in the world as well. The future looks very bright indeed. Yet there are some important issues and struggles ahead that need to be addressed.

CURRENT ISSUES, PROBLEMS AND STRUGGLES

The most obvious problem, although one not necessarily prioritized by those involved in girls' and women's soccer in Canada, is the lack of female leadership. Certainly there are key women leaders – some mentioned in the previous section – but by and large, the sport executives, volunteer administrators, paid staff, coaches and officials who run soccer in Canada are overwhelmingly male. The Canadian amateur sport system, from the local clubs right up to provincial and national sport organizations, requires volunteers to help run it. Traditionally, many more men have been involved in this capacity than women, but in 1998, there was an equal proportion of males and females, a change from 1992 when nearly twice as many men were sport administrators. In the past, approximately 25 per cent of the volunteer sector in amateur sport was female, as was the case with senior executives and technical directors in paid positions.[36] The numbers in soccer are considerably lower.

There are 12 provincial and territorial soccer associations in Canada, in addition to the national sports governing body, the Canadian Soccer Association (CSA). Together, and along with the local clubs and regional associations, the men and women who run these organizations either as volunteer executives or paid staff, are in charge of amateur soccer in Canada. Each of these associations has a Website making it relatively easy to accumulate the necessary statistics (for 2001, and in some cases 2002). Although female participation in soccer is now nearly 40 per cent, only 13 per cent of the volunteer administrators at the provincial and national level are female, considerably lower than the national average of at least 25 per cent. There is also considerable variation among the provincial and territorial associations, with at least one province (Alberta) having no women in a volunteer leadership capacity, and the highest (nearly 30 per cent) in Saskatchewan. Only one province or territory (British Columbia) had a female president at the time of writing. At the national level, there are two women on a 21-member Board of Directors. Of course, this does not take account of the many women who volunteer at the club and regional level, and who actively take on leadership positions in their local areas.

On the professional level, those who are paid to run soccer programmes at the regional, provincial, territorial and national levels, statistics are not as easy to come by. Several provincial and territorial associations do not have a paid staff, or if they do, it is one person responsible for almost everything. Large-scale organizations, such as Ontario and Quebec, have extensive and specialized staffs with a greater proportion of females, although they tend to be in the administrative and programme areas rather than the high-profile executive director or technical positions.

42

Only a few of the provincial and territorial associations have created either a director of women's soccer as a board position, or in some cases, a special women's soccer or female development committee. The Saskatchewan Soccer Association, for instance, has created such a committee whose purpose is to advise and make recommendations concerning female development to the Board, to become aware and take a positive approach towards gender biases and equity, and to foster the development of the female coach, athlete, referee and volunteer.[37] The Fédération Québécoise de Soccer-Football also has a female committee, which has recently completed a study of the viability of a semi-professional women's league in Canada. In 1999, the CSA appointed Sylvie Béliveau as Director of Women's Soccer Development, a volunteer position on its Board of Directors. She in turn created a 'Female Committee', comprised of several women soccer leaders from across the country, each of whom also sits on a CSA committee. So far they have focused their work on improving the climate for women in the national body, updating the CSA harassment policy, and creating better opportunities for elite female coaches through mentorship programmes.[38]

The issue of men coaching girls' and women's soccer is seemingly a non-issue in the sport. There is little evidence that men see it as a problem, and as a result there is little effort by local, provincial, territorial and national associations (overwhelmingly run by males) to initiate specific programmes to bring more women into the coaching ranks. The problem is also exacerbated by the fact that as an increasing number of paid positions become available in coaching women's soccer, these are taken by men who see themselves as more qualified for the positions. For example, among the soccer coaches in Canadian universities offering a women's programme, nearly 75 per cent (32 out of 43) are male.[39] Clearly, there are more and more experienced female players who could now join the coaching ranks, but they need encouragement to take the necessary certification courses, and they also need to be mentored by more experienced coaches.

Similarly, there are not enough qualified female referees in Canada. Of the 18,000 currently registered, approximately 22 per cent are women. Most of these are at the beginner level so there is good potential for women referees to gain more qualifications and experience. At the national level, there are presently four women (out of 56) qualified to referee, and as mentioned previously, Canada has two women on the FIFA referee list. Clearly, there is a need for more female referees at a higher level.[40]

Another issue is the lack of a coherent competitive structure for girls' and women's soccer in Canada. Some of the components are there, but they do not necessarily comprise a seamless system, allowing for the most talented players to be identified, nurtured through their developmental years, and then provided with every opportunity to gain experience at national and international levels. There is no question that the development of elite sport and the winning of medals occupy far more resources than does sport at the grassroots level. The balancing of participation on the one hand with excellence on the other is never easy. Many sports struggle to find the right balance between promoting mass participation, and at the same time developing a seamless competitive system in which the talented few can rise to the top and succeed. In the case of soccer – specifically girls' and women's – right from the club level upwards, it has been only recently that young girls could dream of winning an Olympic medal or playing professional soccer. For Canadian girls, their route to the top may be hindered due to the absence of role models, or a lack of incentives, or more simply a lack of money to play and travel. The latter is a problem not just in the inner centres of Canada's largest metropolitan areas, but also in the far-flung rural areas with few facilities, where ice hockey often takes precedence. In Canada's north, for example, the cost of travel is so prohibitive that teams can rarely travel anywhere to compete.

Even if a talented soccer-playing youngster has all the advantages of a well-sponsored club and supportive family, their route to the top may take them away from home at a young age to seek more competitive challenges. Canada has a viable university system of soccer for women, with most universities offering a competitive team, and there may also be financial assistance in the form of limited athletic scholarships. However, many young women wishing to play soccer and attend university will opt to go to the United States, where the competition is stronger and the financial support often greater. The drain of players to the United States has the effect of watering down the competition in Canada. Those who cannot attend university, or have no inclination to do so, must struggle to gain one of the few spots on the national development teams recently created by the Canadian Soccer Association. For those who aspire to a professional career, they need to play on one of the farm teams (of the W-League), but with only three such teams in Canada (in Ottawa, Toronto and Vancouver), opportunities are severely limited.

While preparing this study, I talked (or had e-mail correspondence) with a variety of women involved in soccer, some with many years of experience in the game. Several told me how soccer had been central to their lives from the time they started playing as youngsters, throughout their competitive careers, to their work now as paid professionals or unpaid volunteers helping to run the sport. I was impressed with their enthusiasm, commitment and vision; however, one person in particular stands out. Her name is Charly Kelly, and she is a First Nation Community Recreation Consultant in Whitehorse, Yukon. She told me about the Whitehorse women's soccer league, which had begun in the mid-1980s. In the beginning, there were six teams in the league, each with 15 players and a coach, and the league flourished. A decade later, the player age-limit was dropped to 16, which meant that younger and more skilled players played in the league. In just a few years, the league died due, in large part, to the clash between recreational and competitive players. The majority of younger players had been playing on representative teams for many years and were looking for a high-level, aggressive, and competitive playing environment. They had also benefited from being intensively coached, and became frustrated with the more recreational players who were unfamiliar with set plays and the finer points of the game. The older players, on the other hand, were divided between those who had graduated from youth representative teams and were looking for a more competitive game, and those who came out simply for fun, friendship and recreation. The recreational players felt intimidated, tensions rose, disputes erupted and the end result was that the recreational players left *en masse* as the league no longer provided them with a 'fun' and supportive playing environment. A couple of years ago, someone had the idea to create a co-ed league with truly recreational rules: before a man can score he must pass to a woman; once a man scores two goals he can score no more; women's goals count more; no referees and certainly no physical contact. This league also flourishes now, along with the more competitive youth leagues. After Charly Kelly told me this story, she showed me something special – the soccer ball tattoo on her foot, also matched on the feet of her six closest soccer friends. Soccer is about more than winning championships, playing for money and winning Olympic gold – it is the game of choice for fun and friendship among thousands of girls and women in Canada – and that's the way it should be.

NOTES

1. Sport Canada, *Sport Participation in Canada: 1998 Report* (Minister of Public Works and Government Services Canada, 2000), p.25.
2. Canadian Soccer Association, '2002 Demographics: Player Registrations', at <www.canadasoccer. com/eng/docs/index.asp>, accessed 26 Feb. 2003.
3. The story of the Dick, Kerr Ladies Football Club is told in Gail J. Newsham, *In A League of Their Own* (London: Scarlet Press, 1997).
4. 'Dominion Soccer Body in Session', *Manitoba Free Press*, 6 Sept. 1922, p.10; 'Lady Footballers on Tour Want a Game in Toronto', *Toronto Evening Telegram*, 2 Sept. 1922, p.33.
5. 'Amazons Stage Terrific Battle', *Lethridge Herald*, 18 Aug. 1922, p.6.
6. 'Want Men to Mind Their Own Business', *Manitoba Free Press*, 7 Sept. 1922, p.10.
7. Newsham, *In A League of Their Own*, p.61. See also Colin Jose, *The Encyclopaedia of Canadian Soccer* (Vaughan, ON: The Soccer Hall of Fame and Museum, 1998), pp.95–6.
8. Arthur S. Lamb, 'Physical Education for Girls', in *Proceedings of the Sixty-Second Annual Convention of the Ontario Educational Association* (Toronto: Clarkson W. James, 1923), p.285.
9. Lamb, 'Physical Education for Girls', p.288.
10. See M. Ann Hall, *The Girl and the Game: A History of Women's Sport in Canada* (Peterborough, ON: Broadview Press, 2002), pp.33–9, for an account of the early beginnings of women's basketball, ice hockey, baseball and softball in Canada.
11. Given the extent of research conducted for my book, *The Girl and the Game*, I am convinced that I would have come across them had they existed. This is also confirmed by Canada's pre-eminent soccer historian, Colin Jose, who claims that after hundreds of hours of research, he has found nothing on women's soccer apart from the Dick, Kerr Ladies tour in 1922 (e-mail conversation with author, 29 Oct. 2002).
12. Jose, *The Encyclopaedia of Canadian Soccer*, pp.15–19.
13. 'Canada: A Brief History of Canadian Soccer', *Canadian Soccer News*, 2, 4 (1972), 17.
14. See Chapter 4 (pp.104–34) in Hall, *The Girl and the Game* for more detail on the post-war era.
15. The Vermont reference is also confirmed in Shawn Ladda, 'Early Beginnings of Intercollegiate Women's Soccer in the United States', *Physical Educator*, 57, 2 (2000), 106–13. It is not known how long the McGill team played, although there is no record of a women's team between 1967 and 1980. It was re-established by the early 1980s with an exhibition schedule.

16. 'McGill Hall of Famer Dorothy Nichol Dead at Age 72', at <www.athletics.mcgill.ca/articles/default.asp?ID=1424&stale=true>, accessed 27 Jan. 2003.

17. Geneva Boucher, telephone interview with author, 10 Jan. 2003. Ms. Boucher spent nearly 30 years as a volunteer administrator at the club, district and provincial levels in Québec.

18. Jim Kernaghan, 'Soccer Growth Scares Officials', *Canadian Soccer News*, 2, 3 (1972), 30.

19. Jack Taylor, 'Calgary Invitational Tournament', *Canadian Soccer News*, 3, 5 (1973), 20; 'The Calgary Girls Invitational Soccer Tournament', *Canadian Soccer News*, 6, 4 (1976), 23.

20. Jeff Cross, 'Women Invade the Soccer Field', *The Magazine* (insert in the *Vancouver Province*), 2 March 1980, 10–11.

21. Information pertaining to these cases can be found in Hall, *The Girl and the Game*, pp.177–82; Cathy Meade, 'The Efficacy of Canadian Human Rights Legislation in Dealing with Sex Discrimination and Gender Inequality in Sport' (unpublished paper, University of Alberta, 1993); Laura Robinson, *Black Tights: Women, Sport and Sexuality* (Toronto: HarperCollins, 2002), pp.177–217.

22. Peter White, 'The Wrong Sex for Soccer', *Globe and Mail*, 1 Nov. 1975, p.1.

23. Meade, 'The Efficacy of Canadian Human Rights Legislation', pp.17–18.

24. 'Girls Win Soccer Tussle', *Globe and Mail*, 2 Nov. 1993, A1.

25. John C. Pooley, 'The Objectives and Programme Priorities of the Canadian Soccer Association', *Canadian Soccer News*, 6, 6 (1976), 11.

26. 'Canadian Minor Soccer Association Changes Its Name', *Canadian Soccer News*, 7, 2 (1977), 21.

27. Kevan Pipe, 'Breakdown of 1977 Participation Figures', *Canadian Soccer News*, 8, 2 (1978), 20.

28. '1978 World Women's Invitational Soccer Tournament', *Canadian Soccer News*, 9, 2 (1979), 28–9.

29. Although the number of registered players in 1980 is known to be 198,927, the number of female players was not available. I have estimated it at 16,000 based on the fact that there were 12,342 under-18 female players in 1977. The statistics for 2000 are found in Canadian Soccer Association, '2000 Demographics: Player Registrations', available at <www.canadasoccer.com/eng/docs/index.asp>, accessed 14 Jan. 2003.

30. Sylvie Béliveau, interview with author, Hamilton, Ontario, 29 Nov. 2002. See also 'Women's World Cup's Only Female Coach', *Soccer Canada*, June-July (1995); Wendy Long, *Celebrating Excellence: Canadian Women Athletes* (Vancouver, BC: Polestar, 1995), pp. 202–203.

31. See 'Museum' at <www.soccer.on.ca/>, accessed 15 Jan. 2003.

32. Joe O'Connor, 'Lightning Striker', *Saturday Night*, 18 Aug. 2001, pp.30–35.

33. Ibid.; Norman Da Costa, 'Canadian Woman Signs Big Soccer Deal', *Toronto Star*, 29 April 1992. Information about the Women's United Soccer Association can be found online at <www.wusa.com>, accessed 16 Jan. 2003.

34. Sonia Denoncourt, e-mail conversation with author, 23 Jan. 2003; Les Jones, 'The Changing Face of Refereeing: The Good Example of Canada's Sonia Denoncourt', *FIFA Magazine*, Dec. (1997), 36–7, 39; Dave Stubbs, 'Ref Denoncourt Still Breaking New Ground', *montrealgazette.com*, 15 April 2000 at <www.caaws.ca/Whats_New/apr00/denacou_apr15.htm>, accessed 5 Oct. 2002.

35. I am grateful to Sylvie Béliveau for telling me about this event.

36. Sport Canada, *Sport Participation in Canada*, pp.44–5; Canadian Association for the Advancement of Women and Sport, *Towards Gender Equity for Women in Sport* (Ottawa: CAAWS and Women's Program Sport Canada, March 1993), p.38; M. Ann Hall, Trevor Slack and Dallas Cullen, 'The Gender Structure of National Sport Organizations', *Sport Canada Occasional Papers* 2, 1 (Dec. 1990), 1–2.

37. 'Female Development Committee' (Section 7 Pg.18, Updated March 2002) at <www.sasksoccer.com/board.html>, accessed 25 Nov. 2002.

38. Canadian Soccer Association, 2001 Annual Report, pp.51–3 at <www.canadasoccer.com/eng/index.asp>, accessed 19 Jan. 2003; Béliveau, interview with author.

39. Marg McGregor, Chief Executive Officer, Canadian Interuniversity Sport, e-mail conversation with author, 23 Jan. 2003.

40. Denoncourt, e-mail conversation with author, 23 Jan. and 26 Feb. 2003.

Will the 'Iron Roses' Bloom Forever?
Women's Football in China:
Changes and Challenges

FAN HONG and J.A. MANGAN

Football has become the 'national' sport of China. It is a passion that cuts across class, gender and ethnicity. It has become a manifestation of Chinese modernity, a link between China and the West, a symbol and symptom of the global sports market. Women's football for its part is one of the fastest growing female sports in China. Women forced their way into this traditional bastion of masculinity in the late twentieth century with a confidence, purpose and determination born of a radical image of femininity stimulated by decades of change. On football fields this confidence was not without foundation. The Chinese Women's Football Team won the silver medal at the 1996 Olympics, were placed second in the Third World Cup in 1999 and won the Asian Cup and Asian Games ten times between 1986–99. Female footballers, in fact, were used as models of resolution to inspire Chinese male footballers to qualify for the 2002 World Cup.[1] The Chinese proudly call these women the 'Iron Roses'. The question now is, can the 'Iron Roses' bloom forever?

BEGINNINGS

Modern football was first played in Hong Kong when Hong Kong was colonized by the British after the Opium War of 1840.[2] British soldiers, merchants and missionaries in Hong Kong played football; in time, so did the Chinese. The game then spread to mainland China in the late nineteenth century. The first recorded match took place in Shanghai in 1902 between St John's University and Nanyang University.[3] Football initially, as elsewhere, was regarded as a men's sport and played at various missionary schools and universities by male students.

The situation changed during the New Culture and May Fourth Movement between 1915 and 1921. The aims of the Movement were to introduce the positivism, equality and democracy characteristic of Western culture to Chinese society, to alert the Chinese to the need for science and a scientific spirit and to inspire China to build a new country.[4] Women's emancipation, mentally and physically, thus became an essential part of the New Culture and May Fourth

Movement. It taught women the concept of individual freedom. It provided a new climate in which women could attempt to free themselves from feudalism, and gave them opportunities to develop themselves, physically and mentally.[5] On the back of dramatic change, in 1924 Sheng Kunnan, a physical education teacher at the Liangjiang Women's Physical Education Institute in Shanghai, translated the English *The Rules of Women's Football* into Chinese and taught the girls at the Institute to play football.[6] The Principal, Lu Lihua, a radical feminist, who saw women's participation in football as a tool for achieving equality and a symbol of sexual liberation, supported his action.[7] However, since there were no other women's team in Shanghai, the Liangjiang women's team had to play against men.[8]

China at the time was a male-dominated society and Confucianism was still the dominant culture. Women were considered inferior to men – physically and intellectually. They had their place – reactive not proactive, subordinate not superordinate – certainly not equal.[9] Therefore, Liangjiang women's football was regarded as the provocative and extreme action of a small band of schoolgirls and failed to win the approval of Chinese society. Nevertheless they persevered until their involvement in modern football came to an end at the beginning of World War II when Japan invaded China in 1937 and occupied Shanghai in 1938. Liangjiang Institute of Physical Education was closed[10] and this brought women's football to an abrupt end.[11] It was reported that a few women students played football at Xibei University in 1939 in Nanzhou. However, it did not make any significant impact on the society.[12] Conservatism was simply too powerful.

The eight-year war with Japan ended in 1945. Immediately China was thrown into the chaos of the five-year Civil War between the Nationalists and Communists. During those years, physical activities, such as gymnastics, athletics and basketball, were promoted by both nationalist and Communists for training men and women for military purposes.[13] However, neither Nationalists nor Communists favoured football. It was regarded as an entertainment rather than a martial activity. In addition, as an entertainment, it was regarded as a man's game and unsuitable for women. Therefore, they were not encouraged to play football anywhere in China from 1945 to 1949.

NEW BEGINNINGS

In 1949 the Chinese Communists established the People's Republic of China. Among other things a new sports culture was created.[14] Its rational was exercise for improving productivity: healthy activity was equated with fit producers. Physical education rather than competitive sport was the immediate concern of the Party.[15] It became a compulsory in schools: girls and boys were required to have three classes a week plus one hour of physical activity after school. However, football was for boys and was included in the national physical education curriculum. Girls were not encouraged to participate. Nevertheless, in order to make the out-of-school activities more interesting, some physical education teachers organized football games for boys *and* girls in Guandong province which was close to Hong Kong, which had a strong football tradition, the legacy of the British.[16] However, these football activities characterized a few schools only.

On the whole, football did not attract particular support from the central government. There were several reasons for this. First, it was not an Olympic sport, so it did not receive sufficient financial and administrative support from central government. Second, it was a foreign sport; therefore, it was believed that only the foreigners, who were physically stronger and technically superior, could play well. Football was not for the Chinese. Nevertheless, there were a few matches played at national level between China and East European countries during the 1950s and 1960s for political and diplomatic purposes – and China always lost.[17] This reinforced resistance to the game and, consequently, football became a minority sport that did not win the enthusiasm of the masses or attention from the government. A few girls playing football in Guangdong did not make any impact on the nation and the women's game disappeared at the beginning of the Cultural Revolution in 1966 when education systems went through turmoil and schools closed down throughout the country.

Meanwhile, outside China women's football developed in various Asian countries, for example, in Singapore, Thailand and Taiwan. It prospered relatively, with the result that in 1974 the Asian Women's Football Association was established in Hong Kong. The first Asian Women's Football Championships took place in Hong Kong in the following year. Hong Kong, Taiwan, Malaysia, Thailand and Singapore participated.[18] These developments did not interest China, particularly since Taiwan was a member of the Association. The Communist China would not participate in organizations in which Taiwan was involved.[19]

Women's football in China did not rise from the ashes until the end of the Cultural Revolution in the late 1970s. Chairman Mao's death in September 1976 brought the ten-year Cultural Revolution to an end. China, under its new leader, Deng Xiaoping, began an economic programme of market–oriented reform. This involved a move away from the central economic planning of the past to a more market economy that allowed a place for the profit motive. To accomplish this transformation China 'opened its door' and joined the capitalist world. Subsequently China underwent dramatic political, economic and cultural change. One of the characteristics of the change in the sports culture was more freedom of choice in schools and communities. Sport was now promoted which, it was believed, would be more interesting to pupils and the wider community than those then available.

As a consequence of liberalization, in the spring of 1979 physical education teachers of two middle schools in Xi'an city, who were football enthusiasts, began to teach girls to play football. Soon football matches took place between the two schools. This attracted the attention of the media and the provincial educational authority. The innovation was praised as a bold initiative, and which gave girls an opportunity to play a boys' game.[20] The other schools in Xi'an now established girls' teams. Eventually, in the early summer of 1979, the provincial educational authority and sports bodies jointly organized an inter-city girls' football competition. After the competition, the first female professional football team was established in Xi'an with 12 female players under the wing of the provincial sports commission.[21]

Following in the footsteps of Xi'an, in the next few years women's professional football teams appeared in the provinces of Yunnan, Liaoning, Yanbian and the cities of Beijing, Tianjin, Datong, Guangzhou, Shanghai and Changchun. These teams were the products of the traditional Communist sports system. They were set up by, and belonged to, their provincial or city's sports commissions,[22] for example, the Beijing women's football team was established in 1982 by the Beijing Sports Commission. Players came from sports schools and they were athletes, basketball players or weightlifters, for the coaches thought that football needed speed and strength. Most of them had no idea of how to play football. However, as soon as they joined the team they became professional players and received wages from the sports commissions that provided them with coaching and accommodation, and organized competitions for them.

Under the management of governmental sports bodies women's football in China expanded steadily. In 1982, the Chinese Sports Ministry organized the First National Women's Football Invitation Competition in Beijing and ten teams took part. Following the success of the first national competition, the second and third competitions took place in 1983 and 1984 and the number of teams increased from 27 to 35.[23] The growth of the popularity of women's football ensured that the Chinese Sports Ministry put women's football on the list of formal competitive sports in 1985 at a meeting of the Organizing Committee of the Sixth National Games. Eventually, in 1987, women's football appeared, for the first time, at the Sixth National Games as a formal event – a major development in the women's game.[24]

Simultaneously, Chinese women's football established international links. In November 1983 Guangzhou (Canton) held the First International Women's Invitation Competition. Singapore, Japan and six Chinese teams competed against each other. After the Competition, the first Chinese national women's professional football team – the Chinese Women's Football Team – was established. The second competition took place in 1984 in Xi'an and American, Australian, Italian, Japanese, the Chinese Women's Football Team and three provincial teams took part. In December 1984, for the first time, the Chinese Women's Football Team participated in the Asian Women's Football Championship and won it.[25]

However, a step forward was followed by a step backward. In September 1987 in Guangzhou, during the Sixth National Games, a strategic planning meeting with the Sports Ministry and all the Heads of provincial sports commissions took place. At the meeting it was decided that women's football would not be an official event at the Seventh National Games in 1991 because it was not an Olympic sport and did not fit into China's Olympic Strategy. According to the Olympic Strategy the National Games, which take place every four years prior to the Olympic Games, is the place to forge teams and to select the best players for the Olympics. It is also the place to assess the work of provincial sports commissions. This is of the greatest importance to the regional sports governing bodies, because their budgets and the promotion and demotion of sports officials is largely dependent on their teams' performance during the National Games. Therefore, when women's football was withdrawn from the 1991 National Games most provincial sports bodies immediately decided to dissolve their women's football teams including Tianyin Women's Team, which had just won the championship at the Games. One of the players recalled: 'When I heard the news I was so disappointed. I was still playing at the Sixth National Games. I wondered what I was going to do after the Games ... I spent all my time, energy and youth on the pitch. I have no educational qualification. I did not even finish my secondary school. I can do nothing, but play football.'[26]

More than 30 professional women's football teams in September 1987 were reduced to just five in December 1987 after the Sixth National Games. Most players retired from professional life and the surviving teams such as Beijing, Dalian, Shanghai, Changchun and Guangdong employed only a handful of players.

Fortunately, the international football body, FIFA, did not sympathize with the internal Chinese situation and was impressed by the rapid growth of women's football in China. In 1988 FIFA invited China to hold an international women's soccer competition and China was delighted. The FIFA Women's Soccer Invitation Competition took place in Guangzhou in June 1988 and was sponsored by Huo Yingdong, a Hong Kong businessman and Vice-Chairman of the Women's Football Committee of FIFA, who had been a major sponsor of Chinese sport since the 1980s, and eventually became a Vice-Chairman of the Chinese Political Consultancy in the 1990s. Twelve countries took part. Norway won the Competition and China took fourth place.

The potential of the Chinese women's football team to win international prizes was noticed by the Chinese FA. After the competition, it decided to raise the standard of the women's national team to international level.[27] However, it did not provide a budget, although it had sufficient funds to support its three domestic professional men's football teams! Therefore, a sponsor for the women's team became an urgent need. Guangzhou Qixing Pharmaceutical Company came to the rescue. Qixing was one of the new and ambitious companies in Guangzhou. It had seen the potential of the national women's football team and believed association with it would promote its business image and products throughout China. Qixing agreed to sign a contract with the Chinese FA to sponsor the Chinese Women's Football Team with 150,000 RMB (£15,000) each year. According to the contract, the Chinese FA would not spend a penny on the women's team but would obtain 30,000 RMB (£5,000) from it as administration fees. Consequently, the Chinese Women's Football Team became the first football team in China to stand on its own feet without state support.[28]

The Chinese Women's Football Team had to survive on a relatively small sum of money. It had to cover their wages, accommodation, food, training facilities and the cost of travelling to competitions. While the national men's football teams received direct and adequate financial and administration support from the Sports Ministry, the national women's football team received nothing from its governing body. To save money, they established their base in Yingde, a small nondescript town in Guangdong province. The players remembered it vividly:

> We trained for 10 hours a day, six days a week. Our training ground was terrible. On wet days the ground became a muddy puddle and we played in it. Tears and rain ran down our faces. We were cold and hungry all the time, for there was no hot water and not enough food because of the tiny budget. We lived and trained in these conditions for five years, five long hard years! We cried to our coaches from time to time that we would not play football in our next life.[29]

However, their determination paid off in their victory in the 1990 Beijing Asian Games, which they won.

FIFA, again impressed by the success of Chinese women's football and China's efficient hosting of competitions, invited China to host the first FIFA Women's Football World Cup in 1991. China eagerly accepted. In November 1991 the World Cup took place in Guangdong province and China came fifth.[30]

This had positive internal repercussions in due course. Women's football obtained full support from the Chinese Sports Ministry both financially and administratively in 1994, following the International Olympic Committee's important announcement that women's football would be a formal sport at the 1996 Olympic Games. Huo Yindong, the Vice-Chairman of Women's Football Committee of FIFA, immediately proposed to the Chinese Sports Ministry that China should pay special attention to women's football with its potential for winning Olympic medals. The Sports Ministry, in response, now changed its attitude towards women's football. It recognized the validity of his claim and included women's football in its Olympic Strategy. The Chinese Women's Football Team was now treated the same as the other Olympic teams: managers for the national team were appointed and the best players were selected from the whole country and trained up to ten hours a day and six days a week in much improved conditions.[31]

The result was dramatic. The years between 1986 and 1999 were the golden age of Chinese women's football. In December 1986 the Chinese Women's Football Team won its first victory at the Sixth Asian Women's Football Cup. It then went from success to success. It won the Asian Cup seven times, the Asian Games three times, the 1993 World Students Games and obtained a silver medal at the 1996 Olympic Games. Finally at the Third Women's World Cup in 1999, the Chinese women's team competed against the USA in the final: the Chinese players lost the final on penalties. The approaching Fourth World Cup is anticipated with relish.

THE RECONSTRUCTION OF FEMININITY

The achievements of the Chinese women's football players have not only made an impact on the national and international football stages, but have also influenced cultural and social change in China. A new femininity had developed in the post-Mao era and the success of women's football has helped reinforce gender evolution that has challenged traditional Chinese culture and gender relations in the post-Mao era, at a time when conservatism has been reasserting itself to the detriment of women. For example, the Marriage Law in 1950 gave women the freedom to choose husbands, and the traditional business of selling women into marriage is coming back since the 1980s. In 1990 alone, the authorities investigated 18,692 cases.[32]

In addition, while women are said to have equal work opportunities, in fact, men get the better jobs and women have to take lower-paid and less qualified jobs. Leadership positions are dominated by men, or given to women simply as window-dressing. There were 12 female vice-ministers among more than 200 male vice-ministers. There were only ten women provincial vice-governors, compared to about 50 men at this level. The present Politburo of the Chinese Communist Party Central Committee has no women members.[33]

Modernization has brought technological reform and freedom from labour intensive work. Consequently female unemployment is rising. In cities female workers are sent home to await work while male workers retain their jobs. In rural areas, since men with machines can do field work by themselves, women are instructed to return to their homes to concentrate on housework.

Women do not receive equal pay for equal work. In urban areas they receive only 77.4 per cent of the pay given to men, in rural areas the figure is 81.4 per cent. In the 1980s and 1990s female graduates from college found it more difficult to obtain a suitable job than men. About 8 per cent of children, at this time, who dropped out of school in rural areas were girls. Concubinage and prostitution, which the Communist Party fought hard to eliminate in the revolutionary years and which largely vanished after 1949, have both reappeared.

In consequence, the belief that women 'can hold up half the sky' is now questioned by women themselves and within Chinese society. A survey in 1991 showed that more than half of the respondents (both men and women) believed that men were superior to women.[34] Women in China have thus failed to 'hold up half the sky' to the extent that Chairman Mao promised they would do if they simply embraced a Communist 'New China'. In short, in China, in the post-Mao era, gender inequality persisted and even increased.

However, there seems to be one exception to this rule: women in sport, especially women in football, who have won enhanced status. On the international sports stage, between 1979 and 2002, the Chinese Men's Football Team lost almost every international game, while the Chinese Women's Football Team won almost every international game. Women footballers have advanced China's image; men footballers have retarded it. At the 1999 Women's World Cup, the

Chinese Women's Team competed against the USA in the final match at the Pasadena Rose Bowl in front of President Clinton and a 65,000 audience. China only lost on penalties. However, the Chinese Men's Team did not score a single goal at the 2002 Men's World Cup final first stage matches. Men's football has only brought humiliation to China, while women's football has brought prestige. Women footballers have done themselves and the nation proud on the international football stage. Their status, unlike that of many other Chinese women, is high in the China of the twenty-first century.

Outstanding female players, therefore, have asserted themselves and have contradicted past and present stereotypes of femininity. They have won the admiration of the nation and the football world with the result that five players have been signed by Japanese clubs and seven by American clubs. One of the best players, the Chinese team's captain, Sun Wen, became an icon for the Chinese – men and women alike. Sun Wen came from a working class family in Shanghai. She went to a sports school in Shanghai in 1985 when she was 13 years old. Her mother was not pleased with her choice of football as a possible career, however her father supported her because he was a football fan. Eventually her mother changed her mind and Sun Wen concentrated on football. In 1991 she played in the First Women's World Cup when she was 18 years old. She then played in the Second and Third World Cups successively in 1995 and 1999. She is now training for the Fourth World Cup in 2003. Her outstanding performance won her one of the Top Ten outstanding Chinese athletes awards and one of the Top Ten outstanding young people in China awards in 1999, and made her one of the 50 sports stars of the People's Republic of China in the period between 1949 and 1999. She also won the title of the Best Female Footballer in Asia and the Golden Boot at the Third Women's World Cup in 1999.[35] She has become an 'inspirational icon' in women's football, nationally and globally.

PATRIOTISM AND PRAGMATISM

Why has women's football achieved so much in such a short time? The answer lies partly in traditional sports patriotism and contemporary sports pragmatism.

Arguably the most severe demands on Chinese sportsmen and sportswomen are the product of the passion of patriotism. Ever since the beginning of the century Chinese athletes have operated in an atmosphere of pervasive and passionate nationalism. From the 1980s onwards, in addition, many Chinese, who have strongly wanted China to gain the admiration of the West, and indeed to out-perform the West, have believed that while China has lost some years on the international sports stage, it can still catch up, move to the top, and become a sports superpower. Chinese athletes' commitment to the need to make sacrifices for China has been translated in practice into the repression of open criticism and the demand for total conformity to political demands.[36] Sports patriotism – and more to the point, sports success – has become a symbol of national allegiance.

Shang Ruihua, the manager of the national women's team from 1988 to 1992, for example, has stated: 'Our girls have endured hardships which ordinary people cannot imagine. All they wanted was victory on the international football stage. They know that they represent our country.'[37]

Yet this sacrifice is exploited. Indeed, it seems women footballers are willingly exploited. A top male football player receives a monthly income of 160,000 RMB (£13,000) while a top female football player receives a monthly income of 700 RMB (£60),[38] and some have to wait for several months to receive their wages.[39] When Liu Ailing, a famous national player, was asked what she thought about this huge difference in treatment she answered: 'I don't compare myself with male players. I play for my country and myself.'[40] The coach of Shanghai women's football club recently claimed: 'We are struggling in a less privileged situation compared to men. However we are excited about our achievements. Through football our girls realised their value and increased their confidence. They are determined to achieve glory for our country and themselves.'[41] Jiang Zemin, the General Secretary of the Party from 1989 to 2003 praised the national women's team as 'inspirational icons for the Chinese'.[42] All well and good. However, it remains a bitter irony that failed men (internationally) are rewarded far more handsomely than successful women (internationally).

The cult of patriotism has been part of a new Olympic Strategy since 1990. Its aim has been for China to become a leading sports power by the end of the twenty-first century. Wu Shaozu, the Sports Minister from 1990 to 2000 once claimed: 'The highest goal of Chinese sport is success in the Olympic Games. We must concentrate our resources on it. To raise the flag at the Olympics is our major task.'[43] Therefore, in 1996 when women's soccer became an Olympic sport, as noted earlier, the Sports Ministry began to pay particular attention to women's football. As stated above, it provided the national women's team with finance, training and administrative support. Their progress was monitored.[44] The efforts of both sides – the sports authority and the players – achieved very satisfactory results. Women's football became a part of the big red machine that has produced hundreds of sports stars and gold medals, and patriotism in itself was considered a sufficient incentive! The question remains, however, why the marked financial discrepancies in men's and women's football – at both national and international level? As will be seen below the consequences for women's football in China have been serious. Among other things, its best players now play elsewhere. Clearly patriotism is not sufficient motive.

SPORTS PRAGMATISM

From 1980 onwards, ideological subscription to ideology, the hallmark of Chinese Communism under Chairman Mao Zedong, has been replaced by adherence to the no-nonsense pragmatism of Deng Xiaoping, who does not care about the 'colour of the cat' so long as it catches 'the mice'. The new pragmatism promises, to a degree, to liberate the Chinese people from the heavy hand of doctrinal politics. Chinese women's football in response is equally pragmatic. Its characteristics are as follows:

Commercialization

Since the 1980s the Chinese football system has been transformed from a highly centralized system to a free market economy. Football has been encouraged to stand on its own feet and not to rely on State support. The reformed sports system encourages corporate sponsorship. This gives coaches and managers more freedom. Thus, regional women's football teams have the freedom, and the challenge, to find sponsors to survive. In the 1980s about 20 regional women's football teams received sponsorship from big companies, such as Wanbao Electrical Group, Dongbei Pharmaceuticals and Beijing Xuehua Company.[45] On the national level in 1988, as mentioned earlier, Guangzhou Qixing Pharmaceuticals signed a contract with the Chinese FA to sponsor the national women's team. This is one of the major reasons why women's football developed in the early 1980s without State support, and survived in the late 1980s when the State withdrew its support. It opened a new chapter in the history of Chinese football. Following in the women's footsteps, men's teams, such as the national youth team, the national junior team and the Olympic team, all signed contracts with sponsors.[46] However there was a big difference between the women's and the men's teams. The national women's team stood on its own feet without State support, whereas national men's teams received both sponsorships and State financial support.[47] The blatant and unfair imbalance does not do credit to the Chinese authorities in their ostensible pursuit and endorsement of equality between the sexes. Little evidence of sexual liberation is to be found in this state of affairs.

After the 1996 Olympic Games, when the Chinese Women's Team won the silver medal, the Chinese FA decided that it was time to promote a women's professional league system called Women's Primary League. The system was a carbon copy of the men's league system which had started in 1994 with the help of the International Management Group (IMG). In 1996 Shanghai TV Station, a commercial organization, bought Shanghai women's football team from the Shanghai Sports Commission and established the first women's professional football club. A similar process took place in other cities and women's football clubs appeared in Beijing, Jinan, Guangzhou, Dalian, Zhengshou, Shijiazhaung, Chengdu and Dalian between 1996 and 2002. Then the Women's Primary League was launched in 1998 with four elite teams.[48] The Primary League changed its name to the Women's Super League in 1999 after the near victory of the Chinese women in the Third World Cup. Eight teams participated in 1999 and ten in 2002. The League was sponsored by Bubugao, a major mobile phone company, with a contribution of 5,000,000 RMB (£416,000) between 2000 and 2002.[49]

Medal Fever and Financial Rewards

In China, national football and regional championships, both youth and junior competitions, take place primarily for the purpose of training female footballers for successful participation in international medal-awarding competitions and the Olympics. Women's football has been unequivocally elitist since the 1990s. The government officially rewards winners, their coaches and relevant officials. The sports authorities officially acknowledge that athletes, like most human beings, desire wealth. In addition, famous female footballers receive money from various sponsors and from commercial organizations. After the victory of the Women's World Cup in 1999, for example, the Chinese Women's Football Team received an award of 3,250,000 RMB (£270,000) from the Sports Ministry and the Chinese FA, 5,500,000 RMB (£250,000) from Chinese companies and 3,000,000 RMB (£450,000) from Huo Yingdong, the Hong Kong millionaire.[50] The team also received three mini vans and 35 motorbikes from car and motorbike manufacturers respectively.[51] Seven top Chinese players transferred to USA teams after 1999 and played there professionally.[52] However, their rewards lagged behind the male footballers.

Arguably, no other Asian nation has been as committed to women's liberation as Communist China and certainly none has been as committed to systematically producing sporting heroines. In general, they are not only distinguished by their patriotism, but also by their ambition, hard training and desire to achieve personal freedom, fame, power and wealth in the new pragmatic cultural and commercial atmosphere with the support of the state and the whole nation. It is no surprise, therefore, that when many of their eastern sisters were still playing the game as amateurs, these Chinese women footballers made a mark for themselves as professionals.

PROBLEMS AND CHALLENGES

The development of women's football has not gone smoothly. There have been problems, setbacks, complications and contradictions. Indeed, in the future some problems may become major obstacles even to the extent of limiting amateur and professional women's participation in competitive football – at home and abroad.

Gender Bias and Lack of Recruits

One looming problem is the continuation of gender bias. Lucian W. Pye, the cultural historian, has recently remarked: 'In China the post-Mao era of "opening to the world" revealed the fact that while China had changed, there was still much continuity.'[53] Traditional culture still strongly influences people's attitudes to femininity and masculinity. This has produced both confusion and complexity. On the one hand, the dominant trend in women's football has been 'to play like a man', to model female action on the values and traditions of men's football in which aggression and physicality are endemic. On the other hand, many sportswomen including women football players playing 'men's sports' like men face criticism and ridicule. The Confucian form of sexism remains extant. The idealized image of the 'ladylike' sportswoman is still praised by most parents and the public.[54] This spills over into football. By way of example, one famous player, Sun Qingmei, recalled that in the 1980s her parents locked her in her bedroom to prevent her going out to play football.[55] Liu Ailing, another famous player, has stated that her parents once confronted her coach and told him that they did not want their daughter, 'such a lovely girl to play a boy's sport'.[56]

Little has changed in the minds of many despite the fact that women's football has achieved such remarkable victories. One young girl interviewed in 2001 stated rather poignantly:

> I love to play football. I went to our local football school and received one year's training. When I was in the last year of my middle school my mother asked me to give up football and to concentrate on my studies in order to get to university. A football career is for boys not for girls. Therefore I gave up football. I am now studying accountancy. Sometimes I miss football.[57]

Another recalled:

> My father is a football coach, therefore, I want to play football. But my mother will not let me. She has told me that if I play football people will think I am not a real girl. It will be difficult for me to find a good boy friend. However, she encourages me to play table tennis. She thinks that is all right, but not football. Football is so violent, it is a game for boys.[58]

These girls' experiences were by no means exceptional. Their experiences were confirmed in the same year by Feng Jianmin, the Director of Women's Football of the Chinese Football Association. He pointed out: 'The lack of parental support is a big problem. In China we have this one-child policy. Parents don't want their daughters to become footballers. Their ambition for their daughters is to go to university and then find good jobs. The belief, widely held, is that a girl should not play football. It is so aggressive and masculine.'[59] In a sentence – traditional gender differences are retained, and in some instances, being reconstructed and reproduced, publicly and privately, in the post-Mao era. Such reactionary manifestations deny change. They endorse a traditional cultural climate, in which femininity should not incorporate equal images of aggression, force and physicality. The consequences are dramatic. There are now no national or regional female football programmes for state schools and the young, with the result that there are few football opportunities for most girls and young women. Therefore, Chinese women's football faces a very serious problem: lack of recruits.[60]

Thus it comes as no surprise that when a junior Coca Cola Cup Competition took place in Beijing in July 1999 – the year in which the Chinese Women's Team won second place in the World Cup – there were 1,666 teams with more than 30,000 young players participating, but there were only three girls' squads comprising 72 players.[61] Zhang Hen, the Chairman of the Organizing Committee and the general secretary of the Beijing Football Association stated anxiously: 'If we don't pay special attention to the change in cultural attitudes ... very soon then our women's football will lag behind the American and European countries.'[62]

There are only ten officially recognized girls' football schools in China. Most of them are detachments of local sports schools.[63] In the biggest football school, the Chinese Football School in Qinghuangdao, there are more than 1,000 boys but only 30 girls. In Shengyang, in the north, a girls' football school with 70 players from age 9 to 15, is attached to the city's sports school. The coach, a former national player, had to take her team to train in Dongwan, in the south, 3,000 miles away from their hometown, due to lack of training facilities and support in the sports school. The lack of support, facilities and money is a big problem. The football school gets no support from regional or local sports bodies. Girls in her school have to pay 4,500 RMB (£375) per year just to cover their boarding costs. Sponsors are depended on to cover the cost of the facilities. She has claimed: 'There are more than 300 girls in Shengyang who want to play football. However, due to their parents' attitudes and due to lack of money (they cannot even pay the 4,500 RMB boarding fee)[64] they have to be excluded from football.'[65]

Girls, in general, do not play football inside or outside school. Those who play football are those who want to become professional players. Self-evidently, they are small in number. In China, in fact, there are, at present, just over 800 girls and women playing professional football.[66]

FOOTBALL SYSTEM

In the wake of the transition of the sports system and sports management in the 1980s, women's football has been struggling. As early as 1979 Han Chongde, a member of staff in the Chinese FA, proposed to the Chinese Sports Ministry that it should pay more attention to women's football. The Sports Ministry replied: 'We are not against it but we do not promote it', and 'We welcome anybody who wants to promote women's football on the condition that it will not affect the budget and training facilities of men's football'.[67] Therefore, women's football in the beginning did not get support from the Chinese sports authority. However, thanks to the change in the sports system from a planned to a market economy, women's football took off in the early 1980s as an unofficial sport. And it became a formal competitive sport at the Sixth National Games in 1987 and an Olympic event in 1996. Its progress followed the model of men's football and a women's football league was established in 1998.

Women's football has existed in uneasy tension with local sports commissions, the Chinese FA and their sponsors. Initially, the selection of players took place in local and regional sports schools. In 1982, for example, when Beijing, Tianjin and Guangzhou started their women's football teams their players all came from local sports schools which belonged to regional or local sports commissions. These players were full time professionals. Their futures were in the hands of the Sports Ministry and the Chinese FA. Therefore, in 1987 when the Sports Ministry announced that women's football would not be included in the 1991 National Games, women's football teams decreased from 30 to five in three months. In 1996 when the Chinese FA decided that women should follow the men and set up a league system, these provincial women's teams overnight were bought by big companies and became professional clubs.

Take Beijing Women's Football Team as an example. The team was established in 1984 under the leadership of the Beijing Sports Commission and has won the national championships six times. It has produced five players for the national team. In 1996 Weikerui Company bought the team and changed its name to Weikerui Company Women's Football Team. In 1998 the company went bankrupt and the women's team became an 'orphan'. The Beijing Sports Commission had to take it back. In 1999 a construction company signed a contract with the Sports Commission to sponsor the team for three years with 7,800,000 RMB (£650,000) and changed its name to Beijing Construction Company Women's Football Team. However, the money only covered basics, like wages, food and accommodation. The Beijing Sports Commission had to provide the team with free training facilities. But the team still needed more money to survive.[68] What was available allowed only for survival on the edge. In contrast half of one year's salary of a foreign coach in Shanghai Shenghua Men's Football Club would cover the whole year's costs of Shanghai Women's Football Club.[69] Such experiences were typical of almost every women's football club. In 2003 there were only nine such clubs in China.

The Chinese football system has undergone major changes in order to successfully meet the demands of the market economy. However, most changes have involved men's football, not women's football. The details of changes, set out below, starkly illustrate the differences in support for the men's and women's games. In 1994 IMG (the International Management Group) signed a contract to assist the Chinese FA to set up a Chinese men's football league system (Jia A and Jia B, equivalent to the English Premiership and first division) with initial seed money of US$1 million from Philip Morris Inc., which wanted the Chinese FA to publicize its Marlboro brand. The same year, IMG signed a five year US$8 million guarantee with the Chinese FA as the exclusive agent for advertising and television rights for the League. It initiated the globalization of Chinese professional football.[70] With the establishment and expansion of these commercial football reforms Chinese men's football has become an international business, involving nationwide professional club networks, player transfer, player agents, sponsorship, television rights and merchandising. Chinese football players play in the top leagues in Britain and Germany, while more than 70 foreign players play in the Chinese Jia A and Jia B league and more than ten foreign coaches are coaching Chinese football clubs. Between 1998 and 2002 a foreigner, Bora Milutinovic, coached the national team. In consequence, the Chinese FA had been singled out as a particularly successful model of Chinese sports adjustment to a market economy.

Regrettably this model applies only marginally to women's football. The Women's Super League was created in 1999, as mentioned earlier, and is controlled by the Chinese FA and managed by the local football associations of Beijing, Hebei, Guangdong, Shandong, Henan and Dalian.[71] There are no foreign coaches coaching women's football clubs. Women players can play in the USA but are not allowed to transfer to clubs within China. When Sun Wen, the international player, came back from the USA in 2002 Tianjin Jinying Women's Football Club wanted to buy her from her Shanghai club. However, the Chinese FA stated that it was not the appropriate time for women's football to introduce the player transfer system. The time was not considered ripe, ironically, to fully introduce market economy system and methods to women's football.[72] The reason remains unclear. The suspicion must be that gender prejudice and discrimination is far from dead in modern Chinese football.

In essence, women's football in the twenty-first century is squeezed between a somewhat unenthusiastic traditional Chinese sports system, which is a product of traditional culture, a weakening socialist planned economy and a surging capitalism and commercialism that favour the men's game. Consequently, after four years in existence the so-called successful Super League faces serious problems: lack of spectators, sponsorship and investment. Clubs rely heavily on their owners' companies and local government. Chinese football clubs (including men's) do not make money! In this situation, men retain more practical sympathy and support than women.

A major reason is that the closed socially hierarchical system still operates in the Chinese sports system. In football, in consequence, the structure of management has not changed. The state controlled Chinese FA is still in charge and its provincial and local commissions make major decisions. The owners (usually big companies) are sponsors but they have little power and influence.[73] Even minor matters must be referred to the Chinese FA and regional and local sports authorities and have their approval. It is no surprise, therefore, that women football players' transfers could not succeed due to the disapproval of the Chinese FA which is run essentially by male traditionalists for men. The Chinese FA's attention is focused on men's football with its greater popular appeal, commercial support and unambiguous gender status.

Thus, the brutal fact is that women's football, although it was a pioneer of sponsorship in the 1980s, as mentioned earlier, has regressed. It is restricted by the still extant 'planned economy' sports system. The Chinese FA recently announced that the future targets for women's football are to concentrate on a few elite U-18 and U-16 teams as sources for the national team, which is expected to win a good medal in the 2008 Olympics in Beijing.[74] Women's football, in short, is for the few not the many, for international prestige not national pleasure, for show not for fun!

MEN'S REJECTION AND WOMEN'S SUBORDINATION

Although football has played a role in changing perceptions of the capacity of female physiology, it has not changed the perception of women's biological inferiority. Women's victory in football is simply victory of women over women, not men. Male superiority is, therefore, not fundamentally challenged. Male privilege, therefore, remains in place. The importance of football as a symbolic representation of ideal masculinity is emphasized by means of the contrasting image of ideal femininity. The demonstration of strength, aggression and musculinity has always been advantageous for men, whereas for women it has always been disadvantageous. Nothing has changed. This catch-22 situation means – you are damned if you do and damned if you don't! The women's game is portrayed as 'boring' and 'slow' while the men's game is praised as 'exciting' and 'fast and powerful'.[75] During the 2001 Women's Super League season, only one or two reporters showed up at matches. On average there were about 100 spectators per match even when the tickets were free. On the contrary, there were more than 3,000 journalists at the men's World Cup qualifying matches in Shengyang in October 2001. The Chinese Central Television Station broadcasted every match throughout China and the stadia in Shengyang were full. As male players become bigger, stronger and more skilled, and the games more confrontational and physical, the question 'how should women play football' takes on added ideological importance. Women's football is played in a context in which men's football performances dominate the media and are the model against which all other versions are compared. Therefore, women's football exists in a situation of invidious comparison with the dominant model. Football, thus, remains a bastion of male privilege, power and prestige – a bastion that is reinforced year by year.

Little will change while women footballers lack the power to make changes to their advantage. They have minimal representation on decision-making bodies, which are powerful male–dominated and dominant institutions. In sport, as in society, men hold most of the major administrative positions at every level, from the Sports Ministry to the Chinese FA, from provincial football management centres to local football offices. To add insult to injury most football coaches are male even in the women's games.[76] It seems men's football lives a charmed life. Men's football teams receive the greatest levels of sponsorship and media attention no matter how badly they perform. As for women, as soon as they lost their matches in the 2000 Sydney Olympics and the 14th Asian Cup in 2002, Bubugao Company, the sponsor of the Women's Super League, decided to withdraw its sponsorship and the League now faces serious financial problems.[77]

Consequently, between 1997 and 2002, the number of men's football clubs has increased while the number of women's professional teams decreased from 30 to ten.[78] The Chinese FA claims that domestic women's football lags behind men's football by at least 12 years – small wonder given the attitude of the Chinese FA.[79] Yet women have out-performed men for decades in the international arena!

CONCLUSION

Women's participation in competitive football, to some extent, has altered gender relations in China. Stars have certainly improved their personal gender circumstances and raised expectations of gender equality in the still conservative Chinese society. But an organizational infrastructure born of communist percept and practice, the longevity of traditional values and indeed their renaissance in an increasingly market economy environment, have adversely affected the growth of women's football in general in modern China. World trends cannot be resisted. Women's football is here to stay – in China and elsewhere. Chinese women's football will grow but slowly. However, gender prejudice and consequent institutionalized discrimination, limited resources and recruitment shortages will have their influence in the short term – and perhaps the long term. When the FIFA Fourth Women's World Cup takes place in the USA in 2003 it is most unlikely that the 'blooms of the Iron Roses' will win first prize.

NOTES

We wish to thank Yan Xuening, Editor of *The People's Sports Press*, and Wu Ping, senior reporter for *Chinese Sports Weekly*, and her colleagues in Beijing for providing us with information on Chinese women's soccer for this chapter.

1. Xiao Ge, 'Nuzu zhengfeng' ['The Rectification of Chinese Women's Football Team'], *Zhongguo tiyu bao* [*Chinese Sports Daily*], 18 Oct. 1999, p.6.
2. Opium War (1839-42): fought between Britain and China; triggered by the British outcry against the Chinese Qing government's confiscation of British opium. Hostilities were initially confined to Guangzhou (Canton) and to the east China coast as far north as Tianjin. When British forces threatened the Yangzi delta city of Nanjing, the Qing government sued for peace, signing the Treaty of Nanjing in 1842 and Hong Kong became a colony of Britain. The conflict with the British opium traders and subsequent British expeditionary forces in 1840 was a turning point in modern Chinese history. For details see Hu Sheng, *Cong yapian zhangzheng dao wusi yungdong* [*From the Opium War to the May Fourth Movement*] (Shanghai: Shanghai renmin chubanshe, 1982), pp.11–13. Jonathan D. Spence, *The Search for Modern China* (London: Hutchinson, 1990), pp.155–9, 802.
3. Guojia tiwei wenshigongzhuo weiyuanhui and Zhongguo zuqiu xiehui [Department of Sports History of the Chinese Ministry of Sport and Chinese Football Association], (Hereafter Guojia tiwei) (eds), *Zhongguo zuqiu yundong shi* [*The History of Chinese Football*] (Wuhan: Wuhan chubanshe, 1993), p.102.
4. Fan Hong, *Footbinding, Feminism and Freedom: The Liberation of Women's Bodies in Modern China* (London: Frank Cass, 1997), p.120.
5. Ibid., p.139.
6. Guojia tiwei, *The History of Chinese Football*, p.71.
7. Liangjiang Women's Physical Education Institute was founded in 1922 in Shanghai. Lu Lihua, a graduate of the Chinese Women's Physical Education Institute, founded in 1912, was the Principal. She believed that if Western women could play football then so could Chinese women. For details

about Liangjiang Women's Physical Education Institute and its football team, see Hong, *Footbinding, Feminism and Freedom*, pp.271–2, 274–5, 285.

8. Wu Zimin, 'Woguo diyizi nuzi zhuqiudui' ['The First Chinese Women's Football Team'], *Tiyu wenshi* [*Journal of Sports Culture and History*], 3 (1985), 30.

9. Hong, *Footbinding, Feminism and Freedom*, pp.43–52.

10. The Institute was closed in Shanghai but moved to Chongqing and changed its name to Liangjiang Women's Physical Education Teachers Training College. In 1940 the College was closed for good. There was no record of women's participation in football in Chongqing.

11. Hong, *Footbinding, Feminism and Freedom*, pp.271 and 285.

12. Guojia tiwei, *The History of Chinese Football*, p. 72.

13. Zhongguo tiyushi xuehui [The Chinese Society for History of Physical Education and Sport] (ed.), *Zhongguo jindai tiyu shi* [*The History of Modern Chinese Sport*] (Beijing: Bejing tiyu xueyuan chubanshe, 1989), passim.

14. Fan Hong, 'Women's Sport in the People's Republic of China: Body, Politics and the Unfinished Revolution', in Ilse Hartmann-Tews and Gertrud Pfister (eds), *Sport and Women: Social Issues in International Perspective* (London: Routledge, 2003), pp.225–7.

15. Ibid., p.227.

16. 'Zhongguo nuzu fazhanshi' ['The Development of Chinese Women's Football'], http://team.china. com/zh_cn/data/women/100000096/20010419/10011681. Accessed on 4 March 2003.

17. Guojia tiwei, *The History of Chinese Football*, pp.115–34.

18. Ibid., p.157.

19. In 1949 the Chinese Communists won the Civil War, established the People's Republic of China (PRC) and controlled all China except Taiwan, to which the Nationalist government had fled. The Nationalists remained there as the Republic of China. Communist China was recognized by the Soviet Union and East European countries, and Nationalist China was recognized by the USA and the United Nations. In 1958 Beijing announced that the PRC would refuse to cooperate with any organization or personnel that recognized 'two China' – Communist China *and* Nationalist China. PRC's sports associations therefore withdrew from many international sports federations including the International Olympic Committee. The PRC did not come back fully to the international stage until the 1970s when she renewed her seat in the United Nations and the International Olympic Committee. For details of the 'two China' issues and sport, see Fan Hong and Xiong Xiaozheng, 'Communist China: Sport, Politics and Diplomacy', in J.A. Mangan and Fan Hong (eds), *Sport in Asian Society: Past and Present* (London: Frank Cass, 2003), pp.319–39.

20. Guojia tiwei, *The History of Chinese Football*, p. 157; Reporter, 'Xi'an nuzi tizuqiu' ['Girls in Xi'an Play Football'], *Shanxi ribao* [*Shanxi Daily*], 29 July 1979.

21. Ibid.

22. Guojia tiwei, *The History of Chinese Football*, pp.157–8.

23. Ibid.

24. Ibid.

25. Ibid., pp.159–60.

26. Liu Zhongyi, 'Yingxiong lei' ['The Tears of the Heroines'], http:www.tjip.net/bcy/etiyu/nz/wz/c.htm. Accessed on 28 March 2003.

27. Ibid.

28. Guojia tiwei, *The History of Chinese Football*, p.161; Liu Zhongyi, 'The Tears of the Heroines', p.2.

29. Liu Chang, 'Huishou Zhongguo nuzu shiwu nian' ['Women's Football: Fifteen Years' Struggle'], http://www.hg.cn.gs/hggxlj/zgzq/ljwj/nz-1.htm. Accessed on 28 March 2003.

30. 'Znhongguo nuzu fazhanshi' ['The History of Chinese Women's Football'], http://team.china.com/zh_cn/data/women/100000096/10011681.html. Accessed on 24 March 2003.

31. Wei Min, 'Zhongguo nuzu yundong zhangdaozhe Huo Yingdong' ['Huo Yingdong: The Promoter of the Chinese Women's Football'], *Zhongguo tiyu bao*, 12 Oct. 1999, p.3; Xu Xiaoli, 'dachu guowei, suli zhongguoren de xinxiang – fang nuzu jiaolian' ['Play for China, Establish the Chinese Image – Interview with the Head Coach of the Chinese Women's Football Team'], *Zhongguo tiyu bao*, 13 May 1999, p.2.

32. S. WuDunn, 'Feudal China's Evil Revived: Wives for Sale', *New York Times*, 3 Aug. 1991, p.7.

33. Li Xiaorong, 'Gender Inequality in China and Cultural Relativism', in Martha C. Nussbaum and Jonathan Glover (eds), *Women, Culture and Development* (Oxford: Clarendon Press, 1995), p.408; Hong, 'Women's Sport in the People's Republic of China', p.233.

34. Wang Jia, '40,000 diaocabiao xianshi zhongguo funu de shehui diwei' ['Data Illustration of the Social Status of Chinese Women: the Investigation of 40,000 Questionnaires'], *Zhongguo funu* [*Chinese Women*], 1 (1992), 24–5.
35. Xu Xiaoli and Ma Yihua, 'Guanyu rongyu de duihua' ['Interview with Sun Wen'], *Zhongguo tiyu bao*, 25 Oct. 1999, p.6.
36. Fan Hong, 'Making Sporting Heroines in Modern China: A Cultural Explanation', *Stadion*, xxxvi, 1 (2000) pp.120–21.
37. Liu Zhongyi, 'The Tears of the Heroines', p.1.
38. Ma Caoyang and Shi Jinmin, 'Zhaoyuguilai gongzhi yiran liubai' ['The Heroines have Won Victory at the World Cup but their Wages are still Six Hundred Yuan'], *Tiyu kuaibao* [*Sports Express*], 12 July 1999, p.2.
39. 'Dongfang meigui, jinqiaoqiao de kai' ['The Eastern Roses Bloom Quietly'], *Qiubao* [*Ballsweekly*], http://ballsweekly.sina.com.cn/9907/071216.html. Accessed on 28 March 2003.
40. 'Zhongguo nuzu zi chuang' ['The Window of the Chinese Women's Football Team]', http://www.ffotballwindom.com/women/ziliao/ziliaodiandi.htm. Accessed on 25 March 2003.
41. 'Guanrong beihou de youtan' ['Behind the Glory'], *Qiubao*, http://ballsweekly.sina.com.cn/9007/070832.html. Accessed on 28 March 2003.
42. Jiang Zemin, 'Gei nuzu de xin' ['Letter to the Chinese Women's Football Team'], 10 July 1999, http://www.footballwindow.com/women/huihuang/mianli.htm. Accessed on 25 March 2003.
43. See his opening address at the Congress of Olympic Movement Studies in Beijing, 1993. Wu Shaozu, 'Olympic Strategy and Sports Reform in China', in Xie Yalong (ed.), *Olympic Studies* (Beijing: Beijing tiyu daxue chubanshe 1993), p.402.
44. Wei Min, 'Huo Yingdong: the Promoter of Chinese Women's Football', p.3; Xu Xiaoli, 'dachu guowei, suli zhongguoren de xinxiang – fang nuzu jiaolian' ['Play for China, Establish the Chinese Image – Interview with the Head Coach of the Chinese Women's Football Team'], *Zhongguo tiyu bao*, 13 May 1999, p.2.
45. Guojia tiwei, *The History of Chinese Football*, p.161.
46. Ibid.
47. Ibid.
48. See *Zhongguo tiyu bao*, 18 Oct. 1999, p.6.
49. Li Haobo, 'Conghui linqing, jimo qianxing' ['The Review of the Women's Primary Football League in 2000'], *Zhongguo zuqiu bao* [*Chinese Football News*], 27 Nov. 2000, p.7.
50. Wei Min, 'Huo Yingdong: The Promoter of the Chinese Women's Football', p.3.
51. Ma Bangjie, 'How Much Reward Has the Women's Football Team Received', *Tiyu quaibao* [*Sports Express*], 22 July 1999, p.3.
52. 'Zhongguo nuzu qimin duiyuan ruxuan quanminxingdui' ['Seven Top Chinese Female Footballers Will Go to Play In the USA'], http://dailynews.muzi.com/II/chinese/63380.shtml. Accessed on 10 Oct. 2000.
53. Lucian W. Pye, *Asian Power and Politics: The Cultural Dimensions of Authority* (Cambridge: Cambridge University Press, 1985), p.4.
54. Xu Xiaoli, 'Shenghuo zai zuqiuzhongde nuren' ['The Real Women Who Live in the Football World'], *Zhongguo tiyu bao*, 4 Jan. 1999, p.7. Zhao Su, 'Liu Ying lun mei' ['Liu Ying's View on Beauty'], *Tiyu tiandi* [*Sports World*], 2 [1999], 9.
55. Liu Chang, 'Women's Football: Fifteen Years' Struggle', p.2.
56. Ibid.
57. Interview in Mianyang, Sichuan, China on 21 Aug. 2001.
58. Ibid.
59. Interview at the Office of the Chinese FA in Beijing on 2 Sept. 2001.
60. Ibid; Ye Ban, 'Cong nuzu yajingsi kan huobei liliang' ['From the Asian Championships See the Problems of Recruits of Women's Football'], *Zhongguo tiyu bao*, 22 Nov. 1999, p.2; Fang Shao, 'Nuzu qishilu' ['On Women's Football'], *Tiyu cankao bao* [*Sports News*], 14 July 1999, p.3.
61. Shi Jinmin, 'Xiaonusheng buai ti zuqiu' ['Girls don't Like to Play Football'], *Tiyu kuaibao*, 15 July 1999, p.3.
62. Ibid.
63. Liu Suyun, 'Woguo chuanjian shijia nuzu qingshaonian jilebu' ['Ten Girls' Football Schools are Established in our Country'], *Xi'an wanbao* [*Xi'an Evening News*], 29 Dec. 2001, p.4.
64. The coach explained that most of the children's parents were unemployed and they got 150 RMB

(£12) per month per person from the government to cover their basic food costs. Therefore they didn't have enough money to pay for their children's football fees. See Wang Hui, 'Shengyang nuzu nanxia shizhong dajiemi' ['Shangyang Girls' Football School Has Gone South'], *Yangchang tiyubao* [*Yangcheng Sports News*], http://www.footballwindow.com/women/xiaonvzu/dajiemi.htm. Accessed on 25 March 2003.

65. Ibid.
66. Ma Chaoyang, 'Nuzu ziyou' ['The Big Problem of Women's Football'], *Tiyu kuaibao*, 12 July 2001, p.4; see also 'Jianming zhiliao' ['Data Collection'], http://www.footballwindow.com/woman/ziliao/ziliaodiandi.htm. Accessed on 25 March 2003. Potential professional girls are trained at specialist football schools from the age of thirteen onwards.
67. Liu Chang, 'Women's Football: Fifteen Years' Struggle', p.2.
68. 'Behind the Glory', see n.41, pp.2–3.
69. Ibid., p.2.
70. Chris Ashton, *China: Opportunities in the Business of Sport* (London: Neil Tyler, 2002), passim.
71. 'Chinese Football Association – Introduction', http://www.fa.org.cn/en. Accessed on 28 March 2003.
72. Reporter, 'Nuzu zuanhui lanshixian' ['No Transfer System for Women Footballers'], *Titan zhoubao* [*Sports Weekly*], 27 Jan. 2003, p.4.
73. Interview at the Office of the Chinese FA in Beijing on 2 Sept. 2001.
74. Huan Yong, 'Fang Zhang Jianqiang, zuxue nuzibu zhuren' ['Interview with Zhang Jianqiang, the Head of Women's Football Division of the Chinese FA'], 24 March 2003, http://sports.sohu.com/51/64/news207526451.shtml. Accessed on 24 March 2003.
75. 'Nuzu huayuan weihenan?' ['Why cannot Women's Football Teams get Sponsorship?'], 30 Jan. 2003, http://sports.tom.com/Archive/1569/1573/2003/1/30-32683.html. Accessed on 26 March 2003. See also 'Meigui jinqiaoqiao de kai' ['The Iron Roses Have to Grow very Quietly'], http://www.footballwindow.com/woman/zhidaoma/0629meigui.htm. Accessed on 25 March 2003.
76. Zhen Guishen, 'Woguo nuzu haobei duiwu de jianshe jidai jiaqiang' ['On the Problem of Recruit of Female Football Players'], *Jianghan daxue xuebao* [*Journal of Jianhan University*], 1 (2001), 108.
77. Luan Kaifeng, 'dui shaosu zhiye zuqiu yundongyuan chaogao shouru de yidian shikao' ['My Thoughts on the High Income of Some Professional Football Players'], *Tiyu wenshi* [*Journal of Sport History and Culture*], 6 (2000), 11; A. Xiang, 'Zhongguo titan de disan shijie' ['The Third World in Chinese Sport'], *Xing shiji* [*New Century*], 1 (1997), 75; Wang Suizhi, 'Zuqiu zhiyehua dailai de kuihuo' ['The Confusion which Brought by Professional Football'], *Banyetan*, 19 (1997), 46–7; 'Guojiao xianjin jiangli renjun yicao 30 wan' ['Top Footballers' Bonus have Reached More than 30 Thousand RMB'], http:www.sportsonline.com.cn/GB?channel12/507/1971/20011026/42520.html. Accessed on 26 Oct. 2001; Xu Xiaoli, 'Sichang haishi hexin' ['Women's Football Depends on Sports Market'], *Zhongguo tiyu bao*, 18 Oct. 1999, p.6. Min Yan, 'Guanyu zhongguo nuzu' ['About Chinese Women's Football'], *Zhejiang ribao* [*Zhejiang Daily*], 13 July 1999, p.4.
78. 'Nuzu chaoji liansai' ['Women's Primary League'], *Zhongguo tiyu bao*, 18 Oct. 2000, p.6.
79. Ping, 'Nuzu shengyan zhiyehua' ['The Problem of Women's Football and Sports Market'], *Zhongguo tiyu bao*, 8 Dec. 1999, p.2; Cao Jing, 'Nuzu de digu jiangshi changqide: Mayuan'an didiao shuo nuzu' ['The Decline of Women's Football will be a Long Period according to the Head Coach Ma Yuan'an'], *Zhongguo qingnian bao* [*Chinese Youth Daily*], 28 Dec. 2001.

4

Chains, Challenges and Changes: The Making of Women's Football in Korea

EUNHA KOH

'Better than Men's Football'
Women's football is winning popularity far beyond outdoing people's
expectations. Excellent play in Tiger Pools Toto Cup International
Women's Football Games is drawing football fans. (...) Some fans suggest
bold investment into women's football, indicating women's football has
better prospects than men's football. Recently, a fan made a cutting remark
that men's football should follow the example of women's football.[1]

The Women's National Team and Women's Football Federation were established
in March 2001, 11 years after Korea sent a women's football team to the 1990
Beijing Asian Games. In August 2001, the Women's National Team won a victory
in the Toto Cup,[2] and also won the bronze medal at the 21st Summer Universiad.
This was the moment when Korean women's football first came into the national
spotlight and became a new icon of Korean sport.

Baseball and football have been the very popular in Korea in recent times.
National surveys show that they are the first and second most popular spectator
sports.[3] Since the professional baseball league was launched in 1982, it has been
the most watched event, and there has been considerable interest in Korean
players who have been transferred to professional leagues abroad. On the other
hand, international events like the football World Cup have attracted huge
attention nationwide. The birth of 'Red Devil' as the nationwide football
supporters group is a good example of football enthusiasm in Korea.[4] The
enthusiasm is evident not only in spectatorship, but also in participation.
Although football participation has decreased slightly because of the rise of
various new sports, nevertheless football is still one of the most popular sports,
with thousands of clubs and community associations.

Given the general enthusiasm for football throughout the country, it was
logical that interest was shown in the Women's National Team following its
successful debut. The team began in the hope that it would establish a new era of
women's football in Korea, just as had occurred in other countries, such as the
United States, Japan and China. However, the glow of success began to fade after
a few months and slumped at the beginning of 2002 when the team was soundly

beaten in three goodwill matches against Australia. Then the Sungmin Wonders, the strongest Korean women's corporate team, was disbanded because of the financial difficulties of the sponsoring company.[5] Furthermore, structural problems within women's football and friction inside the football community have created several problems for women's football.

Were the recent rise and the unexpected prestige of women's football due to the progress of women's sport in Korea, or to other social factors? What is the reason for the collapse of its sudden fame? Was it because of the limitations of women's matches as compared to men's and the perceived inappropriateness of the sport itself to women? What are the possibilities and limitations of women's football in women's sport in twenty-first-century Korea? Will it be able to overcome the present difficulties or will it again become a relatively unpopular sport? What are the forces that will decide the fate of women's football?

To answer the above questions, it is necessary to map out the present status of women's football through a careful investigation of the development of women's sport and football in modern Korea. It is evident that the progress of sport in a particular country or society is closely related to the politics, economics, culture and other aspects of that society. Thus, it is essential to examine the relationship between the traditional values on gender in Korean society and the development of women's sport in general and women's football in particular. The rapid modernization of Korean society has brought about a remarkable growth of sport, elite sport in particular. But conservative gender stereotypes and discriminative gender relations inherited from the Confucian tradition are deeply rooted in Korean society, and have resulted in gender inequality in sport. Therefore, we need to take a dialectic approach to the status of women's football, with the nationalism witnessed in football on one axis and the traditional values on gender relations on the other.

In what follows, the context in which prejudice against women's sport (including women's football) is constructed in contemporary Korea, at the same time as men's sport is celebrated, will be explored. Then the rise of women's football, the challenges and changes it has faced in the twentieth century will be discussed, with an emphasis on the contradictory status of women's football in Korean society. Finally, the possibilities and limitations of women's football in the future will be considered.

CONFUCIANISM AND PREJUDICE AGAINST WOMEN'S SPORT

The male population took possession of modern sport from its introduction into Korea during the age of the 'Korean Empire' from 1897 to 1910. The main reason for this unusual adoption of sport can be found in the Confucian tradition of the Chosun dynasty (1392–1896). The Confucianism that formed the foundation of social values in Chosun was the school of *Sung-ri-hak*, a product of the Song dynasty of China. *Sung-ri-hak* had the most conservative character among the

68

various schools of Confucianism, and emphasized the control of the individual as a way of establishing virtue.[6]

Confucian values strictly divided the domestic and social roles of male and female, and spread the notion of *Nam-jon-yeo-bi* (predominance of men over women), which defined woman as subordinate to men. Confucianism not only separated the domains of the daily lives of men and women under the rule of *Nam-nyeo chil-se bu-dong-seok* (boys and girls over 7 years old should never be in the same room), but also cut off women from opportunities for education. Moreover, the norms and rules of Confucianism produced the 'docile body' of women, to use Foucault's term, by presenting detailed standards for bodily actions and behaviour. It should be noted that Confucianism was weakened and almost disappeared during the Communist revolution in China, where it originated, but that it was still able to exert its influence over contemporary Korean society.[7]

Gender discrimination and the neglect of women's rights and needs have been visible in almost every society. Discrimination in Korea, however, is different from that in the Western countries because of the fact that female bodies were supposed to be hidden from public view. Physical activities were not in accordance with the moral and bodily behaviour expected of women in early-twentieth-century Korea. A good example of this attitude can be found at Ewha School, the first modern girls' school, where gymnastics was taught to girls in physical education classes for the first time in Korean history, but the activity was harshly criticized. It was seen as not only inappropriate, but also immoral, for girls to raise their arms and legs in the air, because upper-class women and girls were supposed to walk with small and dainty footsteps (with a distance of less than a foot between each footstep). Angry parents withdrew their daughters from the school and families held meetings to protect the honour of the family. Parents with marriageable sons swore not to select a daughter-in-law from those who had attended the school, and the Municipal Government forbade it teaching gymnastics classes.[8]

Nevertheless, in time Korean women were exposed to various sports activities mainly through modern schools, and began to open their eyes to modern values. Gymnastics, basketball and tennis were offered to girls and women in 1911.[9] But there was no opportunity for girls and women to participate in any kind of masculine sport, including football, at this time, when even those sports regarded as feminine or neutral were criticized.

MEN'S FOOTBALL AND NATIONAL IDENTITY IN COLONIAL AND POST-COLONIAL KOREA

The introduction and development of modern sport in Korea proceeded in tandem with the modernization of the nation which began in 1876, when the country opened its doors to foreign countries. Most of the modern sports were introduced between 1900 and 1909, during the 'Korean Empire' (1897–1910), by missionaries from the West.[10] When modern sport was introduced into Korea, it quickly established itself as a means of achieving the self-discipline needed to strengthen the country against foreign powers,[11] as well as a school subject within a modern education system,[12] and an important moral tool for Christian missionaries.[13]

At an early stage of the modernization process, influenced by Western civilization, Korea became a colony of Japan from 1910 to 1945.[14] The experience of colonization before full modernization had a great influence on the construction of modern Korea and also on the development of modern sport. Bum-Jang Lim identifies the results as follows.[15] First, the dual structure of values, derived from the contrast between traditional feudalism and modern civilization, created a discrepancy between the modern sports institutions and rules and what survived of the pre-modern way of thinking. Second, during Japanese rule, sport was used to inspire anti-Japanese feelings, and internal resistance was hidden under a disguise of superficial obedience. In other words, sport was pursued at its face value, but underneath, it had an additional value as a tool of nationalism. The aim of physical education was to create mental as well as physical strength, supporting a cherished desire for the restoration of national rights. Sports contests between Korean and Japanese athletes became opportunities for symbolic battle between the two countries. As Korea experienced Japanese rule, liberation, and industrialization, sport in Korean society continued to develop and change. However, old-fashioned conservatism and a strong sense of nationalism, which were the features formed during its early introduction, remained beneath the surface of contemporary Korean sport culture.[16]

The development of Korean football experienced a similar process to that of Korean sport in general. Modern football was introduced in 1882, when the 'Flying Fish', a British warship, disembarked in Chemulpo.[17] In 1904, football was formally introduced as part of the curriculum of physical education in the National Foreign Language School. Afterwards, football spread to other schools and became a major activity in athletic meetings, and was very popular with the public. The first football game was held in Seoul on March 1906, and standard games with international rules and equipment were held from the 1920s.[18] Football fulfilled the important role of enhancing nationalism and the self-respect of the public under Japanese rule. The hunger for victory in international football games was inspired by nationalism in its early stages.

During the regime of Jung-Hee Park through the 1960s and 1970s, a strong sports policy was first instituted to unify the nation, to spread the nation's prestige abroad, and to confirm the legitimacy of political power. This was the age of elite promotion in all areas of sport, including football. In 1961, the government gave financial support to the Korean Sports Council to strengthen the country's competitiveness at international sport events,[19] and made a great effort to win international medals with institutional support for promising sports. This was the era of the Cold War, when victory in sport was internationally regarded as a way of proving the superiority of the state or an ideology. Men's football was at the top of the list of sports of great promise, being the most popular sport in Asia, and worthy of special attention from the Korean government.

This strong support for sport has been maintained until the present day, through two other military regimes (that of Doo-Hwan Jun and Tae-Woo Roh) and the regimes of the new civilian leaders, Young-Sam Kim, Dae-Jung Kim and Mu-Hyun Roh. The hosting of the Olympic Games in Seoul in 1988 was the biggest event in post-war Korea, demonstrating the growth of Korean society in general, and Korean sport in particular, to the world. In spite of failure in both the World Cup and Olympic Games, men's football received continuous support from the government. As a result of long investment, the Men's National team reached the World Cup Finals, and finally won fourth place in 2002. Men's professional baseball and football leagues were launched respectively in 1982 and 1983, during the social reforms of the 1980s. Many games were broadcast through the newly reformed television system. Whereas the professionalization of sport in the West was based on market forces, that of Korea was conducted according to the political decisions of the government and encouraged the participation of industry, and was a way of legitimatizing political power.[20]

Thus, from the introduction of football in 1882 to the winning of fourth place at the 2002 World Cup, men's football has played a key roll in exhibiting and consolidating Korean national identity. However, it is important to note that the national enthusiasm for football was only for men's games, not for women's games. Prejudice against women's sport has formed a glass ceiling since the introduction of football to Korea, which has constrained the growth of women's football to date.

TOMBOYS IN THE PLAYGROUND: THE RISE OF WOMEN'S FOOTBALL

The history of women's football in Korea is more than 50 years old, although it has been only a decade since the sport started to attract much attention. Less than a year after the government of the Republic of Korea was established in 1948 (emancipation from Japan was achieved in 1945), the first official women's football matches were held as a part of National Girls' and Women's Sport Games. This was in Seoul, on 28–29 June 1949, and included track and field, tennis, volleyball, basketball and handball, as well as football. Although only four high-school teams competed in the Games, it was significant that women's football was first presented as a national-level sport. However, from this point onwards, public opinion was opposed to the pioneers who insisted on including girls' football matches in the Games, that is, Eun-Bae Kim, the president of a nationwide daily newspaper, *Seoul Shinmoon*, and Hwa-Jip Kim, the leading instructor in girls' football. Women's basketball and volleyball won public recognition through the Games, but football was seen not only as being unsuitable for women, but also as being unattractive to the public. As a result, the girls' teams were disbanded soon after the event; and there were various other difficulties, among which the lack of public understanding was perhaps the most important.

As discussed in the previous section, the 1960s and 1970s were the age of elite sports promotion in all areas of Korean sport. At this time, sport was often seen as a war that could be waged without weapons. Men's football was one of the sports where national prestige could best be seen as confirming the legitimacy of political power, and it received special attention from the government. On the national level, the Industrial Football Association was established in 1966, and on the international level, Park's Cup Asian Football Games[21] were established in 1971. In spite of the highly visible role that women athletes have played in international sporting events, including winning the first Olympic medal in Korean history, the promotion of women's sport was carried out only at a limited, elite level. Because it was a somewhat less promising and less 'gender-appropriate' sport, women's football was paid little attention by either the government or the general public.

However, women's football survived through these hard times thanks to a few enthusiastic instructors who made continuous efforts to sustain it. A high school team was established in Jeon-Ju in 1969, followed by six more teams in the early 1970s. Efforts made by a few football authorities led to the First National Women's Football Games in 1974. For the first time in the history of women's football, these advocates pushed forward the formation of a national team and claimed that women's football had a greater possibility of international success than men's. This attempt to revitalize women's football, however, ended in failure. Most football authorities did not welcome female challenges and the public was simply not interested. Furthermore, the media ridiculed women's football and it was claimed that 'the behaviour in the games was non-educational and ugly'.[22]

> The football community is strained at the news that women's football is planning to form a national team and go on a playing tour to Malaysia. (...) However, its [skill] level is the lowest of low class as shown in the First National Women's Football Games. Would it be necessary to go on expedition with this low level? A person concerned in women's football asserted women would top the World Cup faster than men. Nevertheless, the football community is too sceptical about the spread of women's football to support the ambitious plan.[23]

The 1980s was the period when the men's professional football league was established. Along with its popularity acquired through international matches, men's football entered a new era and became one of the most popular media sports in Korea. Football was rated as the second favourite spectator sport through the 1980s and 1990s, after baseball, which was professionalized in 1982. International matches have often recorded the highest television viewing numbers, which demonstrates the importance of football in contemporary Korean sports history.[24] In contrast, women's football was not even recognized as a major sport for college entrance, to say nothing of the lack of a professional league. The 'gender transformation'[25] which had been effected in football in England and other European countries after the 1970s did not occur in Korean football, in spite of the changes in the policies of the Fédération Internationale de Football Association (FIFA), the governing body of world football. FIFA's recommendations to facilitate women's football encouraged the Korea Football Association (KFA) to hold women's matches on 3 and 8 February 1985, but these ended with a repetition of past failure. The public did not express an interest in women's football despite the enthusiasm for both spectating and playing in a sport that had been manifested in the 1980s, and the football authorities did not provide any further financial support or recruit players. The conflict between the masculine image of football and the feminine ideals of society meant that football was stigmatized as an inappropriate sport for women. Women's basketball and volleyball, however, have been successfully embraced by the public and the media thanks to the 'relatively acceptable' ways in which they display the female body.

'TAE-GEUK MAIDENS':[26] THE GROWTH OF WOMEN'S FOOTBALL

With shifting gender relations in the world in general, and in Korea in particular in the 1980s, social institutions began to open their gates to women. Laws and regulations were enacted in support of these social changes and women's movement organizations became active in supporting women's right to participate in activities and occupations that have been traditionally regarded as unsuitable for women. The construction of national gender equality is the basis for the growth of women's sport, which has been witnessed in many Western countries. However, the growth of women's sport in Korea experienced a different pattern, mainly because of the unique character of the gender inequality in Korean society, which has been discussed in the previous section.

There have been neither laws or regulations nor any effort of women's organizations to eliminate gender inequality in Korean sport. Instead, a global women's football boom accompanied by international matches such as the Women's World Cup provided a direct stimulus for the growth of women's football in Korea. The failure to construct a basis for women's football in the 1980s in accordance with FIFA's suggestion was not just because football was not seen as a women's sport in Korea, but rather because women's football did not have the opportunities or the exposure likely to enhance national prestige at an international level. It was hard to promote national glory through football when there were no international games except in European countries. However, the sport started to have the possibility of serving 'sport nationalism', as goodwill matches led to a number of international games such as the Women's World Cup and women's football in the Summer Olympic Games. With the prospect that women's football would have a better chance of ranking higher on the international level than men's, the fortunes of women's football started to rise.

The biggest outcome (of Toto Cup) is that the possibility to proceed to the final eight in 2003 China World Cup. Since we have plenty of time until the game, I'm going to set the plan out carefully and push it forward.[27]

When women's football was officially adopted at the Beijing Asian Games in 1990, there was no women's football team – professional or national. The Korean sports authorities decided to form a women's team with athletes from other sports such as tae kwon do, hockey, and athletics and send the team to the Games. The result was defeat in all matches against Japan, North Korea, China and Taiwan. Nevertheless, this appearance of women's football at the international level had a great influence on the development of women's football in Korea. Colleges and corporations started to launch women's football teams through the 1990s and the first annual national women's football event, the Queen's Cup, was held in 1993. With these changes, the ability of Korean female footballers was demonstrated in the 1995 Asian Cup in Malaysia where they won fourth place.

The 1999 Women's World Cup held in the United States is generally recognized as the event which ignited the global interest in women's football. The mass media, football fans and sports authorities all over the world followed the event closely and were impressed by the enthusiasm of the crowded stadium and the dynamism of the players. This event encouraged a rush to play women's football in East Asia, including Korea. The Ministry of Culture and Tourism, which is in charge of sport policy, announced a three-year plan to promote women's football in Korea. The plan included 300 million Won (approximately US$250,000) of sponsorship to increase the number of women's teams from 32 to 70 from elementary school level to corporate level.[28] At the same time, after watching the 1999 Women's World Cup, the Sungmin Corporation and a famous football mogul called Jong-Hwan Park collaborated to establish the Sungmin Wonders, which became the strongest corporate team and a stimulus to other corporate and school teams. At last, the KFA began to invest in women's football and established the Women's Football Federation (WFF) in March 2001 as an independent organization.

In the two years since its foundation, the WFF's players, coaches and administrators have struggled to establish the independent status of women's football, bearing in mind its status as the little sister of men's football. Although the number of girls' and women's teams and players is still less than 10 per cent of the boys' and men's, women's football is one of the fastest growing sports in Korea.[29] More girls wanted to play football as the image of female footballers became increasingly acceptable in Korean society. With the growing interest in participation as well as watching, women's football was first included as an exhibition match in the 'National Sport Games' in 2002. Now, there are exclusive women's competitions such as the Queen's Cup Women's Football Games, the Unification Flag Women's Football Games, and the Spring/Fall WFF Games, not to mention those held in conjunction with men's games on various levels.

The women's team has been successful internationally despite the relatively weak infrastructure of players and finance. Unofficial indicators show that as of November 2001 the Korean women's team had advanced to twentieth place in world women's football.[30] Furthermore, during the 2002 Asian Games held in Busan, Korea, women's football was singled out as an avenue for the exchange of friendship between South and North Korea. After more than 50 years of struggle against prejudice and indifference, by 2002 Korean women's football finally began to gain public recognition both as a participating and spectating sport.

PROBLEMS AND CONTROVERSIES IN WOMEN'S FOOTBALL TODAY

The prestige of the Korean Women's National Football Team began to decline at the beginning of 2002 with its poor results in international competition. It had been less than a year since the team had suddenly become famous. As the glow of victory cooled, various controversial issues and structural problems in the system of women's football became apparent, and friction was created within the football community.

Most of all, it became evident that the most serious problem women's football had to face was its weak infrastructure. The national team did not have a firm basis of school teams to provide sufficient quantity and quality of players. There were a total of 65 women's football teams from elementary school level to professional level, but many of them had been established in the last year or so, intentionally organized by the government.[31] When the situation of countries where women's football has a solid structure is taken into consideration, it can be seen as a miracle that the Korean team has been so successful to date.

In Norway, women's football is one of the most popular sports for women, with approximately 60,000 players at various levels, and it has equal status to men's football. There are more than 4,000 teams for girls aged between 7 and 19, the members of which make up half the total number of youth football players. In the annual youth football games, 25,000 players take part in 3,000 games in one single week. The United States also has a strong base of women's college teams, with 791 teams enrolled in the National Collegiate Athletic Association (NCAA). It is not surprising that it was Norway which won the 1995 Women's World Cup, or that the United States won in 1999. China, which was placed second in the 1999 Women's World Cup, has a corporate league with ten elite teams, and is estimated to be the strongest of the Asian countries. In Japan, there are 1,138 teams, including ten professional teams and 50 college teams with more than 23,000 players.

The reason that these countries have such a broad basis is that players in the school teams enjoy football as a recreational sport. However, at any level of Korean football, it is hard to find recreational players. This is due to the rapid but unbalanced development of sport emphasized in the previous sections. Thus, it is no use to build up more teams or invest more money to train players unless the very nature of sport participation is changed.

The second important issue in women's football is that the Women's National Team and the WFF were constructed hurriedly, with the result that both organizations are immature. The Women's National Team consists of leaders and players from two major professional teams. Most of the players were from INI Steel Red Angels and the former Sungmin Wonders until the latter was disbanded in November 2002. When the Daegyo Kangaroos was launched in the same month, most of the players came from the above three teams. The manager of the team had been Jong-Gwan Ahn, who was the manager of Red Angels until he quit the job in 2002, whereas the president of WFF is Jong-Hwan Park who is the former manager of the Sungmin Wonders. This strange composition of the national team also resulted in its lack of efficient management.[32]

The friction and antagonism inside the women's football system is also one of the serious problems that women's football is faced with. When the WFF was established in 2001, it seemed that Jong-Hwan Park, the president of the association, was supported both by the football authorities and by the public. However, recent newspaper coverage on him and other personnel in the football field has revealed there is a great deal of friction within the administration of the association. He blames other members of the board for the factional strife, whereas they blame Park for his dogmatism and unfairness.[33]

More evidence of the friction and factionalism can be found in the resignations of the secretary of KFF, Sang-Gon Kim and the manager of the national team, Jong-Gwan Ahn. When Kim left his office in early February 2002, the business of women's football was severely affected. Since his resignation meant leaving football permanently, it is obvious that he had a great deal of difficulty making his decision. Ahn sent in his resignation on 19 February. As the manager of INI Steel simultaneously, he experienced difficulties in the selection of the national team players. Some key players were not available. The reason why half of the national team players are from INI Steel is that the Sungmin Wonders wanted to get better results in the domestic league rather than in international matches.[34]

THE FUTURE IS FEMININE? WOMEN'S FOOTBALL IN TWENTY-FIRST-CENTURY KOREA

In the previous section, some of the problems the sport is faced with today were identified. The controversies and problems within women's football are an expression of the contradictions of the sport. The weak infrastructure, the immaturity of the organizations, and the factionalism in sport all result from its history as an unpopular women's sport. As J.F. Larson and H.S. Park[35] suggest, sporting spectacles, which are beamed across the globe to the competing countries and other countries also, are almost impossible to decode without recognizing these nationalistic signs and interpretations. The strong relationship between national identity and Korean sport culture excluded women's football from consideration for a long time, and has supported other sports that were competitive at an international level and popular among the general public. In other words, women's football was abandoned in the course of the 'symbolic process of nation-making through sport'[36] until it recently regained its popularity as a possible source for the expression of national pride.

The social acceptability of sport in terms of gender appropriateness has been a major factor in deciding the future of the sport. With the transformation of football culture on a global level, it can be seen that discrimination in any form will be opposed, and anti-sexism and anti-racism will be advocated as new values.[37] However, to date, football has been seen as a male sport in Korea. The prejudice of the gender inappropriateness of football has limited women's participation in the sport not only at the elite level but also at a recreational level, which has resulted in a lack of players. In addition, the lack of opportunity for women to participate in football resulted in a shortage of women in the decision-making process and in managerial positions, which increased the problems in women's football.

In recent years, as women's football experienced its rise and fall, it seemed at first that the strong nationalism present in the Korean culture would overcome the obstacle of sexism and establish women's football in the mainstream of sports activity. However, as soon as women's football failed to function as a symbol of national identity, the sport lost much of its prestige and was beset with controversies both of an internal and external nature. Will women's football ultimately overcome its present difficulties and recover its prestige, or will it end as an unimportant footnote in the history of sport?

Only the future will tell whether Korean female footballers are successful or not in international competition or in the forthcoming Women's World Cup. The future of the sport will be uncertain unless the entire culture in which it is situated is reformed. Korean women's football needs a different kind of victory in its long struggle with the heavily gendered Korean culture: only then will the young generation be able to fulfil its dream of becoming a Korean Mia Hamm. 'The future of Korean football will be feminine'[38] only when the global trend of gender transformation underway in football is willingly accepted in Korean society, sport and the football world.

NOTES

The author expresses her thanks to Professor Mangan for his additional support.

1. Sung-Wook Choi, 'Better than Men's Football', *Sport Today*, 8 Aug. 2001.
2. A women's football championship established and sponsored by Sport Toto Ltd, a subsidiary company of Tiger Pools Korea, in 2001. The Second Toto Cup was held under the name of East Asian Four Countries Women's Football Championship.
3. Ministry of Culture and Sports, *National Survey on Sport Participation* (Seoul, Korea, 1994). Ministry of Culture and Sports, *National Survey on Sport Participation* (Seoul, Korea, 1997). Ministry of

Culture and Tourism, *National Survey on Sport Participation* (Seoul, Korea, 2000). Ministry of Sports, *National Survey on Sport Participation* (Seoul, Korea, 1989). Ministry of Sports and Youth, *National Survey on Sport Participation* (Seoul, Korea, 1991). The Research Institute of Physical Education, Seoul National University, *National Survey on Sport Participation* (Seoul, Korea, 1986).

 4. 'Red Devil' was the nickname for the Korean National Youth Football Team that played in red uniforms and startled the world by winning fourth place at the World Youth Championship in Mexico in 1983. As a need for a systematic fan culture arose among supporting groups, a national-level football supporters' group was formed in 1997 named after 'Red Devil'.
 5. With no professional women's football league or team, there are corporate teams that are included in the corporate/college league.
 6. Key P. Yang and Gregory Henderson, 'An Outline History of Korean Confucianism: Part ¥±: The Schools of Yi Confucianism', *Journal of Asian Studies*, 18, 2 (1959), 259–76. For the relationship between masculinity, virtue and sport in Korean cultural tradition, which clearly influenced attitudes to men's football in later centuries, see Ha Nam Gil and J.A. Mangan, 'The Knight of Korea: The Hwarangdo, Nhhtarism and Nationalism', *The International Journal for History of Sport*, 15, 2 (1998), 77–102.
 7. Eunha Koh, *Kicking off a New Era for Female Footballers: Gender, Nationalism and Women's Football in Korea*, Paper presented to 'Soccer Nations and Football Cultures': International Symposium in Commemoration of the 2002 World Cup Finals in Japan and Korea (Vienna, Austria, 20–23 March 2002).
 8. Council of Education, Seoul Metropolitan Government, *Educational History of Seoul* (Seoul, Korea: Seoul Metropolitan Government, 1981), pp.80–82.
 9. Young-Il Na, 'Development of Sport in Modern Korea', *Proceedings of 2001 International Conference on Sport Management and Sport History: Humanities and Social Sciences of Sport in 21st Century* (Taiwan, 13–14 July 2001), p.1089.
10. The name of Korea was changed from Chosun to the Korean Empire in 1897, but the country continued to be governed by the Chosun dynasty until its colonization by Japan in 1910.
11. J.M. Lee, 'The Influence of Sport on the State', *The Monthly Journal of Suhbuk Hakhwei*, 6 (1908).
12. Korea Amateur Sports Association, *The 70 Years History of Korea Amateur Sports Association* (Seoul, Korea: Korea Amateur Sports Association, 1990), p.33.
13. Hyung-Ki Kwak, Jin-Soo Lee, Hak-Rae Lee and Young-Moo Lim, *Korean Sport History* (Seoul, Korea: Gisik Sanupsa, 1994), pp.147–8.
14. On the grounds of mainstream sociology that regards industrialization as the starting point of modernization, Korea is an exception exposed to modernity without modernization. Korea turned into a modern nation-state without the basis of industrialization, since the industrialization both in name and reality did not begin until the 1960s.
15. Burn-Jang Lim, *Sport and the Modernisation of the Korean Society*, Paper invited to the 6th Annual Conference of Japanese Society of Sport Sociology (Kyoto, Japan, 26–28 March 1997).
16. See in particular for a further discussion, Ha Nam Gil and J.A. Mangan, 'A Curious Conjunction – Sport, Religion and Nationalism: Christianity and the Modern History of Korea', *The International Journal for History of Sport*, 3 (1994), 329–54.
17. Chemulpo was one of the three ports opened to Western powers according to the 'Kanghwado Treaty' in 1876. It became a city and was named 'Inchon', where the largest international airport in East Asia is located.
18. Korea Football Association, *100 Years History of Korean Football* (Seoul, Korea: Rasara, 1986).
19. Korea Sports Council, *70 Years of Korea Sports Council* (Seoul, Korea: Korea Sports Council, 1990).
20. See Ha Nam Gil and J.A. Mangan, 'Ideology, Politics, Power: Korean Sport Transformation 1945–92', in J.A. Mangan and Fan Hong (eds), *Sport in Asian Society: Past and Present* (London: Frank Cass, 2003), pp.213–42.
21. It was renamed as the 'Korean Cup Asian Football Championship'.
22. Dong-A Ilbo, 'Worries for Women's Football Going on Expedition', *Dong-A Ilbo*, 11 July 1974, 6.
23. Ibid.
24. *National Survey on Sport Participation*, 1986; 1989; 1991; 1994; 1997; 2000.
25. Richard Giulianotti, *Football: A Sociology of Global Game* (Cambridge: Polity Press, 1999), p.154.
26. The nickname for the Korean Women's Football Team, which was named after the 'Tae-Geuk Warriors', the nickname for the Korean Men's Football Team. 'Tae-Geuk' means 'the Great Absolute' in Chinese philosophy, which is the source of the dual principle of Yin and Yang. The nicknames used for football teams symbolize 'Tae-Geuk-Gi', the national flag of Korea.

27. Duk-Gi Kim, 'Possibility for the World Stage: An Interview with Park Jong-Hwan Park, the First President of Women's Football Federation', *Sport Today*, 8 Aug. 2001.
28. Sport Today, 'Ministry of Culture and Tourism's Women's Football Promotion Plan', *Sport Today*, 26 Aug. 1999.
29. As of 2002, there are 65 girls' and women's teams and 1,231 enrolled players, whereas there are 593 boys' and men's teams and 17,106 enrolled players throughout elementary school to professional level.
30. There is no official rank in FIFA. Unofficial sources include: http://home.sprynet.com/~ronkessler/ rankings.htm, http://www.reed.edu/~jones/ratings/ratings.html, http://home.sprynet.com/ ~ronkessler/rsssfarc.htm.
31. There are 16 elementary school teams, 22 middle school teams, 16 high school teams, 9 college teams, and 3 professional teams, which becomes 66 in total at the end of 2001. In 1999, there were 2 middle school teams, 15 high school teams, 5 college teams and 3 professional teams.
32. Data obtained from official websites of KFA (www.kfa.or.kr) in Dec. 2002 and the website of WFF (shut down in Feb. 2002) in Jan. 2002.
33. Kyung-Wan Suh, 'Domestic Trouble: Women's Football Federation in Danger of Collapse', *Sport Today*, 30 Dec. 2001.
34. Eun-Hee Chung, 'Depressed Women's Football with People Leaving', *Sport Seoul*, 26 Feb. 2002.
35. James F. Larson and Heung-Soo Park, *Global Television and the Politics of Seoul Olympics* (Boulder, CO: Westview Press, 1993).
36. David Rowe, Jim McKay and Toby Miller, 'Come Together: Sport, Nationalism and the Media Image', in L.A. Wenner (ed.), *Mediasport: Cultural Sensibilities and Sport in the Media Age* (New York: Routledge, 1998), p.120.
37. Giulianotti, *Football: A Sociology of Global Game*.
38. Quoted from the title of the article 'The Future is Feminine' dated 1995 and posted on FIFA Website: <www.fifa.com>.

5

Forwards and Backwards: Women's Soccer in Twentieth-Century India

BORIA MAJUMDAR

I

England's progress in the World Cup is likely to draw record interest from women, as the notion of the 'football widow', annoyed and alienated during high profile matches, becomes a thing of the past. For the first time, marketing of the World Cup is being directed towards women, particularly younger ones, as companies attempt to cash in on the growing popularity of football. High street stores, including Top Shop, have produced a range of World Cup merchandise, from bikinis to underwear, printed with the cross of St George and other slogans designed to show support for the England team.

Both the Football Association and television companies expect record interest in the tournament from women, and about 15 per cent of England fans in Japan with the official England supporters' club will be female. Pubs and clubs also expect many women will watch England during their morning broadcasts.

Female football merchandise is one of the fastest growing areas in the marketing of the game at club and international level. There has always been England merchandise aimed at men during a world cup, making it a multi-million pound industry, but many firms now feel that similar merchandise for women could prove just as lucrative.

Umbro, which makes the England kit, has produced an England team shirt taking into account the female body, and an England team dress bearing the three lions crest. Top Shop has England World Cup products aimed at women in all of its 300 stores, with a glitter England bikini and England beach towels proving the biggest sellers.[1]

> Football now permeates every aspect of daily life. It was not like this 10 years ago. Companies now realize the huge benefits of trying to tap into women's interest. *Nick Baron, the FA's spokesman for England Fans.*[2]

In contrast to these views portraying the upbeat nature of women's soccer in Britain, this study will demonstrate that Indian women's soccer continues to languish, hardly comparable in popularity to its British counterpart. Women spectators, key to the popularity of football in Britain,[3] are a rarity in India with football still regarded as a male domain, taboo for respectable middle-class women. In contrast to Britain, women footballers in India are members of the lower classes who try their hands at soccer with no other tangible means of livelihood in sight.[4] Women's soccer associations continue to stagnate with financial crisis a permanent companion of the women's game. Leading stars are hardly given due recognition, and jobs on offer on account of their sporting prowess are never higher than the clerical grade. It is commonplace to see noted women footballers starving after retirement, often rescued from such plight by welfare organizations and sports enthusiasts. Faced with the prospect of impoverishment, the Women's Football Federation,[5] it is apparent, can hardly make a difference in the near future. Further, it would be improper to hold them singularly responsible for the gloomy reality surrounding the women's game. Rather, the attitude of the Indian male, the nature of the development of urban Indian societies after independence and the story of women's emancipation in the country have all had a role to play in crippling the development of women's football.

Always keen to relegate his woman to the household, the average Indian male has hardly ever encouraged their women to play soccer. Looked upon as a sport unsuited to women, given their physical build, women's soccer is still taboo in many Indian middle-class homes. Daughters or wives playing football are considered a disgrace to the family, with ostracism from society the outcome of such forays. Under such circumstances, women are often forcibly stopped from playing football, while in many other cases women hardly ever attempt to play, having grown up to understand that football is something alien to them and reserved for men only. The only footballing concession made is in the case of women spectators,[6] but even then, they are hardly ever permitted to look beyond the television screen. The number of women spectators, in comparison to men, is negligible, often less than 2 per cent of the entire spectator base for football in the country. Strangely enough, women themselves have also contributed to this plight. The story of women's emancipation in India has included little attempt by women themselves to encourage women's football and cricket. Most measures undertaken to develop women's football took place in the colonial period, and post-independence women activists hardly consider it relevant to protest against notions that cricket and football, the two most popular Indians sports, continue to be male preserves, barely allowing women's involvement.[7] Such apathy, stimulated and encouraged by the attitude of the Indian male, has made women's football a lower class vocation in modern India.

Using the film *Bend it Like Beckham* as an entry point, which portrays the story of a modern young British Sikh girl who aspires to be a professional footballer, this study attempts to retrieve the lost history of Indian women's football. It also deals with the sad plight of women footballers in modern-day India, the reasons behind the dismal state of the game, and offers comments on the challenges that confront women footballers in contemporary India.

II

Described as the best British comedy since *Bridget Jones' Diary*, Gurinder Chadha's *Bend it Like Beckham* has been accepted as one of the most successful films about Anglo-Indian life of recent years, both in India and abroad. The film's success, as I see it, goes far beyond the marvellous camera work and gripping story line. As a cultural historian, working on the historical centrality of sport in Indian socio-economic and political life, I read *Bend it Like Beckham* not simply as a saga of an Indian girls resistance to familial oppression, or a tale of women's emancipation. The film for me is a commentary, in the filmic and imaginative mode, on the history of women's soccer itself in India today. In this essay, I draw on the representations of soccer in the film to comment on the realities of Indian women's soccer, facts hardly ever mentioned in existing studies on Indian sport. Using the filmic imagination to get an idea of the discursive imaginary, which then helps open up historical questions, I delve into the history of women's soccer in the country, a history that remains 'lost'.[8] Thus, by using *Bend it Like Beckham* as a take-off point, my motive is to question certain assumptions about women's soccer in contemporary India. This questioning, it will be evident from the following narrative, will rectify certain conventional wisdoms about the nature of the women's game, and view it as more than a mere pastime.

III

The film goes deep into the psyche of the Indian masses. It brings together two potent components of Indian cultural life – the magic of cinema and the excitement of the game of soccer. It is therefore a collage of two powerful elements of Indian mass culture, a colourful tale about a talented Indian teenage girl told through the cinematic medium.

The infallibility of this formula is not accidental. Films and sport are pillars of Indian public culture, and unlike other sporting films which have failed miserably at the box-office,[9] the success of *Bend it Like Beckham*, like that of *Lagaan*[10] a year before, has accrued from an ideal blending of the two.

Set in contemporary Britain, *Bend it Like Beckham* is the tale of Jasminder, a young Sikh girl who is a fanatical soccer fan. Her room is full of pictures of David Beckham,[11] in action and otherwise, and when playing in the local park she wears the number seven shirt, used by Beckham while turning out for Manchester United[12] or England. She is the only Indian girl of her age who plays soccer, her mates are all male who appreciate her skills but never forget that she is a girl. It is on such an occasion, when Jasminder is playing with the boys in the local park, that she is spotted by Jules, a regular with the Hounslow Harriers soccer team. The Hounslow Harriers, an all-female team, is coached by an Irishman, a failed footballer himself, and had aspirations of making their mark on the domestic English soccer scene. Having seen Jasminder in action and appreciating at once how talented she is, Jules asks her to train with the Harriers.

When it becomes known to her family that Jess (Jasminder) plays soccer for the Hounslow Harriers, her parents, like most Indian guardians, forbid her to continue. To continue her tryst with soccer, she lies to her family, saying that she is working in a local HMV store. This lie grants her temporary freedom.[13] When her parents discover her deception, they are more determined than ever to stop her from playing soccer, which is, after all, a 'man's game'. She is forbidden from playing soccer by reminders of the rituals of her faith, strict parental control and on grounds that Indian tradition forbids teenage girls from playing physically demanding games like soccer.[14]

Her unabated passion for football made the sport an arena of contestation, individual aspiration against traditional dogma and rejection of parental wishes. The sporting prowess of Jess, and her ultimate success in convincing her father of her ability, helped her emphasize that her 'female' identity was in no way inferior to that of her 'male' counterparts. Women's mastery of a masculine sport, thus, emerges as the leveller between the two sexes. The film, however, goes beyond the soccer field. Unfulfilled aspirations of her father, who was prevented by the whites from playing cricket,[15] and the genuine sympathy of an Irishman for an Indian woman, both born in countries with similar colonial pasts, can be seen as critiques against the practices of racial discrimination and the theories of colonialism.[16]

Indeed, there is an element of the 'feel good' of the Indian blockbuster genre to the plot. But there is much more to the film, and it is this that distinguishes it from other representatives of this genre. Released after the mega success of *Lagaan, Bend it Like Beckham* successfully captures the heart of the Indian sports fan and opens up an entry point for historians to comment on the nature of women's soccer in India.

IV

Historians and commentators of sport in India have always attempted to represent soccer as a masculine enterprise. The links, if any, between women and football are seen as a very contemporary phenomenon. That the two could be linked historically is seen as unfounded and fallacious. The following statement by Peter Velappan, Secretary of the Asian Football Confederation, testifies to this argument:

> Women's football in India is at its infant stage. However, the Indian team has established themselves as a force to be reckoned with after their performances at the 11th Asian Women's Championship in China. Cultural problems are the main factors that are hindering the growth of women's football in India. Eight teams are participating in the National League in 1999. The respective state football associations are responsible for the progress of women's football.[17]

A closer look into the archives of Indian football reveals an entirely different story. The origin of women's soccer in India was closely tied with the movement for women's suffrage and emancipation in colonial India. With the establishment of the All India Women's Congress in 1918, the move for women's suffrage gathered momentum.[18] Around this time, some women commentators espoused the cause of women's soccer, demanding better sports facilities for women. That there was a close link between the suffrage movement and the introduction and/or development of women's soccer was not a new or unique phenomenon. With the establishment of the All India Women's Congress, attempts were made to give women a voice that had been absent throughout the nineteenth century.

With men acting on behalf of their female counterparts, women had, through the nineteenth century, remained a 'site' upon which the colonial state and the Indian intelligentsia had discussed issues of governance and reform.[19] As part of this broader movement for emancipation, sport, especially cricket and football, gained currency among Indian women. Period vernacular tracts commented on the virtues of these sports, claiming that sporting prowess would stimulate the movement for women's emancipation.

The vernacular journal *Meye Mahal* asserted:

> Earlier, sport was for women an extremely limited enterprise. By sport, they understood the playing of cards or other indoor games. By the 1930s things had changed. By this time women had started taking a keen interest in cricket, football and hockey. 'If we are to rise from ignominy, we must take sport more seriously. When the Mohun Bagan Football Club had won the IFA shield in 1911, Indian males had made a huge issue out of it. We should also equip ourselves to achieve a similar victory. Such a victory is only possible in sport.'[20]

It is evident from such tracts published in colonial India that prowess in sport provided a sense of community to Indian women from disparate backgrounds, who, in a patriarchal society, had been united by the expediencies of history. Earliest evidences of Indian women playing football go back to the 1890s. In the closing years of the nineteenth century, a series of matches were organized between men and women, with teams consisting of six members each from both sexes.[21] Despite this early start, women *en masse* continued to stay away from soccer by the turn of the century, and there was a hiatus of almost three decades before organized attempts were undertaken to further the development of football among Indian women.[22] Among other reasons, this period was one of intense political turmoil in the country, especially in Bengal,[23] the home of Indian soccer, forcing women's sport to take a backseat in the province. Even when women became conscious of the importance of the sport from the 1920s onwards, this cognizance remained confined to a minority, with most eschewing rigorous sporting activity.

As in Britain, the inter-war period marked the gradual development of women's soccer in India with the post-First World War period opening up opportunities for women to play the game. But unlike in Britain, where such efforts gathered momentum with the result that by 1920–21 there were 150 women's teams playing soccer,[24] in India/Bengal the spurt was short lived and by the early 1920s soccer had again become a male monopoly. It remains unclear whether the colonial Indian male saw the sporting activities of their women counterparts as a conscious challenge to their hegemony, but it was undoubtedly the case that attempts to extend women's recreation provoked vigorous opposition. It is surprising perhaps to note that strong opposition also came from a section of women themselves. Importantly, this section belonged to the educated stratum of society. Some of them, administering women's educational institutions in the city, thwarted attempts to further sport in these institutions, claiming that such actions would have a corrupting influence on the students.[25]

Also contributing to a decline in women's sporting activity was the emergence of criticism of British sports, such as cricket and football, in Bengal in the 1920s. It was argued by Bengali intellectuals that these sports had been consciously promoted by the British to misdirect the Indian youth:

> By promoting costly sports like cricket and exciting sports like football, the British have aimed to puzzle our youth. These sports require a developed physique, which most Indian boys do not have. In its absence, it was natural for our boys to remain mediocre, inferior in comparison to their British counterparts. Under such circumstances, the British could continue to defeat the Indians, asserting their supremacy over the sporting arena. Indians should play football only after they have developed their body by doing regular exercise in the *akharas*.[26]

While it was possible for boys to go through regular physical drills in the *akharas*,[27] thus developing their football skills, women were not allowed to do so. This was because the *akharas* were considered a male domain and rigorous physical exercise for bodybuilding was considered opposed to femininity. Accordingly, women's football, which was only gradually starting to mature, underwent a rapid decline.

Antipathy towards women's soccer is explicit in the experiences of Brajaranjan Ray in the 1930s. Ray, considered the father of Bengali sports journalism, tried to promote the development of women's soccer in the educational institutions and clubs of Bengal from the late 1920s.[28] In this period, the number of Indian sportswomen in Bengal was minimal. However, women from the English and Anglo Indian communities actively participated in sports like cricket and soccer. It was the Australian-born teacher, Anne Kelleve, who had taken the lead in promoting women's cricket in India.[29] Under her tutelage, cricket was introduced at the Becker Memorial School at Kotayam, Kerala.[30] Following her lead, cricket and football was introduced in some other Anglo Indian schools of the country. However, in the Indian institutions, the story was fundamentally different. In 1928, Ray took the initiative in establishing the National Youth Association at

Calcutta.[31] When one of its members, Purna Ghosh, attempted to play soccer, she became the subject of ridicule in many sections of society.[32] However, the *Anandabazar Patrika*, the leading Bengali newspaper, gave her considerable support, publishing her photographs on more than one occasion.[33] As the traditional women's dress, the saree,[34] obstructed free movement, women had to discard their conventional attire if they were to play the sport seriously. Rejection of the traditional attire provoked another wave of criticism in the province.[35] In this ambience, in which the hostility towards women's football was growing, Ray's attempt to start an annual soccer tournament for women under the aegis of the Women's Sports Association, established in 1929, was met with severe opposition.

> To promote women's soccer in Calcutta, we decided to start an annual tournament for the girls' colleges of the city. It was decided that the tournament would be organized under the aegis of the Women's Colleges Sports Association, which had been formed in 1929 with Harendranath Mukherjee as President. Accordingly, a notice was sent to all the women's colleges of the city, informing them about the tournament. Soon after the notice had reached, there was widespread opposition against the tournament from many quarters. It was argued that the Association was trying to promote vulgarities and that the members of the Association had evil intentions. As a result, only Victoria College and Ashutosh College consented to participate in the tournament. When I met the Principal of Bethune College, she informed me that the college would field a team only if the referee and linesmen were women. Upon hearing that women referees and linesmen were impossible to find, she expressed concern that without women officials, parents would not want their wards to play. When I insisted that I was a professional coach and hence a teacher, she agreed that Bethune would participate provided I was the only male official. As no other alternative was available, I agreed to the proposal dropping linesmen for the time being.[36]

Securing participation for the tournament did not stop the wave of criticism. Even though Bethune College had agreed to participate, they had done so under the precondition that no male spectator would be allowed entry into the stadium.[37] Accordingly, the first women's soccer tournament was held under strict vigil with no male spectator allowed entry into the ground. Some of the women footballers, playing in sarees, were injured and such incidents were widely reported in the media trying to mobilize public opinion against women's football.[38]

Opposition against women's soccer in Bengal intensified further in the 1930s in view of the increasingly close relationship between Bengali soccer patrons and the British Football Association. The 1930s witnessed a bitter struggle between the Indian states, Bengal on the one hand and the Western and Northern Indian states on the other, for the assertion of supremacy over control of soccer in India. In this struggle Bengal drew upon British support at every step, a factor that eventually contributed to the success of the Maharaja of Santosh, the President of the Indian Football Association (IFA), in combating efforts to establish a parallel governing body, the All India Football Association (AIFA) to rival the IFA with its headquarters in Calcutta.[39] Recognition granted by the British Football Association was employed by Santosh to make the point that the IFA was the central governing body for soccer in India.[40] In 1921, the British Football Association had already expressed its aversion towards women's soccer: on 5 December 1921, the British FA had announced that women's teams could no longer use the grounds of any of its affiliated clubs.[41] This move was disastrous for the women's game, 'robbing it of essential facilities and the credibility that use of such facilities conferred'.

> The FA's statement, which accompanied the ban, demonstrated similar sentiments, its council feeling impelled to express their strong opinion that the game of football is quite unsuitable for females and should not be encouraged.[42]

Depending on the FA for support against the united opposition from other provincial soccer associations of the country, it was natural for Bengali sports patrons to follow the actions of their British counterpart, and oppose attempts to promote the women's game in the province.

Despite considerable opposition, the first women's football tournament of the country continued for four years, eventually resulting in the formation of the Women's Sports Federation in 1938.[43] By the third year of the tournament, some college women had discarded the saree and had started playing in shorts, a revolutionary development in colonial Bengal.[44] However, such initiatives were short lived and women's soccer in Bengal had declined by the early 1940s.

V

In many ways the story of soccer as told in *Bend it Like Beckham* brings to light the history of how Indian women had started playing the game, often for reasons more complex than simply trying to emulate their male counterparts. When Jess, played by Parminder Nagra in the film, appears on screen having convinced her father that her presence in the final of the soccer tournament was key to her team's success against white rivals, the audience holds its breath. The final thus became a site for contestation, also one between white and 'black', evident from her father's lament that his daughter would avenge the insult thrust upon him earlier. When he, a young Indian immigrant from Kenya, had wanted to play cricket in an alien land, his attempts had been thwarted by the '*goras*'[45] who had thrown him out of their club. The match also became a site for contestation between the forces of tradition and modernity. The fact that her father allowed her to play in the game, in spite of her sister's wedding, was symbolic of the triumph of modernity over tradition. At the same time, the fact that Jess could not play without her father's permission reinforced the power of the traditional over the modern. In the final, when Jess scores from the free kick, as David Beckham so often does for Britain lending the name of the film credibility, the crowd erupts with joy. The goal can easily be perceived as the moment when dogmas of inferiority, based on both race and gender, are successfully thrown out of the window.

Further, the introduction of soccer in the film, as a sport played and watched by men, is precisely the story of the game in post-colonial India. Soccer in India continues to be treated as a male-female enterprise and female players are hardly ever given equal treatment when compared to their male counterparts. Even after the formation of associations for the promotion of the women's game in the 1970s, the situation did not change perceptibly. These associations were in many cases controlled by women who were related to men of importance in the Indian soccer hierarchy. Often, leading office bearers of the women's associations were wives of male officials, allowing them to exert *de facto* control over the women's game.[46]

Even in 2002, Indian women's football continues to be a sport promoted seriously by only a few Indian states. This explains the Manipuri dominance over the sport since the 1990s. Bengal and Kerala are the only states which have come close to challenging the Manipuri monopoly over women's football. Since 1991, Manipur has won the National Championship seven times out of nine, meeting Bengal in the final on all occasions.[47] It was only in 2002 that Manipur defeated Orissa in the finals of the national championship, *en route* to reinforcing their supremacy over women's football in the country.[48] This statistic is illustrative of the fact that Manipur and Bengal have completely dominated Indian Women's Football in recent years.[49] In the absence of other states advocating promoting the sport seriously, Manipur, which had established its own Women's Football Federation soon after the All India Women's Football Federation was established in 1975, was able to establish its monopoly over the women's game. In 1976, at the Pologround in Imphal, Manipur, the first State Level Women's Football League was held.[50] This tournament marked the beginning of organized women's football in Manipur.[51] Since then, Manipur has contributed a major share of players to the Indian women's team over the years.[52]

However, in Manipur too, the economic condition of the players and the financial condition of the state soccer association are hardly stable. The following comment by Ibotombi S. Longjam bears testimony to this fact:

> In this age of advanced technology, and high quality products, we are far behind. Players do not get any sponsorship of standard Indian brands of shoes and clothing, let alone those of international repute such as Adidas, Nike, Reebok, etc. These players have long wished for good sports wears, which makes the players fit, comfortable and motivated. But in reality, they are struggling to get even a regular daily diet. Despite all the hurdles of

being born in a poor state, their efforts to keep their opponents at their toes have to be appreciated and admired. It is these issues to which I would like to draw the attention of two agents primarily: the State Government and AMFA have to help our players with money.[53]

It has been a persistent complaint in Manipuri sporting circles that the Government continues to neglect its women footballers. Even when the State Government does offer jobs to female footballers, they are hardly positions commensurate with the players' abilities.[54] Accordingly, Chouba Devi, who has represented India on numerous occasions since 1991, was forced to refuse the post, offered by the state police force, of a constable. Speaking to journalists about her rejection of the offer, Chouba Devi, financially well-off, declared that the state police authorities should have realized that they were not doing her a great favour by offering her the job of a constable. The fact is that women footballers, citizens who had won laurels for their country in international competitions, were hardly given their due in the state. She concluded by saying that by offering her the job of a constable, they were insulting an international sportsperson, who has given her best for her country. Finally, she clarified that she was not against joining the police force, but insisted that the rank should be in accordance with her status as an international footballer, who had made her country proud.[55] Others, like Kumari Devi, coming from a lower middle-class family, were forced to accept whatever was on offer. She confessed that as a member of a poor family, she had no other option but to accept the job of a constable after representing the country for many years.[56]

VI

The central problem that continues to plague the development of women's football in India is lack of financial support. The problem has intensified owing to the negligent attitude of the Indian sports officials towards the game. They continue to treat women's football as something unimportant, hardly significant in comparison to men's soccer in the country. Rarely is a women's encounter played under lights in India. The reason given for not playing under floodlights is that at night it might result in a law and order problem, as most spectators are women. It is an acknowledged fact that more than 30 per cent of the spectators in one-day international cricket matches in India, matches mostly played under lights, are women. So the only tenable explanation for not organizing women's matches under lights is that the organizers do not wish to bear the expenditure that will be incurred. They make little effort to market the women's game, so the financial conditions of the players continue to remain precarious.

It is only recently that a US-based Keralite woman, a member of a football team in the US, has returned to India with a mission – to promote women's football in Kerala.

Margaret Miller, along with a few others – including senior national coach Shaji Cherian Oommen – has launched the Kerala Women's Football Club, the first of its kind in the state. It is aimed at regaining the lost glory of women's football in the state. Affiliated to the Kerala Football Association, the team will be attached to the regional coaching centre of the Kerala Sports Council. More than just extending initial funding, Miller, who is the president of the club, hopes to raise more funds from Kerala associations in the US. Her husband, Thomas Miller, is the chairman of the club, brother Giles Francis, the treasurer, and coach Shaji Oommen, the secretary.[57]

These initiatives, if taken up on a far greater scale, might contribute to improving the state of women's soccer in India. Also of significance are efforts by the leading clubs of the country, Mohun Bagan and East Bengal, to form quality women's soccer teams. The IFA, governing body for soccer in Bengal, has recently started a women's soccer league, a tournament expected to play a significant role in stimulating the development of the women's game.[58]

VII

The stagnant nature of the women's game throws up the question as to why Indian sports administrators, over decades, have remained aloof from promoting women's football? Why, in a soccer-crazy society like India, has the women's game remained marginal? Why has this picture remained unchanged after the formation of the Women's Soccer Federation in 1975? Moreover, why is it so in an age when women are matching men in almost all other walks of life in the country, and when in sport, too, a woman earned the only medal for India at the Sydney Olympics?[59]

As depicted in *Bend it Like Beckham*, the origin and development of Indian women's soccer can only be meaningfully analysed by placing it against the wider canvas of colonial and post-colonial Indian society. In other words, considerations of tradition and efforts to reinforce male superiority over the realm have pushed the development of women's soccer, as in the film, to the backburner. The roots of such opposition go deep in an attempt to reinforce patriarchal control over a society where women are gradually coming to challenge male supremacy. Efforts to promote women's soccer, which could have emerged as an index wherein trends governing day-to-day life in India could be assessed, in turn making the sport a contested arena between the sexes, has thus been often nipped in the bud.

In contrast to India, in England, as Vivek Chaudhary asserts:

> Last season, the FA had 61,000 registered women players, compared with 55,000 women classed as netball players. Another 20,000 women are believed to play football informally each week. The FA is drawing up a blueprint for a full time women's professional league, which, it hopes, will be formed within five years.[60]

He quotes Bev Ward, the FA's spokeswoman on women's football, who has declared,

> Football is now the most popular sport among women, and the World Cup will increase their interest in the game. Many companies now realize there are huge financial benefits from having football merchandise aimed at women. The game is more accessible to women, footballers are now like pop stars and their celebrity status has helped attract women to football.[61]

Chaudhary concludes saying:

> Women make up 15 per cent of the 21,000 members of England Fans, the official England supporters' club. The FA has introduced subsidised travel packages for England away matches so that women can travel with children. The ticket allocation system has also been changed to give women a greater chance of buying tickets for England matches.[62]

Unfortunately, in India, the craze for women's soccer or women's attraction for soccer is nowhere near its British counterpart. As depicted in this essay, with initiatives being undertaken by leading clubs and individuals, the prospects for the women's game, however, seem much brighter than a couple of years ago.

VIII

A history of women's soccer in India, as has been evident from this essay, cannot be written without attention to the day-to-day developments in contemporary Indian society. The birth narrative of the women's game in India only makes sense when we take into account the social context, reading this narrative in terms of power equations governing gender relationships in the country. Existing studies on sport in India have hardly given any importance to the women's game. In most studies, the specificity of the women's game and its immediate context is lost. There is hardly any mention of the attempts to develop women's soccer in colonial India, attempts motivated by ideas of self-cultivation and self-worth. Soccer was promoted and played by women in colonial India not simply to facilitate women's emancipation. Rather, the game had become a mirror through which Indian women's identity assessed itself, and in this respect the appropriation of soccer by women could be seen as an early breeding ground of feminism. Such feminist articulations on the sporting field in the minds of many may have been a good enough reason for men to thwart attempts to develop the game in post-independence India.

Finally, it is interesting to note that the release of the film coincided with a period of renewed interest in sporting films in India. If the film had been released a year earlier, its marketable potential would have been in doubt. But with the commercial success of *Lagaan* before her, Chadha had strong reasons to believe that the film would do well at the box office. This close linkage between commerce and leisure in the Indian context, a fact evident from the timing of the film's release, is yet another factor that makes *Bend it Like Beckham* worthy of study. This linkage helps demonstrate the centrality of sport in the Indian socio-economic and political scenario, despite a typically Indian apathy to recognizing this truth, branding it as a mere 'leisure' or 'entertainment' pursuit. Further, the commercial significance of sport in India raises fundamental questions about the value of sport as an 'industry' in the Indian context. This acknowledgement, I feel, will provide fundamentally different explanations about India's industrialization process than the ones hitherto advanced. Finally, the popularity of a film, which shows an Indian woman excel in football, is a telling comment on the changing mentality towards women's soccer in the country. *Bend it Like Beckham* is proof that all is not lost for women, and the years to come may present a different scenario.

NOTES

1. Vivek Chaudhary, 'Women Football Fans Show their True Colours', *The Guardian*, 16 May 2002. In another article written by Chaudhary in *The Guardian*, 'World Cup Marketing Directed at Women for First Time in Attempt to Cash in on Sport's Popularity', he mentions Lucy Palmer, 22, who had already bought an England replica shirt, which she had planned to wear for the World Cup. 'She has entered a television contest where the first prize is an all expenses paid trip to watch England in the World Cup. If she does not make it, she plans to watch the team in the pub. Last season Palmer joined the Tottenham women's team in north London. She also plays for her pub in a five-a-side league composed of men and women players. Her ambition is to get paid for playing football'.
2. *The Guardian*, 16 May 2002.
3. Ibid.; Women make up 15 per cent of the 21,000 members of England Fans, the official England supporters' club. The FA has introduced subsidized travel packages for England away matches so that women can travel with children. The ticket allocation system has also been changed to give women a greater chance of buying tickets for England matches.
4. It is only recently that women are playing football by choice. The game is taking off among Indian immigrants, a fact depicted in the film, *Bend it Like Beckham*. In 1998, Permi Jhooti, a Fulham Ladies Player, had been selected to play for India in the Asian Women's Soccer Championship. For details, see, 'News for the month of October 1999', in .
5. Established in 1975, the organization continues to face severe financial crisis.
6. In accounts describing the passion of fans during Mohun Bagan versus East Bengal contests, it is often mentioned that women do not eat if their favourite team loses; for details see, *Khela*, Sept. 2000.
7. Satires have been written about how women, who go to the cricket ground, spend their time in knitting sweaters, socializing and having a huge feast; *Grahamandal*, Dec., 1960.
8. In all existing works on Indian sport, it has been accepted that women's soccer in the country had started in 1975. There is no mention of any attempt undertaken in colonial India to spread soccer among women.
9. Some sporting films which have failed at the box office are *Awwal Number* and *All Rounder*. Others which have been successful include *Lagaan*, *Ghulam* and *Jo Jeeta wohi Sikander*.
10. A three hour 42 minute film with a budget of 25 crores, Aamir Khan and Asutosh Gowarikar's *Lagaan* has been accepted as the most successful Bollywood blockbuster of recent years. It was nominated for the Oscars in 2002. For details on *Lagaan*, see Boria Majumdar, 'The Politics of Leisure in Colonial India: Lagaan-invocation of a Lost History,' in *Economic and Political Weekly* (1 Sept. 2001).
11. England Captain, Beckham is currently one of the costliest football players in the world. His injury before the world cup in April 2002 had sent shockwaves through England.
12. Arguably the most written about football club in the world, it has more than 15 monographs to its credit.
13. It allows her to tour Hamburg, Germany, as part of the Hounslow Harriers team.

14. The movie starts with a fictional scene where Jess is seen scoring for Manchester United against Anderlecht at Old Trafford. Commenting on the game, Gary Lineker, Alan Hansen and John Barnes see her as the answer to England's problems in the World Cup. However, when they ask her mother, Mrs Bamra, as to whether she is proud of her daughter, she mentions that she is not. Rather, by her own confession, she is ashamed, as her daughter does not know how to cook, a skill expected of all Indian women of her age.

15. Her father mentions that he was a fast bowler and was part of the team, which had won the local cricket championship in Nairobi. However, in Britain the whites discriminated against him and did not allow him to be a part of their club. Humiliated and insulted, he had given up playing cricket.

16. Professor Chris Bayly has spoken of a newly emerging trend in the realm of imperial history – a comprehensive-comparative history of the colonies. Instead of studying colonial histories in isolation, he stresses the viability of studying colonial conditions across the globe. Taking the cases of India and Ireland, both colonies of the erstwhile British Empire, he pointed out a host of affinities in the histories of both these colonies despite their geographical and socio-economic differences. Covering a vast period, 1780–1914, he emphasizes similar strands in the pre-independence and nationalistic movements of both these countries. First Sisir Kumar Bose Lecture organized by the Netaji Research Bureau, Calcutta (29 Dec. 2001). For details on the lecture see, Boria Majumdar, 'History across Continents', *The Statesman*, 9 Jan. 2001.

17. Dato Peter Velappan, 'History of Women's Football in Asia', Keynote address in 'Symposium sur le Football Féminin: Intégralité des interventions'; for details of the speech, see, www.ifrance.com.

18. Through the 1920s, women in most of the Indian states earned voting rights. Sarojini Naidu's campaign for women's suffrage was to a large extent responsible for this development.

19. This argument, advanced by Lata Mani, has been extremely influential in recent writings on Indian History. Lata Mani, *Contentious Traditions* (California: University of California Press, 1998).

20. *Meye Mahal* (Calcutta: 1934).

21. *Anandabazar Patrika*, 13 Aug. 2000.

22. Detailed descriptions of attempts undertaken to promote women's football are evident from Brajaranjan Ray's unpublished account on the genesis of Bengali sports journalism. In this essay, he mentions that it was only in the 1930s that attempts were undertaken to develop women's football in Bengal.

23. The early years of the twentieth century was a phase of intense political turmoil. The partition of Bengal carried out by Curzon in 1905, and the Swadeshi movement launched in protest against the partition, dominated Bengal social and political life of this period. Revolutionary terrorism was also popular, especially in the first decade of the twentieth century.

24. Dave Russell, *Football and the English* (London: Carnegie Publishing, 1997), p.96.

25. Brajaranjan Ray, *Banglay Krida Sangbadikatar Adiparba*, unpublished.

26. Ibid.

27. Gymnasiums, which had become extremely popular in the 1930s.

28. Ray, *Adiparba*.

29. *The Economic Times*, 27 Dec. 1997.

30. Ibid.

31. Ray, *Adiparba*.

32. Ibid.

33. Ibid.

34. Most women wore sarees in colonial Bengal. Things have changed drastically after independence, more so in the course of the last two decades with the result that most women are now seen in modern attires like jeans, salwar kameez and the like.

35. Ray, *Adiparba*.

36. Ibid.

37. Ibid.

38. Ibid.

39. All the leading newspapers of the country, *Amrita Bazar Patrika*, *The Statesman*, *Anandabazar Patrika* carried detailed reports about this ongoing tussle throughout the 1930s.

40. *Amrita Bazar Patrika*, 14 May 1936.

41. Russell, *Football and the English*, p.97.

42. Ibid.

43. Ray, *Adiparba*.

44. Ibid.
45. A term used to refer to the whites. Often used with disgust and anger.
46. This was the case throughout the 1980s and early 1990s.
47. S. Sabanayakan, 'Manipur Unstoppable', in the *Sportstar*, 6-12 April 2002.
48. Ibid.
49. Even in 2002, Bengal was destined to have met Manipur in the finals had it not been for Kerala deliberately conceding two goals against Orissa in the quarterfinal. This resulted in Bengal being pitted against Manipur in the semifinal.
50. Ibotombi S. Longjam, 'Women's Football: Manipur', in the www.manipurpage.tripod.com.
51. Ibid. In this tournament, ESU (Eastern Sporting Union) was the Winner, while TRAU (Tiddim Road Athletic Union) bagged the runner up trophy.
52. Ibid.
53. Ibid.
54. Ibid.
55. Ibid.
56. Ibid.
57. For details see 'NRI boost for Kerala women's football', 2 Aug. 2000.
58. However, rivalry and jealousies among the officials often plague women's football in Bengal. Commenting on Bengal's failure to reach the finals in the national championships in 2002, S. Sabanayakan asserts, 'Bengal's cup of woe was complete when the state body appointed two coaches having their own views on team composition. As the coaches were waging a silent yet sustained war between them, the team suffered badly. Poor conditioning, lack of match practice and above all complacency, typical of most Bengal sides, especially in football, brought forth shame on the state.' Sabanayakan, 'Manipur Unstoppable'.
59. Karnam Malleswari won the only medal for India at the Sydney Olympic Games in women's weightlifting.
60. *The Guardian*, 16 May 2002.
61. Ibid.
62. Ibid.

6

Asserting the Right to Play – Women's Football in Denmark

ANNE BRUS and ELSE TRANGBÆK

In 1970, the Danish Football club Boldklubben Femina (BK Femina) became unofficial world champions. The success of BK Femina women's football team was not a coincidence and should be placed in the context of more than ten years of struggle to get football accepted as a sport for women in Denmark.

Football was, on the organizational level – that is, within the Danish Football Association (DBU) – still a sport only for men. BK Femina's[1] struggle to win recognition for football as a sport for women can thus be described as a process of 'change and resistance to change in what was seen as "accepted" feminine and masculine practices'.[2] From this perspective, the development of Danish women's football in the 1960s can be seen as a steady progress towards the recognition of women's football, with its admission into the DBU in 1972 as its official culmination. However, the struggle for women's football continued after 1972.

On the basis of a theoretical perspective on gender, this study will analyse three consecutive periods in Danish women's football: firstly, the period of the establishment of women's football in Denmark before 1970, secondly, the period around the time of admission in the DBU, 1970–72, and finally, the development of women's football in the DBU from 1972 to 2002.

THEORETICAL PERSPECTIVE

Women's Football or Ladies' Football?

According to the Danish Language Advisory Committee, the term 'women's football' officially entered the Danish language in 1996. Despite this, *damefodbold* ('ladies' football') is still the DBU's official term for women's football. According to *Nudansk Ordbog* [*Dictionary of Modern Danish*] a 'lady' is 'a cultivated, genteel woman', whereas 'woman' means 'an adult female person'. From a linguistic point of view, then, 'women's football' is the more correct term to use, if the intention is to denote women who play football.

There are no official DBU documents explaining why the term 'ladies' football' was chosen in connection with the admission of women's football in 1972. We have interpreted the DBU's intention in choosing the term 'ladies' football' as expressive of a wish to emphasize the contrast between ladies' football and gentlemen's football. There is, for example, no synonym for the term 'gentlemen's football', since, according to the Danish Language Advisory Committee, the term 'men's football' does not exist in Danish. It might be claimed that the DBU, in choosing the term 'ladies' football', was attempting to underline the feminine aspect of women's football. In this connection, it is worth noting that the name of the sport was changed from ladies' football to women's football in the UK as long ago as 1969, in connection with the formation of the Women's Football Association (WFA). 'Ladies play golf – women do athletics and football',[3] as Olive Newsom of the newly-founded association then put it. We have chosen here to use the term 'women's football', as it denotes all women who play football.

Gender and Femininity

For many years, football was the preserve of men – not just in Denmark, but all over the world. When women entered this male-dominated world, they had to challenge the norms regarding a 'real' women's sport. Accordingly, an understanding of historically-determined femininity is an important point of departure for the analysis of women's football.

Gender, as an analytical category, has formed a recognized part of humanistic research for more than 30 years. Despite some disagreement on definitions, the distinction between the biological category of 'sex' and the historically, culturally and socially-conditioned category of 'gender' has been a recognized, if controversial, perspective on the relationship between the sexes.

We will not, here, deal in depth with the debate on sexual categories, but merely mention the Danish historian Birgitte Possing's interpretation of gender as an analytical category. Possing has delineated five distinguishable and different gender categories: 1. Biological gender (boy–girl, man–woman), 2. Sexual gender (heterosexuality, homosexuality, bisexuality, transsexuality), 3. Psychological gender (sexual identity). 4. Historical gender (the social role and functions of gender) and 5. Gender in fiction (as a literary symbol).[4]

When defining historically-determined femininity, it is necessary, according to Possing, to clarify in advance whether you intend to analyse the subjective or the normative category of gender. Subjective gender acts in greatly contrasting ways, both with regard to relations between the sexes, and also within the same sex. Possing points out that subjective gender is a complex mesh of biological, sexual, identity-related, historical and literary elements. Accordingly, it cannot be reduced to a historical category. If, however, we employ normative gender categories, it is possible, according to Possing, to define and describe femininity as a historical category. In this context, femininity is defined in relation to society's understanding of the human qualities, social tasks and functions that should be associated with the respective genders. At the same time, Possing emphasizes the importance of allowing norms and reality to meet, because it is in this process that historical changes occur. Otherwise 'we can easily end up staring blindly at an empty theory that leads to a cliché, and fail to place actual women in the historic perspective'.[5] This approach to the phase of the establishment of women's football has been an important source of inspiration to us. As women's football, from 1959 and up to the time of its acceptance by the DBU in 1972, was not recognized as a sport for women, the development of women's football was very much dependent on the efforts of individuals, who, to use Possing's expression, exploited 'the changes and the ambiguity present in the demographic, economic, social and cultural trends of the time'.[6]

We have been able to identify a number of key events that, in their separate ways, contribute to an understanding of the development of women's football and its recognition as a sport for women.

THE ESTABLISHMENT OF WOMEN'S FOOTBALL BEFORE 1970

Early Women's Football in Denmark

> We all know that ladies can play tennis, row, ride, even sail, but every man has doubtlessly been sceptical of the idea of women as football players. It was thought that this game – the charm of which, more than any other, lies in its forcefulness – would remain forever within the realm of men; but the attempt has now been made to wrest even this branch of sport from their manly grasp.[7]

Historically, various descriptions of football-playing women can be found from the end of the nineteenth and the beginning of the twentieth centuries. In Denmark, it was possible for women to play football in a football club or at school. The attitude towards gender in school however, in contrast to clubs, was very different, and was perhaps more closely connected with these two different environments' understanding of their purpose, than with their view of gender as such.

The leading figures within the educational system made efforts to encourage the participation of girls in ball games, including football.[8] In fact, the educational system emphasized that both the character-forming and health-related elements of the game also applied to girls. The Danish sports historian Ole Skjerk has pointed out that the educational ideals of schools at the time focused on, and sought to enhance, the students' ability to enter into binding social relationships. Consequently, educational ideals were the same for boys and girls. However, despite these ideals and a few attempts by the girls to play football, it did not prove possible to establish football as an educational school sport for girls during the period. Women teachers placed a higher priority on teaching girls to play other ball games, and were apparently more committed to teaching and developing the game of handball. Handball had its own school rules, which were adapted to the school's overall aims of teaching sport as a subject.[9]

Furthermore, on the basis of their perception of the biological body, doctors claimed that women were not suited to the practice of competitive sports, including football. As a consequence, gender came to be viewed as two separate categories in sport. Football was regarded as a sport for men, and in the clubs it was a gender-divided and masculine activity. Football-playing women were seen as presenting a challenge to the masculine football ideal, which it was believed promoted a staunch male character in a powerful male body. The failure of football to establish itself as a sporting activity for women at the end of the nineteenth and the beginning of the twentieth centuries was a consequence of its association with both schools and sports clubs.

Femina *Magazine Takes up the Theme of Football*

At the end of the 1950s, the weekly magazine *Femina* published a number of articles on women's sport. Traditional and less common sports were introduced to the magazine's readers under the heading 'Which sports can I choose?'. In May 1958, football received the following description: 'Football seems to be a forbidden area for the beautiful gender. In Denmark, it is reserved exclusively for men.'[10] However, in the autumn of 1959 a sports club in Slagelse lacked money for their activities. Their manager, Allan Andersen, had seen the student nurses from the nearby hospitals playing football several times as part of their handball training. Andersen got the idea of getting the girls to play against each other during the half-time break at a men's football match.

A journalist from *Femina*, Alf Mørkeberg, was send to Slagelse to cover the game. The game was so entertaining that the journalist realized that 'women's football does indeed have a future in Denmark'.[11] After the game, several of the girls stated that it was much more fun to play football than handball. Andersen, too, spoke in positive terms of women's football to *Femina*: 'I originally suggested to the girls the idea of playing at a football match, and although they were handball players, they were immediately enthusiastic. Since that day, I haven't been able to persuade them to pick up a handball.'[12]

Femina's editor saw the potential of using articles on women's football as material for the magazine, and consequently asked Mørkeberg if it was possible to get women to play football. 'Why not?' replied Mørkeberg, 'We can always try.'[13] The outcome was the *Femina* women's football tournament in spring 1960. Around 29 teams participated, one of which was BK Femina.

BK Femina *of 1959*

The idea for this women's football club came from Mørkeberg. During a guided tour for visitors at the magazine on 18 September 1959, he asked two women who played handball in *Københavns Kvindelige Gymnastikforening* [Copenhagen Women's Gymnastics Association] (KKG) whether they would like to take part in a test football match. 'Ladies' football ... isn't that a bit crazy?' replied one of the two women. 'Definitely not', Mørkeberg answered. 'It was once considered crazy for women to play handball, but now it's completely normal.'[14] Later in the week, Mørkeberg and a photographer from the magazine visited the handball club and again asked the girls if they would like to participate. Five girls replied that they would, after asking their parents for permission! The following week, the handball girls played their first football match. Although the girls lost this first match, they became so enthusiastic about playing football that they agreed to start up a women's football club. Just as women's handball in Denmark – at association level – was born out of the desire of women gymnasts for an activity that could be practised out of doors once the gymnastics season had ended, handball now became in turn the recruiting ground for women's football.

On 13 October 1959, a founding general meeting was held in Valby at the premises of the magazine. Mørkeberg and some of the handball players from KKG were present. At the meeting, the club's articles of association and rules were written down. The name of the club was Mørkeberg's invention, and won him a staff cup 'for the year's best *Femina* idea'[15] – not least because of the considerable advertising value it gave the magazine whenever BK Femina was playing a match.

Measures were taken to ensure that the club would develop. Mørkeberg secured twice weekly training sessions for BK Femina at Valby Sports Ground. In addition, Mørkeberg quickly brought professional trainers from established men's football to the club. The trainers were encouraged by Mørkeberg to make positive remarks about women's football for inclusion in his weekly *Femina* column on women's sport. The interviews were published together with photographs of the 'football experts' and the women players.

The appointment of well-qualified trainers for BK Femina and their media use bears witness, not just to the club's serious approach to performance, but also to Mørkeberg's recognition of the importance of media exposure for getting women's football accepted as a sport for women. Conservatism was still extant. The fact that women also wanted to play football was still seen by some as a threat to the norms of femininity. This attitude to women's football was revealed in public debate. The attitude was often accompanied by attempts to ridicule or even actively oppose the idea of football for women. 'The football amazons from Valby',[16] 'Football is no sport for girls',[17] and 'enjoy yourself at women's football matches because hilariously funny situations arise',[18] are typical examples of the ways in which women's football was discussed in the newspapers. The idea that women become masculine by playing football has roots that can be traced back to the final decades of the nineteenth century. Examples of football-playing women being referred to as 'amazons' can be found during the earliest phases of the establishment of women's football. Mørkeberg's football experts, with their commitment to, and positive statements about, women's football were a counterbalance to such prejudice, helped to make the sport more acceptable and encouraged positive attitudes to the new sports phenomenon.

The positive media attention provided by *Femina* had significance beyond the acceptance of women's football. It also attracted a number of new players to BK

Femina. Interest grew in women's football. In 1960 the *Femina* cup tournament, an indoor Danish women's football championship tournament and an outdoor women's football tournament involving 26 teams from all over Denmark were held. In these competitions, BK Femina quickly established a reputation as the best women's football team in Denmark. The 1960 Femina cup was won by BK Femina, and indeed, the club lost only one of the 30 matches it played in 1960.[19]

Women's Football Becomes Organized

From an economic point of view, BK Femina was closely associated with *Femina* during the first years of the club's lifetime. The magazine provided the players' football kit, and the club's travel expenses. In 1962, however, it was announced at the club's annual general meeting that *Femina*'s financial support for the club was to end. BK Femina would henceforth be required to 'stand on its own two feet and manage all its own problems'.[20] Besides ending its financial support for BK Femina, *Femina* also ceased to cover women's football. In the following years the media's importance in the spread of women's football was reflected by a decreasing interest in playing women's football. Only three clubs in Copenhagen, BK Femina, Rødovre Boldklub and Sundby Boldklub, continued to play. In 1963, the clubs sought permission to hold a tournament under the auspices of *Københavns Boldspil Union* (the Copenhagen Ball Games Association, or KBU),[21] but were refused with no explanation provided. However, a joint overall organization of women's football was now necessary – particularly because there was a need for 'someone' to take care of the standardization of the rules and coordinate the various matches and results. Accordingly, the three clubs formed their own union, *Dansk Kvindelig Fodbold Union* (the Danish Women's Football Union, or DKFU). Until the admission of women's football into the DBU in 1972, the DKFU was responsible for coordinating tournaments, rules and such like.

Besides the clubs already mentioned, there was only a slow and small growth of new clubs. The new clubs were affiliated to firms and regrettably did not last for long. Until 1970 the number of club's playing women's football in Denmark did not exceed ten. Of them all, none of the clubs were able to challenge the supremacy of BK Femina. The club won more or less every championship organized by the DKFU, indoors as well as outdoors. At the same time, the number of participating teams was not large enough to allow a league to be organized. Accordingly, the club tested it's talent against men's teams. As one BK Femina player put it: 'In a period in which we had too little opposition, we were forced to play against junior men's teams and old boys. We would typically win our championship games by 10-0 or 13-0.'[22]

BK Femina also performed at various entertainment events. In this way, the club won media exposure in the company of famous actors, journalists and former men's national team players. In addition, through a partnership with *Fodboldalliancen af 1940* (the Football Alliance of 1940),[23] BK Femina played warm-up matches at several Alliance games at the shrine of men's football, *Idrætsparken* in Copenhagen. The Alliance wanted to get the seal of approval for women's football. The entry of women's football into this masculine preserve was acceptable in the eyes of the DBU, however, only because the Alliance was not the official organ of men's football. The purpose of the games was to raise money for financially hard-pressed men's football clubs, and so the games were not seen as an official recognition of women's football on the part of DBU, but as charitable events. Officially football was still considered as a sport for men. However one newspaper lamented: 'The poor men have nothing to themselves any more – even at Idrætsparken's football stadium.'[24]

The Road to BK Femina's Unofficial World Championship Title

BK Femina did not just seek challenges within Denmark, but were interested, right from the start, in seeking them abroad. In 1962, a tour to South America unfortunately had to be cancelled. From the middle of the 1960s, the club attempted without success to contact other women's football clubs in Germany, Great Britain, the Netherlands and Austria. However, they did make successful contact with a Czechoslovak club, Slavia Praha, and in 1968 BK Femina set off on their first foreign tour to Czechoslovakia. Women's football was well-organized in Czechoslovakia, and the individual clubs were ranked according to their relative strengths. In the best clubs, the women were on professional contracts.

Accompanying BK Femina on the trip was a photographer and a journalist from *Billed-Bladet*.[25] In a report on the tour, the 'femininity' and the 'masculinity' in and out of the field were juxtaposed in both photographs and text. The headline for the article was: 'Hard tackling and light make-up.' Contrasting photographs were used, depicting one BK Femina player in football strip, then in a bikini by the swimming pool. The photograph emphasized the player's breasts. The caption read: 'Let no-one say football players are masculine. [Here] she is relaxing beside one of Prague's open-air pools – sweet, feminine and charming.' The women from BK Femina saw the participation of *Billed-Bladet* in the trip as, in many ways, a recognition of their sport. After several years of being ignored by the media, at least someone had finally shown an interest in women's football. But the media were in control of how the women were presented to the general public. The depiction put an emphasis on personal sexuality rather than professional skill.

The following year, BK Femina again went on tour, this time to Czechoslovakia and Italy. As in Czechoslovakia, women's football in Italy was an organized sport with its own professional league.[26] BK Femina was so impressive that in 1969 it was invited to participate in the first international tournament for women's football, the Europe Cup. As some national European football associations still did not recognize women's football, the event was organized by a privately-financed football association, the Federation of Independent European Female Football (FIEFF).[27] In reality, FIEFF's backers were associated

6.1 In 1959 the BK Femina soccer team played their first match, wearing shirts and shorts sponsored by the weekly magazine *Femina*

6.2 BK Femina players on their way to a match against a male team, 1964

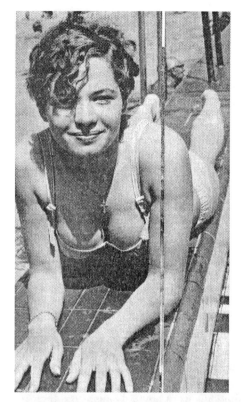

6.3 BK Femina in Czechoslovakia in 1968: 'Let no-one say football players are masculine. [Here] she is relaxing beside one of Prague's open-air swimming pools – sweet, feminine and charming' (text and photo from *Billed Bladet*, 16 August 1968)

6.4 BK Femina won the unofficial World Championship in Italy in 1970. Their players had to wear the famous Milan shirts because their official BK Femina strip had been lost in transit

with several of the privately-financed Italian women's football clubs. The Europe Cup turned out to be a good investment for FIEFF. Good crowds at the games meant good revenues. BK Femina reached the final only to be beaten narrowly by the Italian national team. With this tour, the club had demonstrated that it possessed international class.

WOMEN'S FOOTBALL IN DENMARK IN THE EARLY 1970S

The World Championship in Italy, 1970

BK Femina's performance in the Europe Cup ensured an invitation, the following year, to the first unofficial world championship in women's football in Italy – once again with FIEFF as organizer and sponsor. The event proved another financial success for FIEFF: 50,000 spectators attended the final between BK Femina and the host nation, Italy. BK Femina had their revenge from the year before and beat Italy 2-0. For the BK Femina team, the 1970 World Championship proved to be an unforgettable experience. They were 'top of the tree'!

After winning the world championship title, the team was invited to many public events both in Denmark and abroad. Sponsors began to see the potential of women's football: BK Femina became the first football club in Denmark to receive direct financial support from a sponsor.[28] However the unofficial world champions also proved valuable in other commercial ways. BK Femina was invited to attend a 'Danish Week' in Turin, Italy. Well-known Danish sports stars were the linchpin in a Danish commercial campaign, and BK Femina, having become world champions in women's football, were now a Danish 'product' to show off.

The team's success, especially in winning the World Championship, meant that women's football in Denmark now received a great deal of media attention, leading to calls for the DBU to admit women's football. In the face of these demands, the then DBU chairman, Vilhelm Skousen, made the following complacent, indeed arrogant, statement:

> The girls find themselves in a footballing no-man's-land, with no affiliation to any organized association. But no matter how much sympathy there might be for the lady football enthusiasts, their success is to some extent a result of their own self-promotion. We cannot and will not take this seriously in the DBU.[29]

In short the DBU was not interested in admitting women, even though several men's football clubs had already established women's football teams. Instead of accepting women's football, Vilhelm Skousen chose to reject it. The unofficial world championship nonetheless had opened the eyes of the media to women's football in Denmark. The unofficial world championship produced the first direct confrontation in the printed media between the DBU and their rejection of women's football on the one hand, a demand for the recognition of women's football via its admission into the DBU, on the other.

The World Championship in Mexico, 1971

In the spring of 1971, more than 200 teams registered for the DKFU's women's football outdoor tournament. The recruiting basis for a national team was now large enough for the DKFU to pick a 'real' national team for the second women's football unofficial world championship in Mexico in 1971. Once again, Denmark managed to reach the final where Denmark met the host nation, Mexico, and beat them 3-0. Danish women's football had made its mark by winning the unofficial world championship for the second successive year – a success that the Danish media recognized as a major sporting achievement.[30] Furthermore, with more than 100,000 spectators, the tournament was a commercial success for the organizers.

None of the Danish newspapers, however, had found the world championship interesting enough to send a journalist to Mexico to cover the event 'on location'. The coverage of the world championship was thus in many ways dependent on interviews with the women world champions after their return to Denmark. Consequently, it was very much these women who set the agenda for the media treatment of this sporting event. Once again, the women's wish to have women's football admitted by the DBU was their priority, and this was the message that the Danish media passed on.

However, in all the resounding applause, there was a discordant note struck by some critical commentaries on the tournament that called it 'the Mexican jamboree', more a commercial show than a sporting event. They remarked:

> The women involved played into pink goal frames, beauty parlours were installed in the dressing rooms, and some teams were encouraged to wear hot pants and blouses in place of the normal football strips. As a prelude to matches there were rodeos, baseball games, and displays by semi-clad majorettes. Predictably, perhaps, the tournament was a huge commercial success.[31]

According to these commentators, the 'confections' of women's football, the media and the vulgar entertainment, had very little to do with a World Championship tournament. These external influences on the development of Danish women's football, nevertheless put pressure on the DBU to admit women's football. At the same time, the support of the media and sponsors for women's football created new obstacles to their admission in the DBU.

The Admission of Women's Football into the DBU

Women's football and the commercial staging of the international games was a thorn in the side of the DBU, for whom amateurism was sacrosanct. The chairman of the DBU, Vilhelm Thomsen, now stated: 'No direct association with the DBU can be contemplated for as long as women's football has the backing of magazine publishers.'[32] Once again, the DBU's senior management had revealed their complacent ignorance of women's football. BK Femina had not enjoyed the support of magazine publishers since 1962. The statement also clearly implied a condemnation of BK Femina for accepting sponsorship for their club. In the eyes of the DBU, this represented a break with the principles of amateurism that the association had struggled valiantly to retain since the end of the 1950s and 1960s.

Therefore it was not surprising that a proposal introduced at the start of 1971 to admit women's football into the local associations was defeated at the annual assembly of delegates of the DBU. The following year, attitudes remained the same. At UEFA's annual conference in June 1971, however, UEFA encouraged the national football associations to take control of women's football. This challenge from the DBU's organizational big brother was probably the decisive factor in the final adoption of the proposal to admit women's football into the DBU in February 1972. As one of the participants at the annual assembly of delegates said from the podium, to the considerable amusement of the other participants: 'Let's get this thing up and working!'

THE DEVELOPMENT OF WOMEN'S FOOTBALL WITHIN THE DBU

One of the greatest hindrances to the development of women's football is the way in which the male-dominated football associations have retained 'conventional stereotypes of hegemonic masculinity in western culture. For women to enter the powerful male domains and the controlled world of football, they have had to challenge dominant notions of "appropriate" female sport.'[33] Equally, the hegemonic universe of masculinity is most pronounced in relation to organization and management.[34] This certainly proved to be the case in the Danish football association. With the admission of women's football into the DBU, the threat it represented to masculine hegemony became more blatant. Men now had to share their pitches and changing rooms with women. The outcome was that women were afforded a lower priority.[35] They were allotted the worst training grounds and training times. The DBU, for its part, appointed a so-called 'ladies committee' to 'represent' the interests of women's football in the DBU. One of the first decisions of the 'ladies committee' was to abolish the Danish women's football team. The reason given was that UEFA had decided not to organize women's international tournaments. The decision was incomprehensible to many of the players who had been involved in women's football at both national and international levels prior to the admission to DBU. As one of the players put it: 'The prospect of going to Mexico was a great incentive. Those were the kind of carrots we lost by entering the DBU.'[36]

Both in relation to the development of national and the international tournaments, the DBU's ladies' committee chose a 'gradualist approach',[37] characterized by a 'softly, softly policy'.[38] This gave rise to a conflict between DBU and the women football players. Nonetheless, the first few years of women's football in the DBU were characterized by a non-confrontational attitude on the part of the women football players. The desire to be allowed to play 'organized' football had been fulfilled, and most of the players concentrated on the weekly training sessions and the games at the weekends.

The development of women's football has been examined in a number of the sport's leading countries. Several factors have been identified as possibly significant in these countries: The connection between the pace of development of women's football and the finance available, the degree of autonomy obtained, and the female involvement at managerial level. In this connection, Norway, Sweden, Germany and the USA are nations where former women footballers have occupied important national and international positions. As a result, decisions were taken on the basis of an understanding of women's football, and not in order to construct a mere replica of men's football.[39]

In Denmark, almost 20,000 active women footballers transferred the administrative work, and consequently, the development of women's football, to the men in the DBU. The few women who chose to go down the administrative route learned to adapt to masculine imperatives. One of these women was described in the following manner: 'She abides by the rules.'[40]

Women's football by now had become an everyday affair – but without the national media coverage and support it once enjoyed. Only when the Danish national team won the unofficial European championship in 1979, did Danish women's football again become the subject of media interest. The DBU once again came in for media criticism. The management was criticized for being too 'old' and for opposing the development of women's football – amongst other reasons, because no national tournament for women had been established, even seven years after its admission to the DBU. To this attack the new chairman of the DBU, Carl Nielsen,[41] replied in the DBU's official magazine, that the criticism was ill-informed and revealed an ignorance of women's football. It was most unusual for the chairman of the DBU to publish an article in the DBU's official magazine. This action demonstrated that the criticism had been of a nature that required a response from the highest level of the DBU.

In spite of the criticism DBU failed to change their approach to women's football and, as a consequence, women footballers now adopted a high-profile aggressive approach. But unfortunately they sought influence by working to outflank the official organs: the players and trainers published their own magazine, *Fokus Damefodbold*, and organized themselves into a players' association, *Damedivisionsforeningen* (the Ladies' Division Association). The confrontational attitude evoked only criticism from the DBU. The implication was all too clear: look after your players better and get off the backs of the officials. The chairman of the ladies' committee stated: 'You should take care of your grass roots.'[42]

It took a long struggle to move the DBU forward. It was not until the 1990s that any improvement could be seen in the finances available to women's football from the DBU. The development of women's football now became an area of investment for the DBU. It wished to be the first association under the umbrella of DIF (the Danish Sports Federation) to reach the 300,000-member mark. For the most pragmatic of political reasons, not out of sympathy for the women's game, the Association has recognized that stagnation in the membership of men's football clubs has increased the value of women's football. However, decisions on women's football taken within the DBU can still be seen as expressions of a hegemonic masculinity. The DBU's unwillingness to invest in a women's football elite is the latest example of women's football being an accepted, but still not respected, sport for women. Danish women footballers have still a long way to go to achieve equality.

CONCLUSION

With its tournament in 1960, *Femina* showed that the time was ripe to challenge football's hegemonic masculine universe. At the same time the history of BK Femina shows how the rapid organization of women's football, its competitive attitude and its performance orientation, contributed to gaining media support for the sport – despite the entertainment-oriented and commercial aspects of the international tournaments.

But this promising beginning faltered in its early steps. The history of Danish women's football reveals both the 'proud history of Danish women's sports and the problematic history of Danish women's sports'.[43]

The women of BK Femina wrote the proud women's sporting history. It quickly made its mark as a football club, partly due to the measures employed by *Femina* and by the women themselves: the support of key male football players was secured, show matches were played and the team's profile raised in relation to sponsors and the media. Its early struggle to get women's football accepted, however, was succeeded by a problematic period for Danish women, involving the admission of women's football to the DBU.

The hegemonic masculine universe, as pointed out earlier, is most pronounced in the spheres of organization and management. This became clear from the time of the proposal to admit women's football into the DBU – both in the then chairman's statement to the media on women's football, and in the gender undertones that greeted the proposal. Once women were no longer to be represented outside the football hegemonic masculine universe, the development of women's football was controlled from within the ranks of the association itself. The women left this control to the men in the DBU. Not until the DBU used women's football as an element in its strategy to exceed its 300,000-member mark, did women's football become an area of investment.

Today, women's football is only accepted, and still not respected as a sport for women. Ironically, in view of the early BK Femina success, one of the reasons for this is probably the lack of success at international level: not since the unofficial European championship in 1979 has the Danish team managed to bring home an international title. Other countries, whose football associations were prepared to invest in women's football, rapidly overtook the progress that characterized women's football in the 1960s. In Norway in 1984 there was a marked and positive shift in attitudes to women's football.[44] In contrast, lack of support from the male dominated and reactionary DBU led to Danish women missing out and failing to exploit the possibilities for progress that were created in the 1960s by BK Femina.

The lessons from Denmark are clear. The history of Danish women's football shows that if women's football is to achieve acceptance with respect, it is necessary to make an impact at the highest international level. Only in this way can women's football achieve the media support that is necessary to change the public view of women's football, and bring in its wake, the necessary finances, resources and facilities that will ensure a successful future.

NOTES

The authors express their thanks to Professor J.A. Mangan for his additional support.

1. As BK Femina was the leading women's football club in the 1960s, the development of women's football in Denmark was highly dependent on the sporting progress of this club. For this reason, this study takes the history of BK Femina as its point of departure. In many ways, BK Femina mimicked the organizational methods of men's football. However, the club chose to differentiate itself from men's football in one decisive area: only women were allowed to play football in the club. This decision was to be of significance for the club's leading status within women's football until it became admitted by the DBU in 1972. When decisions were taken, BK Femina had only its own interests to consider – and, thereby, the interests of women's football. Other important clubs that played women's football were attached to men's football clubs, and on the decision-making level, these women's football teams were consequently subject to the boards of the men's football clubs and the decisions that these boards took on behalf of women's football. For further details, see Anne Brus, 'Desserten kom først – om kvindefodboldens udvikling i Danmark frem til optagelsen af kvindefodbolden i DBU i 1972' ['Sweeties Before Dinner – Women's Football in Denmark Before the Admission to DBU in 1972'] (Unpublished Masters Thesis, Institute of Exercise and Sport Sciences, University of Copenhagen, 2002).
2. Gerd von der Lippe, *Endring og motstand mot endring av femininiteter og maskuliniteter i idrett og kroppskultur i Norge: 1890-1950 – med et sideblikk på Tyskland, Sverige og Danmark* [*Changes and Resistance to Changes of Femininities and Masculinities in Sport and Bodyculture in Norway:1890-1950 – Including an Analysis of Germany, Sweden and Denmark*] (Oslo: Norges Idrettshøgskole, 1997), p.5.
3. Sue Lopez, *Women on the Ball: A Guide to Women's Football* (London: Scarlet Press, 1997), p.56.
4. Birgitte Possing, 'Køn og kvindelighed – hvilke historiske kategorier?' ['Gender and Femininity – in a historical perspective'], *Den jyske Historiker* , 58–9, (1992) (Aarhus Universitetsforlag), 38.
5. Ibid., p.50.
6. Ibid.
7. The quote is from *Boldbladet* 6 [*The Game Magazine*], (Copenhagen, 1902). The article is by Copenhagen Women's Ball Games Club and provides a summary of the club's activities, as well as a comment by the chairman on the possibilities for women in sport.
8. Jim Toft, 'Fodboldbanen kridtes op – en analyse af fodboldspillets tidlige historie og udvikling frem til 1911 i København' ['The Football Pitch Is Drawn – An Analysis of the Early History and Development of Football to 1911 in Copenhagen'] (Unpublished Masters Thesis, Institute of Exercise and Sport Sciences, University of Copenhagen, 1990).
9. Ole Skjerk, 'Team Handball in Denmark 1898–1948: Civilisation or Sportification', in Else Trangbæk and Arnd Krüger (eds), *History of Physical Education and Sport from a European Perspective* (Copenhagen: Institute of Exercise and Sport Sciences, 1999), pp.97–108.

10. *Femina*, 21 (1958).
11. *Femina*, 33 (1959).
12. *Femina*, 40 (1959).
13. Grethe Mogensen (ed.), *Femina Fodbold Klub 1959–1984* [*Femina the Football Club 1959–1984*] (Hårlev: Otto Petersen, 1984), p.4.
14. Helle Lydholm Madsen (ed.), *40 år med Femina Fodbold Klub 1959–1999* [*40 Years With Femina the Football Club 1959–1999*] (Hvidovre Kopi,1999), p.8.
15. Ibid., p.6.
16. *Berlingske Tidende*, 24 May 1961.
17. *Berlingske Tidende*, 10 April 1965.
18. *Femina* 25 (1960).
19. BK Femina lost the indoor Danish Championship tournament final against Køge.
20. BK Femina's minute book. According to the minutes of the annual general meeting on 3 Feb. 1962.
21. The DBU is divided into six local associations, of which the KBU is one.
22. Madsen, *40 år med Femina Fodbold Klub 1959–1999*, p.11.
23. The alliance was formed in 1940 from six Danish men's football clubs. The purpose of the association was to organize international matches involving selected players from the respective clubs.
24. *Berlingske Tidende*, 1 June 1960, published as commentary to a picture of a couple of muddy women leaving the pitch at Idrætsparken on 20 May 1960 following BK Femina's first performance at this stadium.
25. *Billed-bladet* is one of the pulp magazines in Denmark.
26. Several of BK Femina's women footballers were later to play on contracts in the professional Italian league. Becoming a female professional football player in Italy was not an economic gold mine for the players, but was rather seen as a personal experience for life. In the Danish and Swedish press, however, the advent of professional football players received a great deal of attention. The thought of professional female football players was apparently shocking, seen in relation to the masculine hegemonic logic in football; the women were described as football Amazons. According to von der Lippe, *Endring og motstand mot endring av femininiteter og maskuliniteter i idrett og kroppskultur i Norge*, p.75, the myth of the Amazons is often utilized as an image of women who are physically strong. When physically strong women with dominance perform in fields in which men also compete, the women tend to be described as unfeminine and in certain contexts as also possessing a different sexuality, even if the women concerned may 'objectively' be both attractive and heterosexual.
27. According to Lopez, *Women on the Ball: A Guide to Women's Football*.
28. According to BK Femina's annual budget, BK Femina received DKK 4,000 (around £400) in sponsorship from Faxe Breweries during the second half of 1970, and DKK 10,000 in 1971.
29. *Berlingske Tidende*, 16 July 1970.
30. The unofficial women's national football team was voted number three in the newspaper *Ekstra Bladet*'s readers' poll for the 'Twelve of the Year'.
31. John Williams and Jackie Woodhouse, 'Can Play, Will Play? Women and Football in Britain', in John Williams and Simon Wagg (eds), *British Football and Social Change: Getting into Europe* (Leicester: Sir Norman Chester Centre for Football Research, 1991), p.97.
32. *Aktuelt*, 17 July 1970.
33. Sheila Scraton, Kari Fasting, Gertrud Pfister and Anna Bunuel, 'It's Still a Man's Game? – The Experiences of Top-Level European Women Footballers', *International Review for the Sociology of Sport*, 34, 2 (1999), 99–111.
34. Jennifer Hargreaves: *Sporting Females* (London: Routledge, 1994).
35. Laila Ottesen, 'Hvornår begyndte kvinder at spille fodbold?' ['When Did Women Start to Play Football?'], in E. Trangbæk, *Den engelske sports gennembrud I Norden* [Dansk Idrætshistorisk Forening Krop og Kultur, 1989] pp.197–214.
36. *Ekstra Bladet*, 28 July 1979.
37. Williams and Woodhouse, 'Can Play, Will Play? Women and Football in Britain', p.96.
38. Ibid.
39. Lopez, *Women on the Ball: A Guide to Women's Football*, p.112.
40. *Fokus Damefodbold* [*Focus on Ladies' Football*], 5 (1983).
41. Carl Madsen, 'Reflektioner på Kvinde fodbold' ['Reflections on Ladies' Football'], *Danish Football*, 6 (Copenhagen, 1979).
42. *Fokus Damefodbold*, 5 (Copenhagen, 1985).

43. Else Trangbæk, 'I medvind og modvind' ['With Success and Opposition], in A. Lykke Poulsen (ed.), *Kvindeliv – Idrætsliv – Om kvindeidræt i Danmark 1850 til 2000*, (Copenhagen: Kvindehistorisk Museum og Institut for idræt, 1998), p.14. The 'proud history of Danish women's sports' concerns the activities to which women have achieved access over the years or have fought for the right to practise. The 'problematic history of Danish women's sports' refers to an impermeable organization culture in which there are apparently insuperable barriers for women to overcome.
44. Roy Kenneth Torkildsen, 'Norsk kvinnefotball – en historisk undersøkelse om norsk kvinnefotballs utvikling' ['Women's Football in Norway – the Development of Norwegian Football in a Historical Perspective'] (Unpublished Masters Thesis, University of Levanger, Norway, 1993).

7

The Fastest Growing Sport?
Women's Football in England

JEAN WILLIAMS

'The Future is Feminine' declared Joseph Blatter, the General Secretary of the Fédération Internationale de Football Association (FIFA), the international governing body of football, in 1995. This pronouncement in *FIFA News*, the official publication of the association, effectively included women players in the family of football on behalf of the worldwide community. At the same time, Blatter, arguably the most powerful man in world football, was careful to distinguish their place within that family. If the place of the announcement was significant, so was the timing. It followed two Women's World Cups (China in 1991 and Sweden in 1995) and the inaugural Olympic women's competition at the Atlanta games in 1996. Blatter's epigram therefore envisaged women's football as firmly established and with tremendous potential for growth but was otherwise, and perhaps deliberately, vague.

Against this background of apparent international growth, the past, present and future of women's football in England is also less than clear. Football is a highly visible aspect of popular culture in 'New Britain'. The views of fans, professionals and investors, for example, are widely debated. In contrast, the entitlements of women players and administrators are not generally discussed. Most British people could name a male football star whether or not they consider themselves to be enthusiasts of the sport. In contrast, the majority of self-confessed football fans could not name a single female player. At the same time, one of the most frequently discussed aspects of women's football in England in the 1990s is the growth in the number of female participants. The starting point for this study was to ask how we have arrived at this moment of obvious inequality and how this disparity sits alongside the idea of football as an increasingly chosen female sport. So little work has been done to uncover information in the specific subject area that it is difficult to draw upon selected themes from writing about the code of association football, about women's experience of team sports (and more specifically football) or female sport generally. *The* history of women's football in England remains to be written and is beyond the scope of this study. Instead, the focus is a discussion of the overall shape of female participation in England and in particular the impact of historical forces on contemporary women players.

While the conventional wisdom now is that women's football is the fastest growing sport in England, the female football player has been part of the social and cultural history of Britain for over a century. What has never been satisfactorily explained is a peculiarly English expression of contempt for women who play association football. Another avenue of enquiry could examine the precise role of the British in exporting this sneering and disdainful attitude, and would surely make the point that throughout the world it is not exceptional. However, the English example is overdue for attention because this condescension has persisted in one form or another for at least a century, but has been juxtaposed in the last 40 years by an increase in female participation. The derision shown to English female footballers simultaneously trivializes their sporting accomplishments (as in the pejorative 'play like a girl') and insists on the female as the object of masculine desire (women are supposed to play at being a woman, not at football). Discussions conducted for this study with women and girls at all levels revealed diverse experiences of playing football, and it became increasingly evident that women's participation in an outdoor contact team sport which involves competition, co-operation and skill is sufficiently celebratory to make negotiating a change in stereotypes worthwhile. Are women playing football in increasing numbers in England and what are the key issues around that participation?

An examination of the recent historical period would be incomplete without considering the early development of women's first participation in football as a sport, a game or a pastime. The beginnings of a female tradition are difficult to pinpoint. In nineteenth-century upper-class Japan women played a courtly form, and Native American women played folk football, but since sport is typically defined as an institutionalized, highly structured, rule-bound physical contest, the British examples are the most significant in the international tradition of women's football as athletic competition. In the final decades of that century British women were agitating for improved economic, social and political conditions. It was also an era of popular entertainment and there were many new 'healthful' forms of recreation covered in the pages of the *Athletic News*, from boat polo for ladies to a feminized form of football on roller-skates. Inverness, in Scotland appears to have hosted the first recorded women's football match in 1888. This can be interpreted as distinct from folk football, like the late eighteenth-century women's games, or mixed holiday games such as the Shrove Tuesday free-for-all in the English town of Atherstone, though it did pit the married against the single women. In the Inverness game, the two teams had uniforms, fixed goals, a fairly stable and even number of members and the game had a limited time span. The first match within Scottish FA guidelines was held at Shawfields Ground, Glasgow in 1892. An association for women was founded in 1894 and began the attempt to link female football with lady-like behaviour that persists today. Nettie Honeyball, the secretary of the British Ladies, organized the English North versus South game at Crouch End, London in 1895. It was followed by games in the Midlands, the North and in Scotland, the most significant of which was the Newcastle fixture with a crowd approaching 8,000. Lady Florence Dixie, the President of the British Ladies' Football Club, youngest daughter of the Marquess of Queensbury and a keen advocate of women's rights, sponsored the tour with the declared aim, 'I am in hopes that the British Ladies Football Club will be able to furnish teams to travel about the country, and endeavour to popularize the sport by playing some matches in different localities'.[1]

Though the trip attracted great publicity from the press, the coverage did not confine itself to the sporting contest. One way that women's football acquired a dubious status for the bourgeois girl around this time was a link with the Rights question. Though there had been some change in public opinion about the place of games for girls in public schools, women who participated in individual and group sports were likely to have their motivation for doing so discussed and criticized in local, national and specialist publications. Whether early women football players were politically motivated, following fashion, or tentative enthusiasts of a sport popular with their male counterparts, the football authorities viewed their involvement as a nuisance. Resentment had become sufficiently widespread by 1902 in England for the FA to issue a ruling preventing men's clubs from playing against 'lady teams'.

Photographs of the time suggest that dress codes were open to interpretation. If on the one hand Rationals allowed for some freedom of movement, it can hardly have been conducive to strenuous or pleasurable play to wear, 'Red blouses with white yolks, and full black knickerbockers fastened below the knee, black stockings, red berretta caps, brown leather boots and leg-pads ... white gloves and ... a short skirt above the knickerbockers'.[2] Little is known about whether girls played football among themselves or with boys at this time. Even less is known about street football involving females. Playing football in a skirt or baggy breeches would as much disadvantage the working class girl who wanted a kick-about in the street as the young ladies of Roedean. Female sports enthusiasts could wield a hockey stick or cricket bat with relative freedom but would have had greater difficulty in receiving a ball to feet while wearing a dress or long skirt. The 1890s cycling craze had spread the popularity of bifurcated garments for women as highly fashionable but risqué. If sport was the enemy of femininity, then the symbolic significance of playing in uniforms which risked compromising women's and girls' status as ladies could only make football challenging to public reaction.

Work, rather than leisure, increased the acceptance of trousers as practical in some circumstances when women moved into new occupations in the First World War. In the first phase of what can be called widespread female popular participation, a defining factor in determining women's play was access to relatively well-paid work outside the home, and the consequent opportunity to pursue collective leisure. Before this time women's football shared aspects of English leisure in that it was born of collective enthusiasm (albeit that the groups were small), largely neglected and unregulated by authorities, though the participants were by no means all working-class. Now, what had been relatively rare exhibition games became more regular fixtures as Britain pioneered football as more widely popular with women and with live audiences. The expansion of women's football organized by workers after 1914, sometimes on the initiative of welfare supervisors, was more pronounced in Britain than anywhere else. Teams included Aberdeen, Belfast, Cardiff, Edinburgh, Glasgow, Llanely, Newport, Renfrew, Rutherglen and Swansea, in addition to English sides like Bennets' of London and Dick, Kerr's of Lancashire.[3] The most eminent team, Dick, Kerr Ladies, travelled to Europe, Canada and the United States to play, and tens of thousands watched women's games. Industries that commonly employed women, for example insurance companies, light engineering and food manufacturing, extended the point that the places where women's teams were created show the changing nature of women's work. After the war Lily Parr, Joan Whalley and other Dick, Kerr players had to move from munitions to nursing to support themselves, but they continued to play in spite of shifts and long hours.[4]

There were around 150 women's teams by 1921 playing regular, well-attended games, though without a league structure. The English FA found this threat to the idea of football as a man's game sufficiently serious. The ambiguous status of women's football was evident in the ban from clubs affiliated to the association and Football League grounds by the English FA which began on 5 December 1921 and was to last until 29 November 1971. The quasi-legal terminology of a 'ban' reflects a social taboo against women's involvement in sport that is more enduring. How significant was this attitude for women's football then and what has its legacy been?

Much has been made of the large crowds that women's teams drew up to 1921 and of the sums of money raised for charity that equate to millions of pounds today. However, it is also important to remember that the Football League had continued with fixtures in the 1914–15 season in the face of much press criticism, some of which raised old prejudices about working class professionalism as a dilution of middle class amateurist values.[5] Games played by women for charity had been one means by which the members of the Association and League could reclaim some credibility through the appeal to patriotism. Thus, the 1921 ruling was not a dramatic about face by the FA, which had debated the financial repercussions of continuing with women's matches for over six months. Two months before the decision, the FA had given host clubs authority to take over the gate receipts from women's games. As a parallel form of entertainment with male professional football, women's football had established itself as a sporting spectacle, watched by a mainly male audience whose entrance fee was donated to charity. The growth of the women's game in England had led, not to a tattered amateurism, but to a tendency toward professional organization in terms of raising large sums of money as the result of consistently attracting large crowds. Banning women as a group could be interpreted as a rather clumsy attempt on behalf of the Association and League to recoup the manly, patriotic image of football tarnished by the continuation of fixtures when other sports had suspended play.[6] With the return of men from the front-line, the association could ill afford to alienate those who had been prime supporters. This was a quick and crudely effective strategy to protect the development of masculine professionalism because without the grounds to stage large contests, women's football was socially, culturally and economically marginalized. Women's football has never recovered its early popularity in terms of status or support. Having established itself as a show, the capacity to perform in locations that held large crowds was vital to guarantee a substantial following. The idea of 'improper' behaviour is still pertinent to the reputation of women's football today when larger numbers of women players participate but in less spectacular surroundings. Geographically and numerically, women's football remains a minority activity in comparison with men's football and female leisure activities generally.[7]

One reason why the FA ban had such impact is that the early split between administrators, entrepreneurs, managers and players, evident in the formation of the Football Association and Football League, did not take place in women's football. In the absence of patronage and sponsorship, football for women was promoted in small collectives based around work or leisure interests that became competitive networks. The Secretary/Manager such as Alfred Frankland of Dick, Kerr Ladies (later Preston), usually dealt with a counterpart to arrange fixtures, in addition to training the team, organizing transport, publicizing fixtures, scouting for new talent and dealing with cash. It was comparatively rare for teams like Atalanta, from Huddersfield, to be run by and for women.

The considerable spectator support and media interest of the 1920s is noticeably absent in the present. Nevertheless, since the 1960s, large crowds and media interest are a growing part of the women's game and participation rates are considerably higher. At the elite level, since the middle of the 1980s, the English national team has gradually become less successful and other countries have progressively overtaken them in international influence. This has not helped the image of women's football in England and social taboos around female participation remain strong.

The English tradition of women's football continued to juxtapose two contradictory factors rather uncomfortably during the twentieth century. On the one hand, works and representative teams continued to play one another through the decades. The organization of the matches continued to show the quite explicit appropriation of early established aspects of the game, such as spectator-supported events, and their reconstitution as a form of entertainment with a female focus; for example, the Hulton Getty Picture Collection has photographs of a female Marks and Spencer's team walking out to play against Invictas in 1933. On the other, football continued to be seen as authentic only when played by males, and the unfeminine effects, in particular of energetic exercise, continued to influence the public image of women who played and this has changed only a little in the twenty-first century. Unfortunately, the cajoling and persuasive tone of the commentary in this 1950s programme, here presented as a form of educational plea, has a contemporary relevance:

> Should ladies play football? Can they play the game? These and other
> questions are often asked. Today you have the opportunity to judge for
> yourself. Many people go to ladies' football matches out of curiosity, but we
> feel sure that before half time you will admit that the girls play the type of
> football that entertains the public; the attacking game with the ball on the
> ground. The girls play for the love of the game. To them football is a serious
> matter. They play with a full-size ball on the regulation size field for the full
> 90 minutes. So please give them every encouragement and in return they
> will give you a good afternoon's sport.[8]

It would appear that the Second World War was much less important to the
growth of women's football in England than the Great War, though there remains
a considerable body of work to be done to ascertain how many teams there were
at this time.[9] After 1945, old contacts were revived and new ones established. In
the 1950s, Corinthians, Fodens (based at a hauliers in Sandbach) and Bolton
toured extensively and the Dick, Kerr works team became a representative
Preston team. By the 1970s Fodens became dominant and played against new
clubs like Warminster and Southampton (originally the Cunard shipping
company team). The emergence of the new teams points to the need for a
thorough investigation into the growth of women's football up to and after the
Second World War. It has various causes and is only partially explained by the
demands of war work and petrol rationing. It is not enough to suggest that
women's interest prior to the 1950s was simply the product of war-time
enthusiasm or largely a form of charitable voluntary work. The endurance of
individual clubs and competitive arrangements, involving business activity,
leisure and social practices requires that a more searching light be thrown on the
communities which have formed women's football.

During the 1960s the status of football altered immeasurably following the
removal of the maximum wage in 1961, and the abolition of the 'retain and
transfer' system in 1963. Against a background of a newly profitable
professionalism, celebrity wealth and the slick marketing of the men's game,
participation football for women grew, but crowds dwindled and the sport became
less about spectacle and more about taking part. Professionalism, as it has
manifested itself in women's football, has been a mixed blessing. In the 1970s
British women players like Sue Lopez, Edna Nellis and Rose Reilly had to choose
between travelling to pursue a professional career and representing their nation.[10]
Rose Reilly and Edna Nellis were respected professionals in France and Italy.
This experience led them to suggest that the newly appointed manager of the
Women's Scottish national team, an unqualified coach with no elite playing
experience, was not the best choice.[11] In return, both received a lifetime ban,
which they feared would cost them their professional contracts. Fortunately this
was not the case; Rose captained the Italian team after being given citizenship and

continued to live in Italy for some years. As the issue of female professionalism becomes more pressing in England, women players will hopefully not have to face similar choices, although the United States collegiate and WUSA (Women's United Soccer Association) professional league are the best option for young talented British women players. Italy and Japan are also developing the media profiles of their long established professional women's leagues.

> The England victory in the 1966 World Cup proved to be the catalyst for a dramatic renaissance in the women's game, and this time the upsurge of interest would be sustained. For a group of women football players in Southampton, it was to be the beginning of a long and successful career.[12]

It is highly unlikely that England's 1966 World Cup victory was a major agent of change for most women players. Manchester Corinthians were formed in 1949 and disbanded in the early 1970s. Fodens began playing around 1955. Stewarton Thistle, a Scottish team that regularly played in England, was formed in 1961. The last game of a depleted Preston came in 1965 before they folded due to a lack of players. EMGALS (a Leicester-based gas company team) began in early 1967. Sheila Stocks and many of the older Doncaster Belles began to play in 1969 after selling Golden Goals tickets at Doncaster Rovers because the job gave them free entry to watch the club they had supported all their lives. Knowing that they could not join a men's team, they clubbed together and initially played at five- and six-a-side until sufficient numbers joined to form a full team. The less well-known example of Homestead Ladies reveals how clubs emerge and disappear: an ongoing situation in women's football, as with other locally-based and volunteer-supported sports. The team originated at a local garage where several women worked as administrators in early 1960. They played on Sundays on Home Ground Memorial pitch and trained under floodlights nearby. The largest crowd of supporters, 3,500, was recorded at a match against the Boston Bombshells at the Mayflower Sports Ground in 1961, but Homestead also played against teams including Gainsborough Worthies, Oldham Ladies, Corinthians and Ripley. They lost the use of the Memorial Ground site in 1964 and ceased to play soon after. The team's performance, incidentally, was the subject of a local history inquiry, still to be published. It includes Linda Dring knocking herself out on her own goalpost; a collision involving Hykeham's Shirley Reid in which a visiting centre forward's arm was broken; a 7-1 defeat at Ripley played in teeming rain and ankle-deep mud; the feats of leading goal-scorer, Audrey Mole, and the leadership of Captain Barbara Duncombe.[13] A more comprehensive picture is needed as to why the team did not obtain an alternative home ground, whether players went on to play for other teams and indeed, the relatively short time it took to get the team underway at the beginning of its career. More local histories of this kind that include references to women's clubs would be invaluable to historians of the women's game in England.

The competitive network of women's football is a distinctive and characteristic aspect of involvement that formalized to an extent into regional leagues after 1969 with the creation of the English Women's Football Association (WFA) with 44 affiliated teams. Some clubs, such as Homestead, have been one-off collections of women playing for short periods of time. Others, such as Corinthians and Ripley, lasted for several years. The network may appear somewhat fluid compared with county-based and regionalized leagues with rules for promotion, relegation and so on. But this loose alliance of interest provided enough of a foundation for women's participation to grow without central regulation or a great deal of bureaucracy in the 1960s. If local histories are one requirement, so is the need for specific inquiries into the continuity of clubs, the involvement of administrators and managers, the movement of players between clubs and the playing careers of individuals.

1966 was not as important or the change in participation as significant as Lopez suggests, not least because football for women became popular at around this time in other countries. Indeed, directives from the Union of European Football Associations (UEFA) regarding the co-ordination of women's competition in the 1970s were strongly resisted by conservative male-dominated associations in the United Kingdom. Change has been painfully slow; for example, the FA of Ireland formally adopted the Ladies Football Association of Ireland into its structure in 1991, the English Football Association and the Football Association of Wales took control of women's football as recently as 1993 and the Irish Football Association agreed a partnership with the Women's Football Association of Ireland only in 1995. The Scottish Football Association took over women's football as late as 1998. The tentative phrasing of the agreements reflects a conspicuous lack of enthusiasm, which means that, after integration, home countries women's teams have increasingly struggled in international competition.[14]

In spite of having world-class players, British women's associations (and this includes women's committees within, or affiliates to, the Football Association of each nation) unfortunately have been prone to internal sparring, particularly about how to make female football acceptable to obstinate and fusty bureaucracies. A recurring pattern from the 1920s to the present time is the lack of influence of women in decision-making roles in positions of power at the top level in their own sport. From Alfred Frankland in the 1920s, to the leadership of the Women's Football Associations and the present English Football Association Women's Committee, men have dominated women's football administration. Women have led teams, leagues and have volunteered as committee members but they tended to rely on male sponsorship to hold high office. This can lead to a conflict of interest as the concerns of professional administrators and the interests of female participants may not be entirely compatible. For example, women's clubs based outside Football League and Premiership grounds do not receive the equivalent subsidy to those that integrate. Football Association administrators see independent women's clubs as an extremely low priority. For example, Doncaster Belles' plans to build a stadium are vital, as without it, the club will not be granted a licence to host a Centre of Excellence. If this situation develops, the opportunity to train young players to build a squad could be affected and the representation of independent women's clubs at elite level is likely to be reduced. The Belles' players are keenly aware of this and they describe their situation as follows:

> In my first year at the Club we did the treble – FA Cup, League Cup and the League. Before that we won lots of things including the League many times. We are not associated with a men's side – so I think we lose out.
>
> Belles' were in the North Notts league, then we went to the Premier league. We fund ourselves – we're not affiliated to a men's club which makes it harder for us. ZARA sponsor our kit and tracksuits, tee shirts, shorts ... they send everything free. Belles have won the cup and league many times, the last being the 1994 double season ... we haven't won anything since then.
>
> The club founded for women 1969 ... Our first sponsor was NPS Healthcare and Forester Health. Our major sponsor for 1998/99 season, Optima International, provided a training ground and other numerous facilities ... it was a major financial input.
>
> The Doncaster Belles were founded in 1969 on the Doncaster Rovers terraces by a group of women who sold the 'Golden Goal' tickets for Doncaster Rovers promotion. For the Doncaster Belles to maintain their high profile on and off the pitch we need to be financially secure. This security can only be sustained by sponsorship as the FA say we don't have facilities to merit a centre of excellence.

To withhold support for independent women's clubs without a certain standard of facility, when these clubs have achieved success in spite of not having these resources is, to say the least, arrogant. In future plans to develop women's football there is little recognition of the tradition that these independent teams represent. There is also a feeling among some women players that plans to develop county-based leagues will actually reduce the level of competition that regional leagues have fostered because of the emphasis on local opposition. Currently the county leagues are more useful for youth and reserve teams who have travel concerns or just want to play an occasional game; the vast majority of women's teams have chosen to remain in regional leagues because of the quality and frequency of competition.

After 1969 participation in women's football grew rapidly until 1985, and it may have been this mushrooming of interest that created the administrative and financial problems of the WFA as a governing body. By 1985, the WFA had seriously under forecast its bid for grant-aid support to the Sports Council.[15] An interpretation favourable to the personnel involved would be that the participation of women consequently grew at a time when the bureaucracy necessary to stabilize development was not in place. A more critical view would be that following the affiliation to the FA and the appointment of Tim Stearn as Chair, the officials underestimated the level of female participation to a degree that indicated little understanding of the extent to which the women's football community had grown. At a time when participation numbers were growing and only one paid administrator was co-ordinating activities, the WFA was under pressure from FIFA and funding bodies (such as the Football Trust and the Sports Council) to integrate with the FA. The appointment in 1988 of Richard Faulkener, the first deputy chair of the Football Trust, signalled the move to an eventual amalgamation. After 1985 there was a slower rate of increase in adult women participating, while the overall number of registered players has increased by tens of thousands. The growth has not been a steady rise nor is the relationship between increased bureaucracy and the development of the women's game very clear as yet.

The WFA, though conservative in their attitude to media representation and prone to in-fighting, were progressive in respects other than the success of their league administration in providing competitive opportunities for women players. For example, they sponsored two women for a full A Licence coaching award and developed junior representative sides. However this was short lived and the WFA was forced to field only a senior squad in international competition due to financial difficulties in 1980. It was not until 1997 that a junior squad was again assembled for representative competition. As a central office administering local league and international competition, the WFA was successful in its early achievements; as a unifying authority it was ultimately a failure.

The axiom that has come to describe British and international women's football over the last decade is that it is 'The fastest growing participation sport for women'. This phrase first became widely used in the public relations material of the WFA at about the time it relinquished control of the female game to the English Football Association. Since its formation in 1969 the association had been chaired by men who wanted the FA to acknowledge, accept and administer women's football. Irrespective of its male leadership, the association had been formed on behalf of women and was mainly staffed by volunteers like Flo Bilton, Linda Whitehead and Sue Lopez. Internal disagreement meant that the WFA had acted as a rather leaky umbrella for the sport, particularly when combined with financial difficulty that became acute in 1985. Tim Stearn's 1987 remarks are the repeated refrains of Chairs of the association as members were asked to leave 'the character assassination of bygone days to the past. Sadly for all of us it lingers on … we must start again and implement constructive policies. If we fail our number will decline further.'[16]

In some senses 1992 could be interpreted as a watershed; the last of 23 years of WFA control before the FA took control of women's football and began to promote it. But in significant ways 1993 was a hand-over rather than a take-over.

In fact the WFA had gradually aligned with the structures of the male game over the years: for example, in 1991 the WFA had introduced a national league, the first in the history of English women's football. There seem to be two distinct but interrelated aspects of the idea of a fastest growing sport that seems to look back to the future. The first is that it emphasizes consumption: women are *doing* football in increasing numbers. The ways that women own, use and appreciate football are not incorporated into this narrative. The second is that this glib assertion suggests a perception of recent female interest that has been successfully fostered by sporting bureaucracies.

The use of quantifiable data to discuss increasing participation is the most recent dimension to the official memory of women's football. However, one difficulty is to assess exactly how many players and how many clubs operate in women's football at any one time. A systematic study of the numbers is difficult to conduct because there is no central archive. In order to test the hypothesis of a steady rise in playing numbers that has accelerated since the FA control in the 1990s, Table 7.1 attempts to summarize our knowledge so far. The 1969 figure of 44 clubs came from two WFA administrators who suggested that the number of clubs should have been 49, but five clubs did not join for various reasons. At this time competitive leagues replaced the calendar of touring teams completing annual or tournament-style fixtures. The participation by Chiltern Valley in the second unofficial Women's World Cup in Mexico in 1971 led to the expulsion of the whole East Midlands Ladies Alliance (of which Chiltern Valley were the champions), and therefore these are under-estimates of the unaffiliated clubs in existence. In 1977 the *WFA News* gave the number of clubs as 257 with over 100 youth teams.[17] John Bale appears to support this approximate number, suggesting 260 teams in 1978.[18] Sue Lopez then gives a figure of 300 clubs with 6,000 players in 1979.[19] Dorothy Miller has the 1987 figure as 187 clubs, a figure she obtained from the WFA Secretary Linda Whitehead.[20] The *FA Factsheet* has the 1989 figures as 263 clubs with 7,000 players.[21] In 1991 and 1992, Lopez has 334 and 380 clubs respectively.[22] The 1991–92 *WFA News* development report says, 'Such is the growing interest in women's soccer that by the end of this next season we could be looking at a total of 500 affiliated clubs.'[23] Table 7.1 summarizes the sources referred to here and the uneven growth year on year. The most significant pattern from this data is that in one decade, between 1969 and 1979, the number of clubs affiliated to the WFA increased six-fold. Compared to the FA figures of approximately 35,000 females in 1,500 clubs in 2000, it has taken 20 years for women's football to grow a further six times.

The attempt to chart the growth in numbers by year has been possible to a limited extent. By compiling lists of clubs affiliated to the WFA in the years 1980 to 1990, including those mentioned in minutes, league fixtures, cup matches and feature articles, it was possible to arrive at figures which reflected perhaps the minimum number of clubs. The names of clubs were checked against previous years, in order to examine continuity but it was not possible to track the withdrawal

TABLE 7.1
NUMBER OF WOMEN'S SOCCER CLUBS IN ENGLAND, 1969–96

Year	Number of clubs	Number of registered female players
1969	44[i]	
1971	100[ii]	
1972	182[iii]	
1977	257[iv]	
1978	260[v]	
1979	300[vi]	6,000
1980	250*	
1982	267*	
1984	260*	
1985	163*	
1987	187[vii]	
1988	166*	
1989	263[viii]	7,000
1990	251*	
1991	334[ix]	9,000
1992	380[x]	
1996	600 women 750 girls' teams[xi]	14,000 and 7,500 respectively
2000	700 women 750 girls' teams[xii]	35,000

Sources: i The Football Association Fact Sheet 3 p.1 says 44 clubs; ii Sue Lopez; iii John Williams and Jackie Woodhouse; iv Sue Lopez; v John Bale; vi Sue Lopez; vii Dorothy Miller; viii The Football Association; ix Sue Lopez; x Women's Football Association, *Newsletter* (July 1992), 4; xi The Football Association; xii http://www.the-fa.org.womens.

of teams. The figures compiled from this source, shown in Table 7.1 as asterisked numbers to the right of the left-hand column, when compared with the other sources detailed in the previous paragraph, have two uses. One is to show a similar pattern of growth until 1985, which roughly corresponds with Miller's figure of 187 in 1987. The plateau of numbers and the subsequent drop reveal irregular developments in that the 300 clubs in 1979 was a high point, not exceeded for over a decade. Whether this reflects a dip in actual participation or inaccurate procedures for recording the number of teams, or both, remains to be established.

It was by no means all bad news for women's football in England in the 1980s, however. It was a time when television was becoming interested in the sport, and when England's success on an international stage was recognized in the press, the figures present a challenge of interpretation. Saturation of the game amongst the post-school-age female population made no sense, as the number of clubs was so small, even in periods of rapid growth. The figures in the right-hand column also suggest a further complication, in that, though the number of clubs in 1989 is fewer, the number of players is greater. This is even more exaggerated in the 1991 figure with an increase of 3,000 registered players, though only 34 more clubs. Rather than one underlying reason, it is likely that the combination of factors which include administrative competence, more clubs with reserve and junior teams, an increase in school-age participation and an established structure of regional leagues facilitated the expansion of participation in the early 1990s after the apparent decline in the mid-1980s. The number of clubs was particularly difficult to ascertain between 1979 and 1989. As this was the decade of increased popularity in the media and success in international competition, the lack of documentation was remarkable and reinforced my impression that increased participation was not matched by, let alone created by, increased bureaucratization.

The nature of the evidence therefore precludes unequivocal conclusions about adopting a radical or liberal feminist perspective in studying women who play football. Some gains appear progressive; including increased funding, more playing opportunities and some centralized administrative coordination. However, these developments have yet to serve as the basis of more far-reaching change to the provision of football for women or to the structures of football itself. Football authorities have not actively sponsored, let alone facilitated, women's play until the last decade, nor have periods of increased female participation in England led in any direct way to the reform of football itself. However, most women players interviewed for this study did not want to play a *very* different form of football either as an alternative to the 'male' game or as a critique of the values of competitive contact sport. In fact, women's right to play the standard form of the game without modification to the size of the field of play, the length of a match, the number of substitutes and so forth remains a moot point. Therefore, how best to collect and collate information in order to assess the balance of conservatism and liberalization within women's football? Two issues conclude the study but are meant to indicate points of departure rather than arrival.

Shortly after the ban on women's football was lifted, the Sex Discrimination Act of 1975 was drafted with the intention to exempt football specifically and other contact competitive sports in general from gains in female equity, and this approach has been reinforced on more than one occasion as still valid.

> It seems to me that football is a game that is excepted from this statute. It is a game in which on all the evidence here the average woman is at a disadvantage to the average man because she has not got the stamina or physique to stand up to men in regard to it ... women have many other qualities superior to those of men, but they have not got the strength or stamina to run, to kick or tackle, and so forth.[24]

This legislation is now almost 30 years old, yet Section 44, the clause that limits female access to competitive sport, has endured in its original form in spite of other amendments. Since the purpose of the Act was to address archaic conceptions of the roles of men and women, to insist on the preservation of essential gender difference in sport is both logically and legally questionable. This is one indication of many that the connection between football and women looks set to remain contentious for the foreseeable future. The clause that limits women's access to competitive sport continues to survive amendment. In spite of the increase in the number of female participants, equality of opportunity and, indeed, outcome in football are currently unrealizable at all levels of the game. One reason for this is that there is no consensus about what equal but different provision means: should, for example, it be a professional league for women or women playing in the present professional leagues?

The reactionary sporting world clearly needs to include some women as members for its cultural legitimacy in the twenty-first century in ways that apparently were not necessary in the 1920s. Consequently, claims for a recent rise of female interest retain the idea of natural gender difference and at the same time reposition women as consumers of many aspects of the sport, of which playing is just one aspect. However, flourishing interest and encouraging changes hardly constitute women's participation in football as sufficiently commonplace and significant to mark a new dawn. The marginalization of women at administrative level and lack of widespread support for women players mean that fundamental issues of control are as contentious now as they have ever been. More striking still is that women's lack of equality in this area appears to be taken for granted by some women players and by elite administrators. The key debates about the relationship between changes in quantity and changes in quality of women's football have yet to take place and the place of legislation in regulating gender-segregated sport is one starting point.

In one sense, the story of perpetual expansion is unthreatening to the football authorities because a change in the number of players has yet to alter the essentially amateur nature of the female game. This brief historical summary illustrates that there has been a widespread tendency to devalue the place of women's football in studies of the sport, women players in their own game and, by implication, participants in sport. In the midst of this debate about what should be done on behalf of women or by women or, indeed, to women to develop the game, the players' voices should begin to emerge and become much louder because at present the agenda is rather static and in need of revision. Players express several kinds of freedom when they participate in football and a sense of self-determination emerges in these few responses to my question, 'What are your earliest memories of playing football?'

> I played with my father when I was about eight. He used to take me to a local football field and taught me different tricks and skills.

> [In the] school playing ground, kicking tennis ball around at break times. About five [years old] in infant school – with lads at break times ... Wearing a shirt too big for me, scoring a goal and my team mobbing me.
> Kicking a ball about with my brother and dad in the garden aged four.

> I was aged seven or eight with the lads at primary school, but my dad taught me to kick a ball when I was a toddler and I played a lot with my elder brother.
> Playing in the streets at home with my dad and next door neighbour – Louise – probably age eight upwards.

The continued commitment of the players to the sport appeared to be more than a lifestyle choice, like belonging to a certain gym. The gendered experience of team sport, involving the simultaneous expression of sameness and difference, was sufficiently celebratory for players to want to play in spite of the stereotypical media slur of players as either 'butch' or 'girly'. This contentious connection between women and football and their negotiation of the meaning of their play requires theoretical analysis as well as historical narrative.[25] In outlining the current tensions and some of their historical roots above, it seems safe to say that women's association with football in England will continue in the foreseeable future to be about much more than sport.

NOTES

1. Sheila Begbie, Head of Scottish Football Association Women's Committee, personal communication 2001.
2. *Manchester Guardian*, 1895.
3. See, for example, The Imperial War Museum, Women's Work Collection, (IWM,WWC) MUN 24/6; MUN 24/15; MUN 24/17.
4. Gail Newsham, *In a League of their Own* (London: Scarlet Press, 1998), p.67. See also Ali Melling, '"Ray of the Rovers". The Working Class Heroine in Popular Football Fiction 1915–25', *The International Journal of The History of Sport*, 16, 1 (April 1998) and Ali Melling, 'Ladies Football: Gender and Socialisation of Women Football Players in Lancashire 1926–1960' (Unpublished Ph.D. Thesis, University of Central Lancashire, 1999).
5. For a discussion of the representation of the professional-amateur divide in popular culture, particularly literature and propaganda, see Paul Fussell, *The Great War and Modern Memory* (New York: Oxford University Press, 1975).
6. Public opinion was divided over whether sport and leisure activities boosted morale or were immoral distractions from the war effort. County cricket for example was suspended for the duration whereas the first year of the war saw much criticism of professional football for continuing with fixtures and for poor results in recruiting campaigns at matches. For a more detailed discussion see T. Mason, *Association Football and English Society, 1863–1915* (Brighton: Harvester, 1980); J. Osborne, 'Sport Soldiers and the Great War', *British Society of Sports History Bulletin*, 11 (1991), 17–34; and J. Bailey, *Not Just on Christmas Day: An Overview of Association Football in the First World War* (Upminster: 3-2 Books, 1999).
7. Ann Bridgwood *et al.*, *Living in Britain: Results from the 1998 General Household Survey*, an inter-departmental survey carried out by ONS between April 1998 and March 1999 (London: Stationery Office, 2000), p.213 figure 13E indicates that, even given the loose definition of sport used in the survey, other leisure activities, such as watching television and listening to music, were at least eight times as popular as football for men and at least 80 times as popular as football for women.
8. Corinthian versus Lancashire Ladies Match Programme, 1951.
9. Gail Newsham suggests that in 1947 there were 17 teams. See Newsham, *In a League of their Own*, p.112.
10. Sue Lopez, *Women on the Ball* (London: Scarlet Press, 1997), p.54; I am indebted to staff at the Scottish Football Museum for providing me with cuttings on Rose Reilly and Edna Nellis in April 2000.
11. Sandy Beveridge, 'Edna – The Sad Soccer Star', *Sunday People*, 31 Jan. 1975; Ruth Wishart, 'Woman on the Wing with a Prayer of Stardom', *Saturday Post*, 8 Dec. 1984.
12. Lopez, *Women on the Ball*, p.31.
13. M.A. Hird, 'North Hykeham' (unpublished manuscript, 1997), p.4.
14. For example, the Women's Football Association of Ireland (WFAI) was formed in 1973, and affiliated to the Football Association of Ireland in 1990. Since 1977 Women's Football in Northern Ireland has been under the administration of the Northern Ireland Women's Football Association (NIWFA), which became an affiliate of the Irish Football Association in 1993. The Scottish Women's Football

Association was formed in 1972 and has held affiliate status since 1998. The incorporation of the English Women's Football Association, formed in 1969, was a more gradual and complex situation as they were invited to affiliate on the same basis as a County Football Association in 1983 and did so in 1984. In effect the demise of the association came with the creation of a Women's Football Committee within the Football Association in 1993 which has the dual purpose of administering national aspects of women's and girls' play but also of representing women's interests within the association.

15. Women's Football Association, 'Financial State of the Association', *Women's Football Association News* (Nov. 1985), 1.
16. Tim Stearn, 'Report on the Future Development of the WFA and The New Regional Set Up', *WFA News* (Jan. 1987), 1.
17. Women's Football Association, *WFA News* (July 1977), 2.
18. John Bale, *Sport and Place* (London: Hurst, 1982), p.26.
19. Sue Lopez, 'An Investigation Of Reasons For Participation In Women's Football', *Bulletin of Physical Education*, 15 (1979), 40.
20. Dorothy Miller, 'A Survey of English Women's Football Clubs' (Unpublished MA Dissertation, California State University, May 1987), p.5.
21. Football Association, *Women's Football Fact Sheet 3* (London: The Football Association, 2000), p.1.
22. Lopez, *Women on the Ball*, p.86.
23. *WFA News 1991* (Action Replay Fusion Creative Products Ltd. c, 1992), p.33.
24. Lord Denning, *Theresa Bennet v. The Football Association Limited and the Nottinghamshire Football Association* (Unreported: Judgment of 28 July 1978), pp.4–5.
25. There is a growing literature on the relationship between historical evidence and the women's football community, for example, Melling, '"Ray of the Rovers". The Working Class Heroine in Popular Football Fiction 1915–25'; Melling, 'Ladies Football: Gender and Socialisation of Women Football Players in Lancashire 1926–1960'; Donna Woodhouse, 'The Post War Development of Football for Females: A Cross Cultural and Comparative Study of England, The USA and Norway' (Unpublished Ph.D. Thesis, University of Leicester, 2001); Jean Williams, 'The Revival of Women's Football in England from the 1960s to the Present' (Unpublished Ph.D. Thesis, De Montfort University, 2002); Jean Williams, *A Game For Rough Girls? A History of Women's Football in England* (London: Routledge, 2003).

8

The Challenges of Women's Football in East and West Germany: A Comparative Study

GERTRUD PFISTER

As their 'squad' of 11 players fight for possession, the German fans chant 'Deutschland vor, noch ein Tor!' ['Forward Germany, another goal!'] – such rituals in conjunction with a multitude of symbols and myths which glorify masculinity and national superiority are connected with football. In this world women have always played a marginal role and this is still true today. Why have women had to overcome so many obstacles just because they wished to play football? Were women football players living in socialist systems confronted with the same problems as like-minded women in capitalist systems? These are the questions that will be answered here, by considering the different ways football developed in the Federal Republic of Germany and the German Democratic Republic.

SPORT IS A MAN'S DOMAIN – THE HISTORICAL DEVELOPMENT OF WOMEN'S SPORT IN GERMANY

Both gymnastics and its German variant, *Turnen*, were conceived by men, for men.[1] The latter, developed by Friedrich Ludwig Jahn at the beginning of the nineteenth century, was designed to bring on young men who loved their 'fatherland' and were willing to fight for it. The grounds on which *Turnen* was practised were not for women.

It was not until the 1830s that occasional demands were made for the 'physical exercise of the weaker sex' in order that 'maidens' cheeks should blossom like roses and lilies, and their delicate limbs should be blessed by the goddesses of grace and beauty'.[2]

From the middle of the century onwards girls were allowed to take part in physical education lessons at a number of schools for the daughters of well-to-do families and could also attend the gymnastics courses provided by some *Turn*-clubs. However, it was only at the end of the 1880s that adult women began to take up gymnastics and join in the gymnastic games initiated by the Games Movement in Germany. These years saw the growth of independent women's sports and gymnastics clubs as well as the establishment of women's sections in men's *Turn*-clubs. The latter, however, were mostly very unwilling to grant the new women members rights even though they were quite ready to put them under all sorts of obligations.

Whereas opposition to women's gymnastics declined after the turn of the century, modern sport in general was considered to be particularly unsuitable for women and quite 'unfeminine' because of its orientation towards performance, competition and record-breaking. In spite of this, women, too, were captivated by the growing fascination of sport and some had the courage, although at first in very small numbers, to take part in various sports ranging from cycling and tennis to skiing.

After the First World War a great controversy arose over whether women should be allowed to take part in competitions. The well-known athlete and sports official, Karl Ritter von Halt commented, for example: 'Contests belong to men by right; but they are totally incompatible with women's natures ... so let us do away with the Women's Athletic Championships.'[3] Von Halt, however, did not get his way and increasing numbers of women took up athletics, which were then added to their Olympic programme in the 1928 Amsterdam Games. Nevertheless the 1920s saw an upsurge of women's sport, though a great number of sports remained taboo for women.

'LADIES' PLAY FOOTBALL – DEVELOPMENTS BEFORE THE SECOND WORLD WAR

Even more than athletics, football belonged to those sports that – according to popular belief – 'was not suited to the female disposition, looked anomalous and deforming, and therefore should be left to the male of the species'.[4]

This, however, did not stop women in England and France from trying out football as a game for themselves.[5] In England it was said that women had taken part in folk games in which balls were kicked as early as the eighteenth century. In 1894 the first women's team (the 'British Ladies') was founded and from 1895 onwards various women's teams in England played matches against each other in front of thousands of spectators, both male and female. Accompanied by the nationalist fervour of the First World War, women's football reached a zenith when football matches were organized between women's teams in order to raise money for charity. In 1921 there were around 150 women's football clubs in England, the most famous and successful of them being Dick, Kerr Ladies FC, founded in 1917. The 'ladies', who all worked in the Dick, Kerr Munitions and Engineering Works, not only played matches against other English women's teams but also against foreign women's teams, for example against a team from France in 1920. After the war charity matches lost much of their significance, and in 1921 the Football Association urged clubs to end their support for such 'spectacles'. In spite of the fact that a Women's Football Association was founded, the ban proclaimed by the Football Association signalled the decline of women's football in England, even if it did not prevent women from playing football altogether.[6]

8.1 Poster advertising France v. England match, 1920.

In France, too, women's football teams were founded during the First World War.[7] In 1917 the first women's football championships were held and in 1922 two football cup competitions were introduced. In the 1920s, moreover, numerous matches took place, not only between French teams but also against women's teams from other European countries.[8] The spread of women's sports in France was partly due to the strength of the women's sports movement, which was also supported by influential men. In 1917 the French Federation of Women's Sport (FSFSF, later FFSF) was founded, whose president, Alice Milliat, was the driving force behind the founding of the International Federation of Women's Sport (FSFI). Right up until the mid-1930s, Milliat and her federation gave particular support to athletic events, which at that time were regarded as unfeminine. In 1932 discussions were even held on the supervision of women's football at international level. Alice Milliat had always had a special affinity with football, having accompanied a French women's team to England in 1920. In 1921 she had also organized an international competition between England and France in athletics and football in Paris. Besides the FFSF was founded as a Women's Football Association in 1933, but it did not survive the 1930s.[9] However, opposition to women's football had long been smouldering, and in the early 1930s this opposition became more and more virulent. It was above all the 'street urchin-like' appearance of the young women that seems to have been a special target for criticism.[10] During the course of the 1930s, news reports of women's football in France became increasingly rare until they vanished completely.

This comparatively tolerant attitude towards women's football in England and France is partly due to the exceptional circumstances prevailing during the First World War; but it can also be attributed to specific constellations of sports politics, not least to the existence of and competition between various women's sports organizations.[11]

In Germany, reports about girls and women playing football are rare. In his book on football published in 1898 Philipp Heineken, for example, reports that 'football has long been played by girls – and they enjoy playing it'.[12] But Heineken does not describe what kind of football the girls were allowed to play. Maybe this was a game where the participants stood in a circle and passed the ball around. Circle football is described in several of the game books of the end of the nienteenth century. After the game of football had become a 'real' competitive sport with the founding of the German Football Association, there was no longer any reference to girls or women taking part in the game.

In spite of repeated reports in the German press of football matches being played between teams of women in England and in France, in Germany the football field was no place for German women.[13] 'All types of sport which go beyond a woman's natural strength, like wrestling, boxing or football, are unsuitable; furthermore, they look unaesthetic and unnatural', was how, for example, Willy Vierath expressed it tersely in his book *Modern Sport*, published in 1930.[14] Consequently, few women dared to expose themselves to the criticism of 'masculinizing' themselves by playing football. Thus, it was not until 1930 that what is claimed to be the first German women's football club was founded in Frankfurt; however, after the press had reported this 'scandal', causing a public outcry, this women's football club was forced to close in 1931.[15]

This brief excursion into the European history of football is intended to show that, although playing football was labelled everywhere as a man's activity, the intensity of the opposition to women entering this male domain varied from country to country. Its aim is also to show that there was always a more or less close association between football and masculinity.

'LADIES' FOOTBALL' IN WEST GERMANY AFTER THE SECOND WORLD WAR

'Can they do that?' – The 1950s

After the Second World War a unified sport system was built up in West Germany on the basis of sports clubs and sports associations. Within this system, both the individual clubs and associations, as well as the German Sports Federation as the umbrella organization, enjoyed autonomy. Although women played only a marginal role in sport, women's membership of sports clubs steadily increased from the 1950s onwards, as did the range of sports they played – a general trend in the West, especially in the 1960s, in response to growing emancipatory attitudes and efforts.

West German women began to take an interest in football again after the Second World War. In the early 1950s, for example, the wives and girlfriends of the Tennis Borussia Berlin football team met for a traditional New Year's football match, at which – according to press reports – the spectators amused themselves exceedingly.[16] Thus, the German Football Federation (*Deutscher Fußballbund –* DFB) was forced to consider the question of whether or not to recognize women football players. Its reaction in 1955 was one of total rejection, forbidding its clubs from either founding women's sections or putting their grounds at the disposal of women's teams.[17]

In spite of this setback, 'neglected football dames' and lonely 'football wives' presented the DFB in 1957 with a 'revolutionary demand: "Equal rights for all! We want to play football, too!"'[18] But the women were not content with simply making demands: football matches were played between women's teams and in 1957 there was even a women's international played between Germany and Holland in the Kornwestheim stadium near Stuttgart. Many spectators had been attracted to the stadium by the promise of a highly amusing and entertaining afternoon. Although it appears that the women played quite creditably, reports of the game contained descriptions of the women covered in mud, but unfortunately failed to mention the result.[19] Spectators and the press made similar fun of a women's football match between West Germany and West Holland, which took place in front of 14,000 spectators at the Dante stadium in Munich in 1957.[20] In the same article appeared which mentioned a 'West German Women's Football Association' with 22 affiliated clubs.[21] The author suggested that the DFB should incorporate women's football and put it under its wing in order to stop sensationalism and profiteering, and prevent women's football from sinking to the level of women's wrestling. Banning women's football was pointless, the author went on, and did not make any sense anyway since ideals of femininity had changed and women had proved themselves in many other types of sport. Opponents of women's football, however, put forward aesthetic and medical arguments ranging from anatomical anomalies such as 'knock-knees' and the difficulty of conditioning female muscles, to the 'diminished ability to reproduce' and the masculinization of women football players.[22] Time and again in 1957 the question was asked: 'Should women play football?'[23]

Women's increasing involvement in sport generally was not enough to change the DFB's mind. On the contrary, in 1957 and 1958 it was reaffirmed unanimously that grounds, apparatus and referees were not to be put at the disposal of women's football teams.[24] Horst Schmidt, a DFB official at the time, named one of the reasons in an interview: 'In those days there were "football manager" types who travelled up and down the country making money with breast-swinging women. This was something we rejected.'[25] Moreover, for the DFB, fighting as it did for the amateur ideal, professional women players represented a double offence.

The DFB cited medicine in support of its arguments. An 'expert' report drawn up by doctors warned of the dangers that women allegedly exposed themselves to while playing football.[26] The doctors were supported by the renowned philosopher F.J.J. Buytendijk, who had remarked offensively in his psychological study of football published in 1953:

> Football as a game is first and foremost a demonstration of masculinity as we understand it from our traditional view of things and as produced in part by our physical constitution (through hormonal irritation). No one has ever been successful in getting women to play football ... Kicking is thus presumably a specifically male activity; whether being kicked is consequently female – that is something I will leave the reader to answer.[27]

In the 1950s and 1960s, then, women were only able to play football 'unofficially' in recreational teams because of the DFB's hostile attitude.

Women's Football Becomes 'Official'

It was not until 1970, at the DFB's national conference in Travemünde, that 'ladies' football' was officially recognized.[28] The reason for this change of mind, as Hannelore Ratzeburg, the best known of the DFB's women officials, notes, was the fear of losing control over the women's football movement.[29] In the meantime, several women's football clubs had been founded, for example '*Oberst Schiel*', a club formed two years previously by a women's team in Frankfurt.[30] At Borussia Berlin, too, a regular team had been formed in 1969 by players' wives along with a number of women handball players; this team went on to place second in the (still unofficial) municipal championship in 1971.[31]

A positive and pioneering role was played, in addition, by women's football initiatives abroad. In 1969 a 'Confederation of Independent European Female Football' was founded,[32] and in Italy, for instance, a first unofficial World Cup tournament was held in 1970 which was watched by 35,000 spectators and in which a selection of women players from German clubs took part.[33] A reporter from the *Münchner Abendzeitung*, who accompanied the women, wrote:

> Just before setting off for the World Championships in women's football, Helga Walluga, aged 28 from Bad Neuenahr, the German eleven's striker, went to the hairdresser's to have her hair smartly permed. Then she joined her 12 giggling team mates in the bus ... There was trouble, too, because the reporters wanted to visit the changing rooms with the women in them. The German women had tried, they said, to keep their bosoms out of the limelight in order to be able to return safely to the haven of matrimony afterwards ... Unfortunately the prettiest team lost.[34]

In short, the journalist ended up writing a 'humorous' and humiliating description of a spectacle that was supposed to be funny because of its absurdity. Incidentally, the Danish women's team won this first championship.

Since women's enthusiasm for football could no longer be suppressed, the DFB decided to follow the principle, 'If you can't beat them, join them'. In 1970, the federation accepted ladies' football. The official term 'ladies' football', which was in use until the 1980s, indicates that football played by girls and women should have a different quality from the man's game. It was also considered that the women ought at least to be 'kept on the right track' by means of suitable guidelines. Thus, in collaboration with a woman doctor, Ingeborg Bausenwein, the DFB's Games Supervisory Committee developed a set of rules on how the game should be played by women's teams. So, for example, women's games should be only 60 minutes, the playing season should be from 1 March to 31 October, and the female players were not allowed to use soccer shoes with piles.[35] In the years that followed, however, these rules proved for the most part superfluous, if not senseless. Furthermore, because of the 'female anatomy', any kind of advertising on the women's jerseys was prohibited. 'Advertising distorts', wrote the DFB in a statement issued in 1976.[36] The reason was possibly that the spectators' attention should not be distracted from the actual game.[37] Today there are no regulations which apply exclusively to women.

The Rise of Women's Football – Milestones of the Development in West Germany

The student rebellion of 1968 triggered off sweeping social changes, ranging from 'sexual liberation' (Oswald Kolle) to the forming of citizens' lobbies and initiatives, and the development of a new women's movement. In this period of upheaval and paradigm shift, women's football, also encouraged by initiatives abroad, succeeded in establishing itself in West Germany.

In the 1970s women's football in West Germany experienced a rapid upswing, reflected in, among other things, the institutionalization of the game: in 1971 the first knockout competitions were organized, in 1972–73 championship matches took place in the regional associations of the German federal states and in 1974 the first German championships were held.[38] At the same time club cup matches at regional level were introduced in which all women's teams could take part regardless of the league in which they played. Since 1980 the winning teams of the 16 regional federations compete for the DFB's Women's National Cup (DFB-Vereinspokal).[39]

In 1985–86 regional and upper leagues were introduced. In 1990 teams were divided into 14 regional leagues (regional league, association league or upper league) and a national league with two divisions of 10 teams each. Since 1997–98, 12 teams have formed a national league with a single division in an attempt to concentrate women's football on the best clubs and thus raise standards of play.[40]

In the 1980s major breakthroughs were achieved in women's football at international level, and German women were among the best and most successful players of the game. The first unofficial world championships in women's football, held in Taiwan in 1981, were won by a German club team named SSG 09 Gladbach, whose members had to finance the trip to Taiwan themselves. Subsequently, in 1982, an 'official' national team was formed from the best players. In the same year the German women's eleven played their first international against Switzerland, which they won 5-1. In 1989 the West German women's national team won the European championship.[41] After reunification the success of German women's football was strengthened, the national eleven winning the European championship in 1991, 1995, 1997 and 2001. The first official world championship was held in China in 1991, where the German team took fourth place. In the second world championship tournament held in Sweden in 1995 the German team lost to Norway in the final, thus coming second in the contest. Women's football became an Olympic discipline at the 1996 Atlanta Games.[42] In the 2000 Olympics in Sydney the German women's team won the bronze medal after defeating Brazil in the semi-finals play-off.

The spread of girls' and women's football was due in part to the establishment of women's committees and the appointment of officials in charge of girls' and women's football within the DFB and the regional associations. Hannelore Ratzeburg (in 1977 the first woman to be made a member of the DFB's Games Supervisory Committee), together with the bodies and individuals appointed to supervise girls' and women's sport in the period that followed, initiated numerous projects and schemes in order not only to establish women's football as a recognized sport, but also to ensure its continuous growth and development.

8.2 Women's soccer in West Berlin, early 1970s (Berliner Tennis Club Borussia e.V)

8.3 Women's soccer in West Berlin, early 1970s (Berliner Tennis Club Borussia e.V)

8.4 Women's soccer cartoons from East Germany (*Die Neue Fußballwoche* 31, 52, 1979, 8)

8.5 Women's indoor soccer, East Germany c.1980 (F. Gahlbeck Sportmuseum Leipzig)

8.6 Frauenfußball Frankfurt 1930 (*Das Illustrierte Blatt*, 27 March 1930)

8.7 West Germany v. Switzerland, 1982 (Hannelore Ratzeburg, Hamburg)

8.8 (West) German National Team, 1989, winners of the European Championship (Hannelore Ratzeburg, Hamburg)

Since the mid-1980s especially, the DFB has increased its commitment to women's football and, in particular, its efforts to encourage and support girls in the game.

WOMEN'S FOOTBALL IN EAST GERMANY

Developments and Challenges

The development of women's football in the German Democratic Republic can only be understood if viewed against the backdrop of the post-war restructuring of sport and sports policy in East Germany. After sports clubs and associations had been disbanded by the occupying forces, a centralized sport system evolved in East Germany whose aim was to achieve first of all recognition, and then esteem, for the socialist state through sporting success. Reasons for the GDR's 'miraculous sporting record' are to be found in the numerous, centrally controlled measures and financial resources for improving performance, ranging from talent spotting to medical and pharmaceutical manipulation; in the resources invested in top-level elite sports; and in the system of material as well as psychological incentives with which top performance was rewarded, for example, with visits to foreign countries – something beyond the reach of most ordinary citizens.[43]

While elite sports were organized in children's and adolescents' sport schools as well as in sport centres, recreational sport and 'sport for all' were organized by 'works sport communities' (*Betriebssportgemeinschaften* – BSG) set up in places of work in both industry and in the public sector.

The ruling party of the state, the SED, controlled sport: 'Physical activity and sport are firmly embedded in the structures of a developed socialist society. Their development is pursued within the framework of the SED's policies in general and its sports policy in particular.'[44]

In East Germany, too, the first initiatives to set up women's football teams date back to the 1950s. These, however, were opposed and obstructed without the provision of official reasons. 'In 1956, when we tried to get women's football established again, we got into serious trouble with the national sport bosses. They even threatened to throw us out of the association.'[45]

It took more than ten years before women's football had a chance in East Germany. In 1968, on the initiative of a Bulgarian student at the Technical University of Dresden, the first women's football team was founded in the German Democratic Republic as a section of BSG (*Betriebssportgemeinschaft*), Empor Dresden/Mitte. Others soon followed this example. Women began to take up football, first in the state of Saxony but soon afterwards in other cities of the GDR. In 1971 Turbine Potsdam was founded, which was to become the GDR's most successful women's team. Women's football soon became popular in rural areas, too. In Spornitz, for example, a village in Mecklenburg with a population of around 1,200, of which every third or fourth resident belonged to the local works sport community, the first women's football match was held in 1972 in which two teams of six women each demonstrated their football skills to an initially sceptical crowd of spectators. But the Spornitz example caught on. Soon a women's football team was founded by the BSG Hydraulik Parchim, and, on the closing day of the *Kreisspartakiade*, an annual district sports meeting for children and young people, the team of Traktor Spornitz played against that of Hydraulik Parchim in front of a large crowd of spectators. Further 'friendlies' were played, until it was decided in the summer of 1972 to organize a regional league.[46] The football 'fever' spread rapidly to other areas, where similar developments took place. In the same year, for instance, the first 'ladies' football match' was played by BSG Asobloc in Neubrandenburg.[47] Doreen Meier, a member of the GDR women's national team in 1990, remembers: 'At village fairs and festivals, at sports meetings, at peace rallies and also as a sort of prelude to first-division football matches, women's football was a special attraction in the 1970s.'[48] Up until the 1980s women's football continued to grow steadily in East Germany. Figures published in the women's journal *Für Dich* ['For You'] revealed that something like 6,000 women played football regularly in their spare time in around 360 teams.[49]

Besides the league games that were played in these years, numerous knock-out competitions were also organized, especially in indoor arenas or on smaller pitches with six players on each side. From the players' reports one gathers that they had lots of fun, the highlights including everyone getting together for an enjoyable evening after a tournament, 'friendlies' and trips, for example, to Poland, as well as birthday and wedding parties.[50] In spite of all this, women's enthusiasm for football gradually faded again. There were various reasons for this: the players often complained that team members gave up football when they moved to another town to study or when they married and started to have children.[51] The spread of football was also probably hindered by problems with the sports grounds – the 'cramped conditions' as the Spornitz chronicles describe them. To this may be added the lack of support on the part of sports officials and the resulting practical difficulties for 'recreational' sportsmen and women in the GDR. As reported in the archive material as well as in interviews, these difficulties ranged from the lack of showers and supervision of the players' children, to the failure to inform players, for example, about team selections. According to Doreen Meier further problems were caused by the great differences in the players' ages and life circumstances, which made it difficult, for example, to plan training sessions.[52] It is also possible that the aura of the new and the exceptional that had guaranteed women footballers special attention in the early years had now lost its attraction. On the whole, though, women's football was not taken seriously in the GDR. This is suggested, at least, by the complaints the players made, the reports and caricatures appearing in the mass media, among others the *Fußballwoche* ['Football Weekly'], and the fact that matches between women's teams were frequently organized as part of the 'entertainment programme' of festivals and celebrations. On these occasions, according to Doreen Meier (1999), the women were often met with shouts of 'beauty competition' or, at the end of the game, that the teams should 'exchange jerseys'. In the *Deutsches Sportecho am Wochenende* it was sarcastically commented that football was 'still sometimes regarded as a man's sport in our Republic. "Moderation, gentlemen!" I would urge.' At women's football matches, the author went on, the spectators would 'snigger' and men would threaten to 'lock their wives out' if they ever had the desire to play football. This short article reveals the numerous strategies that were used with the aim of keeping women in their place. The author concluded: 'There is no question about the popularity of King Football. For his women, though, things are not so easy.'[53]

The Role of the German Football Federation

In spite of the spread of women's football from the 1970s onwards, the sport was never officially recognized as a top-level competitive sport by the East German Football Association (Deutscher Fußball Verband – DFV). On the contrary, women's football was classed as a recreational and leisure sport. Although this meant, on the one hand, that there was no state support for women's football, it made possible, on the other, a development that was largely free of 'official' constraints. Thus, women's football was able to profit from the initiative of a small number of football enthusiasts, both male and female, and was played, perhaps at a lower standard technically, but with great commitment and enjoyment on the part of the players. And in 1971, moreover, the DFV decided that women's football should be organized on a competitive basis but only at the local level.

In 1979 a working group on women's football was set up within the DFV's Commission on Recreational and Leisure Sport/Association Development that extended the organization of women's football to regional and national levels. In the same year competitions took place for the first time to find the best team, but 'official' championships were not held, even though the working group repeatedly demanded the organization of leagues at all levels and official championships.[54] In 1987 the working group concluded, for example, that the 'best team' competitions were not sufficient to motivate girls and women to play football. Further points of criticism were the absence of a regular and frequent sequence of matches as well as the length of football games, which, at two halves of 30 minutes each, did not comply with international regulations.[55] It was not until the 1986–87 season that competitions were held for the DFD (later FDGB) Cup[56] and not until the 1987–88 season that a national league was formed with two divisions and the match length increased to two halves of 40 minutes each. After the political changes in 1990–91 a national league was formed with ten teams in a single division. At the end of 1989, furthermore, the DFV decided to turn the working group on women's football into a commission. All the same, it was intended that women's football should remain rooted in the domain of recreational 'sport for all'.[57] After the fall of the Berlin Wall a women's national team was even formed, whose first international game, however, was also its last. In May 1990, in the final months of the GDR's existence, the women's national team played Czechoslovakia in Potsdam, the East German women losing 3-0 before a crowd of 800 spectators.

After the reunification of Germany the East German Football Federation was incorporated into the German Football Federation as the Regional Football Association (North East) and women's football was 'finally granted the status for which it had fought for 21 years'.[58]

The disadvantages suffered by women football players in East Germany can only be adequately judged when viewed against the background of the privileges enjoyed by their male counterparts. Although men's football in the GDR had no great record of international success, football was not taken off the list of sports that were given special assistance and support since this would have provoked great opposition in a country of football enthusiasts. For the players this meant a life of luxury, as the wife of a player in the national team reported in an interview: 'We … got a car after only a short wait. And, when we needed it, furniture, a telephone connected up or even a bigger flat. In short, we were privileged and enjoyed a living standard that would have taken years, or even decades, for the average citizen in the GDR to reach.'[59]

WOMEN'S FOOTBALL IN EAST AND WEST – A COMPARISON

Here I can only put forward a number of hypotheses about the reasons for the different development of women's football in East and West. In doing so, I will concentrate on the ideology of sport and the gender order in sport as well as on its organizational framework and its structures. I will also examine the significance of sporting success in both systems.

The starting point of my analysis is the fact that, in spite of numerous differences, the gender order in the Federal Republic undeniably exhibited similar structures to those of the GDR: in East and West women were under-represented in executive and policy-making bodies; and in both systems women were responsible for the family and children, for example.[60] The claim that women's emancipation in the GDR had been achieved with the removal of class distinctions, that is, through the liberation of the working class, is not borne out by the facts.

While ideals of womanhood and myths of femininity made access to top-level elite sports difficult for women in the West, sports competitions were by no means a male preserve in the GDR. On the contrary, East German women were given intensive support in elite sports – and with great success. This is not true of all sports, however; aggressiveness, physical contact and consequently football appear to have been men's prerogatives in East and West Germany alike, in spite of the

GDR's claim that it had put 'women's emancipation' into practice. Thus, traditional ways of thinking and sport ideologies seem to have prevailed in both countries even though the roles of sports women and the sport systems were different.

Nevertheless, the sport systems of the two countries must be taken into consideration on account of the considerable influence they had on the development of sport. Characteristic of the West German sport system, based as it was on autonomous clubs and federations, was, for example, the limited degree of centralization, the relatively large amount of independence that the individual associations and clubs had, and the absence of generally recognized directives. The GDR's sport system, by contrast, was integrated into the labour force; it was financed to a large degree by the state, and thus centralized and hierarchically structured. As in all other areas of society, the overriding political precept was the SED's absolute rule, the 'claim to leadership of the party of the working class'.[61] Consequently, despite similar attitudes in general, women's football had different opportunities and different challenges in East and West.

Thus, whereas in the West the fear that women's football could become commercialized or that a women's football association might be founded (threatening the unity of the sport) contributed to women's football being incorporated into the German Football Federation, in East Germany the Football Federation did not need to give in to the wishes and demands voiced by the advocates of women's football, since there was no fear of competition or commercialization.

It must also be taken into consideration that, although in its striving for international recognition, the GDR placed much emphasis on sport, priority was given to sports promising great success and prestige, in other words Olympic medals. In 1969, for example, it was decided to concentrate on 'medal-winning' sports. As a result, numerous types of sport were excluded from the country's 'intensive backing'.

Women's football, however, was not even recognized as a 'serious' performance sport. This meant, of course, that it had no backing from the state; on the other hand, though, it allowed a relatively autonomous development that was largely free from 'official' directives and controls. Thus, women's football was able to profit from the initiative of a small number of football enthusiasts, both male and female, and was played, perhaps, at a lower standard technically but with great enjoyment on the part of the players. Whereas the motto in the West was 'you must integrate in order to control', the GDR's precept was 'you must control in order to prevent integration'.

WHY IS FOOTBALL A MALE PRESERVE?

After reunification women's football experienced a further upswing. In 1996 the German Football Federation (DFB) had 706,346 women members. Today, in spite of the rapid growth over the last years, girls and women still only represent a small minority of 12 per cent of DFB members. Moreover, it can be assumed that the majority of girl and women members of the DFB do not play football, at least at competition level. In 1996 there were, in effect, only 4,760 girls' and women's teams registered with the DFB, that is a mere 3 per cent of all teams. This means that only about 10–15 per cent of the DFB's female members take part in official DFB-organized games.[62]

The continuing development and the record of success in women's football over the years should not be allowed to cover over the fact that women football players are still confronted with numerous problems today. The question arises as to why, in football of all games, women in both East and West met with such serious opposition in the past and why they have faced all kinds of discrimination right up to the present day. Every one of the 20 West German women footballers interviewed as part of the project 'Sport in Women's Lives' could remember experiencing hostile attitudes.[63] They reported that they were not taken seriously, that they were labelled 'lesbians' or that they had to come to terms with the lack of interest and support.[64]

Both the long exclusion of girls and women from football, and the fact that they were only slowly accepted as football players, are connected first of all with the image of the game. In contrast to gymnastic games like team races and tambourine ball, football was considered in Germany from the late nineteenth century onwards to be competition-oriented, strenuous, aggressive and potentially dangerous. Therefore, well into the twentieth century, physical education teachers did not allow even their male students to play football, which they described deprecatingly as 'kicking a ball around'.[65] If playing football was not suitable for boys from well-to-do families, one can imagine that it was considered entirely irreconcilable with the prevailing ideals of femininity.

Even today football is associated with rough and aggressive play and, therefore, the view is widespread that women who play 'real' football can't be 'real' women. Women players interviewed in various surveys agreed that, now as before, football is regarded as a man's sport and that they have to live with the stigma of not being 'feminine'.[66] The interviews carried out as part of the project 'Sport in Women's Lives' also revealed that almost all the women interviewed judged football to be a rough and masculine sport. Thus, in East as well as West Germany, women's football was considered unaesthetic and unfeminine.

The labelling of sports as 'masculine' or 'feminine' is by no means idiosyncratic. The body, physical activities and ways of presenting oneself – including through sport – play an important role in the reproduction of the gender order. To the present day, sport or certain types of sport have served to construct and demonstrate masculinity. The enactment of gender, or 'doing gender', is something that continuously takes place in everyday situations and, hence, in sport too.[67] As Eric Dunning was able to show using rugby as his example, sport gains particular importance as a source of male identity in times when a shift takes place in the balance of power between the sexes.[68] Football teams can be interpreted – from their rituals and enactments – as male bonding groups – alliances founded above all on the exclusion of women and the rejection of both femininity and all the qualities related to it such as gentleness, consideration and empathy.[69] This ideology of the 'polarity of gender traits' (that is, unchangeable, innate differences between the sexes), does not only play an important role in male bonding, but is anchored in society as a whole, be it East German or West German society. For many, women who play football have transgressed the socially-fixed boundaries between the sexes; they pose a threat to ideals and myths of masculinity and call into question the prevailing gender order – and with it the whole social order. Thus, the attempts to keep women off the football pitch were by no means just simply a question of sport but were concerned with the structure and the legitimacy of the social order as a whole.

Finally, it must be borne in mind that football is a national sport, with which much of the male population identifies. National sport and myths of masculinity are here interwoven in a particular way: 'In the national sport of any given society a specific male identity is produced and nurtured. This explains why the national sport in every society is not only a male preserve ... but is also bound up with sexual claims, needs and anxieties.'[70]

In many societies football is a stage upon which masculinity can be produced and staged. Involved in the building of the stage and the staging of the play/game are social structures, institutions and norms with their gendered scripts, just as much as individuals engaged in 'doing gender'. Since gender, gendered scripts and 'doing gender' are specific to a culture and not unalterable, practices which are labelled 'masculine' or 'feminine' – and these include sports – can open themselves up to admit members of the other sex, experiencing as it were a 'sex change'. The popularity of women's football in the United States, for example, could become 'infectious' and spread, thus improving women football players' chances of attracting the public's attention and receiving the support they deserve all over the world. Whether men would then withdraw from the football field and let women take over is a moot question. It must also be asked whether the price to be paid for the recognition of women's football is that of commercialization and sexualization.[71] In my view the scenario drawn up by E. Thurner is a realistic one: 'In spite of the current obstruction strategy and faltering development ... (Western capitalist) societies will "swallow" women's football, too. As long as football kicking women only want to be "equal" and do not intend to break the rules of "bread and games" politics, in future they will even occasionally be given the main venues – depending on performance and profitability.'[72]

CONCLUSION

Although the development of football in both German states reveals numerous similarities, there are also fundamental differences. Women's hesitant attempts to play football in the 1950s, for example, were successful in neither the West nor the East. Moreover, women's football spread at about the same time in both countries (that is, in the 1970s); and in both countries women football players lived a life on the margins of sport. However, unlike their counterparts in the East, West German women succeeded in obtaining official recognition for women's football as a top-level competitive sport and also succeeded in playing an important role at the international level. Women's football in the German Democratic Republic, on the other hand, in spite of the SED's claim to have achieved the emancipation of women, failed in its attempts to be included in the list of sports receiving state (and financial) backing. The gender orders prevailing in the two countries were identified as the cause of the marginalization of women's football. Women's football in the West profited from the autonomy of sports associations whereas women players in the East had to submit to the supremacy of the cost-benefit principle. Since there were no Olympic medals to be gained in women's football and thus no political impact was to be expected, an upgrading of women's football to a top-level competitive sport did not seem to be worth any investment of financial resources. The socialist claim of guaranteeing the equality of men and women was thus renounced for political and financial reasons.

NOTES

1. On the history of women's sport in Germany, see G. Pfister, *Frau und Sport: Frühe Texte* (Frankfurt: Fischer, 1980).
2. J.A.L. Werner 1839, quoted in A. Bluemcke, *Die Körperschule der deutschen Frau im Wandel der Jahrhundertwende* (Dresden: Limpert, 1928), p.81.
3. Quoted in W. Kühn, 'Wohin führt der Weg? Eine kritische Betrachtung zur Frauensportbewegung', *Die Leibesübungen*, 2 (1926), 193.
4. *Sport und Gesundheit*, 5, 1 (1932), 16.
5. On women's football in other European countries, see G. Pfister, K. Fasting, S. Scraton and B. Vasquez, 'Women and Football – A Contradiction? The Beginnings of Women's Football in Four European Countries', *The European Sports History Review*, 1, 1 (1998), 1–26.
6. D. Williamson, *Belles of the Ball* (Devon: R & D Associates, 1991); J. Williams and J. Woodhouse, 'Can Play, will Play? Women and Football in Britain', in J. Williams and S. Wagg (eds), *British Football and Social Change* (Leicester: Leicester University Press, 1991), pp.85–111, 94; S. Lopez, *Women on the Ball* (London: Scarlett Press, 1997); see also F. Brändle and C. Koller, *Goooal!!! Kultur- und Sozialgeschichte des modernen Fußballs* (Zürich: Orell Füssli Verlag, 2002). See also *Sport und Gesundheit*, 5, 1 (1932), p.16; *Sport und Sonne*, 3 (1927), pp.24–7.
7. On the development of women's football in France, see. L. Prudhomme, 'Sexe faible et ballon rond. Esquisse d'une histoire du football feminine', in P. Arnaud and T. Terret (eds), *Histoire du Sport Féminin* (Paris: L'Harmattan, 1996), Vol.I, pp.111–26.
8. *Organe bimensuel de l'education physique et sports féminins.* Publiant l'Officiel de la Fédération féminine sportise de France, 1, 1 (1926), pp.10ff.
9. Proudhomme – Poncet, *Histoire du football fémimin au xxe siècle* (Paris: L'Harmattan, 2003).
10. *Sport und Gesundheit*, 5, 1 (1932), 16.
11. In France, there existed two main women's sport organizations: the Union Française de Gymnastique Féminine (UFGF, founded in 1912) and the Fédération des Sociétés Féminines Sportives de France (FSFSF, founded in 1916). Both bodies had a complicated history with many struggles between them. The UFGF was concerned with 'feminine' physical activities, especially gymnastics; the FSFSF was concerned with 'real' sport, also 'masculine' types of sport.
    In the 1920s, the UFGF merged with the Fédération Française Féminine des Sports

Athlétiques (a body which had only been in existence for a few months) to become the new Fédération Française Féminine de Gymnastique et d'Éducation Physique (FFFGEP), which existed until 1940 when it was forced to be reduced to a women's section of the very ancient, prestigious - and male - Union des Sociétés de Gymnastique de France (USGF). The FSFSF existed until 1936. Finally, women could also do sport in other organizations such as the Fédération Gymnastique et Sportives des Patronages de France (FGSPF), a Catholic organization. See for the history of women's sport organizations in France, T. Terret 'Femmes, sport, identité et acculturation' *Stadion*, 26 (2000), pp.41-55.

12. P. Heineken, *Das Fußballspiel* (Hannover: Schäfer, 1898), p.226.
13. On women's football in other countries, see, for example, *Sport und Gesundheit*, 11, 9 (1938), 18.
14. W. Vierath, *Moderner Sport* (Berlin: Oestergaard, 1930), p.61.
15. B. Schreiber-Rietig, 'Die Suffragetten spielten Fussball', *Olympisches Feuer*, 43, 2 (1993), 36–41. See also *Das Illustrierte Blatt*, 18, 27 March 1930. On the development of women's football in Austria, see M. Marschik and C. Eder, 'Männerspiel – Frauenspiel. Die Männlichkeit des österreichischen Fußballs und die Versuche, Frauenfußball zu etablieren', *SWS-Rundschau*, 36, 2 (1996), 317–27. In Austria, too, women's attempts to play football in the 1920s and 1930s met with serious opposition and eventually had to be given up.
16. F.J. Brüggemeier (ed.), *Der Ball ist rund* (Essen: Klartext, 2000), p.300.
17. See the typed report of Hans Hansen in the name of board of consultants of the DFB (15 Nov. 1969; 6 pages). This paper contains an overview of the decisions of the DFB concerning women's football and the proposal for a resolution on behalf of the acceptance of women's football. A copy of this paper was sent to me by Liselott Diem (letter from 25 July 1978). Cf. H. Ratzeburg and H. Biese, *Frauen Fußball Meisterschaften* (Kassel: Agon, 1995).
18. *WFV-Sport*, Nr.7, 11 April 1957.
19. *Christ und Welt*, 19 Sept. 1957.
20. *WFV-Sport*, Nr.7, 11 April 1957.
21. Ibid.
22. *WFV-Sport*, Nr.11, 13 June 1957.
23. *Sport im Spiegel*, 14 June 1957; this is a manuscript of the Carl-und-Liselott-Diem Archive (folder 334).
24. L. Diem, 'Frauen-Fußball – ein Stück Emanzipation?' *Das Parlament*, 22–23 June 1978, p.11.
25. B. Fechtig, *Frauen und Fußball* (Dortmund: sFeF, 1995), p.25.
26. Ibid.
27. F.J.J. Buytendijk, *Das Fußballspiel. Eine psychologische Studie* (Würzburg: Werkbund Verl., 1953), p.20.
28. See the report of Hans Hansen, above.
29. DFB (ed.), *Damenfußball – Grundlagen und Entwicklung* (2. Aufl. Frankfurt: DFB, 1983); Fechtig, *Frauen und Fußball*, p.31.
30. Cf. Ratzeburg and Biese, *Frauen Fußball*. In addition, use was made of numerous reports and articles on sport that appeared in the magazine *dieda*.
31. http://www.tennis-borussia-frauen.de/dt-hist.htm.
32. Brändle and Koller, *Goooal!*, p.224.
33. H. Ratzeburg, 'Fußball ist Frauensport', in S. Schenk (ed.), *Frauen – Bewegung – Sport* (Hamburg: Czwalina, 1986), pp.85–94; Fechtig, *Frauen und Fußball*, p.31.
34. Brändle and Koller, *Goooal!*, p.225.
35. See Fechtig, *Frauen und Fußball*, p.33.
36. http://www.pawlitta.de/fun-box/fun-box-zitate07.htm.
37. Printed in DFB, *Damenfußball*, p.12ff.
38. Fechtig, *Frauen und Fußball*, p.35.
39. Ratzeburg and Biese, *Frauen Fußball*, pp.21ff.
40. M. Kröger, 'Frauenfußball in der öffentlichen Diskussion – Entwicklungen und Veränderungen seit 1970' (Unpublished Master's Thesis, Freie Universität Berlin, 1996), p.31.
41. On the record of success of the German women's national team, see also G. Bisanz, 'Mannschaftsführung aus psychologischer Sicht am Beispiel der deutschen Damen-Nationalmannschaft', in G. Gerisch (ed.), *Psychologie im Fußball* (St Augustin: Academia, 1995), pp.23–9.
42. *Frankfurter Rundschau*, 3 Aug. 1996.

43. See G. Pfister, 'War Without Weapons', forthcoming.
44. Quoted in J. Baur, G. Spitzer and S. Telschow, 'Der DDR-Sport als gesellschaftliches Teilsystem', *Sportwissenschaft*, 27, 4 (1997), 371.
45. http://www.abc08.de/chronik1.htm about the history of the club Aldershofer BC 08.
46. H. Esch, *80 Years of Sport in Spornitz. A Chronicle* (Spornitz: Eigenverlag, 1990), p.39. Cf. D. Meier, 'Frauenfußball in der DDR', in Ratzeburg and Biese, *Frauen Fußball*, pp.29–42. Since 1972 some articles on women's football have been published in the East-German football magazine 'Fußballwoche'.
47. The development of women's football in Neubrandenburg is recorded in a comprehensive chronicle in six volumes with reports of matches, photos and newspaper clippings from the archives of the former Neubrandenburg Agricultural Engineering BSG. I thank Mr Werner Lenz for making these chronicles available to me.
48. Meier, 'Frauenfußball in der DDR', p.15.
49. *Für Dich*, 12 (1982), 8.
50. Cf. the reports of women players belonging to BSG Asobloc in the above-mentioned chronicle of the village Spornitz.
51. Cf. the reports in the chronicle of women's football in Neubrandenburg, archive of the former BSG Nahrungsgütermaschinenbau Neubrandenburg Agricultural Engineering, Werner Lenz.
52. D. Meier, 'Frauenfußball in der DDR', *Sportmuseum aktuell*, 7, 2 (1999), 14–17.
53. *Deutsches Sportecho am Wochenende* [German Weekend Sports Echo] 3, 115 (1980), 2.
54. 'Best team' competitions were not officially recognized as championships; they neither led to prizes or awards, nor did they entitle those selected to take part in international contests. The players were thus deprived of the privileges connected with 'official' championships.
55. Letter from officials and coaches to Secretary-General Zimmermann of the DFV dated 9/10 April 1983; minutes of the working group on women's football 26 March 1986; minutes of the working group 11 Dec. 1987; archive of the former BSG Nahrungsgütermaschinenbau Neubrandenburg, Werner Lenz.
56. DFD – Demokratischer Frauenbund Deutschlands; FDGB – Freier Deutscher Gewerkschaftsbund.
57. Minutes of the FES/VE commission of the East German Football Association dated 23 Oct. 1989; archive of the BSG Nahrungsgütermaschinenbau Neubrandenburg, Werner Lenz.
58. Meier, 'Frauenfußball in der DDR', p.37. See also the minutes of the working group/commission on women's football, archive of the BSG Nahrungsgütermaschinenbau Neubrandenburg, Werner Lenz.
59. Quoted in Fechtig, *Frauen und Fußball*, p.151; on the development of football in East Germany see A. Milios, 'Zur Rolle des Fußballs im Sportsystem der DDR' (Unpublished Master's Thesis, Freie Universität Berlin, 2000).
60. G. Helwig and H.-M. Nickel (eds), *Frauen in Deutschland 1945–1992* (Bonn: Akademie Verlag, 1993); K. Gottschall, 'Geschlechterverhältnisse und Arbeitsmarktsegregation', in R. Becker-Schmidt and G.-A. Knapp (eds), *Das Geschlechterverhältnis als Gegenstand der Sozialwissenschaften* (Frankfurt: Campus, 1995), pp.125–63; S. Diemer, *Patriarchalismus in der DDR* (Opladen: Leske und Budrich, 1994).
61. Baur, Spitzer and Telschow, 'Der DDR-Sport als gesellschaftliches Teilsystem', 371. This contains a detailed description of the East German sport system.
62. DFB members' statistics; see also K. Linsen, 'Frauen im Fußballsport', in U. Henkel and G. Pfister (eds), *Für eine andere Bewegungskultur* (Pfaffenweiler: Centaurus, 1997), pp.245–60.
63. See G. Pfister and K. Fasting, 'Disrupting gender? A Cross-national Study of Female Soccer Players Perceptions of Masculinity and Femininity'. To be published in *Dansk Sociologi*, 3 (2004).
64. See G. Pfister, *Sport im Lebenszusammenhang von Frauen* (Schorndorf: Hofmann, 1999).
65. On the general opposition to the game of football, see G. Pfister, 'Sport auf dem grünen Rasen. Fußball und Leichtathletik', in G. Pfister and G. Steins (eds), *Vom Ritterturnier zum Stadtmarathon. Sport in Berlin* (Berlin: Forum für Sportgeschichte, 1987), pp.68–96.
66. See, for example, Linsen, 'Frauen im Fußballsport'.
67. J. Lorber, *Paradoxes of Gender* (New Haven, London: Yale University Press, 1994).
68. E. Dunning, 'Sport as a Male Preserve: Notes on the Social Sources of Masculine Identity and its Transformations', in N. Elias and E. Dunning (eds), *Quest for Excitement* (Oxford: Blackwell, 1986), pp.267–307.
69. See the various contributions in G. Völger and K. Welck (eds), *Männerbande Männerbünde* 2 Vols

(Köln: Rautenstrauch, 1990); see also E. Dunning, 'Sport as a Male Preserve', pp.267–307.

70. M. Klein (ed.), *Sport und Geschlecht* (Reinbek: rororo, 1983). On the connection between national symbols and myths of masculinity, see U. Gerhard and J. Link, 'Zum Anteil der Kollektivsymbolik an den Nationalstereotypen', in J. Link (ed.), *Nationale Mythen und Symbole in der zweiten Hälfte des 19. Jahrhunderts* (Stuttgart: Klett-Cotta, 1991), pp.17–42.
71. See also R. Diketmüller, 'Frauenfußball in Zeiten der Globalisierung', in M. Fanizadeh, G. Hödl and W. Manzenreiter (eds), *Global Players* (Frankfurt: Brandes and Apsel, 2002), pp.203–27.
72. E. Thurner, *Nationale Identität und Geschlecht in Österreich nach 1945* (Innsbruck, Wein, München: Studien-Verlag, 2000), p.126.

9

Small Country – Big Results: Women's Football in Norway

KARI FASTING

It's a fascinating game ... One which permits individuals to be creative, to do things on their own, to find new ways of solving a problem, which may surprise your opponents ... what can I say ... how can I explain it, it's really problem solving, how we, together as a team, can manage. (Norwegian elite female football player)

Football, with over 70,000 active female players, is the largest female sport in Norway today.[1] But the sport does not only have a broad base, it also has excellence. As shown in Table 9.1, the national women's football team has won many medals in international competitions, of which the gold medal in the 2000 Olympic Games in Sydney is the most prestigious. An interesting question is why Norwegian women's football has had such a positive development both at the grass roots and the elite levels? The purpose of this study is to contribute to an understanding of why and how this has happened. This will be done not only by describing the membership development of women's football in Norway, but also by analysing the work of the Norwegian Football Association (NFA) in its effort to promote the sport for girls and women. The positive and the negative experiences of some footballers themselves are also added to this discussion.

THE BEGINNING

The Norwegian Football Association was founded in 1902, but it was many years

TABLE 9.1
OUTSTANDING ACHIEVEMENTS OF THE FEMALE NORWEGIAN NATIONAL
FOOTBALL TEAM

Gold	Olympic Games	2000
Bronze	Olympic Games	1996
Gold	World Cup	1995
Gold	European Cup	1987, 1993
Gold	FIFA World Tournament	1988
Silver	World Cup	1991
Silver	World Cup	1989, 1999

before women decided to play the game seriously. According to a note in a German magazine, a football match between a women's and men's team took place in Kristiania, the capital of Norway, as early as 1919.[2] It seems as if this game was not taken seriously but was looked upon as a rather amusing spectacle. This attitude was typical of the 1920s. So-called exhibition games often took place between a women's team and a team of untrained men, and was looked upon as entertainment.[3] This appears to be the case in Brumundal in the summer of 1931. Here also a women's and a men's team played against each other. The announcement in the local newspaper read, 'Humorous football match. Women's team against old men.' However, this match apparently inspired some sports women in the district to start a women's football team. There seems not to have been any other women's football teams in Norway at that time, consequently games consisted of matches between the players of that club.[4] Later the same year the first registered soccer match between two Norwegian women's teams took place. A team from Hamar Sports Club, which included women from the Brumundalen area, played against a club called the Kapp Sports Club.[5] This historic moment, however, did not seem to lead to an increased interest in the sport.

According to M. Goksøyr and F. Olstad, there was some interest in the development of women's football, but this interest died out, either because of resistance from the outside or because of an insufficient amount of persistence from within the movement.[6] Many years passed before Norwegian women became seriously involved in football. This was probably due to a multiplicity of factors. In general there was, at that time, a resistance to competitive sport for women in Norway. Competition was not looked upon as acceptable female behaviour.[7] In addition, athletics itself was held to be incompatible with femininity. Furthermore, the fact that football with its 'toughness' and 'body contact' was very popular among men, and accordingly was characterized as a masculine sport, made it less suitable for girls and women.

THE RECENT DEVELOPMENT OF WOMEN'S FOOTBALL

Many Norwegians believe that a football match in 1970 was the first women's match ever played in Norway and that it was the start of women's football in the country. As has been noted earlier this is not the case. However, there was a period of almost 40 years when there was no progress. The match in 1970 was arranged by Målfrid Kuvås and others and was played in Grimstad, a small city in the southern part of Norway. It was Målfrid Kuvås, representing the sport club BUL who lead the way in developing football for women in Norway. She has often been called the 'mother of football'.

This first match was the curtain-raiser entertainment before an international athletics competition. There was an audience of 5,000, in spite of rainy weather. Though the match was probably taken seriously by the female players who participated, it was generally looked upon as an 'enjoyable form of entertainment' by the spectators. Many of the players were recruited from handball teams, a trend that seemed to last through the 1970s.

Several developments occurred over the next few years which seem to have contributed to the acceleration of the development of Norwegian women's football. A football club in Oslo, named Frigg, sponsored, with a newspaper, an 'unofficial' Norwegian football championship for women in 1971. Sixteen teams participated in the first year.[8] Two years later some private leagues were started at various places in Norway.

Another factor, which may have contributed to the development of women's football in Norway, was the establishment of the Norway Cup. Norway Cup is said to be the largest football tournament for children and youth in the world. It started in 1973 and from the beginning was open to both girls and boys. In the first year, 15 female junior teams participated. This tournament became an important showcase for girls' and women's soccer.[9]

In the first years, women's football was not a part of the Norwegian Football Association. The pressure for official acceptance by the association steadily grew. The 1970s was the right moment in time. Discussion about women's football took place when the second wave of feminism happened and the debate about women's rights had begun. Equal and human rights, plus democracy, were important concepts in the debate about women's position in society in general. The outcome was the establishment of the Norwegian Council for Equal Rights in 1972. This body covered all areas including equal rights for girls and women in sport.

The breakthrough for women's football seems to have come in 1975, partly due to a debate on the subject in the media – particularly in some major newspapers. Among those men who promoted the right for girls and women to play football was a very well known sport editor of *Dagbladet*, Leif Isdal. He wrote in an article that 'the Norwegian Football Association should promote the sport for women, and not work against its development'. *Dagbladet* also claimed that the NFA with its attitude of 'lets wait and see' was one of the few associations in Europe that was saying 'no' to women's football.[10]

However the NFA did give a trophy for the unofficial Norwegian championship in 1975. This was looked upon as a victory for women's football. Members of the board of the Football Association also announced in public that they were interested in accepting women's football into the association. The same year the association started to register girls and women teams. According to I.-M. Vingdal, this first registration revealed 91 girls' and women's teams in 17 different football districts.[11] The Football Association also published a pamphlet titled 'Its fun to be a football girl'.

It was in February 1976 that developmental work for female football accelerated as the outcome of the general assembly's suggestion that a women's committee should be appointed. This advice was followed and a women's committee began to work systematically in developing football for Norwegian girls and women. From 1978 an annual official Norwegian championship has been held. In this same year a female national team was established. The first international match was played against Sweden, a match that Norway lost 1-2. In 1979 the first district league was established. It was soon followed by leagues in different districts around the country.

THE GOLDEN YEARS

The development of female football has been a great success. In 1980, 305 women's teams and 362 girls' teams were registered with the NFA. In 2002 these figures had increased to 449 female adult teams, and 3,502 teams for girls. The membership growth is shown in Figures 9.1 and 9.2. Figure 1 shows the increase in female members in the organization every fifth year from 1985. It demonstrates that more and more girls and women have started playing the game. Figure 9.2 shows the same increase, but separates the girls (up to 17 years of age) and the women. It demonstrates that the greatest increase in membership during recent years has taken place among girls and not among women.[12] Figure 9.3 gives an overview of the latest membership statistics (2001) seen in relation to both gender and age. For both girls and boys, football is most popular among the six to 12 year olds. After that the number of active members diminishes. It is of interest to note that the gender difference is the least among those less than five years of age, 1,658 boys compared to 1,325 girls. When the other age groups are compared, the figures show that the largest gender difference in membership is found among the six to 12 year olds, and the smallest difference among the 19–25 year olds. In spite of the fact that football is the largest sport among girls in Norway, the age group of six to 12 years still seems to offer recruitment potential.

Parallel with this successful growth of teams and individual membership, developments involving different levels of leagues in different parts of Norway

9.1 FEMALE MEMBERSHIP OF THE NORWEGIAN FOOTBALL ASSOCIATION, 1985–2000

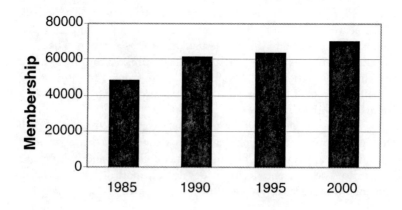

9.2 FEMALE MEMBERSHIP OF THE NORWEGIAN FOOTBALL ASSOCIATION, 1985–99:
GIRLS UNDER 17 AND WOMEN OVER 17

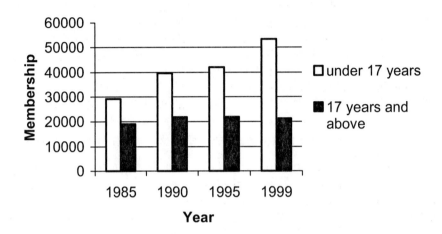

9.3 ACTIVE MEMBERS IN THE NORWEGIAN FOOTBALL ASSOCIATION
IN RELATION TO GENDER AND AGE, 2001

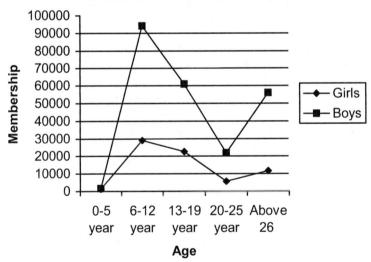

took place. In 1982, for example, a first division league for the middle of Norway was started. That same year, in the eastern part of the country, a second division league was initiated. In 1983 a league was created in the western part of the country, and in 1985 a league for the northern part of Norway was founded. Two years later the first national league was set up. It consisted of the ten best teams in the country, independent of where they were geographically situated. From 1984 girls got the same leagues based on age groups as the boys. It is also important to mention that simultaneously the number of female football players increased and the female national team had considerable success, as shown in Table 9.1.

THE WORK OF THE WOMEN'S COMMITTEE (1976–92)

What are the reasons behind the success of the development of football for women in Norway? Why is it that football today is played by many more girls and women than the traditional Norwegian female sports, such as skiing, handball, gymnastics and athletics? In addition to the fact that this happened at a time when there was a strong focus on women's equal rights in Norway, the main reason may be found inside the NFA itself. From the moment that it accepted women's football in 1975–76 there were women and men inside the organization who worked hard to develop women's football. Various innovations resulted. Most important was probably the establishment of a Women's Committee in 1976. For the first two years the chair of this committee was Nicolai Johansen. He was a very powerful man in the organization and had changed his opinion about women's football from a negative to a positive attitude. The fact that he became the first Chair was also a strong signal to the Norwegian male-dominated world of football that women's football should be taken seriously. The other two committee members were women, Grete Einarsrud and Ellen Wille. Ellen took over as the Chair after two years and held this position until 1986. She became the leading figure in the development of women's football in Norway in this period.[13]

The primary tasks for this first Women's Committee in football were: the development of rules; the establishment of leagues for women and girls in all districts in Norway; the creation of an official Norwegian championship; the establishment of a women's national team. It has been shown earlier that they reached many of these goals relatively quickly. From 1980 the committee's priorities became: the recruitment of new players; the education of female managers, coaches and referees/officials; the cooperation with other committees in the association; the development of tournaments for girls in the different districts; and the establishment of a junior national team for girls. In setting up these goals, they worked systematically with very detailed plans of action including separate budgets for the different tasks that they planned to carry through to reach their goals. They also monitored their work, which included the compilation of different kinds of gender status statistics. These then became a base for future work.[14]

The conclusion to be drawn from these sets of objectives is that the Women's Committee in the NFA was not simply concerned with enrolling more female players. Parallel with this work they systematically worked to recruit girls and women to leadership, coaching and referee positions. In 1985 Ellen Wille became the first woman ever on the NFA's executive committee. In the same year the association decided upon a kind of 'mild quota', that is, that there should always be a minimum of one woman on each of the central committees. One year later, in 1986, Ellen Wille became the first female speaker ever at a meeting of the International Football Federations (FIFA). In her speech she proposed that a world championship for women should be held. This idea was realized in 1991.

After the first 13 years, the Women's Committee sent a questionnaire to all the football districts to get an overview of the involvement of girls and women in all kinds of football roles. Table 9.2 shows the representation of women on the executive committee, in elected and appointed subcommittees, and female participants at the general assembly from 1985 to 1989. In the general assembly the number of women increased from three to ten during these years. In a comment relevant to Table 9.2, the women's committee wrote, 'the representation of women in the elected committees is still small, and it was first in 1987 that a woman was elected to the election committee'.[15]

TABLE 9.2
FEMALE REPRESENTATION IN THE NORWEGIAN FOOTBALL ASSOCIATION 1985–88

Org. level	1985	1986	1987	1988
Executive Board	1	1	1	1
Elected committees	0	0	1	2
Appointed committees	8	9	9	7
Participants at the General Assembly	3	7	11	10

The same report discussed the importance of having a larger representation of women among the sport administrators, and mentioned three major reasons: First the question of democracy, that is, it was important to have a correspondence between the number of female members in the federation and the number of females in decision-making positions. Secondly, the question of resources. Many sports organizations had, and still have, problems with the recruitment of leaders. It was therefore important to use the resources represented by the women. Thirdly, the question of interests. Since women and men are socialized differently, they have often developed different interests and have different values. The committee also asked if women's football was developed enough according to women's own wishes, a debate that they thought should continue. This report also showed that more women were taking leadership courses at different levels, and that many teams for girls and women now seemed to have some women among their support personnel. Statistics about women taking some kind of coaching training also showed some positive trends, though at the lower level. The first woman to take the highest level of coaching training in the Association was Eva Alme in 1989. During these first years, girls and women were also participating in refereeing courses. By 1988 there were about 200 active female referees. But as the report states: 'This only counts for less than one female referee for every 10 female teams.'[16]

THE INTEGRATION PERIOD – 1990 ONWARDS

At the end of 1992 the women's committee of the NFA was disbanded. The organization now started a more active integration policy. Two years earlier it was required to elect a minimum of two women to all boards and committees. This was a result of a quota regulation concerning gender-representation that had been adopted by The Norwegian Olympic Committee and Confederation of Sport at their General Assembly. This regulation was also introduced into Norwegian sport law. It stated that the number of female members on boards and committees should be equal to the representation of women in the organization, with a minimum of two women on each committee. The reason for this last point was to avoid female membership on committees being merely tokenism, which so often had seemed to happen when one woman had become a member of a male-dominated organization.

Karen Espelund became the most dominant female leader during these years. She was first elected to the executive board in 1988, and advanced to the post of first vice president in 1996. This was the first time that a woman had reached such a high position. At that time three of the eight members of the executive board were women. Three years later, in 1999, Karen Espelund became the first female secretary general of the NFA.[17] This is one of the most powerful positions in Norwegian sport. She still holds the position in 2003.

During the final years of the twentieth century more and more women became involved in all kinds of football roles. It is not that surprising, therefore, that Bente Skogvang, another pioneer, was appointed to officiate at the Sweden World Cup in 1995. It was a landmark for Norwegian female referees. Norway failed to get to the final of the first Olympic Games which included women's football – Atlanta in 1996 – the Norwegian Bente Skogvang, nevertheless, refereed the final between China and the USA.

Many female football players have started playing with the boys in the street and/or with their fathers and/or brothers.[18] It was therefore not uncommon to find girls playing in boys' teams during the first years of the development of women's football. The same seems to have happened in other countries. After 1979, however, when the Secretary General stated that both the international (FIFA) and the European (UEFA) football associations had decided that mixed gender teams were not permitted, only the youngest girls were allowed to play on the boys' teams.

In 1996 the General Assembly of the NFA decided that girls and women could play on all teams of boys or men, something which according to M. Goksøyr and F. Olstad, was unique in the international world of football. Norway also became the first country that did not distinguish between women and men in their efforts to develop highly talented players.[19] Since 1991, elite teams have received specially earmarked money in order to work towards a higher degree of professionalism.

Other initiatives have also been taken to recruit more girls and women into football. One of the most recent is a project named 'The Football Girls Project 2000/2001'. The aim of this project was 'to recruit more girls' (6–12 years of age) to the game. It involved 75 clubs, and 5,000 T-shirts and 1,500 balls have been given to clubs which have started new teams for girls in 2000 and 2001. There has been an increase of 30 per cent over these two years: in 1999, there were 1,367 girls' teams below 13 years; in 2000 this had increased to 1,519, and in 2001 there were 1,776 girls' football teams below 13 years of age. As a part of this project the NFA did a survey with the aim of finding out what the clubs could do to get more girls involved in football. The main results were: establish a football environment especially for girls by inviting them to practise, create a milieu for girls in the club, have girls-only teams for girls aged six to 12 (many girls have had to play on boys' teams) and recruit more coaches and administrators to girls' football.

Resistance

From the development described above, it might be thought that everything went smoothly after the formal acceptance of women's football into the Association in the middle of the 1970s. This was of course not the case. Resistance, negative attitudes and scepticism did not change overnight. Ellen Wille stated in an interview that people attended women's football matches to see the women 'miss' the ball. There was no one who took women's football seriously. Eventually when the 'establishment' understood that women really wanted to play the game of football, other kinds of problems appeared. When Wille was travelling around in the country she was met with questions like: 'Do we have to get rid of the little boys' league now, so that the girls and women can get time to play on the field?' This negative attitude lasted to the end of the 1980s. People invented problems instead of discussing how the real problems could be solved.[20] The media had also been unhelpful to women's football. Female footballers have never been presented in the media to the same degree as their male counterparts. Certainly, as the performance of the women's Norwegian national team has improved, the media has given more space to cover them. However, in spite of the fact that the women's national team's performance has been better than the men's, the presentation in the media remains extremely skewed. This can be seen both in relation to photos and text. Furthermore, the term 'national team' still seems to mean the men's team, with the result that compared to men, it is more difficult for women's teams to get sponsors. The same is true of individual women players.

HOMOPHOBIA

In short, in spite of the work for full integration since the 1990s, many women players have experienced both resistance and suspicion from the male-dominated football environment.[21] Some have focused on, and questioned the sexuality of, the female football players. As a Norwegian study presented below shows, women players have experienced homophobia irrespective of their real sexual orientation.

Homophobia is normally defined as the irrational fear or intolerance of homosexuality in men and women, but it can even include behaviour that is simply perceived to be outside the boundaries of traditional gender expectations.[22] It is well documented that the institution of sport promotes compulsory heterosexuality (expectations and acceptance of heterosexuality as the only appropriate sexual orientation). Women footballers can be said to have entered a man's playing field. In Norway, as in many other countries, football has been looked upon as 'the masculine sport'. In addition a woman footballer's appearance may sometimes differ from the feminine stereotype. There is then the definite possibility that she is labelled 'lesbian'. The attitude that a women football player cannot be 'a real woman' characterizes this kind of reasoning. P. Griffin expresses it as follows:

> Homophobia is a powerful political weapon of sexism. The lesbian label is used to define the boundaries of acceptable female behaviour in a patriarchal culture. When a woman is called a lesbian, she knows she is out of bounds ... Because women's sport has been labelled a lesbian activity, women in sport are particularly sensitive and vulnerable to the use of the lesbian label to intimidate them.[23]

P. Griffin wrote of sport in the culture of North America. The Nordic countries have been known to have a more open-minded view on sexuality. Indeed, in relation to legislation and rights for homosexuals, Norway is also looked upon as more radical and democratic than many other countries. But when it comes to sport and the daily life of female athletes how accepting are Norwegians? With this as a frame of reference, ten elite female football players went through a qualitative interview in which their experiences in different areas were discussed. One of these areas was homophobia. This was a part of a larger European study whose aim was to explore women's individual and social experiences in sport, to discover the ways in which women integrate sport into their lives, and to find out what sport and exercise mean for them.[24] The study, which was undertaken in the mid-1990s, revealed that all football players have experienced some form of homophobia, particularly from men outside sport. This is illustrated in the following quotes from the players. It shows what kind of barriers the female football players had to overcome: 'In my community many believe that everyone who plays soccer in my club is a lesbian' (Turid); 'it quickly becomes suspicious if you play soccer and look somewhat masculine, then it is very easy to start a rumour that you must be a lesbian' (Kari). Beate expressed it this way: 'When people such as John ask: are there many of "those" on your team? My answer is "no". Because it is not his business. I don't bother to talk about it, because it is not positive. I don't bother talking negatively about my club or about female soccer in general.'

When these interviews took place, none of the elite women athletes were open in public about their homosexuality. However, during the last five years one of Norway's best-ever female football players has 'come out'. So has one of the women on the national handball team. Norway also has a 'legal partnership law' for homosexuals, and some of their most famous politicians have been open about their homosexuality. It is therefore the author's impression that homophobia in society at large is not as strong as it was only a few years ago. The fact that 'football' sometimes has been 'marked' as a 'lesbian' sport may have had some negative outcomes for some individuals in the past, but in terms of the huge strides women's football has taken in recent years, it seems little affected by a 'homosexual stamp'. Football for women could have a problem if homophobia in the society had been so strong that it was a barrier to recruitment. But with more than 70,000 female players, it is clear that this has not been the case in Norway.

Changing Gender?

In any consideration of the development of women's football in Norway it is relevant to ask what it is that makes football so fascinating and attractive to women. Can the development be interpreted as a kind of protest movement, because in the past women have not been allowed by men to play football? Or is it something to do with the sport itself that makes it so attractive not for only men, but also for women. The women in the above-mentioned study were asked about this. Most players gave as their main reasons for playing the game: a good social milieu, togetherness, female team friends and belonging to a team and succeeding with others. But they stressed that the game in itself was fun. The interviewees particularly mentioned: scoring a goal, handling the ball and playing, using the body, feeling the body perform and feeling in good shape. Some also appreciated the satisfying body contact and tackling as well as the challenges that the game offers. Else expressed it this way: 'It's a fascinating game ... One which permits individuals to be creative, to do things on their own, to find new ways of solving a problem, which may surprise your opponents ... what can I say ... how can I explain it, it's really problem solving, how we, together as a team, can manage.' Solveig challenged traditional forms of femininity when she stated: 'To run into a slide tackle, for example. I like physical contact, to use my strength, and to win when an opponent and I fight to head the ball ... I think that's fun.'

'Doing' gender is not about acting out a fixed role, although as Judith Butler argues, failure to 'do gender right', or the act of 'performing one's gender wrong', can initiate punishment. To 'do gender right' means to conform to dominant cultural expectations about femininity.[25] When Norwegian girls and women started playing football they 'did the gender wrong', which can explain some of the resistance that they experienced particularly in the 1970s and 1980s. As girls and young women, they challenged conventional standards of femininity. But even if the first female footballers 'did the gender wrong', they played the men's game. The development of women's football seen in such a perspective may be said to be an expression of liberal feminism. Women adopted the men's game, made by and for men. A more radical approach would have been to develop a women's version on the game. This has never happened. Thus, the development of women's football in Norway can be looked upon as a clear example of how girls and women can succeed in 'invading' a traditional masculine sport. By doing so female footballers may contribute to a transformation of the concept of 'femininity' and gender in society at large.

NOTES

1. NIF/NOK, *Årsrapport 2001* (Oslo: Norges Idrettsforbund og Olympiske komite, 2002).
2. *Damen-Sport Damen-Turnen* (1919), 156.
3. M. Goksøyr and F. Olstad, *Fotball. Norges Fotballforbund 100 år* (Oslo: Norges Fotballforbund, 2002).
4. R.-K.- Torkildsen, 'Norsk Kvinnefotball. En historisk undersøkelse om norsk kvinnefotballs utvikling' (Masters Thesis, Høgskolen i Levanger, 1993).
5. Kretsstyrets møteprotokoll. Bergen og Fylkenes Arbeideridrettskrets 1932-1934.
6. Goksøyr and Olstad, *Fotball. Norges Fotballforbund 100 år.*
7. G. Pfister, K. Fasting, S. Scraton and B. Vazquez, 'Women and Football – A Contradiction? The Beginnings of Women's Football in Four European Countries', *The European Sports History Review*, 1 (1999), 1–26.
8. H. Hanneborg and K.M. Paulssen (eds), Fotballboka (Oslo: N.W. Damm & Son, AS, 1992), pp.192–5.
9. Goksøyr and Olstad, *Fotball. Norges Fotballforbund 100 år.*
10. Torkildsen, 'Norsk Kvinnefotball. En historisk undersøkelse om norsk kvinnefotballs utvikling'.
11. I.-M. Vingdal, 'Norsk kvinnefotball på høgt nivå' (Masters Thesis, Oslo: Norwegian University of Sport and Physical Education, 1988).
12. From the year 2000 the membership statistic in relation to age is presented in a different way (see Figure 3). This is the reason why the figures from 2000 are not presented.
13. Hanneborg and Paulssen, *Fotballboka*, pp.192–5.
14. Ellen Wille, *Arbeid med handlingsplaner for kvinnefotballen i Norges Fotballforbund* (Oslo: NIF, 1985).
15. NFF's kvinneutvalg, *Ressursrapport – norsk kvinnefotball* (Oslo: NFF, 1989), 6.
16. NFF's kvinneutvalg, *Ressursrapport – norsk kvinnefotball* (Oslo: NFF, 1989), 9.
17. Goksøyr and Olstad, *Fotball. Norges Fotballforbund 100 år.*
18. S. Scraton, K. Fasting, G. Pfister and A. Bunuel, 'It's still a Mans Game? The Experiences of Top-Level European Women Footballers', *International Review for the Sociology of Sport*, 34, 2 (1999), 99–111.
19. Goksøyr and Olstad, *Fotball. Norges Fotballforbund 100 år.*
20. Hanneborg and Paulssen, *Fotballboka*, pp.192–5.
21. Goksøyr and Olstad, *Fotball. Norges Fotballforbund 100 år.*
22. J. Krane, 'Lesbians in Sport: Toward Acknowledgment, Understanding, and Theory', *Journal of Sport and Exercise Psychology*, 18, 3 (1996), 237–47.
23. P. Griffin, 'Homophobia in Women's Sports. The Fear That Divides Us', in G.L. Cohen (ed.), *Women in Sport. Issues and Controversies* (Newbury Park: Sage, 1993), pp.193–203.

24. K. Fasting, S. Scraton, G. Pfister and A. Bunuel, *The Experience and Meaning of Sport and Exercise in the Lives of Women in some European Countries* (Oslo: Norwegian University of Sport and Physical Education, 1999).

25. J. Butler, *Gender Trouble. Feminism and the Subversion of Identity* (New York and London: Routledge, 1990).

10

Women's Football in the Republic of Ireland: Past Events and Future Prospects

ANN BOURKE

Women's football (soccer) in Ireland has a relatively short history (approximately 35 years) and this chapter provides details of its evolution, an update on the current situation and a review of the future prospects for the game. It draws on both theory and practice with a view to providing insights on the reasons for the growing popularity of the game, the forces (organizational, social, economic, cultural, etcetera) that have ensured the game's development and identifies the main issues which need to be addressed to advance the game further. The women's game in Ireland is organized and coordinated by the Women's Football Association of Ireland (WFAI) a self-governing organization with its own National Council, Executive Committee and sub committees. It is an affiliate of the Football Association of Ireland (FAI). Affiliates of organizations have certain responsibilities and powers and this examination of the women's game is undertaken bearing this in mind.

Over the years little has been documented in relation to women's soccer in Ireland, consequently the secondary source material available is rather fragmented. In this study it is drawn primarily from a single source. The information utilized in the preparation of this study was compiled drawing on Ladies Football Association of Ireland (LFAI) documentation such as annual reports, programme notes for both international and domestic competitions, LFAI News and recent WFAI newsletters.[1] Other source material used included consulting reports and strategy documents, journal articles and features in sports magazines, newspapers, plus material from various web pages. To celebrate the twenty-first anniversary of the LFAI in 1994, it was planned to publish a history of the association but, as yet (2003), this project has not been realized. To complement the secondary source material the author undertook a number of semi-structured personal interviews with selected personnel associated with women's soccer in Ireland. These included a representative from the Women's Football Association of Ireland (WFAI, formerly the Ladies Football Association of Ireland), three FAI Regional Development Officers (RDOs), a college's officer and four current soccer players (female) who have played at the highest level. As the secondary source material for this project is rather limited, these interviews were designed to overcome this limitation, but for many interviewees, it soon became apparent to the author that current issues and future prospects for the game rather than past events were their primary concern.

The chapter is divided into five parts. In part one, a brief overview of the main developments in women's soccer which have occurred during the past 30 years in Ireland is provided, while part two reviews the organizational structure and strategy which exist for the game. Part three examines the issues surrounding the game's infrastructure, both physical and human. In part four, drawing on figurational sociology, the football figuration is defined and utilized as the basis for identifying the factors and parties that have both enabled and constrained the development of women's soccer in Ireland. In the final part, pointers for the future progression of the game are provided.

MAIN DEVELOPMENTS

While soccer is the national sport in England, in Ireland for many years it was considered by various people to be anti Irish and was commonly referred to as 'the garrison game'.[2] The men's game in Ireland is not fully professional as the majority of personnel (players, mentors, coaches, medical and administration) attached to clubs are employed on a part-time or voluntary basis; few are employed on a full-time basis. Soccer is a popular team sport in Ireland. During the 1998/99 season there were 187,000 players registered to play soccer in the Republic of Ireland, with just over 4,000 clubs.[3] The greater proportion of these players and clubs are located in the Leinster (which includes Dublin) and Munster (which includes Cork) regions. There are 86 leagues organized in the Republic, with ladies soccer leagues being one fifth of the total.

At the outset, it is pertinent to identify the more important developments that have occurred during the past 30 years with respect to women's soccer in Ireland. Reflection on each of these and their impact on the organization and key 'players' is the recurrent theme of this study. These major developments include the following:

a) Setting up the Ladies Football Association of Ireland.
b) The growth in the number of domestic leagues.
c) Ireland's involvement in international competition.
d) The initiation of development plans.
e) The appointment of a women's development officer by the FAI.

Ellis Cashmore[4] notes that the experience of women in sports virtually replicates their more general experience – that they have been treated as not only different to men but also inferior in many respects. While women in Ireland have participated in various sports (hockey, tennis, golf, basketball and netball among others) over the years, it was only during the 1970s that women's football (Gaelic and soccer) became popular in Ireland. For both codes, there were humble beginnings with teams and clubs emerging on an *ad hoc* basis. With respect to the emergence of Gaelic football teams, at the outset they were associated with firms and places of employment. By 1974, the Ladies Gaelic Football Association (LGFA) was given formal recognition by the games governing authority – Gaelic Athletic Association (GAA).[5] Its overseeing body ultimately assimilated the LGFA, and competitions are organized on a county, provincial and national basis. It currently has approximately 80,000 members.

a) Ladies Football Association of Ireland (LFAI)

At the same time several women's soccer teams were formed and leagues emerged which were associated with the manager's, the coach's or the player's place of employment (Civil Service, An Comhairle Oiluna (ANCO), Bank of Ireland). Given the increased number of players and leagues, in 1973 the LFAI was established to coordinate women's soccer in Ireland. At the outset, it was independent of the FAI and relations between leading personnel in both bodies were not particularly warm.

However, things began to change during the mid to late 1980s and the LFAI attained observer status on the Junior Council of the FAI. By 1988, there was a further improvement in relations between the two associations due largely to the efforts of the late Dr Tony O'Neill (former General Secretary, FAI) with the opening of discussions involving the women's game and the future of the LFAI. In 1991, the LFAI gained full status on the Senior Council of the FAI and currently has two representatives. These representatives are actively involved in the business of the FAI and bring issues directly concerning women's football to the discussion table. They also represent the FAI at international meetings and conferences, and are members of the FAI international committee and the domestic and development committees. At the Annual General Meeting held in December 2001 it was agreed to change the name of the association from the LFAI to the Women's Football Association of Ireland (WFAI). This is designed to capture a more modern ideal and is in keeping with the common description of the game across Europe.

Some years ago individuals in the LFAI were conscious of the public's lack of knowledge about the association and its activities. In an attempt to redress the balance, an insertion detailing its main activities was included in *LFAI News* in January 1991 as shown in Table 10.1.[6]

While the LFAI was an independent body, its reliance on external funding and its *de facto* dependent relationship with the FAI is evident from the procedures employed to upgrade its technological infrastructure in 1992. The LFAI had just assumed responsibility for player registration (formerly with the affiliated leagues) so it was recognized by members of the executive committee that its technology needed upgrading. The following year the association applied for and received grant-aid from the National Lottery for the acquisition of a new

TABLE 10.1
WHAT DOES THE LADIES FOOTBALL ASSOCIATION OF IRELAND DO FOR YOU?

Administration	Activities	Regulation	Representation
Admin support for Leagues	National competitions	Player registration	Represents ladies football on FAI committees
Newsletter	Coaching	Discipline	
Handbook	Seminars	Appeals	
	Publicity	National rule making body	
	National teams		

Source: *LFAI News*, 1, 4 (Jan.1991).

computer. This development (receipt of money to purchase a computer) was given much publicity in *LFAI News* at the time, and is a clear illustration of the dearth of resources available for sports administration. The activities performed today (2003) by the association executives are possibly little different from those undertaken ten years ago, yet the context in which the organization operates (internal and external environment) has changed in many respects.

b) Domestic Leagues and Competitions

The number of domestic leagues in Ireland has almost doubled during the past 11 years. During 1991 there were nine affiliated leagues; currently there are 17. These leagues (see Table 10.2) cater for 6,500 registered players playing for 350 teams. An interesting aspect of the league arrangements is that geographical boundaries are disregarded. There are four provinces (Munster, Leinster, Ulster and Connaught) and 26 counties in the Republic of Ireland. As at 1991, there were separate leagues operating in Munster and Limerick (Limerick is a county in Munster), similarly in Leinster there were leagues from Dundalk (town in County Louth, and in Leinster) and Leinster affiliated to the LFAI. More recently the anomalies regarding the provinces in the league structures have been removed, but the areas covered in a number of leagues cross a couple of county boundaries – the Midland Women's League being a case in point.

c) International Competition

The Republic of Ireland senior team first participated in an international competition in 1974 when the opposition was Northern Ireland. One hundred people attended this match and the Republic won 4–0. During the early days, the national teams had little success in international competition so a decision was taken in 1992, as a result of a LFAI development review, to withdraw from these competitions for three years in order to engage in team development. Ireland's

TABLE 10.2
LEAGUES AFFILIATED TO THE WFAI

League	Area	Age Group
Cork League	Cork	Senior, U 18, 16, 14, 12
Donegal League	Donegal and Innishowen	Senior, U 16
Dublin Women's Soccer League	Dublin, Meath and Wicklow	Senior, U 16, 14, 12, 10
Galway Ladies Soccer League	Galway Country	Senior
Inishowen League	Innishowen Electoral Area	Senior, U 16, 14
Limerick Ladies League	Clare, Limerick and North Cork	Senior
Mayo Assoc. Football League	Mayo	Senior
Mayo Schoolboys and Youths Association	Mayo	U 16, 14
Midland's Women's League	Offaly, Westmeath, Longford, Laois, Kilkenny	Senior
Roscommon & District Ladies	Roscommon and District	Senior
Roscommon & District Ladies League	Roscommon and East Galway	U 16, 13, 11
Sligo/Leitrim League	Sligo, Leitrim and parts of Roscommon	Senior
Tipperary League	Tipperary	Senior, U 16
Waterford School Girl's League	Waterford	Senior
Wexford & District Ladies Soccer League	Wexford	Senior
WSCAI	Nationwide	Senior

Source: WFAI, 2002.

participation in international competition resumed in 1995 and since then the Republic has participated in World Cup and European Championship qualifiers at various levels and with some success.[7]

d) Development Plans

Sports organizations need to engage in planning and development on a regular basis. The first LFAI development plan was undertaken in 1992 to deal with the lack of team success in international competition. The outcome of this plan was the implementation of a strategy in relation to national team management and young player development. The second plan published in 2000 was devised to deal with the association's changing relationship with the FAI.[8] This resulted in the LFAI rearranging its organizational structure, specifying basic requirements for the management of clubs and formulating strategies for the development of the game. But there was an overlap in this scheduling, as while the LFAI was planning its strategic changes its parent body (FAI) was also working on a Development Strategy published in 2001.[9]

e) Appointment of Women's Development Officer

In line with FIFA's assertion that women's soccer is the fastest growing participation sport and the fact that few resources (apart from budgetary) have been directed to the women's game in Ireland, in 2001 the FAI appointed a

Regional Development Officer with special responsibility for the women's game. Regional Development Officers are appointed to provide support for local initiatives, and lend assistance with various FAI programmes that strive to develop talent and potential such as coaching, education and elite squad development. The women's development officer is employed by the FAI, works closely with WFAI personnel and is actively involved in many projects designed to achieve increased participation in soccer among young girls.

Such developments (a–e above) could be referred to as the 'high points' in relation to women's soccer in Ireland. While women's sport in Ireland has been considered for some time now as the 'poor relation' to men's in terms of funding, infrastructure, media attention, participation, coaching and management, there is evidence to suggest that in some respects changes (administrative, strategic, social and cultural) are being realized. Certain infrastructure improvements have occurred, yet there are signs that all is not rosy on the women's soccer playing fields and beyond, as detailed in the following sections.

ORGANIZATIONAL STRUCTURE AND STRATEGY

One of the key aspects in relation to promoting sport in any country is having an adequate organizational structure in place, along with a strategy formulated and implemented to achieve strategic goals. To appreciate the progress (or lack of it) made with respect to women's soccer in Ireland, the objects and governance arrangements within the WFAI are outlined together with its organizational strategy. The nature and the extent to which developments within the FAI affect processes and procedures within the WFAI are considered in this section.

The objects of the WFAI are to:

a) promote and improve women's and girls' football in the Republic of Ireland through the medium of the Association and,

b) foster international relationships and the cultivation of friendships between all nations.[10]

The association is currently governed by the National Council initially composed of representatives of each of the affiliated divisional leagues. Amendments have been made with respect to membership of the National Council which now include the following:

- Members of the executive committee
- Three delegates from each of the provincial councils
- Three delegates from the Women's Soccer Colleges Association of Ireland (WSCAI)
- Any person elected as an Honorary Life President of the association
- Such representation from the FAI as is provided for in the rules.

This Council formerly met four times a year, but it is now specified in the rules that it should meet twice each year and on any other occasions that may be found necessary. At the opening meeting, the Council shall appoint sub-committees, ratify the operation of an appeals panel and appoint a disciplinary committee. The Executive Committee shall act on behalf of the Council and consist of the officers of the association: Chairperson, Secretary, Treasurer, Underage Officer, Coaching and Development Officer, Competitions Officer, Public Relations Officer and International Officer.[11] Committee members are engaged on a voluntary basis and the FAI assists the WFAI with its day-to-day administration. The only person employed on a full time basis directly associated with women's soccer is the Women's Development Officer.

FAI and WFAI – Dependency Ties

From an organizational (operational and management) standpoint, the WFAI is relatively autonomous from the FAI, but this does not apply when reviewing financial arrangements. The administrator from the WFAI clarified the funding arrangements that exist for the WFAI. Each year the WFAI submits a budget to the FAI and an agreed amount is then transferred to the WFAI. Details of the amounts given by the FAI to the WFAI are as shown in Figure 10.1 during the four-year period 1998–2001.

10.1 FINANCIAL GRANTS TO THE LFAI

Year	Amount
1998	£44,000
1999	£42,500 + cost of international activities
2000	no figure revealed – change in year end for FAI
2001	£10,000 + international expenses.
	£66,410 for y/e 31 March 2002.

Source: LFAI Annual Reports, 1998–2001.

The WFAI use the major part of the funding received from the FAI to support the activities of the international teams. Currently, the Republic of Ireland has international teams at Senior, U-20, U-18 and U-16 levels. Apart from the cost and time associated with identifying talented players, organizing international activities can be very demanding especially for an organization whose personnel are not employed on a full-time basis. The technical staff for each of these teams now includes a manager, an assistant manager, and a kit manager.

The vision for sport in Ireland as expressed in the Irish Sports Council's (ISC, 2002) strategy document includes the aspiration that Irish sports men and women achieve consistent world-class performance, fairly.[12] To that end, from January 2001 the Council allocated funding on 'a core and challenge basis'.[13] While the authors of the document provide a definition of both core and challenge funding, it is not clear as to which applies more succinctly in the case of women's soccer. It is probable that funding for women's soccer by the ISC is directed via the FAI.

To alleviate financial shortfalls many sports organizations actively seek and acquire sponsorship. The 'success' of women's Gaelic football in Ireland was discussed with the administrator from the WFAI. She maintained that this 'success' stems from their organizational structure (using the county and provincial system adopted by the GAA) and the receipt of a major sponsorship deal during its early days, which provided the impetus it needed. Women's soccer has not had the same good fortune and over the years sponsorship deals have in general been for small amounts. The LFAI news carries many references to the various firms that have provided funding for the game – Lifestyle Sports, Electricity Supply Board (ESB), Waterford Glass, Opel, Media Sport and Coca Cola to name but a few. In 2002 the WFAI benefited from the FAI sponsorship arrangements particularly in relation to the national teams. Eircom sponsors both the women and men's national teams. In addition to Eircom, other sponsors include Umbro, Ballygowan, Master foods, Ray Treacy and Sports World. The WFAI also has a three-year deal with an Irish insurance firm – O'Driscoll/O'Neil to the tune of €25,000 per annum and this money is used to support its domestic activities such as coaching schools, administration, travel and organizing competitions.

Organizational Strategy: The FAI and WFAI Connection

Rumult considers strategy as the constant search for ways in which the firm's unique resources can be redeployed in changing circumstances.[14] Henry Minzberg[15] distinguishes between planned and unplanned strategy. He regards strategy as a pattern in a stream of decisions or actions, the pattern being the product of whatever intended (planned) strategies are actually realized and of any emergent or unplanned strategies. For most firms, strategies are a mix of intended and emergent. All strategy walks on two feet, one deliberate and one emergent. A common thread among the definitions of strategy is its dynamic nature as customer needs and wants are constantly changing. With respect to sports organizations, according to Trevor Slack the senior members' first step in the formulation of a strategic plan involves defining a mission statement.[16] While the WFAI sets out two general aims (detailed earlier), it is difficult to determine exactly what are its strategic objectives and goals. The purpose of the association, the business it is in, and its principal customers, users, or clients is not clarified in its documentation or by way of a mission statement.

David Waldstein and Stephen Wagg note that in the United States association football has been promoted mainly via the national teams instead of having the domestic game produce the national team as happens in virtually every other country.[17] This situation is somewhat similar to that pertaining to women's football in the Republic of Ireland. Sue Lopez provided an overview of women's soccer in 1997 in selected countries and mainly focused on initiatives that have impacted on the development of the national team/s.[18] She set out a diary of the main events from the national team perspective. Ireland's participation in international competition commenced in 1974. During the first 20 years, the Republic of Ireland international team did not achieve much competitive success, and in 1992, as noted above, an assessment of the situation was conducted. Again as noted earlier, it was decided to withdraw from international competition for three years. At that juncture, the FAI authorities agreed to provide funding for a development plan, the main outcome being organizing our national teams at U-16, U-18, U-20 and the reformation of the national senior team for the European Championships 1995–97, participating in the 'B' qualifying section – the section for the weaker nations.

Towards the end of the 1990s, in view of the changed relations between the LFAI and the FAI and changes in the game, members of the Executive Committee spent a substantial amount of time considering the outline of a Development Plan for the Association. Details of this plan are outlined in an undated booklet entitled *LFAI Development Plan*.[19] Recommendations were made to meet current and future needs of the association using the following headings:

a) The *organizational structure* – which detailed proposed changes in the administrative arrangements now incorporated into the Rules and Regulations (2002).[20]
b) The *club structure* – this section focused on essential details for the organization of any club and included a recommendation for a women's national league.
c) Designing strategies for *development of the game* – this part focused on strategies to be employed to develop the game using the following headings – developing the underage game, developing the adult game, expanding numbers involved in support areas and developing career opportunities.

This plan was worked on by LFAI personnel for almost two years and finally launched in May 2000, but the timetable for implementing specific recommendations (Provincial Councils) was not met. As indicated in the following year's Annual Report (2001), the implementation of the development plan was somewhat 'overtaken' by the emergence of the FAI Development Strategy launched in December 2001.

Due to a change in government policy at that time, the FAI was informed that extra funding would become available to develop soccer. The FAI then formed a grants strategy committee chaired by the President of the WFAI with a view to formulating a response to this situation. A development strategy document was compiled drawing on input from many parties including the government, and involving detailed consultation with what is termed the *Irish football community.*[21] The *areas of participation* were highlighted, such as underage, women's, men's, and people with special needs. Areas for potential were addressed, as was the association's (FAI) governance structure.[22] The development of women's football is given special mention,[23] suggesting that any plan to expand the game should be undertaken in a planned manner and be catered for through the existing structures rather than building parallel ones. As there are few people who would disagree with this stance, the process commenced with the appointment of a women's development officer as an RDO.

The FAI strategy document entitled *One Association, One Game*[24] is long and detailed with many aspirations being set out using vague terminology. The idea of a mission statement is overlooked and the research design and methodology employed is rather simple. There is some confusion with respect to the development of elite players. It is stated that the development of elite teams at regional, national and international level is a priority.[25] However, among the weaknesses identified in the SWOT (Strengths, Weaknesses, Opportunities, and Threats) analysis of Irish football[26] is the neglect of '*non-elite football* such as *women's football*, people with special needs; and the overemphasis on competition in underage football'. Clearly, there seems to be a little ambition in relation to the development of female elite players. While the fact that the neglect of women's football was recognized in an FAI strategy document is to be welcomed, it does beg the question as to the meaning of elite – men only?

IRELAND'S FOOTBALL INFRASTRUCTURE – PHYSICAL AND HUMAN

Due to the recent success of the national team (men's) in international competition and the subsequent increased media exposure, more young boys and girls are playing soccer. In the case of young boys, many aspire to pursuing a career in professional football and, as detailed by Ann Bourke, the practice of youngsters leaving school and home at an early age to join an English club is common.[27] So what career ladder exists for girls wishing to pursue a professional playing career? In order to advance their playing career, girls tend to seek to join an English club or pursue higher education in the US by taking advantage of a soccer scholarship. The 'brawn drain' is evident in women's soccer as seven members of the Irish senior squad who played in the final World Cup qualification game (May 2002, Group 6) were registered with English clubs during the 2001/02 season. Ireland is considered a fertile country for young soccer talent, and scouts from US universities regularly attend underage matches with a view to recruiting university students. Among the senior Irish squad, three players were pursuing higher education in the US on soccer scholarships. Nigel Crawford[28] provides insights on sports scholarship packages offered by US universities. He maintains that entry standards are not as high in the US universities as for equivalent courses in Irish institutions. Sports scholarships in the US are awarded for the duration of the degree programme rather than on a year-to-year basis, as is the case in Irish universities and colleges. University College Dublin (UCD) is the first Irish university to award soccer scholarships to two female students in the current academic year – 2002/03.

Crawford noted that for Irish students taking advantage of sports scholarships at US universities, the most positive aspect of their experience was having access to excellent sports facilities and sports administration. Three player interviewees confirmed that this was the case and two of them stated that it was a far cry from their experience on bumpy pitches used for training during their secondary school days. Such pitches were not for exclusive use by soccer players as they were shared with other sports personnel. There is no national soccer stadium in Ireland and given the recent economic downturn (the Irish government is now seeking private investors to build the stadium) building a new stadium looks unlikely for some years. Dublin's Lansdowne Road (the home of Irish Rugby and used by the FAI for soccer internationals) is an adequate stadium but it is not used for women's international matches. These are played in venues made available by clubs such as Tolka Park, Richmond Park and Flancare Park.

There are 17 women's soccer leagues in Ireland and probably the most developed and extensive one (in terms of area covered) is the Dublin Women's Soccer League (DWSL). This league was founded in 1993 and originated from the amalgamation of two leagues formerly serving women's soccer in Dublin – the Leinster Ladies League and the Civil Service League. It caters for over 140 women and schoolgirl teams. Clubs participating in this league are in general from the Dublin area, but there are several which are not. The league is divided into three sections: senior, intermediate and schoolgirls. League and cup competitions are played during the summer months – May to September – whereas other leagues (Mayo, Wexford and the WSCAI) operate a winter schedule. Some interviewees referred to the national league, and when questioned about its existence responded that the DWSL is national. When asked why the title was not changed the interviewees asserted that it was perceived to be the leading league in terms of quality and hence there was little need to change the name.

Quite a few women's soccer clubs were established independently of men's clubs (Castle Rovers, Rathfarnham, Benfica, Lifford). One of the more successful clubs in women's soccer is Shamrock Rovers – formerly Castle Rovers. This is an example of an effective and efficient 'marriage' of two clubs, whereby women can benefit from the infrastructure in place for the men. Attendances at women's soccer league games are rather low, so the earnings from the men's activities at the club are used to meet the financial shortfall from the women's activities. Shamrock Rovers participate in the DWSL and their dominance in that league is very evident. Gerry McDermott highlights the 'success' achieved by this club.[29] During the season just ended (2002), they played 20 matches and won 19, winning the League Cup, but when going for seven-in-a-row WFAI Cup they were beaten by University College Dublin in the final. Shamrock Rovers is the first Irish women's soccer team to participate in the Women's UEFA Cup.

Many sports organizations in the Republic of Ireland rely to a great degree on the input of voluntary personnel, especially at club level. The key contributors are either individuals who are largely interested in the sport or parents of youngsters who play the sport, and may not have the credentials (apart from having played the game as a child or in their youth) or qualifications with respect to coaching or management. The FAI has in recent years developed and promoted courses for aspiring managers/coaches. These courses are open to both male and female participants but they are not attracting as many female participants as desired. Apart from the deficiency in coaching and managerial standard at community-based clubs, there is also a scarcity of suitably qualified referees available – especially at the elite level.

Schools and Colleges

S. Stroot notes that parents organize opportunities for very young children to participate in formal and informal physical activities and provide financial and emotional support to encourage their involvement.[30] In general, participation in most sports in Ireland is initially facilitated through the school system either at primary and secondary level or via local community-based clubs. Gaelic football, hurling, rugby, camogie, netball, hockey, cricket and basketball are the more popular team sports in Irish schools both at secondary and primary level. Youngsters who may wish to develop their talent in other sports such as swimming, golf, tennis or soccer are obliged to join their local community-based club, as their individual needs are unlikely to be catered for adequately within the school setting. The player interviewees commenced their playing career at an early age – between 6 and 8 years old, all four played soccer with their local community based club, and two played soccer while attending their secondary school. Gaelic Athletic Association (GAA) personnel have always actively promoted their games within primary and secondary schools in Ireland by way of organizing competitions and fostering links with the parish clubs. One of the major changes occurring within soccer is the employment of this tactic to encourage girls to play the game. This could be interpreted as a WFAI policy change – going for the bottom up rather than the top down, or perhaps it reflects the interest and ability of the women's development officer.

The Football Association of Ireland Schools (FAIS) represents the schools (boys and girls) sector and was established in 1968 with five schools. Since then school membership has grown considerably and now stands at 1,200. The association oversees inter-school competitions both at secondary and primary level and is organized using a provincial structure. For girls aged between 12 and 18 years competitions are organized at U–13, U–15 and U–17. It is customary for many youngsters to play soccer outside school with their community-based club. These clubs are members of the Schoolboy Football Association of Ireland (SFAI), catering for girls aged between 12 and 18 years. Personnel in both bodies (SFAI and FAIS) organize soccer camps to facilitate player development. In recent months the girls' section of the Ulster branch of FAIS arranged a coaching workshop at which 17 women and three men from various schools attended. This workshop was facilitated by the RDO for Donegal South and the Women's Development Officer. The FAIS is also involved in introducing soccer to second level schools during students' transition year (post junior certificate year – aged 15/16 years). This allows girls who do not normally play soccer to do so. While many have found the experience a very positive one, certain schools have encountered the usual lack of interest from the girls and it has been discontinued.

Similar advances are also occurring in Irish primary schools. Since the appointment of the Women's Development Officer and a schools officer (RDO), greater attention is being paid to providing younger children with the opportunity of playing at school. Children in many schools aged between 8 and 11 years participate in the Ribena Sixes - a nationwide competition. It is initially organized on a county basis, then provincial winners emerge and finally the semi-finals and finals are played in May of each year. In order to progress this within primary schools it is crucial that teachers are familiar with the game and how to deal with younger age groups. To this end, the FAI (due largely to the efforts of the RDOs concerned) offers an introductory coaching course for primary teachers during the first week of July. From the teachers' perspective this is a welcome development as the Department of Education and Science recognize this course as an in-service course. For those teachers who have completed the basic course, it is planned to offer advanced courses each summer.

In 1983, women's soccer in third level institutions was finally given the recognition it deserved when University College Dublin hosted an intervarsity tournament. Due to the growing popularity of the game among college students, in 1987 the Ladies Soccer University Association of Ireland (LSUAI) was formed to oversee developments in the game. Over the years combined universities sides have provided the opposition for the Irish senior and U–18 national teams. Playing the game at this level contributes to player development with several students progressing into the senior national squad. Student teams are limited with respect to international competition and depend on invitational events or quadrangular tournaments. Efforts were made to enter an Irish combined universities team in the World Student Games in 1993, but there was difficulty making the 'cut' as entry is associated with the overall ranking of the national team. It is unlikely that a universities team will gain entry into the Games in 2003 as Ireland's current European standing is around the mid-20s. In 1997, a combined universities team from Ireland (32 counties) participated in an invitational tournament against university teams from England, Scotland and Wales, and won. With the introduction of the British University Games, the combined universities team from the republic is no longer eligible – a team drawn from Northern Ireland would be allowed to participate.[31]

Initially, the universities were to the fore in the development in women's soccer, but in the early 1990s other colleges (Institutes of Technology, Post Leaving Certificate Colleges) were granted affiliation to the association. The LSUAI changed its name to the Ladies Soccer Colleges Association of Ireland (LSCAI) in recognition of the changed membership. By the mid-1990s the association title was changed once again to the Women's Soccer Colleges Association of Ireland (WCSAI). By 1998/99 the association had 27 affiliated colleges and this included colleges from Northern Ireland. The WSCAI leagues are organized on a national and regional basis and there are other competitions such as intervarsity, freshers, indoor intervarsity and inter-provincial competitions.

As in the men's game, in many clubs the facilities for women's soccer are rather basic – but this is not the case in the colleges sector. Due to the importance of sport in higher education institutions and the availability of funding, many colleges have a high quality sports infrastructure covering facilities, equipment, support personnel and coaching. Various colleges have designated sport officers for each of the main sports – Gaelic games, soccer and rugby. While some soccer clubs have clearly made strides in promoting the women's game (especially at schoolgirl level) in the sense that top class facilities are available on demand, in many cases there are difficulties organizing venues for women's league matches, and involving poor quality pitches and inadequate changing rooms. According to two interviewees, conflict still exists at times over the use of the dedicated men's pitches for women's games, even in the colleges sector. They state that reasonable cooperation exists in some quarters, but that the view is often expressed that 'they are only women' when requests for use of facilities are being considered.

THE FOOTBALL FIGURATION

The concept of figuration refers to the webs of interdependencies that link and both *enable* and *constrain* the actions of individuals.[32] Drawing on Clark's[33] football figuration cited by Eric Dunning,[34] the complex web of interdependencies is identified below. It involves at the highest levels the following interlocking groups and organizations: the owners, sales and administrators, and other non playing personnel of clubs; overall controlling organizations such as the FAI and the Eircom League; players, managers and coaches; the mass media increasingly in recent years, television both terrestrial and satellite, and finally the fans. These figurations stretch over time and space and are marked by a series of tension balances. This concept is used as a basis for discussion of the factors that have both facilitated and hindered the development of the women's game to date and which will impact on its future progress.

Figure 10.2 is a modified version of Clark's football figuration for women's football in the Irish context. Throughout this study, the main parties (FAI/WFAI, schools/colleges personnel, coaches, managers, sponsors, other sporting bodies) and administrative arrangements (leagues and cup competitions) that

10.2 WOMEN'S FOOTBALL FIGURATION

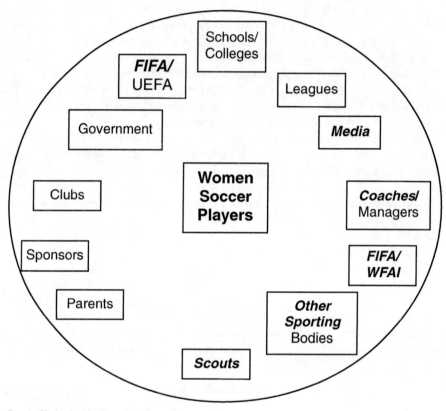

Source: Clark, cited by Dunning, *Sport Matters* (1999).

have influenced the progress of the game in terms of such matters as participation, funding and planning, have been identified. However, there are other factors and parties that must be considered when assessing both the game's evolution and current practice.

One of the main factors is *culture*, both national and organizational. As noted at the beginning of this study, soccer was viewed for many years in Ireland as 'the garrison game' by a large proportion of the population. The removal by the GAA of Rule 21, which banned GAA members from participating in foreign games such as rugby, soccer and hockey, has diluted this perception, but according to one RDO interviewed for this research, there is still a strong traditional resistance to soccer in certain parts of the country. He contends that some parents and siblings actively dissuade their daughters/sisters from playing soccer for that reason.

Participation in professional men's soccer in the Republic of Ireland is, by and large, only possible on a part-time basis (only a couple of clubs employ fully paid professionals such as Bohemians and St Patrick's Athletic), whereas in the case of women's soccer it is mainly recreational. Consequently, the culture within the organizations overseeing the game reflects this situation to some extent. A large proportion of personnel (managers, coaches, administrators) associated with the men's game are involved on a voluntary basis, and in the case of the women's game it is even more pronounced. David Watt accepts that volunteerism is part of sport and recognizes that the voluntary commitment shown by many people is enormous.[35] But he strongly advises that this commitment should be matched by a serious professional attitude being adopted by such people to a level that does not embarrass or cause performers any difficulties, and will deliver their requirements on a consistently high level. The culture that prevails within the WFAI is very much part-time, as several management personnel are not free to devote the time and energy needed for business matters as they must operate within the constraints of a day job. There have been occasions where, due to work commitments, designated managers or coaches have been unable to accompany the team overseas to participate in international competition. In view of these problems associated with women's teams, the national teams have acquitted themselves well in recent competition, especially the U-19 national team.

It is pertinent to identify the factors that both enable and constrain contemporary women's football in the Republic of Ireland. Obviously, the key factors that facilitate the development of the game are the presence of talented youngsters and the existence of a social and physical infrastructure that allows their talent to be recognized early and developed. While much of this study has focused on the governance of women's soccer at present, and some gaps are still apparent, the appointment of a full time Women's Development Officer is a positive move, and her planning efforts (especially at schools level) are likely to reap rewards in the future. The supportive efforts of the FAIS have continued

10.3 The Republic of Ireland Under-19 team.
Source: FAI files.

over the years, and equally the support rendered by players' parents is in most situations a positive element, especially when their children are very young. Another facilitating force in the development of the game in the Republic of Ireland is the colleges sector. It boasts a good quality infrastructure with modern exercise and training facilities that allow all students to play the games of their choice and, at the same time, pursue their academic studies.

The main constraint is the lack of a top down professional approach to management of the various aspects of the game at executive level and at club level. Slack notes that the key to management in sports organizations is that personnel do not have to have participated in the sport at the highest level, but rather have an understanding of the sport.[36] There is a practice in many sports organizations of appointing people without management expertise who insist that they will pick it up as they go along. One area in which women's soccer has a large deficit is media exposure. Given the tremendous interest in sport among the Irish public it is difficult to fathom the reasons why women's soccer gets so little publicity. The WFAI has a PR officer (employed on voluntary basis), yet few details of the Association's activities gain media attention (unlike its parent body). Club fixtures' lists and results (domestic and international) are given scant attention and are normally only available on designated web pages.

Apart from the unawareness of the importance of management structures, there is also a lack of awareness regarding the role of information and knowledge as key resources. The transmission of information is greatly facilitated now by technology and many packages exist both to compile and disseminate information. Sports bodies are notorious for failing to encourage new insights, or adopt procedures and methods using the latest technology. There are situations when particular individuals (Alex Ferguson at Manchester United; Gerard Houllier at Liverpool) have adopted a modern approach. But in many cases, even at national level, there is evidence of resistance to distinguishing between best practice as opposed to current practice.

Finally, a major constraint is the lack of funding for the women's game coupled with the inability or unwillingness of senior executives to channel funds to women's organizations in the most effective manner.

CONCLUDING COMMENTS

The Irish Sports Council (ISC) has the responsibility to plan, lead and coordinate the sustainable development of sport in Ireland. It employs various bodies to assist it in achieving its objectives such as national governing bodies (NGBs) of sport (FAI, WFAI and the like) and other sport bodies (Olympic Council of Ireland), the National Coaching and Training Centre (NCTC) and local sports partnerships. The FAI as the overall governing body for soccer in Ireland receives an annual grant each year (€145,459 for 2000) to fund its activities. The governance structure for soccer currently in place is hierarchical and divisive, and is mirrored in many instances at club level. Few National League (Eircom) clubs are actively involved in developing the women's game, if one is to judge from the scarcity of references to women's football on each club's home page on the web. At schoolboy level, things are more positive as certain schoolboy clubs (Stella Maris, St Joseph's Boys and St Kevin's) are now actively promoting and developing schoolgirl teams. The LGFA was governed independently of the GAA during its early days but is now part of the GAA. Following its assimilation, and with active promotion of the women's game through its club network, the male/female divide has become less obvious, and now all club personnel take an interest in and promote both games. The LGFA has recently completed a new sponsorship deal for its National League, and during the year various matches are shown on national television by TG4. Perhaps there is a lesson here somewhere for WFAI and the FAI executives.

The Genesis report[37] reviewed FAI structures with respect to organizing and managing affairs of the senior team at the World Cup in Japan and Korea. The outcome of this study pointed towards serious flaws in the management set up and made recommendations for improvements. Senior personnel are now getting assistance with the implementation of these recommendations. This is strange, as the Genesis review assessed the FAI's ability to engage in project management rather than how it organizes its affairs on a day-to-day basis. There are implications for the WFAI executives here, as new structures (positions) are likely to emerge. Of course, the Genesis findings are useful, but they are most pertinent to project/event management. The inability of the senior personnel to notice this fact is disappointing and does not augur well for future planning and organizational strategy.

To improve the administration of the game and raise its profile, it is essential to appreciate the need for and engage in serious research to identify key aspects (either administration or playing) that need attention; to compile a database in such a manner that it can be updated regularly; to have efficient personal communication channels in place; to utilize appropriate services marketing techniques; to employ people who are confident and comfortable and understand the job to be done, and most of all have a vision for the women's association and the ability to put in place the strategies to strive for the best for its key 'players'.

The appointment of the Women's Development Officer by the FAI has led to many new initiatives such as the publication of a newsletter, the organization of workshops in relation to coaching and the formation of new leagues. As there is only one full time officer/administrator associated with women's soccer in Ireland, it is difficult to conclude that the football authorities are serious about the potential of the game. This brief review lacks depth and detail, but despite this it is should be obvious that the Irish soccer authorities (FAI/WFAI) need to take action in relation to streamlining the governing authorities, to adopt a more professional approach to the promotion, management and co-ordination of the game, its infrastructure and playing personnel.

NOTES

The author wishes to acknowledge with thanks the assistance given in the preparation of the study by personnel from the Women's Football Association of Ireland, the Football Association of Ireland, the Women's Colleges Soccer Association of Ireland and the four current players.

1. Documentation provided by the WFAI includes copies of: LFAI News (various issues); Annual Reports (1998–2001); LFAI Development plan, 2000; WFAI Newsletters, 2002; WFAI, *Rules and Regulations*, 2002, Dublin.
2. D. Hannigan, *The Garrison Game* (Edinburgh: Mainstream Publishing, 1998).
3. *Football in Ireland – An Overview* (Dublin: The Football Association of Ireland, 1999).
4. E. Cashmore, *Making Sense of Sports* (London: Routledge, 2000).
5. The Ladies Gaelic Football Association History, see http://www.ladiesgaelic.ie/history/htm retrieved 25 Nov. 2002.
6. *LFAI News* (Jan. 1991), p.31.
7. The 'success' of National senior women's team can be gauged from the World Cup group results – played six games, won four lost two. Yugoslavia qualified from this group having beaten Ireland on both occasions – away 5–0 and at home 1–0. The other countries in Group 6 were Moldova and Greece. The Republic of Ireland senior team has been invited to participate in the Algarve Cup (March 2003) – the most prestigious invitational women's tournament in the world. At U19 level in the European championships the Republic of Ireland team have qualified for phase two which was played in April 2003.
8. *LFAI Development Plan.*
9. *One Association, One Game* (Dublin: Football Association of Ireland, 2001). The FAI abandoned its proposal to build its own stadium and participate in the Irish government's Stadium Ireland project. This change in policy by the FAI led to government funding (19m each year for 3 years) being available for the development of the game so it was decided to review all aspects of soccer. This strategic review covered the period 2002–2006 and was published in 2001.
10. WFAI Rules and Regulations, 2002.
11. Ibid.
12. *A New Era for Sport* (Dublin: Irish Sports Council, 2000).
13. Core funding will be used to develop and support the structures and systems essential for the effective administration and development of Irish sport. Challenge funding will be used to promote specific, targeted and generally time-limited initiatives which will make sustainable differences in the way Irish sport is planned, coordinated or delivered (*A New Era for Sport*, pp.27–8).
14. R. Rumult, 'Towards a Strategic Theory of the Firm', in R. Lamb (ed.), *Competitive Strategic Management* (Englewood Cliffs, NJ: Prentice Hall, 1984), pp.556–70.
15. H. Mintzberg, 'Crafting Strategy', *Harvard Business Review* (July/Aug., 1987), 66–75.
16. T. Slack, *Understanding Sport Organisations* (Champaign, Ill.: Human Kinetics, 1997).
17. D. Waldstein and S. Wagg, 'Unamerican Activity? Football in the US and Canada', in S. Wagg (ed.), *Giving the Game Away* (London: Leicester University Press 1995).
18. S. Lopez, *Women on the Ball* (London: Scarlet Press, 1997).
19. *LFAI Development Plan.*
20. WFAI Rules and Regulations, 2002.
21. *One Association, One Game.*
22. Ibid., pp.24–7.
23. Ibid., p.18.
24. *One Association, One Game.*
25. Ibid., p.23.
26. Ibid., p.3.
27. A. Bourke, 'The Road to Fame and Fortune: Insights on the Career Paths of Young Irish Footballers', *Journal of Youth Studies*, 5, 4 (2002), 375–89.
28. N. Crawford, 'Sports Scholarships and the Internationalisation of Higher Education' (Unpublished MBS Thesis, Smurfit School of Business, UCD, 2002), Ch. 6.
29. G. McDermott, 'The Other Shamrock Rovers', *Sports Monthly: Irish Independent* (30 Sept. 2002), 4–9.

30. S. Stroot, 'Socialisation and Participation in Sport', in A. Laker (ed.), *The Sociology of Sport and Physical Education* (London: Routledge, 2002).
31. The All-Ireland university team was deemed ineligible as the competition was then organized for British Universities that would only include those located in Northern Ireland, which is part of the United Kingdom.
32. E. Dunning, *Sport Matters* (London: Routledge, 1999); G. Jarvie and J. Maguire, *Sport and Leisure in Social Thought* (London: Routledge, 1994).
33. A. Clark, 'Figuring a Brighter Future', in E. Dunning and C. Rojek (eds) *Sport and Leisure in the Civilizing Process: Critique and Counter Critique* (London: Macmillan, 1992).
34. Dunning, *Sport Matters*.
35. D. Watt, *Sports Management and Administration* (London: E & F Spon, 1998).
36. T. Slack, *Understanding Sport Organisations* (Champaign, Ill.: Human Kinetics, 1997).
37. Genesis Review Football Association of Ireland: Preparation and Planning for the 2002 FIFA World Cup, www.genesis.com retrieved 12 Nov. 2002.

11

A Breakthrough:
Women's Football in Sweden

JONNY HJELM and EVA OLOFSSON

The first women's football team was established in Sweden in 1917. Their opponents were usually so-called '*gubblag*' or old-boys' sides. One of these matches attracted 1,700 spectators. The first match between two women's teams took place in Stockholm in 1918 in front of approximately 500 spectators. Male football experts did not appreciate this independent initiative by women. The influential sports newspaper *Nordiskt Idrottslif* made its position clear:

> There are not words strong enough to berate women's football – if the girls or their advocates want to be taken seriously. Sure, they can wear gym shorts and kick a suitable ball around now and then, but certainly not under the pretension of having anything to do with playing football. Several other women's competitive sports already exist that are completely objectionable, and women's football would become the most reprehensible of them all.[1]

The predominant attitude was that it was all right for women's football teams to participate in exhibition matches against old-boys' sides with the proceeds going to charities; however, they wanted nothing to do with a serious women's team.

In this study, we both describe and analyse the emergence of women's football in Sweden between 1965 and 1980. We examine the reasons behind why the pioneers within women's football began to play football, as well as how their struggle for recognition was met by the institutionalized football movement – that is to say, by local football clubs, the regional football organizations and the national Swedish Football Association (SFF). The actions of the pioneers within women's football and the football movement itself are placed in a social as well as sporting context. Particular emphasis is placed on the social changes that occurred during the 1960s and at the beginning of the 1970s and, among other things, how shifting values undermined SFF's attempts to ignore the rise of women's football and how instead, thousands of women were encouraged to become 'norm-breakers' and challenge the existing gender order within the football movement.

This study is based in part on E. Olofsson's study of the manner in which leaders within the Swedish Football Association, as well as the organization itself, dealt with women's football during the 1970s and 1980s. The details were published in her doctoral thesis *Do Women have a Sporting Chance?* completed in 1989.[2] The study is also partly based on J. Hjelm's study-in-progress on the development of Swedish women's football in local clubs and regional organizations between 1965 and 1980. Olofsson's study is based on SFF minutes, annual reports, policy documents etcetera, while Hjelm's study uses interviews with about 60 women's football players, coaches and managers and the minutes and annual reports from local sports clubs and regional sports organizations, in addition to press clippings. Hjelm's final report will be published towards the end of 2003 or the beginning of 2004 under the provisional title *The Football Amazons* [*Fotbollsamazonerna*].

'THE SWEDISH MODEL'

The Swedish Sports Confederation (Riksidrottsförbundet) was established in 1903 and ever since then has been the umbrella organization for all organized sports in Sweden. The federation is composed of 67 different sports associations including the Swedish Football Association established in 1904. In turn, the various national associations have regional organizations based on geographical divisions within Sweden. The Swedish Football Association covers 24 regional districts. A local football club belongs to both its regional as well as the national association. This means that all of Sweden's approximately 22,000 sports clubs belong to the Swedish Sports Federation. This form of organization is often referred to as 'the Swedish model' or ideal, although similar kinds of organizations also exist in other Scandinavian countries. What is unique about this model is its quality of a popular movement and its democratic construction. The primary function of the individual national associations is the formation of policy. They also maintain the right to make decisions concerning rules and regulations and systems of organized competition. The primary task of the regional associations is to organize competitive and educational activities within the district. The actual sporting events take place in local clubs, apparently independent of control from the central level, but remaining within the framework of the centrally determined system of rules.[3]

THE SWEDISH FOOTBALL MOVEMENT

The first men's football team in Sweden was established towards the end of the 1800s, and in 1896, the first Swedish national championship was played. However, a national league (Allsvenskan) for men's football was not started until 1924. During the period 1930–60, interest in football increased and grew to become the most popular national sport among Swedish men. In 1959, there were 2,849 football clubs in Sweden, and that same year the men's national league set an attendance record of an average of 13,000 spectators per match, which is still the current record. One factor contributing to the increase in the popularity of football was the success of the men's Swedish National team during the 1940s and 1950s.

Average attendance for the men's premier league dropped somewhat during the 1960s, and decreased even more during the 1970s. A similar trend was observed in the lower divisions as well. Contemporary commentators explained the decrease by claiming that the quality of play had become poorer and that Swedish football had become too constrained by a system of play which was too defensive and 'boring'. The commentators also pointed out that new recreational interests had become popular, with people seeming to prefer participating in sport to watching other people compete. In addition, more football matches were being shown on television. Since the end of the 1960s, football fans have been able to enjoy men's football – especially English football – at home in front of the television.

Although the number of Swedish football spectators decreased during the 1970s, quite the opposite was true regarding the number of football players. Between 1970 and 1980, the number of licensed players increased from barely 110,000 to over 170,000. This development took the SFF by surprise, as they had predicted an increase in the number of men retiring from the game as well as tougher competition from other sports. The two most important explanations for this increase were the investments made in youth activities and the rapid expansion of women's football. In 1970, there were 728 licensed women's football players, and in 1980 the number had increased to 26,000.

Today the thousands of clubs across the country form the foundation of the football movement. Day to day activities are managed by the club board of directors and – if the economical situation allows – by employed staff. More important decisions are made at the annual meetings when all of the club members are invited to participate. The ideal of amateurism was long a part of the Swedish football movement, and not until 1967 were the amateur rules rescinded. Since then, it has become increasingly common that clubs employ staff and that clubs with men's football teams in the highest divisions pay their players. However, a large majority of football clubs are still completely dependent on volunteer efforts by members, and most football players – particularly women players – cannot support themselves by playing football.[4]

WOMEN'S FOOTBALL AS A PUBLICITY STUNT

As mentioned earlier, during the late 1910s and early 1920s, several women's football teams were formed that primarily played against '*gubblag*' or old-boys' sides. The proceeds from the matches went to charities and to the clubs that arranged the matches. At this time an attempt was also made to invest more seriously in women's football, that is to say, to start regular matches between women's teams and eventually form a women's league. However, as we pointed out in the introduction, male football experts vigorously attacked such initiatives. It was with much satisfaction and sympathy that *Idrottsbladet* in 1921 informed its readers of the fact that the English Football Association had decided to forbid clubs to open their football fields to women's football teams.

> In England and France women have begun to play football in alarmingly high numbers, and in England it is generally believed to have gone too far, as football is no sport for ladies. Women's soft bodies do not benefit from bumps and hard treatment. Thus, women should not play football and should instead participate in swimming, field hockey and other more noble sports.[5]

In Sweden, suspicions also arose that English (and Swedish?) women's football was a step in women's struggle for increased equality between the sexes, something that received strong disapproval.[6] According to the historian Torbjörn Andersson, men's opposition during the 1920s and 1930s (both within and outside of SFF) provides the most significant explanation for why Swedish women's football did not develop into an established competitive sport during the inter-war period.[7]

The first women's football league in Sweden was in Umeå, a coastal city in the northern part of Sweden. In 1950 and 1951, teams competed for the title of 'Umemästarrinnorna' (Umeå women's champions) in a football tournament organized by a local newspaper.[8] The same four teams participated both years. Two teams were made up of employees from one of the city's larger work places, so-called 'korplag' or company teams, while players on the other teams were primarily handball players from two of the city's sports clubs. These matches attracted the attention of the local press, who generally described the matches in a serious and positive manner, and in addition attracted a paying crowd of spectators, sometimes numbering close to 100. Several of the women's teams also played publicity matches against old-boys' sides. On such occasions, however, a sexist and whimsical tone characterized the match commentary. For reasons unknown, the women's football league did not continue in 1952.[9]

Apart from the women's football league in Umeå, before the middle of the 1960s there were no women's leagues in Sweden. On those occasions when women played football during the 1950s and the first half of the 1960s, it was in teams put together in order to play against old-boys' sides. Women's football games had, as in the inter-war period, a publicity-stunt character about them. The primary aim was to entertain the spectators.

THE EMERGENCE OF MODERN WOMEN'S FOOTBALL: 1965–71

Local Initiatives

In 1965, a football tournament for female students was arranged for the first time at Stockholm University.[10] In 1967–68, similar tournaments were held at the universities in Gothenburg and Lund. By this time, other women's football teams in addition to the university teams were emerging, teams that wished to play against other women's teams, preferably in organized leagues. These developments were taking place in several different parts of the country and were due to initiatives of women by themselves or together with relatives or male friends. The initiatives were not coordinated and women from different regions did not seem to know that there were women's football teams in other parts of the country. Up until May 1968, women's football had hardly received any attention from the media. In the beginning, these teams had regular practices and played sporadic matches against old-boys' sides and other newly formed women's sides. The next step was to try to start a football league for women.

Öxabäck IF women's football team (established in 1966) was one of the teams that made a serious effort to establish women's football, and quickly received recognition as the first 'modern' women's football team in Sweden. The team was significant to the early growth of women's football in central Sweden, and after several years of struggle managed to start a league in the Västergötland district in May 1968. However, during May and June 1968, women started leagues in other parts of Sweden as well.[11] Company teams appeared to have participated in some of these leagues, although many played with only seven players and on a smaller pitch than usual. In at least two of the leagues, however, it was primarily a matter of sports clubs entering sides in the leagues and these teams played with 11 players on a regular-sized pitch. Match time, however, was shorter for women's than it was for men's matches.

During the following years, the number of women's teams rapidly increased and several new women's football leagues started up throughout the country. In 1969 in Sweden's three largest cities – Stockholm, Gothenburg and Malmö – women's football leagues began. Also in 1969, Sweden's largest youth football tournament, St Eric's Cup in Stockholm, invited girls' teams to participate for the first time.

There were 728 licensed women's football players in Sweden in 1970, and 4,901 in 1971. Thus during 1970–71, the number of women's football players as well as women's football teams experienced a significant increase. In 1971, 403 of the 2,971 sports clubs in Sweden that included football in their programmes also had a football team for women. Altogether, there were 59 football leagues for women, and only seven of Sweden's 24 regional football associations lacked leagues for women.

The Swedish Football Association's Regional Organizations

Before 1971, the Swedish Football Association had not taken a single initiative to support newly-started women's football teams or women's leagues (more about SFF's actions in the next section). A few of SFF's 24 regional districts were more active however. For example, in 1968, Västergötland's Football Association provided Öxabäck IF and other teams in the league with practical assistance and moral support. Cooperation between Öxabäck IF and other teams in the league and Västergötland's Football Association increased during 1969–71. In 1969, two of the regional associations, Närke's Football Association and Stockholm's Football Association, started 'official' women's football leagues (the associations administered the leagues). Before 1970, the participating teams and their clubs administered most of the other leagues in the country. During 1970–71, several of the regional associations increased their involvement.

Women's Football and Journalists

Between 1968 and 1971, the mass media generally portrayed women's football in a positive light. It was common during this period for the media to take up the issue of women encroaching on areas previously dominated by men. This included sport (women in motor sports, for example), but most often it concerned jobs and career choices (women ministers, police, military and so on). The journalists sympathetically described how women struggled against traditional attitudes regarding appropriate jobs and activities for women. One example of the positive attitude newspapers had towards women's football involved Öxabäck IF's first match in 1968, when Sweden's largest evening newspaper *Expressen* started the 'Öxabäck Fan Club'. In addition, the newspaper *Arbetet* took the initiative in forming the women's football league in Skåne as well as administrating the league between 1969 and 1972.

This does *not* mean that women's football was treated in the same manner as men's football – sexist comments such as 'football amazons' and 'Valkyries' were used when talking about the women footballers, and accounts of the matches did not always deal with the actual football played or the personal performances. Women's football received considerably less attention in the mass media, and matches and tables were irregularly reported and were listed after men's senior and junior results. Nor does it mean that the majority of sports journalists exhibited particularly positive attitudes towards women's football. However, strikingly many of those who wrote about women's football at that time, and who became 'women's football experts' for their newspapers, held a positive fundamental tone and willingly reported on the criticism the pioneers within women's football aimed at SFF or at other local opposition to women's football. For example, when SFF's secretary in 1968 claimed that 'we do not have any women's football in Sweden', the press covered the story and wrote about the irritation his comments had caused among advocates of women's football.[12] The newspapers also noted that the women's football matches often attracted as large a crowd, or larger, than men's second division football or lower divisions, and that the crowd enjoyed watching women's football. The pioneers within women's football experienced the attention by the press as positive which encouraged them to continue their involvement with football.

Four Categories of Women's Football Teams

The women's football teams that began before 1972 and played in organized leagues can be divided into four categories: a) company teams; b) handball teams; c) 'sports-widows' teams and d) girls' teams.[13] *Company teams* were made up of work colleagues. These teams did not exist for long and dropped out of the league after a few years. When this happened, the better players, especially those who were willing to devote a considerable amount of time to training, moved on to other teams. *Handball teams* were probably numerically the largest among the four categories. Many of the first women's football teams were composed of players who played on sports club's handball teams (although other common sports were bandy, volleyball and basketball) during the winter and who wanted a team ball-sport that they could play during the summer. Since handball was a sport that included rough body contact and a high risk of injury, these women had a difficult time accepting the claim that football was too 'tough' a sport for women. They were generally members of a club that included several sports, that is to say a club with several sections that included competitive sports for both men and women. The prospective women's football players were thus already members of the club, they had played a team ball-sport before and they had experience of organized practices. Thus, the formation of a football team and participation in a league did not seem so strange. *'Sports-widows' teams* were formed by women who had husbands, boyfriends, brothers or male friends who played football. Over the years they had followed the men's/boys' matches and had tired of simply being passive spectators. These women were often good friends and acquaintances living in small rural communities, and the social companionship that they found within the women's team strengthened their spirit of community and gave them something meaningful to do for recreation. Finally, *girls' teams* included younger girls (sometimes as young as 11–12 years) who started playing football in clubs that began investing in youth activities around 1970. In this way, girls also became involved in the official activities of the clubs' football teams. There were also girls' teams coached by youth centre leaders (within the framework of youth centre activities).

Before a club's women's team could be entered in a league, the club board of directors had to give their approval. Sometimes this decision could be taken at one of the annual meetings. Men associated with the club were assigned jobs as coaches and managers, and a certain amount of equipment and balls was also provided. As for the rest, the women's football team was expected to organize and finance their own activities. Home matches were played on one of the county-owned pitches to which the club had access.

Coaches and Managers

At the club level (which formed the basis of the Swedish football movement), thousands of coaches and managers kept the team activities going through their voluntary efforts. Here we also find a minority that, early on, willingly helped the women who wanted to play football. At the club level, we can identify three categories of coaches: top level coaches, youth coaches and general sports coaches. Coaches belonging to the first category showed no interest in becoming involved with women's football or in supporting it in any way. Instead, their focus was on the club's senior men's team. Within the two categories 'youth coaches' and 'general coaches' we find those coaches who were positive about the emerging women's football and who were also willing to accept positions as trainers and coaches for women's and girls' teams. These coaches emphasized the fostering of social values and good health, for young men as well as for older athletes. Participation in sports had a value in itself and the emphasis on winning was toned down. This category of coaches had a particularly important role during the second half of the 1970s with the expansion of girls' football.

Was Swedish Women's Football a Result of International Influences?

It has been suggested that during the mid-1960s, the Swedish pioneers within women's football were inspired by the women's football that was being played in Denmark, where serious women's football teams, leagues and tournaments had existed since 1959. The women's football league started by the newspaper *Arbetet* in 1969 in Skåne (a region in southern Sweden quite close to Denmark) was inspired by Danish women's football.[14] However, aside from this league there is nothing to suggest that the women's football that emerged in Sweden before the summer of 1969 was inspired by Danish women's football. In general, representatives of men's and women's football had no knowledge about women playing football in other countries. During the summer of 1969, however, newspapers began to include reports of women's football teams, which even had professional players, in countries such as Czechoslovakia and Italy. This was surprising as well as exciting news for Swedes interested in women's football.

THE SWEDISH FOOTBALL ASSOCIATION'S DECISION TO INTEGRATE WOMEN'S FOOTBALL

At the beginning of the 1970s, women already played football in clubs that were members of SFF and some of the regional associations had begun organizing women's leagues. These activities resulted in two problems for SFF's central organization. What rules of play should women footballers use? And could women obtain players' licences, that is to say, were they eligible for the player's insurance system that was included with the licence? Such decisions were made at meetings of the so-called Representative Assembly, which was composed of representatives for the clubs in the two highest divisions in men's football. In 1970, the Representative Assembly decided that women should use the same rules of play as men (with the exception that match time should be shorter) and that women should become licensed in the same manner as men. Despite these historical decisions, women's football was not mentioned at all in the board of directors' annual report for that year.[15]

The following year, 1971, a committee of four men and two women was appointed with the task of 'working out recommendations concerning women's football in Sweden'. Developments both nationally and internationally induced this decision. The committee described the current national situation as 'a very rapid and partially out-of-control development'. International experiences had shown, or so they claimed, that there was a risk of commercialization and an egoistical exploitation of the sport.[16] Information had also reached SFF that UEFA had appointed a women's football committee. In 1972, with the committee's recommendations as a basis, SFF decided that women's football should be organized under the leadership of SFF and that women should be incorporated into all the organizational levels.

With reference to the fact that internationally there were several 'special provisions' in the rules for women's football compared to men's football, a group of medical experts was assigned the task of, among other things, investigating whether there was 'any connection between hard blows to the chest region and the occurrence of breast cancer'. The medical experts found that 'there was no evidence that football or any other team sport was especially full of risks or was dangerous for ladies'.[17] The experts' opinions supported the decision to employ the same rules of play as used in men's football. Referring to physiological differences between men and women, the medical experts pointed out that it was inadvisable for men and women to compete on the same team, but that this could perhaps be acceptable in the case of girls and boys who had not yet reached puberty. For these same reasons, the experts were negative towards the idea of matches between men's teams and women's teams.

At the time of the investigation, a relatively widely-spread system of district leagues already existed. However, competitive leagues or events had yet to be established that covered the entire nation. SFF decided that the formation of a system of leagues, tournaments and championships should be modelled after those existing within men's football.

Regarding the need of women's football for pitches and economic resources, the investigation maintained that in order for the development of women's football to continue, it was necessary for social support to increase concurrently with the development of women's football. In addition, they argued that women's football should be equivalent to a new special association within the Swedish Sports Federation, thus receiving an increased proportion of the federation's resources. A cutback within one or the other of the federation's 'current areas would be inconceivable', according to the investigation.

THE GROWTH OF WOMEN'S FOOTBALL IN SWEDEN DURING THE 1970S

Women's Senior Football and Girls' Football

During the 1970s, the number of women's teams, women's football leagues and women's tournaments continued to increase rapidly. The greatest growth came in those regions where SFF's regional associations became involved in women's football. These regional associations arranged regular matches between the different district teams, where the best players were provided the opportunity to meet and show their abilities.

TABLE 11.1
THE NUMBER OF FOOTBALL PLAYERS' LICENCES FOR WOMEN AND MEN, SELECTED
YEARS DURING 1970–80

Year	Women	Men	Total
1970	728	108,544	109,272
1972	9,387	113,304	122,701
1974	13,097	118,163	131,260
1976	16,816	136,237	153,053
1978	20,731	140,224	160,955
1980	26,522	144,299	170,821

Source: Swedish Football Association's annual reports 1970–80.

Official district championships (tournaments administered by SFF's regional associations) that were organized as elimination tournaments began in most of the districts during 1970–71, and in 1973 the first official Swedish championship was played, and won by Öxabäck IF. The regional associations also began organizing training for women's football coaches and players at this time. In a few of the districts, clubs started girls' football teams at the beginning of the 1970s, but in general, it was not until the latter half of the 1970s that girls' football experienced its greatest period of growth in Sweden. It was also during this period that youth tournament organizers began inviting girls' teams to participate.[18]

Official and Unofficial International Women's Football Matches

The first known (and very unofficial) international match took place in 1964 when a team from Löberöd in Skåne met a Danish national team composed of players from several Danish clubs. The Danish team won easily 7-0. In May 1968, a Swedish team (which the newspapers designated as the 'Swedish National Team') faced the Danish team *Femina* in Denmark (the Swedes lost, 0-7). Before the match, the team, which was made up of students from Lund University, was trained by a male footballer from the highest division who had also played on the National team. In 1969 a team from Skåne, which was meant to represent the talent within Swedish football, competed in a tournament in Denmark against teams from Denmark and Czechoslovakia. During 1970 and 1971, Swedish teams with players primarily from the Skåne, Västergötland and Stockholm regions played four unofficial international matches against Danish teams. They also played against the Danish National team, which had won the unofficial World Championship in Mexico. One of the matches that took place in Copenhagen was seen by 6,400 spectators and was a fantastic experience for the Swedes in spite of the 3-4 loss. A journalist from the newspaper *Arbetet* played an important role in these unofficial international matches, as he was the one who, in spite of some criticism, and with very limited resources, organized the matches and selected competitive sides.[19]

In 1973, the Swedish women's team played their first official international match (0-0 against Finland). The following year, they played several additional international matches and participated in the Nordic Three-Nation Tournament. At first, only Sweden, Finland and Denmark participated, but in 1978, Norway entered the tournament for the first time. During 1974–76, Denmark won the tournament, while Sweden won in several of the following years. In 1975, the Swedish National team played against a non-Nordic team for the first time. Sweden won two matches against the English National team – one match was played in England and one in Sweden. At the home game against England, a new Swedish attendance record was set with almost 3,000 spectators attending. In 1978, Sweden beat Switzerland 7-1 and in the following year Sweden participated in the first – but unofficial – European Championship in Italy. Denmark won the championship with Sweden reaching third place.[20]

DID WOMEN'S FOOTBALL BECOME INTEGRATED?

What did SFF do after the decision was made to integrate women's football, giving them official control over the women at the same time as women's football was increasing in popularity?[21] Was SFF active in its goal of stimulating and developing women's football, or did the association act as a gatekeeper and thus as an obstacle to development?[22]

The control over women's football that SFF established meant control exerted by men. During the first decades of women's football, there were no female board members on the SFF board or any women within central management. No women participated in the annual meetings or were elected to the Representative Assembly. In 1978, the 'Premier League Association for women's football' was formed and included representatives from the clubs in the highest divisions, acting as a counterpart to the men's Premier League Association. The women's association, in contrast to the men's Premier League Association, was not allowed to vote at the annual meetings and in the meetings of the Representative Assembly, although they were allowed to attend.

One of the leadership positions at the central level that has both high status and a great symbolic value, but that is not among the elected decision-making bodies, is that of the national team manager. The first women's national football team manager was hired in 1975. Between 1975 and 1980, three different men held this position.[23] At the beginning of the 1970s, it became clear why there were few female coaches and managers. The first report on women's football said that 'the explanation is simple; there is hardly any tradition in women's football, and leaders with knowledge of football can only be found among men'.[24] In the report, as well as in articles in SFF's magazine *Svensk Fotboll*, a hope was fostered that women's football would help alleviate the lack of leaders – and not only within women's football. Gradually, the official comments changed character. In several contributions to the magazine, it was argued that the women themselves had to address their own problems. SFF's chairman wrote:

> With the risk of again being called a fat male chauvinist pig, I will say that it is significantly more important that the girls take care of their problems. Themselves. Better than spending time on long-winded complaints. In the mass media. SFF will do its best to see that women's football is a success. Then it is up to the girls. And, as a rule, their male coaches and managers – whatever the reason for that is.[25]

When SFF informed its members of its decision that they should consider women's football as a part of their football programme as a whole and that women's football should be integrated into all of SFF's organizational levels, many districts interpreted this to mean that they should *not* establish special women's football committees. Accordingly, the expansion of women's football leagues was to be dealt with within the district competition committees, the efforts to start girls' football were to be handled by the youth committees, and so forth. In some districts, however, this resulted in women's, and in particular girls' football not receiving enough attention. Thus, after pressure from women's football advocates, many districts established women's football committees and/or assigned someone to pay particular attention to women's and girls' football during the middle of the 1970s. This resulted in problems that concerned women's and girls' football becoming visible, allowing appropriate actions to be taken in order to curtail them.

Various solutions also appeared at the club level, often depending on the size of the club, the number of competitive sports within the club and how serious they were about top-level competition. However, within the small- and medium-sized clubs with both men's and women's football, the women's football team was generally not a part of the football section. Instead, women's football was placed in the women's section, the women's football section or in the youth section. Thus, organizationally the clubs did not follow SFF's integration principle, but seem initially to have preferred an organization based on gender divisions. One reason for this was that the leading advocates of men's football had a difficult time accepting women's football as 'real' football.

In 1979, a second report on women's football was conducted under the auspices of SFF. This report revealed an ambivalent attitude on the issue of integration due to, among other things, the fact that during the 1970s many deviations had been made from this principle at the club and district levels. Those clubs that had been established for women's football alone turned out to be 'more competent to work for the development of women's football than what had been the case when they had been acting as a section within one of SFF's traditional member clubs'. In spite of the fact that these deviations from the integration principle had been successful, it was seen as desirable that even in the future, women's football should become integrated into the existing organization. Consequently, many of the issues within women's football remained invisible – both the problematic issues as well as the successful ones.

RULES AND SYSTEMS OF COMPETITION –
MEN AS THE NORM WHEN IT IS CONVENIENT

After women's football had been officially accepted in 1972, the fundamental principle regarding the rules of play were that they should be the same as for men's football and that they be interpreted and applied in the same manner. While agreement was generally good as to the rules of play, disagreements were greater regarding the organization of leagues, tournaments and other forms of competition. Since 1972, the design of the leagues has been a perpetually problematic issue for the board of directors and the representatives. The 1971 report concluded that the system of competition within women's football should use the organization of men's football as a model. Gradually, the system of competition for women's football, both nationally and internationally, became more like the men's system. The opposition that existed primarily concerned the national leagues and, in particular, the formation of a premier league for women. Two differing opinions can be discerned here. On the one side were those who saw the development of football as the most essential principle. They claimed that competition between equally good teams was a requirement in order for women's football to increase in quality. Because of this, they wanted to form a league pyramid with a pinnacle, similar to the one that had characterized men's football since 1924. The other side believed that the clubs would find it difficult to finance the long trips that a league that included teams from the entire country would require. Thus, meagre economic resources would result in a limitation in the possibility of expanding the league system. This was similar to the opinion in the 1971 report, which stated that 'it is questionable whether women's football can bear the costs involved with play beyond regional borders'. In addition, the report ascertained that experience from other team sports had shown that 'to a great extent, women are willing to invest their own resources in order to realize their desire for competition'. The side claiming that economic resources limited the possibility of expanding league play dominated the Representative Assembly during the 1970s.[26]

From the middle of the 1970s, the board of directors and the Representative Assembly received considerable criticism from advocates of women's football, as well as from journalists, for their strategy in dealing with the issue of league play, and in particular for their passivity, which critics believed had slowed the development of women's football. The association defended themselves by arguing that a gradual development was more positive in the end and that women should stop making demands but instead take responsibility for their sport. This was a responsibility which they had a hard time taking, at least at the national level, since the integration of women's football meant that the men in the Representative Assembly and on the board of directors were responsible for all of the decisions concerning women's football.

NORM-BREAKERS INSIDE AND OUTSIDE THE FOOTBALL MOVEMENT

It is important to be clear that the development of modern Swedish women's football was not a result of international influences (with the exception of the southernmost part of Sweden), and neither was it a process initiated by SFF. Instead, football spontaneously developed from below when hundreds, and after a few years, thousands of women began playing the game. As we have shown earlier, the arduous work was accomplished at the club level where the women were also sometimes helped by individual male coaches and trainers. Together they challenged the hegemonic masculinity – using R.W. Connel's words – that existed within the football movement. The foundations of the football movement's masculinity ideal were laid during the end of the nineteenth century when football was described as a hard physical sport for 'real men', which was also an attitude that became stronger during the twentieth century when football spread and increased in popularity. Thus the women's teams that, in spite of everything, existed before the middle of the 1960s were reduced to playing publicity matches against old-boys' teams.

Why did the women's football teams of the 1960s succeed better than their predecessors? How did the women's football leagues around the country succeed in 1968–70, when a comparative effort – with one exception – had failed earlier? In our opinion, this was due to the increasing number of women employed outside the home as well as the shift in social values, particularly those that had to do with attitudes towards what was 'feminine' and 'masculine', which inspired women to overcome traditional norms within sport also.

Liberalization and Radicalization during the 1960s and 1970s

During the post-war period, the Swedish welfare state expanded rapidly and the material standard of living improved continuously. Each year employees received substantial wage increases, the number of working days per year became fewer and during the 1960s and 1970s, an increasing number of young people were offered the opportunity to attend university. Housing quality improved and unemployment was quite low – compared to international levels and in a historical perspective – and during the 1960s, a labour-force shortage was the labour market's primary problem. One solution to this was to make it easier for women to enter the labour market leading to the number of wage-earning women increasing from the beginning of the 1960s.[27]

From the latter half of the 1950s, traditional value hierarchies and so-called 'fixed values' within cultural, ethical and political fields came to be questioned, initially by only part of the intellectual elite and by liberals. Within the cultural debate in the 1960s, there was a nihilistic element in which value judgements were not perceived as universally true or false, but simply a means to express emotions. One result was that within the sphere of cultural politics, seemingly populist points of view were formulated, which emphasized the consumer's right to decide for him or herself what was good versus what was bad culture. This was an idea shared by many that were active within the rapidly expanding popular culture and mass media sectors.[28]

It is difficult to ascertain with certainty the extent to which the journalists who wrote about women's football held this standpoint. However, it seems reasonable to argue that there were journalists who were willing to defend women's rights to decide for themselves what acceptable athletic activities were, and that it was this attitude they expressed in their coverage of women's football. The criticism against those in positions of power in the football movement and their methods of dealing with women's football were also in line with the more aggressive, more investigative style of journalism that emerged during the 1960s.[29]

During the first half of the 1960s, an intensive debate also took place regarding gender-roles, particularly women's roles, and how these could change. Strong criticism was also voiced here against the traditional attitude that a woman's 'natural' place was in the home and that, if they must work outside the home, women should primarily act as a reserve labour force.[30]

During the second half of the 1960s, the public debate became further radicalized and politicized and we observed the emergence of new organizations, often influenced by socialist ideals and loosely composed groups outside of the established political parties. These came to question traditional norms and values in society to an even greater degree. Within these groups and organizations, people questioned, among other things, the working conditions of industrial workers, nuclear families, traditional holidays, the authoritarian structure of universities, patterns of consumption (materialism) and so forth. The new women's movement criticized the gender order in society and the patriarchal and capitalistic structure that created and upheld this gender order.[31]

Afterwards, the established political parties, particularly the governing Social Democrats, also came to formulate a more outspoken feministic policy. At the 1972 party congress, Prime Minister and party leader Olof Palme gave an opening speech where he talked about the situation for women and maintained that equality between the sexes must increase. The speech was considered an important symbolic gesture and during the 1970s, a number of reforms and laws were introduced that indicated that the government had assumed a new position regarding the issue of gender-roles. 'The goal was to create an improved balance between men's and women's rights, duties and opportunities.'[32]

Pioneers within Women's Football as Norm-breakers

The Swedish pioneers within women's football were driven by a longing to play football and have fun together, just like Swedish boys and men had been doing for decades. Many of them had played football when they were young, with friends, brothers and sisters, and had thus experienced the satisfaction that playing football could give. However, unlike their male co-players and opponents who could start playing football for a club when they grew older, the girls were instead reduced to playing sporadic publicity matches.

For many people, participating in sporting activities in order to have 'fun' and experience 'togetherness' is an important reason for participation in athletics. The Swedish academic Lars-Magnus Engström has called this the 'intrinsic value' of sport. One does not participate in sport primarily in order to achieve something, but instead, the activity 'is (self) sufficient in itself'. Participation in sport provides a special experience or satisfies certain immediate needs. To have fun, to feel excitement or to have the opportunity to relax from the demands of the day are all reasons given as primary explanations for participation in athletic activities. 'Now is what matters – not the future.'[33] According to Engström, alongside the self-sufficiency of athletics are the investment values that motivate people to participate in sport. This is partially an investment in health and physical status and partially an investment in the future. In both cases, it is about the fact that the athletic activity awards the participant a special status in relation to other people.[34]

Initially, for the women football pioneers, the investment value of sport was probably of less significance. Information from the interviews as well as information from press clippings unequivocally indicate that the intrinsic value of football was the most important motive behind the formation of women's teams and the attempts at starting women's leagues. Most of the women did not feel that playing football *in itself* gave them a higher status within society, but that their social status was positively affected when they broke traditional norms that dictated how women and men should act. Consequently, it was not their initiative to play football that affected their status, but the fact that they refused to accept the traditional gender order that existed within the football movement, which prescribed that boys and men played football while girls and women were passive onlookers or did volunteer work within the clubs. There was a positive value in breaking the norms and values that dictated how life should be lived.[35] Questioning the traditional sex-roles was not something new, but with the development of the 'new women's movement' at the end of the 1960s it came to attract increasing interest. However, the women's football pioneers did *not* feel like they were feminists, and they hardly shared – on a conscious level – the values found within the new women's movement.[36] Neither does anything indicate that the advocates of the new women's movement at the end of the 1970s found the women's football pioneers' struggle something worth supporting.[37]

The pioneers of women's football were norm-breakers who, through their actions, challenged and exposed the gender order existing within the football movement. This was not their actual goal; they 'only' wanted to play football. In reality however, they questioned male hegemony within the football movement and inspired many other girls and women to follow them. During a certain period, norm-breakers can herald a behaviour that later becomes more generally accepted.[38] Whether the norm-breakers' behaviour is later accepted or not depends on how the leading resource-rich actors in a specific context – in this case the advocates (local, regional and national) of the football movement – manage to uphold and defend the traditional norms. The prerequisite for succeeding in this is naturally affected in turn by if, and to what extent, the norm-breakers manage to mobilize support for their behaviour.

Women's initiative to start playing football was supported in general by their families and friends. It was rather the criticism and pronounced scepticism from people in their local environments that motivated them to try even harder to create a 'we'll show them' mentality. This was particularly the case when self-appointed experts on football voiced these kinds of opinions, or when ministers and others worried about the effect women's football would have on their morals.[39] As we have shown, however, even the pioneers within women's football had support from some of the coaches, trainers and journalists. The latter described women's football as something new and exciting, and articles about women football players became a feature in the 'women-can' discourse of the late 1960s. Journalists contributed by spreading information about women's football and put the pressure on SFF. The power to create opinion held by journalists should not be underestimated. Thus, journalists had a completely different attitude towards women's football when compared with journalists during the inter-war period.

Naturally, sex-roles, the equality debate as well as the political parties' growing involvement in the issue of equality all meant that, on the level of the individual, it became easier to challenge the masculine hegemony within football. In addition, at about the same time national and county initiatives aimed at making the sports movement into a genuinely widespread popular movement as well as a youth movement. The latter meant that the social- and health-promoting aspects of sport were emphasized and that the concept of 'sport for everyone', which was the name of a governmental report (1969), became something of a guiding-star for those who believed that everyone could participate in sport, regardless of age, ability or sex.[40]

Taken together, this led to SFF's leadership having a difficult time in publicly criticizing or ridiculing women's football, and the association chose instead to wait and see. The passivity among the leaders in SFF and other representatives of men's football was due to, among other things, the criticism they received when they publicly expressed condescending or critical remarks about women's football and the women players. Remarks claiming that women could not play football, that it was physically dangerous for women or that football was 'unwomanly', which had been common during the decades between the two World Wars, also occurred now, but did not win any great acceptance, and most importantly, did not discourage the women footballers. The opinions, and those who expressed them, were seen as being conservative, 'old-fashioned' and uninformed. SFF's own report of 1971 had already shown that there were no medical arguments against women playing football. Using the excuse that the football movement's resources (the volunteer work, pitches, travel monies, and such like) were limited and only available to men's and boys' teams was probably judged as challenging to people's ideas of fairness and thus even more impossible to express in public. The primary strategy became, therefore, to wait-and-see if women's football was, as they said, 'a fad'.

BEING MADE INVISIBLE AND SUBORDINATE

When football advocates realized that women's football was not a whim, but continued to grow, the decision to incorporate women into the organization of football was more natural than to exclude them and have no control over them. They probably thought that taking control would bring with it the ability to restrain women's football – by exerting control so that women's football did not expand at the cost of men's football and by seeing to it that the game remained intact, that is to say, that women played real football. The principle of integrating women footballers into the organization meant that the existing board of directors, committees and working groups in the districts and clubs could take responsibility for women's football as well. Integration can lead to invisibility and in turn, invisibility is seen as one of the domination techniques available to those in power and control.[41] What happened then? During the entire 1970s, women's football, for example, was relatively invisible in the association's official documentation, annual reports and newsletters. Some commentators argued that SFF deliberately delayed over issues concerning the league system, and that this can be explained by the fact that women's football and its supporters were not included in the decision-making bodies. As we have shown, the principle of integration had less pervasive force at the district and club levels. Here, women's football became more visible and gained a forum where their questions and issues could be addressed. Thus, women's football advanced its position regionally as well as locally. Consequently, the control that the central organization tried to exert was not complete.

The integration principle was only applicable at the organizational level. When it came to the actual playing of football, the principle was the opposite; that is to say, men and women were kept separate.[42] In spite of this, the fundamental principle concerning the rules of the game for women ever since women's football first began was that the rules should be the same as those used by the men, as well as be interpreted and applied in the same manner. This attitude was shared by the association and by the women footballers. The fundamental idea of football, like other competitive sports, is that the players adjust themselves to the rules of the game. Those who wish to play real football should play using the rules that had been developed in men's football. When the women knocked on the Football Association's door, they were seeking the same rules of play as those applied to men's football. Perhaps no other opinion was viable at the beginning of the 1970s. An equality discourse was taking place in society at that time – that is to say, an idea that equality between the sexes meant that women and men were more alike than different and that because of this, women could do the same things as men. Thus, the prevailing view of women and the fundamental ideas concerning football went hand in hand.

By deciding to use the same rules, male norms came to be applied to women's football. This led to the situation that women's football could be directly compared with men's football. Often, the quality of women's football was compared to men's football; that is to say, men's football was the norm by which women's performances were judged. Women's football did not always lose out in such comparisons, even if it was understood that women's football was subordinate to men's football. When a comparison was made over time, the judges agreed that the quality of play within women's football had gradually improved and that the improvement occurred more quickly than might have been predicted. During the 1970s, an increasing number of commentators pointed out differences that were favourable to women's football. That women's football had more finesse and technical skill were some of the things that were particularly emphasized, and further, that women's football had less of the dull system play and lack of freedom that was seen within men's football. Some claimed, especially in the media, that women football players were not as serious as the male players were. It was also argued that women, unlike men, prioritized values such as social time together rather than the actual football game.

CONCLUSION

Since the beginning of the 1970s, the advocates of men's football have assumed the point of view that women's football should be integrated in the football movement and that the expansion of women's football should not occur at a cost to men's football. In principle, this means that women's football should be self-financing. In practice, this has meant that Swedish football since the 1970s has experienced numerous conflicts in the clubs that have both men's and women's football. One reason for this is that it is often almost impossible to identify what percentage of the costs and profits come from men's football and women's football. When the clubs' common resources are distributed (for example for practice and match time) by the clubs' board of directors and other authorities – where advocates of men's football often make up the majority – women's football has been pushed to the background. This has of course led to criticism and even resulted in some of the women's football teams forming their own separate women's football clubs. Many women's football advocates also critically allege that the regional associations and SFF have not prioritized the needs of women's football adequately enough.

In our opinion, the maintenance of a separation between women's and men's football contributes to the preservation of the dichotomy between women and men. This is a situation found within most competitive sports. At the same time, the breakthrough of women's football has caused attitudes about what is feminine and what is masculine to alter – a process of change that is continually taking place despite the preservation of the dichotomy.[43]

This breakthrough has brought about the expansion phase of women's football in the 1970s, which continued into the 1980s and then levelled off. Since the end of the 1980s, the number of women football players has fluctuated between 37,000 and 40,000. In Sweden in 2002 there were approximately 200,000 licensed players (16 years and older) and of these, about 37,000 were women footballers and 240,000 were youth footballers (of which approximately 85,000 were girls).[44]

Ever since the middle of the 1970s, Sweden has had one of the best women's football teams in the world. In the beginning, their strongest opponents were Denmark, Italy, England and France, but during the 1980s and 1990s, Norway, China and USA have emerged as new, strong competitors. Since the second half of the 1970s, interest in the Swedish Women's National Team has gradually increased, as well as mass-media coverage, and many see the Swedish National Team's participation in the European Championship 2001 (where Sweden won the silver medal) as the definite breakthrough. At the same time, coverage and interest is not nearly as intensive as when the Swedish Men's National Team plays international matches or participates in European and World Championships. However, perhaps a change is in the air. For the Women's World Championship in China 2003, a Swedish commercial television channel has purchased the broadcasting rights (for Sweden) and announced that they see this as a good investment, as they see an increased interest in women's sports. There is, of course, a danger that traditional sexual stereotypes are focused on here. The marketing value of women athletes is not only influenced by their athletic performances. Emergence onto the international sports stage at the top level also brings with it the pressure to secure media interest and commercial sponsorship.[45] Whatever the problem ahead, however, women's football in Sweden is here to stay.

NOTES

1. Quotation taken from T. Andersson, *King Football. The Cultural History of Swedish Football from the End of the 1800s to 1950* [*Kung Fotboll. Den svenska fotbollens kulturhistoria från 1800-talets slut till 1950*] (Stockholm: Symposium, 2002), p.312.
2. E. Olofsson, *Do Women Have a Sporting Chance? Organized Sport and Women in Sweden in the Twentieth Century* [*'Har kvinnorna en sportslig chans? Den svenska idrottsrörelsen och kvinnorna under 1900-talet'*] (Doctoral Thesis, Umeå University, 1989).
3. Olofsson, *Do Women Have a Sporting Chance*, p.16.
4. Andersson, *King Football*; Tomas Peterson, *The Game that Turned Serious. Halmstad's Ball Club Between Popular Movement, the State and Market* [*Leken som blev allvar. Halmstads Bollklubb mellan folkrörelse, stat och marknad*] (Lund: Arkiv, 1989); Bill Sund, *Football's Domain of Power* [*Fotbollens maktfält*] (Stockholm: Svenska Fotbollförlaget AB, 1997).
5. Quotation taken from Andersson, *King Football*, p.314.
6. Ibid.
7. Andersson, *King Football*, pp.305–23.
8. A similar tournament for men's sides was also organized by the newspaper.
9. J. Hjelm, *The Football Amazons* [*Fotbollsamazonerna*] (unpublished manuscript, Institutionen för historiska studier, Umeå University).
10. Information included in the section entitled 'The Emergence of Modern Women's Football: 1965–1971' is based on Hjelm, *The Football Amazons*, unless specifically stated otherwise.
11. Leagues were started in, among other places, Bollnäs (ten teams), Eskilstuna (five teams), Perstorp, in northern Skåne (12 teams) and in Umeå (five teams).
12. *Expressen*, 14 May 1968.
13. These categories, as well as the different categories of sports leaders in the next section, are ideal typically constructed.
14. Claes-G. Bengtsson, 'From a Few Enthusiasts to an Established Popular Sport' ['Från ett fåtal entusiaster till etablerad folksport'], in Göran Havik, Tomas Glanell, Ester Kristiansson (eds), *25 years with Swedish Women's Football* [*25 år med Svensk damfotboll*] (Stockholm: Svenska Fotbollsförlaget AB, 1998), p.7.
15. The information included in the section 'The Swedish Football Association's Decision to Integrate Women's Football' is based on Olofsson, *Do Women Have a Sporting Chance*, pp.145–8.
16. The recommendations gave no examples of how this commercialization would be expressed. It appeared that the committee was referring to certain examples in Austria where advertisements had been published looking for 'beautiful, attractive, shapely women for interesting work within the world of sports'. Olofsson, *Do Women Have a Sporting Chance*, p.147.
17. During the course of development of modern athletics in Sweden, as well as internationally, medical arguments have been brought forward as reasons for barring women's participation in certain sports. Particular interest has been in the risk of damage being done to women's reproductive abilities. For a description of the situation in Sweden, see Olofsson, *Do Women Have a Sporting Chance*, pp.63–4. For a description of the situation in North America, see Alethea Melling, '"Charging Amazons and Fair Invaders": The 1922 Dick Kerr's Ladies' Soccer Tour of North America – Sowing Seed', in J.A. Mangan (ed.), *Europe Sport, World, Shaping Global Societies*, The European Sports History Review 3 (London: Frank Cass, 2001), p.167. For a British perspective, see S. Fletcher, *Women First. The Female Tradition in English Physical Education 1880–1980* (London: The Athlone Press, 1984), pp.26–9.
18. In 1981, the first top-level training camp for girls was arranged (312 girls between 15 and 16 years old); its counterpart was the boys' top-level training camp that had existed since 1956. Tomas Glanell, 'Year for Year' ['År för år'], in Göran Havik, Tomas Glanell and Ester Kristiansson (eds), *25 Years with Womens' Football in Sweden* (Stockholm: Svenska Fotbollsförlaget AB, 1998), p.32.
19. Hjelm, *The Football Amazons*.
20. Glanell, 'Year for Year', pp.14–29.
21. This kind of control is not unique to Sweden. Duke and Crolley summarize their description of 'her story in football' by ascertaining that men's football as well as women's football is male-dominated and male-controlled. See V. Duke and L. Crolley, *Football, Nationality and the State* (Harlow, Essex: Addison Wesley Longman Limited, 1996), p.144.
22. Information included under the headings 'Did Women's Football become Integrated?' and 'Rules and Systems of Competition – Men as the Norm when it is Convenient' are based on Olofsson, *Do Women*

Have a Sporting Chance, pp.148–60.

23. In 1988, a woman was hired as the national team manager for the first time. Olofsson, *Do Women Have a Sporting Chance*, p.166.

24. A Premier League for women was not started until 1988. Olofsson, *Do Women Have a Sporting Chance*, p.155.

25. The percentage of wage-earning married women in Sweden in 1960 was 23 per cent, and in 1975, 58 per cent. Walter Korpi, *The Working Class in Welfare Capitalism* [*Arbetarklassen i välfärdskapitalismen*] (Stockholm: Prisma, 1978), p.72.

26. Kjell Jonsson, 'What Was Cultural Democracy? Tactics in the Early 1960s Debate on a Democratic View of Culture' ['Vad var kulturdemokrati? Linjer i det tidiga 1960-talets debatt om en demokratisk kutursyn'] *Nordisk Kulturpolitisk tidskrift*, 1 (2002).

27. Lars-Åke Engblom, 'Why Professionalization?' ['Värför professionalisering?'], in Agneta Lindblom Hulthén (ed.), *The Journalists' Book 1901–2001* [*Journalisternas bok 1901–2001*] (Stockholm: Svenska Journalistförbundet, 2001), p.267.

28. Christina Florin and Bengt Nilsson, *Something that Looks Like a Bloodless Revolution ... The Politicization of the Equity Between the Sexes During the 1960s and 1970s* [*Något som liknar en oblodig revolution... Jämställdhetens politisering under 1960- och 1970-talen*] (Umeå: Umeå University, 2000).

29. Kjell Östberg, *1968 When Everything Was on the Move* [*1968 när allting var i rörelse*] (Stockholm: Prisma, 2002); Thomas Forser and Ingvar Johansson, 'The Left's Years' ['Vänsterns år'], in Peder Aléx and Jonny Hjelm (eds), *After Work. Investigations into Swedish Recreation* [*Efter arbetet. Studier av svensk fritid*] (Lund: Studentlitteratur, 2000), pp.74–100.

30. Florin and Nilsson, *Something that Looks Like a Bloodless Revolution*, p.74.

31. Lars-Magnus Engström, *Athletics as a Social Marker* [*Idrott som social markör*] (Stockholm: HLS förlag, 1999), p.40.

32. Ibid.

33. Forser and Johansson, 'The Left's Years'.

34. This was something that our informants emphasized during the interviews, together with those interviewed within the framework for the investigation of the development of women's football in Skåne. According to Hargreaves, the politicization of women's sports is unusual, see J. Hargreaves, *Sporting Females. Critical Issues in the History and Sociology of Women's Sports* (London and New York: Routledge, 1994), p.254. Hall adopts a similar standpoint and defines politics as 'the struggle to define and control women's sport: its meanings and values, the structures required, and the debates over policy', in M.A. Hall, *Feminism and Sport Bodies. Essays on Theory and Practice* (Champaign, IL: Human Kinetics, 1996), p.100.

35. This conclusion is based on an examination of *Kvinnobulletinen* 1971–80, *Vi Människor* (which in 1968 was called *Vi kvinnor*) 1968–80, *Rödhättan* 1975–80, as well as interviews with representatives of the new women's movement. For a more thorough account, see Hjelm, *The Football Amazons*. We would however like to mention that one of the new women's movement's leading figures, Barbro Backberger, in an interview in *Arbetet* in 1969 explained that women's football was 'something fun', but that it was not an 'effective weapon' in women's struggle for liberation. 'By the way, I am not a sports fan. Sports is terribly male dominated.' *Arbetet* 5, 9 (1969).

36. Kajsa Sundström-Feigenberg, 'Women's Lives During Five Decades – Life Histories in Medical Science' ['Kvinnors liv under fem decennier – livshistorier i medicinsk vetenskap'], *Kvinnovetenskaplig Tidskrift*, 1 (1989), 36.

37. In *Expressen*, the priest in Öxabäck explained that 'Here at the parsonage, we are not pleased about women's football. No one will believe that the spectators come to watch football. They will come to watch the girls. Football is too tough for girls.'

38. The report also led to an active effort on behalf of women's sports (later referred to as sex equity) within the Swedish Sports Federation with the goal of gaining more women athletes and coaches. Olofsson, *Do Women Have a Sporting Chance*, pp.69–76.

39. B. Ås, *Women Together. A Liberation Handbook* [*Kvinnor tillsammans. Handbok i frigörelse*] (Malmö: Gidlunds, 1982), pp.37–42.

40. The Swedish women's historian, Yvonne Hirdman, maintains that the gender system's two fundamental principles are dichotomy, that is, separateness, and hierarchy, that is, men as the norm. Yvonne Hirdman, 9, 3 'The Gender System – Reflections on the Social Subordination of Women' ['Genussystemet – reflexioner kring kvinnors social underordning'], *Kvinnovetenskaplig Tidskrift*, 9, 3 (1988), 3.

41. Within post-structuralistic feminism, the woman-man dichotomy is questioned, just like the 'natural' connection between female/male, feminine/masculine, heterosexual. With such an approach it becomes relevant to ask questions like Larsson does in a study of the Swedish sports movement: Why are sports divided between just women and men? H. Larsson, *The Staging of Gender in Sports* [*Iscensättning av kön i idrott. En nutidshistoria om idrottsmannen och idrottskvinnan*] (Stockholm: HLS publishers, 2001), p.267. For a further discussion, see also Susan Birrell, 'Feminist Theories for Sport', in Jay Coakley and Eric Dunning (eds), *Handbook of Sport Studies* (London: Sage, 2000), pp.68–72.
42. The statistics are taken from SFF's official Website November 2002 (with the exception of the youth statistics, which are from SFF's Website September 1999).
43. See Nancy Theberge, 'Challenging the Gendered Space of Sport: Women's Ice Hockey and the Struggle for Legitimacy', in Sheila Scraton and Anne Flintoff (eds), *Gender and Sport: A Reader* (London: Routledge, 2002), pp.292–301.

12

From Heydays to Struggles:
Women's Soccer in New Zealand

BARBARA COX and SHONA THOMPSON

The whistle blows – it's the end of the game. Twenty-two players come to a standstill. Some throw their arms up in delight, the others slump in dejection. Then they begin to move again, shaking each other's hands. It's been a hard game – New Zealand versus Australia. As the central defender, I have been under constant pressure to prevent my opposite number from scoring. Today is not our day; the Aussies have won, 2-1. As I trudge wearily to the changing room I keep my head down. I do not want the small crowd to see my face, nor do I want to stop and talk to anyone. Why? Because I am drenched in sweat, especially my face, and I need a shower. It's 1981 and the old saying, 'Horses sweat, men perspire but ladies merely glow' is still very much part of my understanding of what it is to be female.

Soccer is a minority sport in New Zealand. It is overshadowed by several others, mainly rugby for men and netball for women. It is, nevertheless, growing rapidly in popularity, particularly at the youth level. Girls' soccer, for example, has been recorded as the biggest growth sport in secondary schools over the past five years.[1] Typically, on Saturday mornings, hundreds of five, six and seven-year old girls now take to the fields throughout the country to play soccer alongside their male counterparts. This is a new phenomenon.

While there are recorded accounts of the game being played as far back as the 1920s, women's soccer was not established as an organized sport in New Zealand until the early 1970s. In 1973, a game between teams representing Auckland and Wellington was played as a 'curtain-raiser' before an international men's game at Newmarket Park, the home ground of Auckland soccer, drawing 'internal criticism'[2] and many raised eyebrows from those who disapproved of women playing soccer.[3]

Nevertheless, by 1975 three of the major cities, Auckland, Wellington and Christchurch, had established women's soccer associations, with organized league and knockout competitions within the local areas. The inaugural Asian Cup was held in Hong Kong that same year. A letter from the Asian Ladies Confederation, inviting a team from New Zealand to participate in this event, hastened the formation of the New Zealand Women's Football Association (NZWFA). Its first job was to select a national representative team and to help raise the NZ$10,000 required to pay for the team's travel expenses to Hong Kong. Much to their surprise, at what was New Zealand's first foray into international competition, this team won the tournament, beating the highly-favoured and well-supported team from Thailand 3-1 in the final.

Fuelled by this success, women's soccer developed rapidly in New Zealand and soccer associations sprang up throughout the country. Some were affiliated to their local men's associations, but most were directly affiliated to the NZWFA in which the control, organization and promotion of women's soccer was vested. During the 1980s soccer was the nation's fastest growing sport for women.[4] Competition extended to a National Tournament for provincial representative teams, youth tournaments, and a regular programme of international games. At this time, national representative teams from New Zealand were ranked amongst the top four countries in the world. Arguably, this was the sport's heyday, a period of ten years stretching from 1981, when a New Zealand team was runner-up in the World Women's Invitational Football Tournament in Taiwan, to 1991 when they were contestants at the first FIFA Women's World Cup in China.

Today, New Zealand women's soccer can no longer claim to being highly ranked internationally. As the sport grew in popularity in other countries, where more resources were made available for their female players, New Zealand found it increasingly difficult to keep up. Other major changes occurred. The administration of women's soccer is no longer from within a purposively-defined women's organization, the NZWFA, which was solely responsible for and answerable to female players. In 1999 this organization was subsumed by the men's national organization, New Zealand Soccer (NZS).

In this study we present an overview of the context in which women's soccer in New Zealand has developed, tracing the way in which it has needed to forge a position for itself within a culture in which other, highly gendered, sporting codes have traditionally dominated. One of the authors, Barbara Cox, has been involved in soccer since its beginnings in the 1970s, as a player, a coach and an administrator. Some of her recollections from those early years have been included as a recorded dialogue, providing a personalized account of those experiences and reflections on the changes that have occurred. A further dimension of Barbara's involvement in soccer has been as a researcher, in which capacity she conducted participant observations and in-depth interviews involving the members of a club team competing in the premier women's soccer league, run by Soccer Auckland. Results from this qualitative research are presented, highlighting some key issues that were identified as salient to the experiences of these elite soccer players in the mid-1990s. Finally we discuss some observations regarding the structure and organization of women's soccer in New Zealand today, focusing on recent changes.

EARLY DAYS

Women's soccer in New Zealand cannot be understood without first examining the way that sports developed in this country – a small, isolated nation colonized by Great Britain in the 1800s. The forms of sport that became popular, and the sporting opportunities for women, were greatly influenced by this history.[5] The earliest sports to be established in New Zealand were those popular with the middle classes in Britain, such as cricket, tennis, golf, lawn bowls, rowing, polo, rugby and horseracing.[6] Men's rugby, which developed as the dominant sport was, in its earliest days, a generic form of folk football that appeared to be a mixture of soccer (Association Football), Australian Rules (Victorian Rules Football) and rugby (Rugby Football Union). The debate over 'hacking' and the use of hands, which precipitated the formation of two separate sports in Britain, association football and rugby football, also occurred in New Zealand. As a result, rugby began in New Zealand at the Nelson Rugby Club in 1870[7] and soccer, as it is commonly known here, began with the Auckland Association Football Club in 1887.[8]

Men had been playing soccer in Auckland, Wellington, Christchurch and Dunedin for some time before the New Zealand Football Association (later renamed NZS) was established in 1891. Information from those early days, however, indicates that rugby was already becoming established as the most popular winter sport.[9] It lent itself well to the pioneering New Zealand conditions, requiring very little equipment, minimal playing field preparation and suiting a society disproportionately populated by young men in work camps developing the infrastructure for a new nation.[10] The advent of professionalism in football in England is also cited as a reason why rugby so quickly gained the affections of New Zealand colonials. A more plausible explanation, however, might be that New Zealand, a distant colony, more readily attracted ex-pupils from the newer, less prestigious schools which played rugby rather than the older, elite, soccer-playing schools such as Eton.[11] The adoption of rugby as a compulsory part of the curriculum in New Zealand boys' secondary schools in 1905, and the success of the National team's tour of Great Britain, France and North America in the same year, elevated rugby to an importance beyond that of sport itself,[12] and entrenched its reputation as embodying New Zealand masculinity.[13]

Rugby's subsequent association with hegemonic masculinity and national identity has had long-term effects on soccer in New Zealand. Not only did it consign the game to a minority status, but also men who played soccer were collectively labelled 'wimps', 'sissies' and 'girls' on the basis of the belief that to be a man was to be a rugby player. It was not until a New Zealand representative team gained a coveted place in the FIFA World Cup Finals in Spain 1982, following the conflict surrounding rugby which resulted from the 1981 visit to New Zealand of a white South African rugby team,[14] that soccer became better recognized and its ambivalent association with masculinity overcome.

For women's sport to be recognized in New Zealand, therefore, it had to struggle against ideological beliefs that deemed sport to be a highly valued, almost sacred, male terrain on which they were encroaching. As Sandra Coney commented:

> New Zealand has been called 'a man's country' and nowhere has this been more true than in sport. Sporting contest has been a male proving ground, sport a source of national identity and pride. Traditionally, the nation's heroes have won their colours either on the battlefield or the sports field.[15]

Early attempts by women to play rugby and cricket, the sports most popular with New Zealand men and the most symbolic of the Victorian cult of masculinity, were fiercely resisted.[16] For example, a proposal in 1891 for a women's rugby team to tour the country was met with such a 'public roar of outrage' that the idea was quickly scrapped.[17] The sport of netball, however, introduced from Great Britain at the turn of the twentieth century, quickly found favour as an activity for girls and women which did not compromise dominant notions of femininity or appropriate female behaviour. It was promoted as a sport particularly suitable for females because the rules prohibited physical contact, and physical exertion was limited by a small court area, stepping rules and restricted zones of play. Also, because it was played only by girls and women, the sport distanced itself from the dominant men's sports and thus it was allowed to flourish.[18] Its history and popularity have contributed to its status as the most recognized and 'appropriate' sport for New Zealand females.

With this background it is hardly surprising that, when women's soccer was introduced in the 1970s, it did not meet with universal approval. The image of sportswomen, epitomized so strongly in the controlled, clean, non–contact, short-skirted, throwing game of netball, was compromised by the contrasting images of wide-ranging runners and kickers in short shorts and mud, images that were viewed as 'unladylike' and 'unfeminine'. Furthermore, the encroachment of women players into 'male terrain' was seen as an invasion. 'It's no place for a woman' and 'It's a man's game', were common refrains from both inside and outside the sport. Few people, at the time, thought that women might be equally attracted to a sport that had captured the attention of millions of male players, or that they had the right to be active for fun.

Nevertheless, women's soccer has grown. From its earliest days it has been governed by a simple, tiered system common to most sports in New Zealand. At the 'grassroots' level, most women players belong to a soccer club. These clubs, established solely for soccer, are usually governed by a committee of volunteers who undertake to organize and control the sport according to the agreed regulations of their constitution. In the main, these are non-profit making, incorporated societies. The next tier of organization is based around provincial regions, of which the Auckland Women's Football Association (AWFA) is one. All clubs affiliate with and pay a subscription/team levy to participate in the various competitions run by the provincial organizations. In turn, these organizations affiliate to the national body, the NZWFA. Most provincial organizations and the

NZWFA are also affiliated to parallel men's organizations. Secondary schoolgirl soccer players have several options. They can play in a school-based team against other school teams in mid-week competitions; and/or they can play in a community club team or a school team entered into the women's weekend regional competitions. Secondary schools have their own governing systems but they are also registered with their provincial and national organization that is, in turn, affiliated to the NZWFA.

REFLECTIONS ON CHANGE: A DIALOGUE

Scene: Auckland, New Zealand, 2002. In Barbara's study, a large sunny room, the walls of which are hung with many framed photographs of women's soccer teams dated between 1975 and 1998. Barbara and Shona, leaning over a coffee table, are leafing carefully through a thick scrapbook. Its cover is long-gone and its edges are tatty. The pages and newspaper clippings within it have all yellowed with age. The earliest clipping is dated July 1973 and documents the establishment of two women's soccer associations, one in Auckland with ten teams, the other in Wellington with five.[19] It stimulates the following discussion.

Shona: Barbara, you have lived the history of women's soccer in this country. We should incorporate some of your reflections into this study. You can tell us so much about what it was like at the beginning, simply by recalling your experiences. You could describe how it developed, what were the problems, what have been the main changes. And it would make much more interesting reading than trying to report all that in academic-style prose.

Nobody knows New Zealand women's soccer better than you do. Just look at your record! You have played it for 30 years; you hold the record number of appearances for Auckland – 120 caps; you played for New Zealand during the period 1975 to 1987 and captained the team for many years; you were the first woman in New Zealand to get your National Coaching badge, paving the way for other women to follow; you were Soccer Auckland's Coach of the Year in 1991; you have a Level 3 Coaching certificate from Oceania Football Confederation and were the national women's coach for Tahiti in 2000; you were secretary for Auckland Women's Football Association (AWFA) from 1978 to 1992 and served for many years on Soccer Auckland's Board of Control and the NZWFA; you were inducted into the Soccer Hall of Fame in 1995 and a year later awarded an MBE for services to soccer, one of only five ever honoured for soccer in this country and the only woman. What's more, your husband coached both New Zealand and Auckland teams for many years, was instrumental in setting up NZWFA and was its first president. Plus, both your daughters have played premier league soccer and been selected for Auckland and New Zealand teams. On top of all that, women's soccer was the focus for your Masters thesis research. Phew! So, tell us what it was like to be a player in the beginning, in the 1970s?

Barbara: Well, we took it really seriously but we were treated as a bit of a joke. And, oh my God, we played on some terrible grounds. Some barely had the correct markings, or had markings for another sport, which was highly confusing. Some had no facilities. If you needed to go to the toilet you hopped behind a tree or a car and hoped no one could see you. And it was just too bad if the field was a quagmire. We had to get back into our cars filthy dirty because there were no showers at the fields. We got used to changing in the car park or on the sideline and thinking nothing of it. For example, we would have only eleven shirts, the goalkeeper's and ten others, so if we needed to substitute a player she would come off the field, whip off her shirt and give it to the sub to put on. Whip off, whip on. People would laugh and say that's why we got lots of male spectators to our games – because we regularly stripped off our shirts on the sidelines. I remember I took a team to Dallas in the USA in 1989. At one field there were no changing facilities so our players, quite casually, as per normal, got changed on the sideline. Well, the American women were shocked, absolutely horrified. If you think about the furore when Brandy Chastain took her shirt off after the 1999 World Cup final. Now, that was ridiculous. The media made such a big deal of that, but it was simply something we'd been doing regularly, for decades, out of necessity! And of course by then we had sports bras. It's not uncommon now for our players to train in their sports bras, with no shirts, especially in the summer when it's so hot.

Shona: What about the structure and administration. How was it set up? What relationship did you have with men's soccer, which was well established by that time?

Barbara: Well, as I recall, there were three major problems. One was that Sunday had been chosen as the day for women's soccer to be played. This was

12.1. Eden Saints Team, Auckland, New Zealand, prior to departure for a nine day Australasian Tournament in Sydney, Australia, March 1974. The tournament involved six teams – three from Auckland and three from Sydney. (Photograph: Barbara Cox collection)

210

12.2 Three Kings United Team, Auckland, New Zealand, winners of the SWANZ Cup, a National KO tournament, 1998.

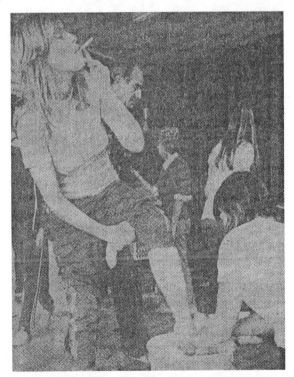

12.3 Elaine Lee receives treatment during an attempt by ten Auckland women's soccer players to break the 63-hour world record for continuous playing set by two English men's teams. (Photograph: Barbara Cox collection)

211

mainly so it wouldn't clash with the men's games played on Saturdays. Most of the coaches of the women's teams were male soccer players. Also it was thought that, while the men played on Saturdays, their wives/girlfriends/families would watch and support and the reverse could then happen on Sundays. But not all the soccer clubs had fields available on Sundays. Sometimes this was because of the condition they were left in after Saturday's play and sometimes because of Regional Council by-laws which prevented Sunday use of playing fields, a hangover from early Puritanical influences in this country whereby Sundays were designated for church-going – certainly not for playing sport. For many years our games were often played on school grounds, and some teams could go a whole season without one home game.

The second problem was a lack of referees. Initially the Auckland Referee's Association wouldn't officially appoint referees to women's games. Ostensibly this was because the AWFA wasn't affiliated to the Auckland Football Association (later known as Soccer Auckland), but even after this affiliation happened in 1974 it was a further two years before a Referee's Appointee was designated for women's soccer.

The Referee's Associations were definitely chauvinistic in those early years. I'm sure they just wished we would go away! And they were so illogical at times. I remember when we went to our first international tournament, the Asian Cup in Hong Kong. We wanted to take a referee with us and chose one who had refereed for us, voluntarily, week in and week out, all season. But, oh no, according to the Referee's Association he was not acceptable. We would have to take someone from the 'highest level', no matter that this person had never ever refereed a women's game. In the end we took no one. In spite of urgings from the AWFA and refereeing courses being available, few women have taken up refereeing and women's soccer is still adjudicated mainly by male referees. However, FIFA's insistence that the Women's World Cup be officiated solely by female referees has had a significant impact and more effort is now being made to attract and develop women referees in New Zealand.

The third problem was a general lack of acceptance of women's soccer in clubs and the New Zealand school system. When my daughters went to their high school Principal in the early 1980s, to ask if they could enter a soccer team in the regional schoolgirls competition, they were refused permission and told, 'It is not the sort of sport we want our girls to play!' Again, there were not enough coaches, not enough facilities and, if you were in a co-ed school, it was very likely your playing strip were 'hand-me-downs' from the boys' first X1. However, there have been huge changes in secondary schoolgirls' soccer recently. Today, in Auckland, there are over 200 girls' teams playing after school on Wednesdays, in regular league and KO competitions spread over five geographically-based areas. Each year, 28 teams from all over the country come together to compete in a week-long tournament for the national title and a NZ Secondary Schoolgirls team is selected. Also, during the same week, a further 62 teams compete in three regionally based tournaments. This is really significant for the future of women's soccer, given that those tournaments represent a huge amount of support from the schools. Some schools are paying to get good coaches, and approaching Councils and clubs for permission to use their fields.

But it was common-place for women to be treated as 'second-class' citizens in the club scene in the early days, exemplified by this quote from the history of Metro Football Club.[20] The women were told, 'You can't train on [that field]. The first team (that is, the men) are playing on it on Saturday.' In another instance, a group of women who wanted to play in the first year of competition in the Auckland region were given permission by the management committee to enter as Mt Wellington AFC but, 'as long as it wasn't going to be at a cost to the club'.[21] Today the clubs are much better about women's soccer but there still exists the feeling, and it's very strong, that the first men's team is *the* team, even when the first women's team is more successful in terms of winning major trophies or producing national representative players.

Shona: Did women 'do their own thing'? Was women's soccer ever run separately from the men's?

Barbara: No. It was generally accepted that we needed men's assistance for the development of the game. Most women players joined their local men's clubs but, in the Auckland region for example, the control and administration of women's soccer was vested in the AWFA and its decisions were binding on the clubs. The inaugural Executive Committee of this association consisted of four women and two men, and this gender ratio continued, more or less, throughout its entire history. By 1980 the AWFA, as a sub-association of the Auckland Football Association (AFA) had accrued sufficient credibility to gain representation and a vote on the Board of Control. This was the first time in New Zealand that women's soccer had a voice at this level of administration. There has been regression since. In Auckland I don't think we have anywhere near the same voice or control of our sport as we did in the 1970s and 1980s, but we're going to talk about that later in the study.

Shona: How were the women involved within the clubs? From my research in tennis, I've seen how much work they did to keep the club going; work that usually benefited the men more than the women and was often at the expense of their time playing the sport.

Barbara: Yes, well we did too! We helped out. There's an apt quote here from the history of Mt Wellington AFC, 'the girls were more than willing to help out where necessary round the club, such as gate duty, bar duty, waitressing on "Ankletappers and Dribblers" night and painting the changing rooms. We painted them pink one year – the boys never liked that colour!'[22] It was the same in my club. We did fundraising; we organized the social functions, but we didn't see it as exploitative, as serving the men, because it was *our* club. It was our fun too. Best of all was organizing discos for the visiting overseas teams, men's mainly. Look, the soccer club was our social centre. It's not like that now. Young players today hardly ever go to the clubrooms, maybe out of obligation on a Sunday after a game, for speeches and some food, but very few of them would use it as the base for their social lives. They have other alternatives now, like bars and nightclubs. But we went to the club, always. We'd have a dance in the clubrooms every month. Everyone went; you wouldn't miss it. I remember, often, getting home at 5 a.m. after partying all night and being up four hours later to play a game, and thinking nothing of it. Everyone did it.

Those who approved of women's soccer saw it as a way of encouraging heterosexual partnerships. Many women did, in fact, meet their husbands through soccer. It was considered a healthy, and safe, way of encouraging men and women to meet and develop relationships, although probably the thought was never publicly articulated at the time.

Shona: Why did you stress 'safe'?

Barbara: Well, people looked out for each other. For example, as my children got older they would use the soccer 'grapevine' to find out about guys they, or their friends, might be going out with; to find out if they were decent people. It was a network. It's sad, in some ways, that this social aspect, the mixing amongst the clubs, has all but disappeared. But I heard just recently that one club, which runs 7-a-side tournaments during the off-season, has noticed social relationships developing between young male and female players because the teams are mixed. I think that's great.

Shona: Do you think the game itself is now taken more seriously?

Barbara: Oh, definitely! As it became more institutionalized I noticed the fun aspect seemed to disappear. Maybe not so much in the lower grades but definitely in the Premier League. When National Tournament began in 1976, it provided more competition at a higher level and meant there was a bridge between club, provincial and national level competition. As long as you played well at that tournament you would more than likely get selected for the National team, because that was the major identification process for national team players. But now it's necessary to play consistently well all season. You notice this in the way people behave before games. Partying is no longer that acceptable, and there is much less alcohol drunk. The players mostly disapprove of drinking, especially if someone has a bad game and it's discovered she'd been drinking the night before. You're seen as not being serious enough about your sport if you drink and 'bloody selfish', letting the team down like that. At the inaugural Women's National Federation League dinner held recently for the winning team, none of the players drank any alcohol. Now that's definitely changed behaviour from a decade or two ago!

And smoking! Nowadays smoking is a huge no-no. Women players who smoke will go away and hide so that no one knows about it. The national coach will lecture them against it. But look at this photo, 1975 (referring back to the scrapbook). Isn't this a shocker? It's wonderful. We were doing a fundraising marathon, trying to break the world men's indoor soccer record of 64 hours of continuous play. We were sponsored. Look at the caption, 'A smoke and a bucket of ice help ease the aches and pains of more than 24 hours of soccer for Elaine Lee in the YMCA stadium today.'[23] Well you certainly wouldn't see a photo like that anymore. But I remember, of that first New Zealand representative team who travelled to Hong Kong in 1975, about a third were smokers.

Shona: Tell me more about the fundraising.

Barbara: We did incredible things. We'd do marathons, wash cars, anything, but the worst was when we had to raise money to get to Hong Kong for the Asian Cup. We went into pubs with a bucket and asked, 'Could you please give us some money for women's soccer?' And these drunken men would say, 'Yeah, sure Love, if you'll give us a kiss first.' So you'd have to kiss these awful men just to get, say, 20 cents. And we trudged up and down streets doing the same thing. We'd get our bums pinched, we'd be made fun of, we'd put up with all sorts of abuse just to get the money to play for our country. It wasn't just at National level. Jackie Davies, a founding club member of women's soccer once pointed out that initially the women forked out for all their own kit and trophies, etcetera.[24] You had to accept that fundraising was part and parcel of being a female soccer player. Invariably, if you wanted anything more than the regulation two or three balls per team and a playing strip, you had to fundraise. It wasn't worth the hassle of going to the club committee to ask for support.

You know, the inequalities that were there in the early days haven't really gone away. Sure, the women now get better gear, the top team has bags, track suits and playing strip provided, but they don't always get their team subscription fees paid for by the club, as the top men do. And the coach of the women's team still doesn't get paid as much as the men's. Maybe, if they're lucky, they'll get an honorarium of $1,000 while the men's coach might get between $5–8,000 plus bonuses.

Shona: Let's go back to your scrapbook. These articles and photographs are all from newspapers, magazines and match programmes from the 1970s. Looking through them now, what strikes you most about them?

Barbara: Three things mainly. One is the way the photographs are all very posed. The women are not shown actually playing the game. Even this one here, of three players going to head the ball, the action is obviously contrived. They look awkward and there's lots of hair flying about. It seems important to show them as women first, soccer players second, and not very competent ones at that. It's obvious that women playing soccer were still a huge novelty to the journalists at that time, and they're certainly not out there capturing the real action on the field.

Next, what strikes me, is how many articles stressed beauty, describing players with words such as 'lovely', 'pretty', 'gorgeous', 'glamorous', 'shapely', 'graceful' and 'poised'. Several feature a player with the main point being to report that she won various beauty contests, including runner-up in the Miss New Zealand contest.[25] There is a sense of surprise and contradiction. Take, for example, this report,

Why does a beautiful girl play a knicker-ripping, pantyhose-laddering, hairstyle flattening game like soccer? What does hubby or the boyfriend think? Despite the glamour shattering misgivings of the game, over 200 active beauties have taken to the field this season.[26]

And thirdly, there is an insistence that all the players are married, or at least coupled. Partly because that helped explain how women became involved in the sport in the first place, such as here where Jan Innes, the first secretary of AWFA, is quoted explaining why women want to play soccer, 'because the girls want to share a common interest with their husbands, boyfriends and children'.[27] Family relationships within soccer were often highlighted, like this, for example, 'Margaret Hodge, secretary of the East Coast Bays club and wife of its chairman, did a good job in goal for Bays and was given a hint by the referee at half-time that she could hold the ball longer while looking for an opening.'[28] Or this example, 'The slim, attractive, mother of two ... could be a model.'[29]

When I think about it, there were a few players back then who were married and with children, but we were definitely in the minority. And we were made to feel like bad mothers for playing sport. When I first started playing soccer, my daughters were aged five and two and I often took them to training with me. They loved it, particularly when the field was muddy, which it usually was in the winter. They would play behind the goal, sometimes with no clothes on because, they said, that was 'to save Mummy from having to wash our dirty clothes!' But there were several club members who thought my mothering skills very inadequate, or that I shouldn't have been there with my children in the first place. It seems that the point being made in these press articles is that, despite playing soccer, we were still good, feminine women doing the 'right' things – having boyfriends, getting married, raising happy, healthy families. In press reports about sportswomen today there is usually no mention of marriage, unless she is married to a notable sportsman.

Another very obvious thing I notice in these photos is the hair, which is really interesting because soccer players' hair was an issue which came up in my research, as being something the players understood as a strategic signifier of femininity.[30] In the photos in this scrapbook, all the players have long hair reaching well below shoulder length, cascading halfway down their backs. Now this was the fashion in the 1970s, and very few would tie it back, even to play. Some would put it in two pigtails, which was fashionable, but many just let it flow. So, can you imagine, 'here comes the ball, hair across my eyes, hand up to push it away, woops, missed it, it's gone!' It would have been impossible to head the ball with the wind blowing hair all over your face. But that's how we wore it at the time, all females had long flowing hair in the 1970s and soccer players wouldn't have been prepared to cut their hair. Later, as fashion became more flexible, short hair was OK. Also, players took their game more seriously and paid more attention to their performance so their hairstyles had to be more practical. But there's no question in my mind that, as women have become better and more highly trained players, their bodies have come to resemble more androgynous, boyish-like figures, making it difficult to differentiate them from males. Hair, long hair, is the way they do it, which is why, I think, it's come back into fashion amongst soccer players. The unisex action figure with a soccer ball and a ponytail was the logo for the Women's World Cup in USA in 1999. Its use continues for China 2003, albeit in a different way, so I think you could say the ubiquitous ponytail is here to stay as a symbol for female soccer.

Shona: The players in your research talked about hair. Perhaps this would be a good opportunity to move on to your research findings.

EMBODYING SOCCER: SOME RESEARCH RESULTS

In 1997, Barbara Cox undertook research involving a team of women, elite soccer players in Auckland, New Zealand, to help understand something about the corporeal experiences of being a soccer player and what these meant in terms of how the players constituted themselves as sportswomen.[31] The research involved participant observations and in-depth interviews with 16 members of a club team competing in Auckland's premier soccer league. Fifteen of these women had competed at either international or provincial levels. They ranged in age from 18 to 33. Most had completed tertiary education and all were in full-time employment. Two were married; six others lived in *de facto* relationships of which three were with men and three with women. None had children. Five players identified themselves as Danish, Dutch, Norwegian or Chinese nationals. The remaining eleven were New Zealanders, two of whom were of Maori descent. This heterogeneity reflects the more cosmopolitan make-up of Auckland as the largest of New Zealand cities, rather than being representative of soccer teams throughout the country.

The ways in which the football players spoke of their involvement in the sport suggested that there were several identifiably distinct, yet highly interconnected bodily experiences associated with being a female football player.[32] These were shaped by discourses of sport, gender and heterosexuality, and required the interviewed football players to continually negotiate ways of constituting themselves as sports players and as women. Whilst the multiplicity of discourses allowed room for liberating experiences, challenging, for example, restrictive forms of femininity, there was also conflict, particularly through the extent to which homophobia is associated with women's experiences of football.[33]

The players had all played football for a long time. It had become part of their lives and any possibly contradiction associated with being women and playing a traditionally masculine game seldom occurred to them. They saw it as a 'natural' feature of who they were as women, along with other aspects of being feminine. In this aspect, the players closely align themselves with Judith Butler's view of gender as a 'set of repeated performances that congeal over time to produce the appearance of a natural sort of being'.[34] However, their eagerness to adopt some conventional feminine traits, their awareness of the conventions surrounding netball, and detailed consciousness of muscularity suggest there are still lingering levels of conflict between football and femininity.

Netball's popularity as a sport for women has impacted on women's soccer in various ways, the early acquisition of specific skills being one of them. As one male football coach commented in 1974,

> You see a 5 year-old boy on the beach playing with a ball and what is he doing? He's kicking it. You see a 5 year-old girl and she's throwing it. Most women can't kick a ball accurately 20 yards as a result, whereas most men can.[35]

As a marker of appropriate female behaviour, it also defines perceptions of what sporting women should look like. As one woman footballer explained,

> People are a little surprised when I say I'm playing soccer and I think it's just because a lot of people have got that sort of stereotype in their mind of what soccer players look like because there are some tomboy-looking people. You never get the funny reaction when you say, as a girl, I'm playing netball. I mean, netball is already seen as a more feminine sport. (Clarissa)

Another described her resentment when discussing how lightly men dismissed the fact she played soccer at an elite level. She said,

> If we were playing netball – those guys have got a high opinion of netball for some reason. That's about the only sport in New Zealand, apart from the individual ones like swimming, that has any standing, I reckon, in men's eyes. (Fiona)

Netball is the only women's sport in New Zealand that commands regular media coverage, particularly television. Consequently, members of the 'Silver Ferns', the national netball team, have become household names and are often thought of as the 'complementary partners' of the All Blacks, the national male rugby players. In a society organized around the 'normative' principles of heterosexuality, qualities of femininity and masculinity are usually defined in dichotomous terms. Netball symbolizes some of these differences in a sporting context, for example, being played in skirts rather than shorts, throwing rather than kicking, being non-contact versus contact play, and being spatially regulated rather than a 'free-for all'. Neither, as noted earlier, does netball trespass on male terrain, being a sport almost exclusively played by females. Hence, in a gender-structured society such as New Zealand, females who choose not to play netball feel the pressure of having digressed from the gendered norm.

Defining the female body as different from the male body in terms of physical strength is another normative principle of heterosexuality that evoked conflict amongst the interviewed players. Physical strength is most commonly linked with masculine power and muscularity, which frequently operates as a means of coding the 'naturalness' of bodily difference between men and women.[36] Within sport, physical muscularity is most commonly linked to power and muscularity of the male body, which in turn becomes a signifier of masculinity.[37] Thus, the 'weaker' female body may have muscles as long as they are sleek and firm, whilst the 'stronger' male body may have muscles that are highly visible, big and powerful.[38]

Another conflict confronted by the interviewed players related to their physicality and the embodiment of power and strength expressed in soccer. It hinged on concerns about the degrees to which female muscularity could be developed. In the players' eyes, it was not the muscularity *per se* that defined masculinity but the degree of muscularity. Thus, there was a fine line between developing muscularity and it impinging on perceptions of femininity. This understanding was clearly reflected by one woman's comments, talking about her friends at the school gym,

> They only go there to tone themselves. They don't go there to put on muscle because they think putting on muscle is masculine, 'cause if you're all muscley, well, that's gross, that's not nice. (Melissa)

Most of the interviewed players talked about having muscles in terms of being 'toned', 'cut' or 'defined so that when someone's running, you can see the muscles moving in their legs' (Kirsty). These attributes were greatly admired. Some thought femininity was an outdated concept ('Do we really need it in the 1990s?' remarked Holly), and were unconcerned about well-developed muscles, as long as they were not excessively bulky or big. In other words, it was acceptable to have obvious musculature, or muscles that 'stuck out' as long as the overall body appearance was slender and obviously 'feminine', such as 'having breasts, clearly defined hips and waists' (Clarissa). Bulkiness, therefore, was defined as a masculine trait and to be avoided. Players accepted that it was normal to have bigger legs because 'we rely so much on our legs. It's inevitable, really, to get bigger muscles in those areas' (Nicky), but one, for example, expressed anxiety about her thigh muscles when she was away from the soccer environment:

> I find sometimes that I'm a bit insecure when I'm wearing dresses, especially the short ones, 'cause my quads do bulge out quite a bit. Although to other girls that I've asked, they find that it looks better than just being a stick, but to me, oh God, I wish I wasn't so developed in that area. (Marilyn)

Most of the players delighted in their developed muscularity because they associated it with physical strength, which they highly valued. This was seen as not only useful for improving their performance on the soccer field, but they also saw benefits in a wider context. Donna felt that the strength she developed through soccer would help her to secure a position in the nursing profession because, as she said, 'nursing is a physically demanding job'. Fiona found the apparent contradiction of being strong but small in stature highly satisfying, particularly when playing sport against men. She said,

> When you're playing mixed Touch with guys who don't necessarily know
> that you're a New Zealand soccer player, and guys run into you and then,
> they fall over. They just get up and, like, look at you, and that makes me
> laugh … Because I'm not very big, they think oh, you know, whatever. But
> I'm so strong compared to them.

Nicky also commented on the way her strength challenged perceptions of
female physicality, defying the notion that only boys come to experience their
bodies as a physical presence that speaks of latent power.[39] She commented,

> I think of myself as stocky and strong whereas a lot of people see me as very
> small and petite, so when I pick up boxes at work, anything like that, and
> people go, 'Are you alright?' and it's, like, why can't they see me as strong?

Some players expressed this sense of empowerment in terms of confidence
when speaking in public or taking on leadership roles in group situations. Others
felt their strength and body size allowed them more freedoms, and that they were
less likely to be 'victimized' by men. For Rowena, this was expressed in terms of
safety:

> Actually, 'cause of my size and everything, I think I feel a bit safer about
> walking around certain areas than, say, probably someone who's a bit
> smaller and a bit more fragile than the sort of build that I am. You feel more
> confident having to walk somewhere knowing that it was dark.

Despite the obviously advantageous outcomes for women who develop
strengths through playing sport, women's soccer players in New Zealand have
always needed to deal with negative responses to their play, especially if they are
committed to high levels of training and playing in elite competition. The
development of a strong, capable, female body through participation in sport
challenges perceptions of femininity and problematizes the essentialist view that
physical attributes such as strength and power are inherently masculine.[40] This
association of sporting attributes as masculine has traditionally been an inhibitory
factor, keeping females from participating in sports that lie outside the narrow
realm of those considered appropriate for them. In contrast, these interviewed
players have learnt to develop their physical capabilities since early childhood.
They all have confidence that their bodies can run, jump and execute skilful
movements, confidence that has carried over to other aspects of their lives.
Nevertheless, they have been aware of the challenges and contradictions this
poses, and of their need to balance these by 'doing gender' in other ways.

The soccer players in New Zealand appeared to have no major concerns about
'doing gender' in terms of being more conventionally feminine. Clarissa summed
up the team's attitude, saying,

I really don't feel that, with playing soccer, I need to do things to feel more feminine. I don't even really think about it that way. I think, even in our team, when you look at them, no one goes out of their way to put make-up on or anything like that. I would've thought that would've been something that people would do if there was concern about being feminine. That would be one of the first things you would do.

The expectation to appear feminine is felt most when the players' sporting lives intersect with commercial and media interests. For example, when Fiona received personal sponsorship from an international sporting goods manufacturer, she explained how she had deliberately chosen to wear a skirt to her first meeting with representatives from the company, on the understanding that a skirt would make her look more feminine than would wearing trousers. Recent examples from another team sport in New Zealand, field hockey, has highlighted the extent to which individual women players, whose appearances fit popular conventions of femininity, beauty and heterosexual appeal, are singled out for media profiling and commercial marketing of the sport.[41] An increasingly strong mix of media and corporate interests has recently developed around women's sport in New Zealand and some sport associations are paying particular attention to the 'image' of their national women's team.[42] Women's soccer, however, has so far escaped this pressure. Being a minority sport in New Zealand, it attracts exceedingly little media coverage or sponsorship, meaning that players have, to date, felt less constrained by or obligated to present images of heterosexualized female attractiveness. If this sport were to gain a higher profile it is quite possible that the players would experience closer public scrutiny of their appearance and behaviour and, with it, greater expectations to 'do gender' by enhancing perceptions of femininity. Notions of acceptable femininity, however, are changing to include more physically active definitions.

Barbara Recollects:
Today is September 27th, 1997. The finals of the Chatham Cup and the SWANZ Cup are being held in Napier. These cups are presented to the winners of the national soccer knock-out competitions for men and women respectively.

The whistle goes – the game ends. The coach and I (the team manager) jump up from the bench with absolute delight and run onto the field to hug our players, who have just won the SWANZ Cup, 7-5. The television camera waits for the coach's and captain's after-match comments. The team climb the stairs to collect their medals. And then the celebrations begin – the press photographs, the hugs from team-mates and family, flowers and the spraying of champagne. All this happens in front of the main spectator stand. The players break off to run to the opposite side of the field to applaud our Club supporters, nearly all males, who have driven from Auckland through the night to cheer us on to victory. Not for these players, the hiding from the crowd, the quick, embarrassed exit into the *dressing rooms. With faces reddened by effort, sweating bodies, hair in disarray, there seems to be no conflict today between being a woman and an athlete as they demonstrate to the crowd their pride and delight in their achievement. Their effort, commitment and determination throughout the season has been rewarded. This is so very different from my experience 16 years ago. Yet, in spite of these many changes, changes that could be termed beneficial and progressive, the inequalities are still very apparent. Prize money of $8,000 for the men, nothing for the women, Olympic style medals for the men, small metal pins for the women. The match tickets carry information only of the men's game, even though the day is sponsored by money from 'Smokefree', a governmental organization funded by New Zealand taxpayers.*

CONCLUSION: CHANGES STILL TO COME

By the late 1990s, radical changes had happened to the administration and structure of soccer in New Zealand. The AWFA had merged with its male counterpart to become one body, Soccer Auckland. There has been a huge growth in players of women's soccer but the numbers of volunteers necessary to run the organizations has fallen. The control and running of women's soccer was vested in a Women's Management Committee within Soccer Auckland, which, with its full time staff, did all the necessary routine administrative duties. This was a very happy arrangement.

In 1997, New Zealand Soccer (NZS) introduced a rule that placed all women's soccer under its control, with the operational authority to be vested in a Women's Committee. However, NZWFA (now known as Women's Soccer Association of New Zealand – WSANZ) continued to function very much as before, remaining a separate and largely autonomous body, but no longer with control of its international functions. By the end of 1999, affiliated soccer players voted in favour of a federation system instead of provincial organizations. Soccer was to be divided into seven designated areas, based on geographical and numerical strength to ensure no one federation was disadvantaged by having less numbers or area than another. WSANZ was also to be disbanded which meant that, by the end of 2001, the control and operation of women's soccer had been taken over entirely by NZS.

While the future of women's soccer in New Zealand is unknown, it will continue to remain a paradox. In this country, and commonly worldwide, it is controlled and defined by male dominated organizations. Yet it is increasingly apparent that the men in whom the power is vested are reluctant or strongly averse to bringing about the changes necessary to realize the full potential of the women's game. At the same time there are a large number of women, and some men, who strongly desire to promote and develop the game but are powerless to do so because they have no voice at the highest levels where key decisions are made. Meanwhile, in New Zealand, as in other parts of the world, the number of girls and women playing the game is exploding. We are yet to see what this will mean to the sport.

NOTES

1. Hillary Commission for Sport, Fitness and Leisure, 'Sportfacts', http://www.hillarysport.org.nz/sportfacts/members/shtml (accessed 4 Aug. 2001).
2. 'Soccer Girls Land Big-game Prelude', *The Auckland Star*, 8 Sept. 1973, p.10.
3. Roy Cox and Jeremy Ruane, *Coxy: Coach or Clown?* (Auckland: Privately published, 1997).
4. Barbara Cox, 'Multiple Bodies: Sportswomen, Soccer and Sexuality' (Unpublished M.A. Thesis, University of Auckland, 1998).
5. Shona Thompson, 'Women and Sport in New Zealand', in I. Hartmann-Tews and G. Pfister (eds), *Sport and Women: Social Issues in International Perspective* (London: Routledge, 2002), pp.252–65.
6. Bob Stothart, 'The Development of Sport Administration in New Zealand: From Kitchen Table to Computer', in C. Collins (ed.), *Sport in New Zealand Society* (Palmerston North: Dunmore Press, 2000), p.87.
7. Ron Palenski, *Our National Game* (Auckland: Moa Beckett, 1992).
8. Terry Maddaford, *The First 100 Years: The Official Centenary History of the Auckland Football 1887–1987* (Auckland: Auckland Football Association, 1987), p.8.
9. Tony Hilton, *An Association with Soccer: The NZFA Celebrates its First 100 years* (Auckland: New Zealand Football Association, 1991).
10. Jock Phillips, *A Man's Country?* (Auckland: Penguin Books, 1987).
11. Ibid.
12. Scott A.G.M. Crawford, '"One's Nerves and Courage are in Very Different Order out in New Zealand": Recreational and Sporting Opportunities for Women in a Remote Colonial Setting', in J.A. Mangan and R.J. Park (eds), *From 'Fair Sex' to Feminism* (London: Frank Cass, 1987), p.161.
13. Phillips, *A Man's Country?*
14. Trevor Richards, *Dancing on our Bones* (Wellington: Reed, 2001); Shona Thompson, 'Challenging the Hegemony: New Zealand Women's Opposition to Rugby and the Reproduction of a Capitalist Patriarchy', *International Review for the Sociology of Sport*, 23, 3 (1988), 205–12.
15. Sandra Coney, *Standing in the Sunshine. A History of New Zealand Women since they Won the Vote* (Auckland: Penguin Books, 1993), p.238.
16. Ibid.
17. Crawford, '"One's Nerves and Courage are in Very Different Order out in New Zealand": Recreational and Sporting Opportunities for Women in a Remote Colonial Setting', p.169.
18. Coney, *Standing in the Sunshine.*
19. Dorothy Simons, 'Soccer's Definitely not a Joke for the Girls', *8 O'Clock*, 7 July 1973, p.39.
20. Jeremy Ruane, *Metro: A Century in Soccer* (Auckland: Metro AFC, 1999), p.43.
21. Jeremy Ruane, *'C'mon The Mount': The Fifty Year History of Mt Wellington AFC* (Auckland: Mt Wellington AFC, 2002), p.25.
22. Ibid., p.26.
23. *Star Weekender*, Saturday 31 May 1975, p.20.
24. Ruane, *'C'mon The Mount': The Fifty Year History of Mt Wellington AFC*, p.25.
25. 'Soccer Star', *New Zealand Herald*, 26 July 1976, p.1.
26. 'Our Soccer gets a (shapely) Leg up', *Sunday News*, 28 September 1973, p.5.
27. Simons, 'Soccer's Definitely not a Joke for the Girls', p.39.
28. Ibid.
29. 'Taking to the Field,' *Central Leader*, 22 August 1975, p.5.
30. Cox, 'Multiple Bodies: Sportswomen, Soccer and Sexuality'.
31. Ibid.
32. Barbara Cox and Shona Thompson, 'Multiple Bodies: Sportswomen, Soccer and Sexuality', *International Review for the Sociology of Sport*, 35, 1 (2000), 5–20.
33. Barbara Cox and Shona Thompson, 'Facing the Bogey: Women, Football and Sexuality', *Football Studies*, 4, 2 (2001), 7–24.
34. Judith Butler, *Gender Trouble: Feminism and the Subversion of Identity* (New York: Routledge, 1990), p.140.

35. Coach Gary Jenkins, quoted in an article by Ann Lloyd titled, 'Kickers in knickers', *Sports Digest*, 10 September 1974, 18–19.
36. Susan Bordo, *Unbearable Weight* (California: University of California Press, 1993).
37. Lisa McDermott, 'Toward a Feminist Understanding of Physicality Within the Context of Women's Physically Active and Sporting Lives', *Sociology of Sport Journal*, 13, 1 (1996), 12–30.
38. Pirkko Markula, 'Firm but Shapely, Fit but Sexy, Strong but Thin: The Postmodern Aerobicizing Female Bodies', *Sociology of Sport Journal*, 12, 1(1995), 424–53.
39. Robert W. Connell, *Gender and Power* (Cambridge: Polity Press, 1987).
40. Mariah Burton Nelson, *The Stronger Women Get, The More Men Love Football* (New York: Harcourt Brace, 1994).
41. Jan Corbett, 'Hot property', *Weekend Herald*, 20–21 Jan. 2001, p.14.
42. Thompson, 'Women and Sport in New Zealand', pp.252–65.

13

Football Feminine –
Development of the African Game:
Senegal, Nigeria and South Africa

MARTHA SAAVEDRA

In December 2002, a fortnight after deadly riots led organizers of the Miss World Beauty pageant to move the contestants and venue from Abuja, Nigeria to London, England, the Third Women's African Cup of Nations began in the same country without engendering a similar response. This may not be surprising given that Nigeria is a vast and complicated place where many seemingly contradictory things can take place. Nonetheless, in addition to the contemporaneity of both events, they also share what has been a contentious and complicated issue across time and place (and not just in Africa) – that is a public performance by women involving a display of their bodies and physical talents. With regard to football, the immense popularity and weighty social meaning of the men's game in Africa, has made it that much harder for a women's game to develop. Even where other sports for women, such as netball, handball, athletics and basketball, have flourished, women's football has been met with scepticism, neglect and sometimes outright hostility. Yet, women's football has nonetheless emerged. Though the trajectories vary tremendously from one country to another, the current African Women's Championship in Nigeria attests to the growth of women's football across the continent.

By tracing the development of women's football in three African countries, Senegal, Nigeria and South Africa with reference to other African experiences, this study begins to explore the major issues facing the development of African women's football. Wide variation across the continent as well as comparison to women's football elsewhere in the world provide a rich comparative basis for examining the complexity of local, national, regional and global factors that impede and promote the development of the game. Special attention will be given to interactions with supranational and global actors such as the Fédération Internationale de Football Association (FIFA), the Confédération Africaine de Football (CAF), and various sponsoring agencies and corporations, as well as the impact of the increased visibility and marketing of the Women's World Cup. This study will only begin to suggest the many avenues for research, policy and advocacy; in the future in such a volume as this, rather than one study on Africa, there would be several.

225

I will begin with a quick review of the evidence and methodology employed. This is important, as there is so little available in wide circulation on the topic. This is followed by an exploration of questions, assumptions and contexts which must be invoked in order to situate this discussion within larger debates on gender, popular culture, power and political economy in African settings. I then address the specifics of the three cases. In addition to providing some general historical and sociocultural context, I also situate the women's game *vis-à-vis* the football establishment whose priority is the men's game. The study concludes with a comparative analysis of the major achievements, challenges and opportunities for women's football in Africa.

EVIDENCE AND METHODOLOGY

The first thing evident about women's football in Africa is its absence in research and documentary materials. Not many scholarly pieces have been written on women's sport in Africa,[1] and much of what has been done is not in wide circulation. Indeed, scholarly studies addressing African football in general are only now beginning to appear and they inevitably address the men's game or the politics of CAF and national federations, which up until now have been mainly concerned with the men's game.[2] The qualifier 'in wide circulation' is important since, based on my experience in Senegal, I assume that scholars, administrators and activists throughout Africa have written relevant research studies and reports addressing women's involvement in sport, including football. Yet, these tend to remain on shelves and in drawers in libraries, offices and archives or are only locally distributed. Advocacy organizations such as the African Women in Sport Association (AWISA), based in Namibia and formed after the 1998 Windhoek meeting of the Second World Conference on women and sport, will presumably have relevant material. However, because of communication and finance problems, AWISA is mainly active in Southern Africa (Zone 6 among 7 of the Supreme Council of Sport in Africa – SCSA).[3] What sort of documentary and analytical material they may collect or produce is unknown. Efforts to promote the game in Africa should include efforts to seek out and incorporate such work and those who are engaged in it.

Primary documentary material from organizations is scarce and ephemeral. When it does exist, visits to offices and archives are necessary, although documents still may be sparse or unavailable. Even the archivist at CAF reports that the organization does not have significant material on women's football, despite the fact that CAF does have a Women's Committee. For instance, CAF did not produce technical reports for the last two African Women Championship tournaments.[4] If a researcher is lucky, sympathetic individuals may provide personal copies of documents. Increasingly, the web is becoming a great source of material. For instance, significant information about women's football in South Africa can in fact be found at the South African Football Association's database-

226

driven Website.[5] Yet, the Web is also ephemeral. Organizational restructuring, lapses in domain maintenance, lack of server space and personnel changes can all lead to expired links. Furthermore, policy and design decisions can change the availability of internal reports or other analytical documents.[6] For the researcher seeking organizational documents, the Web is both tantalising and frustrating.

The Internet offers more extensive access to another important source – journalistic accounts. Newspapers and magazines have long been important sources of information. Yet, few places within or beyond Africa maintain large collections of African news sources.[7] News sources with a global reach and deep pockets such as the BBC have developed Web interfaces that allow unprecedented access to reports on all aspects of football, including the women's game in Africa. Other ventures such as AllAfrica.com, the largest electronic distributor of African news and information worldwide, aggregates, produces and distributes news from across Africa. With a searchable archive dating back to 1997, it provides unprecedented access to African journalistic accounts. Football and women are two of about 25 special topics highlighted. While a systematic study of media coverage and African women's football is begging to be done, it is clear that coverage and accessibility has increased. African women's football is not invisible. Furthermore, the content is not nearly as often marked by surprise or ridicule as in the past, but more often shows respect and furnishes a straightforward account of events. Still, the men's (and boys') game in all its glory and infamy receives dramatically more attention. Women's competitions receive irregular coverage, often with only the bigger tournaments attracting comment. The technology of the Internet also reveals just how far the journalistic endeavour will go. While the BBC broadcast live over the Web the men's 2002 African Cup of Nations, no such effort was made for the December 2002 Women's Championship.

This study is based on a combination of sources. There is my own experience as a soccer player and coach, and as an educator and scholar. I played soccer as a youth, in college and in a women's soccer league in the Bay Area. I now coach my son's under-10 boys' team. I am a veteran of Title IX battles over varsity status for my college team in the early 1980s. With a doctoral degree in political science and a focus on agrarian politics and ethnic conflict, I began to teach on women and sport in 1993. In 1997 I decided to follow my passion and take up the topic as my next research project.

The section on Senegal derives mostly from two months of fieldwork in 1998–99. My purpose on that trip was to explore the general situation for women and sport in the country.[8] During that time I conducted interviews with players, coaches, advocates, administrators, government officials and scholars involved in various aspects of women's sport. I also spent much time at the Institut National Supérieur de l'Education Populaire et du Sport (INSEPS) reading remarkable and broad ranging student theses. I collected an assortment of documents and newspaper articles, and attended many basketball games and practices as well as

227

track meets and handball tournaments. Alas, the short women's football season was months away, and was only announced as I left the country. While I did meet players, coaches, referees, advocates and officials, I did not witness girls or women playing football.

The rest of the material has been culled from newspapers, newsletters, magazines, Web pages, Internet chat sites and secondary sources. Without actual fieldwork in Nigeria and South Africa, I will doubtless miss obvious factors, misconstrue the facts and generally only provide the most schematic understanding. More fieldwork in all three locations and beyond is required. This study attempts to pull together what evidence is available, fill in some of the research gaps, and suggest where further research might be done. The prospects for women's football in Africa are exciting given the enthusiasm of the young women and others involved, and deserving of scholarly and institutional recognition.

GENERAL QUESTIONS, ASSUMPTIONS AND CONTEXTS

The incredible diversity along multiple dimensions within Africa is the first point to be made. Generalizing is fraught with misrepresentation. With over 53 countries and a range of geography, climates, resources, languages, cultures, and histories, an African 'story' cannot simply be told. Instead, general questions can be posed with only very specific, spatially situated and historicized answers suggested. This study examines the experience of women's football in three countries, two in West Africa and one in Southern Africa. Even within these countries, experiences vary. Hence, any conclusions will beg further, more localized research.

Another concern is the goal of this assessment. Is it to judge the 'success' of women's football, and if so on what basis? Is it the appearance of a national team at a FIFA-sanctioned international competition? Is it the development of a professional league? A regular export of players to leagues in Europe or the United States? Or is it the development of opportunities to play at multiple levels that might include elite and international level, but also considering recreational and competitive opportunities for women of different ages, different skill levels, different income levels, and different locations (for example, rural, urban)? Such questions certainly are familiar in the historical discourse surrounding women and sport in the United States.[9]

This study must also navigate arguments about obstacles to women's football that point to 'indigenous' African culture(s) as the main reason why the sport has not progressed as much as it has on other continents for women, as opposed to global and local political economic contextual questions pointing to poverty both at the individual and institutional level resulting from centuries of exploitation, imperialism, colonialism and domination. More specifically, in the context of football, is the situation for women in Africa more the result of a hierarchy that has held all of African football well behind Europe and Latin America in a predicament which is only now beginning to change?[10] While there are many other possible obstacles as will be discussed below, local culture versus global structure pose two opposite ends of analysis.

Women's football in Africa is also affected by the development of the game internationally and specifically by what FIFA and CAF are or are not doing to promote the game. From various newspaper accounts, it is clear that the Women's World Cup tournaments have made an impression, and a broader section of the population is ready to at least consider women's football. National football associations have begun to pay lip service to developing opportunities for women based on nudging from FIFA and the IOC. Potentially, FIFA has a powerful tool in forcing national associations to implement policies for women in their Financial Assistance Program, in which national associations receive $1 million over a four-year period to do things such as improving grass-roots development. FIFA is willing to suspend associations that do not adequately fulfil other obligations under this programme.[11] However, even as 'the future of football is feminine', Sepp Blatter told women to lobby for their share of the funds.[12] This is an unlikely scenario in most associations, which are heavily dominated by male interests. For instance, after failing to qualify for the 2002 African Women's Championship, women football supporters in Uganda claimed that promised support for women's football was only used as an election gimmick for the current president of the national association with no subsequent effort made on the part of the association. For its part the association claims to have a plan for women, but no funds to implement it.[13] There may be some change on the horizon following the December 2002 decision by the FIFA executive committee that obliges national associations to use at least 4 per cent of the financial support received from FIFA for their 2003 budget to promote the development of women's football.[14] This amounts to US$10,000, which is not much, but can go a fair way in many African economies.

FIFA also has an extensive development programme in Africa, but it is unclear if women are specifically targeted. In its *Futuro* education programme, short courses are offered for coaches, administrators, referees and medical sport personnel. While FIFA's material for these courses includes a small section on developing the women's game,[15] there is little indication that these forums are used specifically to promote the women's game, or that there is any special effort to recruit women to participate in these courses. If national associations are responsible for recruiting, then current levels of representation are likely to be replicated. The *Goal* project, instituted in 1999 by Sepp Blatter, seeks to empower national associations in four areas, infrastructure, administration, education and youth football. Programmes are tailored to meet the needs of a national association, and are worked out with FIFA upon application from the national association. In the case of Senegal, this has meant the beginning of plans to build a new headquarters with a FIFA donation of $400,000.[16] Once again there does not seem to be any clear indication that development of the women's game is particularly a part of this project. Promoting women did become part of discussions between FIFA and the Football Association of Tanzania in 2001 when Ashford Mamelodi, chairman of the FIFA project to promote women's football, addressed Tanzanian sports administrators on the topic, as part of his visit for their *Goal* project to build a technical centre and renovate their headquarters.[17]

The regional body governing football in Africa, Confédération Africaine de Football, has established a women's committee. However, little information on its structure, funding, activities and accomplishments can be found. The committee is responsible for organizing the African Women's Championships. Five of these have taken place since 1991; the first two determined on a home–away basis and the last three with a single location for the final tournament. Often characterized by disorganization and last minute changes, the competitions seem to have been treated as an 'afterthought' by CAF.[18] Yet, CAF can and has influenced national and sub-regional groups to move on the women's game, as evidence by the development of a proposal in 2002 for a Women's cup competition to be staged by the Council of East and Central Africa Football Associations.[19] The Southern Africa confederation already has a championship for women, and West Africa is planning one. Advocates are calling on CAF to organize a women's continental club championship as well.[20] CAF has made the gesture of instituting the African Female Player of the Year Award, which will be awarded for the first time in April 2003. Ghana's Alberta Sackey will be its first recipient.[21] The Nigerian women's team, the Super Falcons, has also been nominated for the 2002 CAF African Team of the Year. Whether they win or lose,[22] this is another indication that the organization recognizes the value of the women's game.

Outside of the football establishment, other sporting bodies at both national and international levels can have an impact. If the International Olympic Committee takes a women's sport seriously, including offering technical and financial assistance, the national Olympic committees at least take some notice. For French-speaking Africa, an important organization is La Conférence des Ministres de la Jeunesse et des Sports des Pays Ayant le Français en Partage (CONFEJES). Established in 1969 to strengthen the bonds of solidarity and cooperation among youth of Francophone countries, since the 1980s CONFEJES has been taking on projects to promote the integration of women into sport. In 2000, they formed a workgroup, Groupe de travail chargé de la promotion de la participation des jeunes filles et femmes aux activités de jeunesse et sports (GTCF), to promote women's sport. Although not exclusively an African organization, they are headquartered in Senegal, and their activities, for example, workshops in sports administration and management training for female coaches, officials and referees, both in focus and location have been particularly sensitive to African situations. With respect to women's football, however, they did not enter the fray until 2002. For women, the sports that they have concentrated on are handball, basketball, volleyball and track and field. For the first time, they will sponsor a training course for female coaches in partnership with the French

Ministry of Foreign Affairs.[23] Given the relatively good track record of CONFEJES on promoting women's sport, if they do seriously become involved in women's football, positive outcomes can be expected.

What are the Obstacles?

While the official approach of Mr Blatter and FIFA is optimistic in emphasizing what the opportunities for women's football are, in assessing the possibilities for women's football in Africa, addressing the obstacles first offers itself as a more realistic approach. In the following pages, general possible obstacles to women's opportunities to play football in Africa are outlined. Each case study then examines specific obstacles and opportunities.

Indigenous Cultures Mitigate against the Participation of Women in Sport

A position often asserted, it contains many assumptions. If 'modern' sport only came to Africa in the colonial period, 'traditional' cultures would not have any prohibition against sport as such – they would have to be created. One would have to look at the nature of 'modern' sport and how 'traditional' cultures handle different aspects of sport. This suggests the whole question of modern versus traditional, which I argue is a dead-end analytical path, since all culture is 'modern' as its creates, reacts to and integrates all the specific historical spatial institutional economic inputs that make up life in a particular time and place. Any consideration of culture must recognize the dynamic, historical and contemporary nature of culture, not to mention its spatial variability. In unpacking the cultural obstacles to women's participation, there is a need to look carefully to see the interaction between what might be an 'indigenous' obstacle versus those effectively imported with the game and its institutional structures. Indeed, the whole colonial, imperial, postcolonial and global experience has impacted on these societies in ways that affect the trajectories of all developments. In other words, cultural inhibitions may be just variants of the patriarchy and sexism that women face elsewhere.

African football, like football everywhere, operates within a highly charged political and personalistic milieu. What should we make of this situation? In November 2002, Zimbabwe's senior football team coach threatened to resign amid reports that the Zimbabwe Football Association (ZIFA) had seconded him to the technical department of the women's side. He is reported to have said that he would rather quit than work with the women's side. The team, the Mighty Warriors, was preparing for the African Women's Championship. Was this a sexist position on his part? Or was he reacting to high-handed moves by ZIFA?[24]

Political Economic Realities for Women in Africa

While it is a gross generalization, it could be argued that most African girls and women have limited leisure in which to pursue activities like football. This incorporates to some extent a cultural argument in which the division of labour for household reproduction falls more heavily on girls and women than boys and men. It may also recognize the continuing economic 'crisis' that much of the continent has been weathering in various forms since the oil shocks of the 1970s. The heavy workload, often referred to as the 'double-day', could be true either for women in rural areas who are involved in agriculture or other primary product production, or in urban areas where they may be economically active in trade, service or manufacturing sectors, whether formal or informal. In either case and in between, most African women have overwhelming and intensive household reproductive obligations that leave little time to regularly play and develop skills in football. The lack of time as well as minimal resources also prohibits participation in and organization of football.

Limited Access for Women in Africa to International Opportunities to Play

When the Senegalese men's national team beat France in the 2002 World Cup, it marked more than the trumping of the former colonizer by the colonized. While this was indeed a major aspect of the moment, their win also marked several other global currents in football. All but one of the Senegalese players play for clubs in Europe, and many of the French players have roots in Africa or somewhere outside of France. Academies of football are springing up all over Africa encompassing the hopes of coaches, children, parents and national associations that new talent can be found to be exported to the rich markets in Europe. These academies by and large train only boys. It might be argued that this is so because there is not yet a lucrative market for female footballers in Europe or the United States. While this argument also may speak to 'indigenous' cultural prohibitions to the participation of women in sport, it most clearly reflects the international difficulties that women have had pursuing football around the world. It also is another element which questions whether what might be seen as local cultural obstacles to women's participation are in fact imported cultural assumptions that have come from Western influences, including missions, educational institutions, international non-governmental organizations (NGOs) and other organizations.

Playing internationally within Africa is also difficult. As Fran Hilton-Smith, the former national coach of the South African women's side and now the U-19 women's coach, points out the cost of airfares within Africa is high and land travel is dangerous.[25] Stories of whole teams being lost in accidents are all too common.[26] For many reasons, the governing bodies do not schedule enough inter-African matches and competitions. In addition, those matches that are scheduled are often cancelled or postponed, or opposing teams withdraw due to lack of funds or support from their football federation. Such circumstances are disruptive to preparation and training. Without competition among African women's national teams and clubs, the level of play and the visibility of women's football will not easily progress.

Low Social Priority? Limited Allocation of Limited Resources

Institutionally, resources may not be devoted to the development of women's football because there are many more pressing issues in other sectors, such as the economy, public health, education and internal and national security. Even if one is just looking at women's issues, one might argue that developing opportunities to pursue sport in general is simply a low priority when faced with other issues such as low literacy rates, high maternal morbidity and mortality rates, HIV/ AIDS, malaria, respiratory ailments, high unemployment and underemployment, domestic violence, personal insecurity, war, internal displacement, drought, land mines, structural adjustment, and so on. With respect to sport, much activity is concentrated on a few sports, mainly for men and mainly at the elite level. Even for men's sport, there are continual calls for development at *le bas*.[27] On the other hand, governments and international agencies promote sport as a tool to combat juvenile delinquency, drug use, unemployment, and contracting educational opportunities in societies which are overwhelming young. As a tool of development, funding often follows. Yet, despite increasing rhetoric about the value of women's participation, choices made by individuals and organizations at national and international levels still often result in the neglect of the women's game.[28] One encouraging example comes from the Mathare Youth Sports Association near Nairobi, Kenya. Begun in 1987 as a self-help club for boys that linked sports and environment, it has evolved into an organization that sponsors hundreds of male and female football teams as well as community service and educational programmes. Influenced by seeing women playing football on a 1992 trip to Norway, members began a girls' football programme. The programme has been so successful that girls from Mathare now dominate women's football in Kenya. Perhaps more important, the programme has encouraged girls to develop leadership and decision-making skills, confidence and agency, and has begun to change attitudes about gender roles and norms among boys.[29]

CASE STUDIES — SENEGAL, NIGERIA, SOUTH AFRICA

Senegal

At the end of the twentieth century, after men's football and wrestling, women's basketball was the most popular spectator sport in Dakar, Senegal. Women's basketball has enjoyed much success witnessed by vibrant and competitive leagues and a successful national team, at least within the continent of Africa.

This is in stark contrast to developments in women's football in Senegal. Despite, and because of, the popularity of men's football, the women's game has had to struggle stubbornly against the odds to build and maintain a tenuous foothold. Young female athletes who pursue basketball will find a much more encouraging climate than girls whose passion and talent is football.

The history of women's football in Senegal highlights some key points about women and sport in general in Senegal. The work of a few individuals is key, but without the support of the sport's establishment, the organization of the sport for women does not develop easily. Among the first on the African continent to field a women's football team, Senegal's programme for women has since lagged behind other countries such as Nigeria, Ghana and South Africa. The football establishment, including the federation and the sports clubs, has been resistant to the development of women's football. With many other issues in the men's game to distract them,[30] women's football has not garnered much interest. Yet, a few individuals have persevered to develop the game. That and pressure felt from the outside, especially as women's football has become more prominent elsewhere in the world, has led to more effort on the part of the federation.

Organized women's football in Senegal began in 1974 with the visit of a team from Milan, Italy. Eliot Khouma, a former track athlete, ran a football school for boys at the Sacre Coeur, a Catholic school in the SICAP area of Dakar. He began to coach some girls informally. An Italian friend proposed to bring a women's team from Milan. The arrangements were made and he had one month to prepare a team, the Gazelles. They lost the 1974 match to the Milan team 5-2. With support from the municipal government of Dakar and the Football Federation (though not much from the latter), the Gazelles then went on a tour around Senegal staging matches with boys' teams. This inspired other teams to form. In 1979 the Gazelles won a second international match, 3-1, against the Republic of Guinea, Conakry at the Iba Mar Diop stadium in Dakar.[31] Ten years later, with the help of the Mayor of Dakar and Madame Abdou Diouf, the wife of the then President, the Gazelles travelled to Italy for a tournament. Later in 1989 they went to Côte d'Ivoire for another tournament. In 1991, they were invited to participate in the first African Championship for women, but withdrew before the first round because the Senegalese Federation declined to send a team.

For the most part, the Senegalese Football Federation was not involved in organizing the games or league play of women's football through the early 1990s.[32] Eventually, through the advocacy and organizational efforts of Françoise Seck, a self described fan of the game, and others, the federation increased their involvement in women's football in 1993, although even in the late 1990s many teams were not part of the Federation, much to the chagrin of some in the Federation. By the 1990s there were several other women's teams, mostly in the Dakar region, but also in Theis, Mbacke, Kaolack and three in St Louis. The Federation began to sanction league play, championships and international friendlies for the women. The staging of league play, tournaments and championships was patchy, however. In 1994, the Gazelles won the first football tournament for women in Senegal. Other teams such as the Sirenes, established in 1987 and based in the Grand Yoff area of Dakar, rose to prominence by winning tournaments and attracting players. In 1997–98, the Dakar regional league had registered six women's teams: Croisement FC, Diankhe Medina, Gazelles, Murenes, Pantheres and the Sirenes. At the same time, it had 29 registered men's team in four divisions. Twenty-six of those teams licensed 2,690 male players at four levels of play (seniors, juniors, cadets and minimes). With Françoise Seck placed in charge of women's football, in 2000 the national Federation stepped up its commitment to the game by instituting a new national football league with 12 teams throughout the country.[33] The Federation reportedly provides uniforms, pays coaches and provides transport for teams.[34] Providing some basic *moyens* is critical. Paying coaches is particularly important for drawing attention to the endeavour, especially in an economy with very serious unemployment. The support from the Federation has had results. In 2001, 10 teams competed for the national championship. In 2002, there were 12. In February 2003, 20 teams contested for the title. Still, the selection for a national team to contest in the 2002 African women's championship only took place a few weeks before the first scheduled match against Guinea-Bissau (who eventually withdrew).[35] Senegal's 'Lionnes' went on to the second round where they lost 0–3 and 1–3 to Ghana, the eventual runners-up.[36]

Neighbourhood leagues, schools and the established clubs offer the main venues for athletes to participate in organized sport. None of these entities have promoted female football. Significantly, the development of women's football in Senegal has taken place outside of the established sports clubs, which sponsor not only the main men's football teams, but also the successful women's basketball teams and organize other sports, including handball and track for both sexes. Over the past two decades, declining resources have limited the ability of schools to provide physical education for their students. Most students are licensed for individual sports such as track or even Scrabble. For boys, the most popular team sport in school by far is football; for girls, it varies between basketball and handball, and only occasionally do they play football. In addition to the clubs and school opportunities, sport is available through neighbourhood leagues. Though they do engage in other activities and have sponsored girls' handball, the neighbourhood teams 'organized' in the *nawetaan* (Wolof) or *navetane* (French) league largely concentrate on football for young men. These *nawetaan* have gained notoriety for violence and profits, but also play a significant role in defining a distinct urban youth culture.[37] What has not been sufficiently analysed is the gendered implications of these clubs, their leagues and the violence, youth culture and material resources that emerge from them. Mention of activities for girls and young women is nearly absent from material written about them. Those wanting to form women's football teams have had to establish their own clubs, often registering them as *associations sportive et culturelle* (ASC) with the Ministry of Interior.

Perhaps not surprisingly, when discussing obstacles to women's participation in sport with sport administrators, official discrimination on the part of the sport establishment is discounted (*'pas de discrimination'*). Rather, cultural inhibitions are presented as the major obstacles. Nestled in the cultural argument is a concern that sport, particularly football, will masculinize women and girls. Unlike discussions in the West, a consideration of muscles, femininity and sexuality in Senegal is not (yet) an issue about suspected lesbianism, but about fertility and socio-economic status. Competing femininities reflect this: the rural, muscled, toiling agrarian woman versus the more privileged, urban woman who need not labour physically. In the urban milieu where sport is most common, there exist two idealized femininities that are decidedly non-muscular: the *disquette* (young, slim, Western-oriented) and the *drianke* (large, soft, round and economically established).[38] Beauty contests extolling both ideals are popular. Athletic women have to navigate around these images.

The history of a sport and the success women may have had in a sport in the past are critical for how 'feminine' it appears. A 1994 study in four Dakar schools, found that secondary school students ranked handball as the most feminine sport, followed by basketball, volleyball and gymnastics. Interestingly enough in that study, judo, a combative sport in which some Senegalese girls have reached international levels, was ranked sixth, while wrestling, traditionally practised by men in many parts of Senegal and only by Dioula women in the southern province of Casamance, ranked last at tenth. Football, a sport introduced by French soldiers, ranked ninth.[39] Even as women's football was beginning to grow, many expressed in interviews I conducted that women's football suffered from an image as 'too physical and brutal', whereas basketball was considered 'graceful' and 'feminine'. Nevertheless, observers of women's basketball matches can attest to the hard physicality of the game and the players, who are neither *driankes* or *disquettes*.

These concerns about the masculinization may be held internally by girls and women themselves. Physical education is required in secondary schools, yet at one elite school, girls avoided it by obtaining doctors' notes excusing them because of some 'malady'. When the school administration discovered the ploy, they required a school doctor to verify the disability. Even female athletes have mixed feelings about how training affects their femininity. Many of the successful basketball players I surveyed eschewed weight-lifting, some believing it would make their muscles too big. Girls with athletic talent often might also choose sports which they thought would not interfere with their fertility (for example, handball as opposed to track).

Families also have concerns about allowing their daughters to pursue sport should their safety and honour be endangered. They may question the intent of a male coach. To allay these concerns, in the 1970s Khouma went on a 'tour de thé', visiting the families of potential players to convince the parents that playing football would not harm their daughters. Yet, as elsewhere in the world, the position of coach is one of power and influence and is subject to abuse. A few male coaches of various sports mentioned in interviews that it was difficult to get their female athletes to train properly, and one offered the fact that he used to beat them. Some players intimated that abuse had taken place, but did not elaborate.

Most Senegalese are Muslim, but this was not raised as a major concern preventing women from playing sport or even football. Islam in Senegal is characterized by tolerance and tempered by a long history of collaboration between the religious brotherhoods and a secular state, first under colonialism and then after independence. While some who practise a more orthodox Islam have said women should not participate in sport, their opinion does not predominate. While most do not, a few female athletes wear the *hijab* and modest Islamic dress. However, this does not mean Islam is dismissed with regard to sport. Serious studies and seminars are devoted to examining how Islam and sport can co-exist.[40] In a show of post September 11th solidarity, peace and friendship, Senegal was one of four African countries (including Sudan, Congo and Uganda) to send athletes (three) to the Third Muslim Women's Games in Tehran in October 2001.[41] Note that while football was not a featured sport, futsal was.

In Senegal, other practical concerns for individuals, teams and leagues are *les moyens*. Resources are always insufficient. Players had difficulty obtaining funds to pay for transportation to practices and games, fees for licences, equipment and uniforms. Teams and leagues were also short of the resources necessary. All sport in Senegal is supposed to be amateur, but in the most popular, this is not observed. While female basketball players are not paid outright, the best clubs find jobs for them, and pay for many of their expenses. The financial rewards of basketball were made strikingly obvious when after winning the 1997 African Championships in Nairobi, each team member received a home or flat from the President Abdou Diouf. In an environment where unemployment is high, opportunities are limited and women have not been traditionally excluded from productive activities, sports that offer financial and social reward and potential overseas opportunities to women, such as basketball, have come to be defined as 'feminine'. Football has yet to achieve that lure.

Of course, the question is not just about women playing football, but also about them being involved in other ways as coaches, referees and administrators. I met several women who were coaching students, boys and girls, at the Catholic school Jeanne d'Arc and elsewhere. Football was just one of many sports in which they were qualified. Senegalese women have also qualified as referees, even for men's matches. One, Fatou Gueye, has been qualified at the international level since 1996, and two others are qualified at the international assistants level.[42] It is also about women becoming active in the administrative side of football. I did not meet any women involved in management and administration of the women's football clubs. There are two women prominent in Senegalese football circles, Françoise Seck, head of the women's committee, and Madame Fatou Ba-Sarr. Madame Ba, because of her work within the Ministry of Foreign Affairs and because in university she wrote a thesis on the politics of sport, was appointed to represent Senegal in the Confédération Africaine de Football (CAF) where she serves on the sub-committee for youth competitions and as an assistant to the chief of protocol.

At the moment, women's football is on the rise in Senegal. Still the Senegalese future is still very much wrapped up in the men's game, especially with long desired international success for the Lions de la Teranga finally at hand. Women footballers can hope that the rising boat will lift them as well.

Nigeria

In international competition, Nigeria's national side, the Super Falcons, are the best that Africa has. They are, in fact, among the nominees for CAF's Team of 2002, vying with two men's teams from Senegal and Cameroon. They have convincingly won every African Women's Championship so far. Several of the Nigerian players have joined professional leagues in the United States and Europe. The Nigerian Football Association successfully staged the 2002 championship even after the debacle of the Miss World Pageant a few weeks prior. Female football clubs abound and there are several leagues throughout the country.

Yet in February 2003, the northern Nigerian state, Niger, banned women's football. The state governor, Abdul-khadir Kure, said, 'I don't see anything rewarding about it as it is not in conformity with our culture.' His action came after meeting with officials of the Niger state section of the Youth Sports Federation of Nigeria who argued that football is specifically meant for men and not women who can pursue other sports like athletics and volleyball.[43] Niger is at least the second state in northern Nigeria to ban women's football. In 2000, when the state of Zamfara declared that *shari'a*, Islamic law, would be implemented, women's football was immediately targeted. The state director of sports said it was outlawed because 'the sport is against the teachings of Islam'.[44] For many northern Nigerian girls, a governmental ban is moot since their parents already prevent them from playing football. While there are girls who do play football in northern Nigeria, as of 2001 none had made the national team.[45]

Nigeria is a country of 130 million people with vast historical and cultural differences in its regions, which are currently carved up into 36 states and the federal territory of Abuja, the capital city. While there are Muslims throughout the country, they are predominately in the North. Christians and non-Muslims are in the majority in the South. Unlike Senegal, during the colonial period, the strong, centralized Muslim states in the North were essentially left to rule themselves under British indirect rule. The particular form that Islam took was less tolerant of the secular. With regard to women, it became more restrictive of their presence in public, and many practise female seclusion.[46] In the current national and international climate, Islamic identities are hardening in the north and being influenced more by Islamicists from Saudi Arabia and elsewhere in the Muslim world. Most likely it is the very success of Nigerian women's football, its challenge to gender norms, and its connection to practices in southern Nigeria that has caused the Islamic leaders to focus on it.[47]

Given the size and diversity of Nigeria's population, it is not surprising to find such drastically opposing circumstances for women's football throughout the country. The current federal government under President Olusegun Obasanjo is not sympathetic to efforts to impose *shari'a* law. Except in those few states where it has been banned, women's football continues to experience success and growth in popularity. However, if national politics become even more confrontational, as they might in the upcoming national elections, women's rights in general and possibly the right of girls and women to play football could very well become part of the political battle, albeit as just one more element in a larger struggle over identity and resource control in the petroleum producing nation.

Women have been playing football on a regular basis in Nigeria only since 1978.[48] Prior to that if women were athletic, they were directed towards netball, field hockey, handball, certain track and field events and basketball. As was the case with the Gazelles in Senegal, a male football enthusiast, Christopher Akintunde Abisuga, formed the first all women's football club, The 'Sugar Babes' Ladies FC. Abisuga's employer, Nigeria Hotels Limited, sponsored the club. They played exhibition matches against young boys in the National Stadium in Lagos, and fuelled the establishment of other clubs. A few years later the club was disbanded. Abisuga said that Nigeria was not ready for women's football and FIFA was not supportive.[49]

Another factor, he writes, was social and religious resistance in that 'people felt that women should be confined to the kitchen and that they had no business on football pitches'.[50] When Ann Chiejine, the Super Falcons goalkeeper, was a child, her parents opposed her playing because 'they felt that football would make me so muscular that no man would want to marry me and I would end up being unable to bear children'.[51] Now Chiejine has three children and even played when she was five months' pregnant in the 2000 African Women's Championship. While some would see that as too risky, it is certainly proof that Chiejine's parents did not need to fear about her fertility.[52] Other players found their parents to be supportive. The father of Mercy Akide, now a forward on WUSA's San Diego Spirit, bought her first pair of cleats, backing her against the objections of his family.[53]

By 1987 several clubs existed, including the Jegede Babes, launched by Princess Bola Jegede, a Lagos businesswoman and eventual official of the Nigerian Football Association (NFA).[54] Owners of the teams came together to form the Nigerian Female Football Organizers Association (NIFFOA). The president of the NFA, Pa Ikpeazu, told them that if the state football associations registered enough female clubs, then national competitions would be held. If the standard was high enough, he would even support Nigeria trying to get a place in the inaugural Women's World Cup to be held in China.[55]

By 1989 there were at least 28 clubs, although some later disappeared because of lack of resources. That year the federal Sports Ministry approved the National

Sports Commission's request to include female football as one of the events in the national Sports Festival held in Lagos. The women's impressive performance at the tournament convinced the NFA to organize the first national female football championship in Lagos in 1990. However, it was not the NFA, but Princess Bola Jegede, who financially supported the tournament and supplied the trophy.[56]

From this tournament a national team was selected that went on to play in the 1991 Women's World Cup. Initially, the NFA was not going to help prepare the team for the qualifying matches unless they had sponsorship. Once that was known funds came pouring in. Contributors included Cadbury Nigeria PLC, Chief Mrs Simbiat Abiola, Julius Berger PLC and Mrs Maryam Babangida, the First Lady. Once they secured the African championship and their berth in the Women's World Cup, the federal government rewarded the team with cash prizes and gifts.[57] While they lost all three matches in China, it was a great achievement to get to the international stage in one year, whereas it took the men's team 32 years to get there.[58]

Women's football in Nigeria flourished through the 1990s. Many sponsors, including women such as Simbiat Abiola and Bola Jegede, sponsored teams. Iain Nelson, a native of Scotland and international marketing manager for the Seven Up Bottling Company (Pepsi), was a major source of support for both the men's and women's games. Many of the women's teams can offer professional contracts and some are even signing players from other African countries. Several of the women on the national team have received endorsements from Pepsi. Many of them have also been able to invest in successful businesses and are the breadwinners for their families. The coach of the national team from 1991 through mid-2002, Ismaila Mabo, has opened a football academy in his hometown of Jos in North Central Nigeria.[59] Clearly, women's football in Nigeria can be lucrative. In a country with serious economic problems and high unemployment just as in Senegal, this can certainly attract female players.[60]

Despite the bans, women's football in Nigeria is certainly vibrant. Women are active not only as players, but as referees (four each international and international assistant referees), financiers, administrators, officials and advocates. This may reflect a history of activism among Nigerian women, especially in the South, but not unknown in the North. The Aba women's war in the colonial period is well-known and presages current activism among women in the Niger Delta region, where the 2002 Championship tournament took place. Women have taken over oil platforms to demand better treatment from the oil companies and the petroleum industry as a whole. Nigerian women have also been economically active, particularly in the markets. Again this is not only true for women in the South, but also for women in the North, where Hausa women often run trading operations in seclusion from their homes. The women's movement, as such, is not monolithic in Nigeria. Activity, advocacy and rhetoric come from several different quarters of society and the political realm. This is its strength in that it is diffuse and permeates through different social paths.

While for some, especially certain Islamic leaders, the money, prestige and notoriety may be enough for them to continue to prohibit their daughters from pursuing football, for many these very factors have influenced them to accept, even become passionate about the women's game. The women themselves have become role models for younger girls. However, some fear that if the government and the NFA do not show more commitment to the women's game, Nigeria's dominance on the continent will soon be challenged, especially by the South African side.[61] One can just recall that Nigerian women's field hockey was internationally competitive in the 1970s, but now can barely field a team.

South Africa

The history of football in South Africa begins in the mid-nineteenth century with matches among white settlers in Pietermaritzburg.[62] By the twentieth century, mainly Black Africans, Indians and working class white immigrants played this sport, while the Afrikaaner and English-speaking white populations preferred rugby and cricket, respectively.[63] The sport of the majority, football became a vibrant part of Black popular culture and national identity, and as such played a significant role in struggles against apartheid.[64] Whereas colonialism, anti-colonialism and the postcolonial experience delimit so much of the Nigerian and Senegalese context, apartheid, the struggle against it, and its aftermath set the stage for football in South Africa.[65] An ideology and system of racial segregation that privileged the white minority, apartheid meant systemic oppression and violence, inequitable resource distribution, and structural neglect of all aspects of life and livelihood for the majority of the population. With its nationalist and patriarchal tendencies, apartheid also carried both ideological and structural implications for gender. The politics and practice of football are intricately imprinted with this legacy.

With the electoral victory of the Nationalist Party in 1948, more and more apartheid practices became law and new policies to ensure white supremacy and the spatial segregation of the races were developed. Sport came under the legal purview of apartheid in 1956.[66] At the same time, the international football establishment, FIFA, was just coming to terms with the development of the game outside of Europe, specifically in South America and Africa. In 1957, South Africa joined with the other independent African countries, Ethiopia, Sudan and Egypt, to form the Confédération Africaine de Football (CAF). Almost immediately South Africa fell foul of a key principle of CAF; CAF barred South Africa from its first tournaments in 1958 and 1959 for refusing to field a multiracial team. CAF formally expelled South Africa in 1961. The non-racial South African Soccer Federation (SASF), established in 1952 and representing 46,000 players, unsuccessfully sought to have FIFA recognize it as South Africa's representative, and expel the white dominated Football Association of South Africa (FASA), established in 1892 and representing only 20,000 players.

Throughout his tenure as the president of FIFA, Stanley Rous gave significant support to FASA. Nevertheless, due to growing pressure from non-European FIFA affiliates, FIFA first suspended and then in 1964 expelled South Africa for its discriminatory policies.[67] They were only readmitted into FIFA in 1992 under a newly integrated organization, the South Africa Football Association (SAFA). Indeed, the issue of South Africa was a key factor in the election of João Havelange as FIFA's president in 1974, and in the emergence of Africa and Latin America as challengers to European control of the global football establishment.[68]

For both men and women playing football in South Africa, this meant three decades of isolation from competition, coaching and advancement of the game internationally. Apartheid also meant extreme inequities in resources and facilities. Despite the isolation and poverty, football maintained its popularity among the Black majority. Sport administration, especially of football leagues and clubs, became a key arena for the practice of leadership and entrepreneurial skills as well as political activity and resistance, as other political venues were denied to nonwhites in South Africa.[69] In the early 1960s, opponents of the apartheid-controlled establishment formed a multiracial professional men's football league, the South African Soccer League, which had a very successful five-year run. It was so successful that the white establishment eventually undermined it and caused it to shut down. Black Africans, Coloured and Indian footballers, administrators and fans could continue as long as they operated within the system that was endorsed by the apartheid regime. By the 1970s, football was the most segregated it had ever been and suffered for it. The non-white leagues had woefully insufficient resources and facilities. Movement was made difficult by pass laws. Even the white leagues that had plenty of resources and quality facilities still lacked competitive and international exposure. All around this was a stultifying and stagnating experience for football.[70]

Under apartheid, South African society was not only segregated by race, but also by sex, in a system that exacerbated patriarchal 'traditions' across different cultural groups. Interestingly enough, this did not mean that women were excluded from sport in general. In fact, due to the influence of the British public school system and the Christian mission school experience, sport was considered an important part of education and central to the development of a national identity. Hence anyone attending a government school was required to practise a sport until she graduated.[71] However, the activities that were encouraged for girls were limited to those considered feminine or ladylike, for example, netball, tennis, hockey, athletics, softball, volleyball.[72] Football was excluded. Even in the contemporary period attitudes persist that would prevent girls from pursuing football. In a 2001 letter to the sports column, Soccer Buzz, in the popular magazine, *Drum*, a 21-year-old woman complained that despite the success of the national women's football team, Banyana Banyana, when she played the game she encountered sentiments, apparently hostile, that football was meant for boys.[73] Likewise in schools, there is some resistance due to a fear of injury to girls.[74]

Despite the attitudes and the lack of scholastic opportunities, girls and women have pursued football. Women have long been involved in the sport as spectators and supporters. According to the current SAFA president, Molefi Oliphant, 50 per cent of football fans are women.[75] Peter Alegi establishes that women were spectators and supporters of the teams in the non-racial SASL of the early 1960s, with some women very involved in the support organizations.[76] Perhaps it is not surprising that the first historical reference I found to women playing football in South Africa, concerns a group of women who began playing 'curtain raiser' novelty matches prior to the games of Mother City, one of three Western Cape SASL professional teams. An October 1962 *Drum* article profiles the Mother City Girls. Started as 'a bit of fun', the women became extremely 'keen' on the game and were longing for more competition. Never losing a match, they played young schoolboys and mixed-sex scratch teams made up mostly of boys. Despite the somewhat condescending tone and the emphasis on the sexual attractiveness of the women, especially in the photo captions, the unnamed author of the piece seems to be genuinely impressed with their skills. Indeed, their sexual attractiveness is heightened by their abilities on the pitch in contrast to much discourse that would categorize their skills and aggressive play as distinctly unfeminine and, hence, unattractive.[77]

Over the next three decades, doubtless more and more women did begin to play football. However, information on women's football in South Africa before the 1990s is scarce and scattered and will require more in-depth research.[78] It is clear that women's football developed along segregated lines through the 1970s. In 1974 the South African Women's Football Association (SAWFA) was formed exclusively for whites and Coloureds, but controlled by whites.[79] The Cape Town area seems to have been the heart of the women's game, where football was particularly popular among Coloured girls and women.[80] Regular competitions were staged in the Western and Eastern Cape, well before other regions.[81] In 1990, Black township women organized their own leagues and competitions. With increasing numbers, in 1991 they formed the South African Women's Soccer Association (SAWSA).[82] As with other sport codes in South Africa, in the aftermath of apartheid, these organizations and the interests attached to them fell into a power struggle with each other and the new national organizations to establish control, authority and access to resources.

From 1990 onward, much more information can be gleaned from the SAFA Website (http://www.safa.net), which SAFA has made a priority for disseminating information about their organization, programmes, teams and players.[83] While the amount of information on men's football far outstrips that presented on women's, since 2001, SAFA has posted significantly more information on the women's game albeit in bits and pieces throughout the site. The following chronology is based mainly on information from the SAFA site.

In 1992, SAFA was readmitted to FIFA and CAF, and immediately a men's national team, Bafana Bafana, was organized and entered the World Cup qualifying rounds.[84] That same year, South Africa was formally readmitted to women's world football at the first Women's World Conference on Football held in Switzerland in October 1992. Because of the struggle between SAWFA and SAWSA, both associations were dissolved, and existing local clubs and emerging new teams[85] were reorganized under an appointed committee, which eventually became the South African Women's Football Association (SAWFA) and an associate member of SAFA.

In 1993, the first non-racial competitive league matches for women were organized. The national women's side, Banyana Banyana, was selected, and in their first friendly international on 30 May 1993 in Johannesburg, they beat Swaziland 14-0. Later that year, they travelled to Harare and won two friendlies against Zimbabwe.[86] With no losses, in 1994, Banyana Banyana entered the qualifying stages for the Women's World Cup.[87] They ultimately made it to the third round by first beating Zambia in Johannesburg and Lusaka in 1994 and Angola in 1995, but lost to Nigeria in the third round at the end of 1995.[88]

Factional struggles within SAWFA continued, as did difficult relations with SAFA over expectations of communications and support. Eventually, these difficulties were brought before the Pickard Commission in July 1996. The Pickard Commission had been appointed by the Minister of Sports, Steve Tswete, to probe into the problems of the administration of football in South Africa. For the women's game, the Pickard Commission recommended two options: 1) find means to make associate membership more dynamic, or 2) restructure women's football by incorporating existing, but often weak, provincial structures into SAFAs provincial associations, and create a subcommittee on women's football which would be accountable to the National Executive Committee of SAFA. Discussions among interested parties continued that year without resolution. Ultimately, SAFA made the decision that SAWFA would remain an associate member. In September 1996, SAWFA elected a new executive committee, amended their constitution and began evaluating budget proposals and looking for sponsorship.[89] However, the autonomous SAWFA's new organizational lease was short-lived.

When Banyana Banyana failed to qualify for the Women's World Cup in 1997, SAFA backtracked and apparently choose to follow the Pickard Commission's second option. It formed a women's steering committee chaired by Nastasia Tsichlas, the national association's first female executive committee member. (In 2000, she was appointed to the CAF Women's Committee as well as the FIFA Football Committee.[90]) SAFA then began organizing training camps, competitions at the senior provincial level and more international matches. In addition, they introduced an U-19 level, with the national team nicknamed Basetsana, to form the core of future Olympic squads.[91]

In 1998 as South Africa announced its intention to bid for the 2006 FIFA (men's) World Cup Finals, Banyana Banyana made it to the inaugural CAF Women's Championship Finals in Nigeria.[92] Ultimately, they lost to Cameroon and Ghana, and Nigeria won the tournament.[93] Perhaps as a response to this performance, in 1999, SAFA held a Women's Football Indaba that led to the development of a policy blueprint that was to be implemented by the Women's Football Committee.[94]

While earlier that year, South Africa lost their bid to stage the 2006 men's World Cup, they did stage the 2000 CAF African Women's Championship at Vosloorus. The final match between Nigeria and South Africa was abandoned with 18 minutes remaining because fans protesting Nigeria's second goal began throwing objects and invaded the pitch.[95] Nigeria was awarded the win and cup on the basis of their 2-0 lead. Despite the trouble, SAFA seemed to be proud of Banyana's runner-up status, suggesting that the reorganization of women's football contributed to that achievement.[96] Capitalizing on this, South Africa has announced that it intends to bid to host the 2007 Women's World Cup.

While clubs had been long been competing locally and provincially, 2001 marked a new phase with the implementation of the SAFA Sanlam National Women's League, encompassing over 300 teams from all 25 SAFA Regions. Champions from each of the nine provinces compete for the national title in the Sanlam's Halala Cup tournament.[97] SAFA expects the league to contribute to the long-term development of women's football. Players for both Banyana and the U-19 national team play in the league and presumably can stay fit when not in training camp for the national side. According to Oliphant, SAFA's president, the League will also 'stabilise and strengthen women's football at regional level and will lay the groundwork for the formation of a professional league for women by 2003'.[98] Even as the Sanlam league was announced in 2001, Banyana players did not know when or if there were any training camps planned. Furthermore, no friendlies in preparation for upcoming competitions had been scheduled, leaving players unclear about their training.[99]

The league marked another advancement for women's football in South Africa: corporate sponsorship. Sanlam, a financial services company, contributed 15 million Rand over three years to support the league. In the same year, Vodacom began sponsoring a Women's Inter-Regional Tournament, a week-long event contested by representative sides of the 25 SAFA Regions and the national side of the SA Students Sports Union (SASSU). And at least within the Football Association of Border, one of SAFA's regional bodies, Cadbury sponsors an U-12 girls tournament and Nike an U-15 one.[100] Nevertheless, the relative disparities in resources and efforts given to women's football are still great. The Banyana players get a win bonus and a daily allowance only when in camp, whereas the men's bonuses and allowances are much greater and they get appearance fees. The men also get to keep their kit, while the women have had to hand it back. Yet, many of the Banyana players are happy with what little they do get, as they are unemployed, unlike the male players who have professional options both in South Africa and abroad.[101]

Women's football has definitely increased in popularity in South Africa. There are at least 50,000 female footballers nationwide. Even alternative football structures for lesbian players, such as the Inter-Africa Women's Soccer Tournament held in 2002, are emerging.[102] The new leagues and competitions should raise the interest and level of competition. While there are no international female referees from South Africa, there are several women involved in administration. South Africa also has the only female coach for a national team in Africa, Fran Hilton-Smith. Women's football is also gaining attention from the media and the fans. Banyana players are known across the nation. Desiree Ellis, one of the top Banyana players over the past decade, avoided a mugging in 2001 when the would-be assailant recognized her.[103] The SAFA Website lists all the players, past and present, on both teams, with a link providing information on their playing history. Furthermore, each match is listed back to 1993 and some details of all those matches are available. SAFA is paying closer attention to developing the women's game. In the forward to Paul Darby's book on Africa and FIFA, Danny Jordaan, the CEO of SAFA wrote:

> A new sense of purpose, like that which typified the 1950s and 1960s, must unite African players, administrators and managers. Such unity will be essential in promoting and strengthening the game in all its facets in Africa for both male and female footballers. The development and participation of women footballers in Africa is not only essential for the growth of football in the continent. It is also a vital component of the gender development of the game in Africa and internationally.[104]

Presumably, these sentiments reflect commitment on the part of the football establishment in South Africa to go even further in promoting the women's game.

CONCLUSION

Based on evidence collected from the Internet, women are playing organized football in at least 30 African countries and probably more.[105] Leagues and tournaments are popping up everywhere across the continent. The continental championship is over a decade old. African national teams have not yet been a threat internationally, but professional teams abroad are recruiting African women. While cultural barriers are still cited as inhibitions to girls playing, the push (for example, international directives) and pull (for example, lucrative financial gains in Nigeria and abroad) of more resources are drawing more into the game. For each case, though, the general economic troubles and the lack of resources overall is still perhaps the most serious hindrance. Even the bans on women's football in Northern Nigeria may be indirectly linked to this. The three cases do share some commonalities that derive from the colonial experience, globalization and the current economic 'crises', and problems seemingly inherent to the football establishment everywhere (for example, corruption, mismanagement, elitism, etcetera). Still one cannot generalize. Each of the three cases has particular factors that have affected the development of the women's game.

If we take the fielding of an elite squad that plays internationally and is competitive enough to make it to the Olympics or the World Cup as a sign of success, what can be learned from our three case studies? Two factors along which differences emerge are the size of population, that is, the existence of critical mass to draw on, and whether there is enough relative wealth in the country to support the development of women's football.

On the basis of elite performance, Nigeria has been the most successful. South Africa and Ghana vie for second place. Senegal lags far behind. What is the basis of Nigeria's success? They have been able to draw from the largest population, approximately 130 million people. Despite the very prominent recent bans on women playing soccer in two or three of the northern states, many girls and women still have the opportunity to play. On the factor of relative wealth, there has been commercial sponsorship of women's football. Economically, Nigeria is in dire straits now and has been for some time. However, the presence of oil has allowed some to accumulate wealth. A further study of the Nigerian situation would evaluate whether or not this has been a factor in supporting women's football, especially relative to men's football. A key factor in directing these resources towards women's football, I would argue, has been the very active women's movement in Nigeria. By the very nature of the discourse combined with the sheer size and diversity and complexity that is Nigeria, women's football has found a supportive constituency. The bans of specifically women's football by a few Islamic states is a sign of the success of women's football in Nigeria.

It may not be surprising that South Africa has done so well. The country has a large population base of about 44 million on which to draw to find good players. Despite economic difficulties, South Africa is the most industrialized country in Africa and has a relative wide range of institutions and available resources to promote women's football though it seemingly has not done nearly as well as Nigeria in gaining sponsorships at the club level.[106] Furthermore, in the post-Apartheid era, there has been at least a rhetorical commitment to providing resources and opportunities to previously disadvantaged groups, which in this case means sporting opportunities (better resources, better fields, better coaching and so on) for women in general and for Black and Coloured populations. Within the South African Football Association, while there has been some feeling of neglect, relative to many other football associations in Africa, there has been a serious commitment to raising the number and quality of opportunities for women and girls to play football. With this combination of advantages, one may wonder why the South African national side does not dominate African women's football. It may be that they are still feeling the effects of three decades of isolation due to the sanctions imposed on South Africa because of apartheid.[107] While the men's side is competitive, it does not dominate African football either. On the other hand, South Africa is very competitive in cricket and rugby, sports more traditionally played by whites. Other African countries tend to put fewer resources towards those two sports, while (men's) football in even a very poor African country will garner huge effort and resources on the part of both government and the private sector. So it may be just a matter of time, before the South African women's side is able to draw on the relative strengths of national wealth to develop into the dominant African team. On the other hand, other African countries, particularly Nigeria and Ghana, will not necessarily stand still while South Africa moves forward. Furthermore, as sports is seen as an integral part of public health and development programmes, more and more development agencies and NGOs may have a positive impact on developing opportunities for women in football elsewhere, such as the Mathare Youth Sports Association Football Program for Girls in Kenya has done.

What does the Senegalese case tell us? Senegal is a small country with a population of around 7 million. On this account relative to both Nigeria and South Africa, it may not be unexpected that they have not been able to field a competitive women's football team. However, they have been able to rise to the top on the men's side, and in addition have been very successful with women's basketball. It may be that as a small country they will only be able to excel in a small number of sports. And in the picking and choosing, women's football until recently simply has not fared as well. Senegal also demonstrates that Islam is not an inhibition to the development of the women's game. It will be interesting to see whether external pressures from CONFEJES, FIFA, the IOC and the like, the need for prestige, and internal pressures from men and women who want to play and promote women's football, will have an impact on their football establishment with regard to the attention and resources paid to women's football.

What all of the cases show is that the rise of women's football elsewhere has for the most part encouraged the development of *football féminin* in Africa. Hopefully, this will also lead to more documentation and research on the developments that have happened and are yet to occur.

NOTES

1. The scholarly work in wider circulation that I am aware of includes C.A. Abisuga and H. Awurumibe, *Genesis of Female Soccer in Nigeria* (Lagos Nigeria: Starmark Consultants, 1991); J. Adedeji, 'Social Change and Women in African Sport', *International Social Science Journal*, 34, 2 (1982), pp.209–18; B. Erraïs and S. Erraïs, 'Le Sport Féminin à l'Épreuve de l'Intégrisme Religieux: Le Cas du Maghreb', in P. Arnaud and T. Terret (eds), *Histoire du Sport Féminin: Éducation et Société*, 2 (Paris: L'Harmattan, 1996), pp.81–94; J. Hargreaves, 'Women's Sport, Development and Cultural Diversity: The South African Experience', *Women's Studies International Forum*, 20, 2 (1997), pp.191–209; A. Mazrui, 'Africa's Triple Heritage of Play: Reflections on the Gender Gap', in W.J. Baker and J.A. Mangan (eds), *Sport in Africa: Essays in Social History* (New York, London: Africana Publishing Company, 1987), pp.217–28; J.C. Omoruan, K. Venkateswarlu and F.B. Adeyanju (eds), *Multidimensional Perspectives of Women Participation in Sports* (Kaduna: Nigerian Association of Women in Sports, 1992); C. Roberts, *Against the Grain: Women and Sport in South Africa* (Cape Town, S.A.: Township Publishing Co-operative, 1992). Wagner's volume also includes some information about the status of women's sport in various countries. See E.A. Wagner (ed.), *Sport in Asia and Africa: A Comparative Handbook* (New York, Westport and London: Greenwood Press, 1989). This recent

reference work includes entries for many African countries. K. Christensen, A. Guttmann and G. Pfister (eds), *International Encyclopedia of Women and Sports* (New York: Macmillan Reference USA, 2001). Deville-Danthu's groundbreaking study on the history of sport in Francophone West Africa does not directly address women's involvement in sport. See B. Deville-Danthu, *Le Sport en Noir et Blanc: Du Sport Colonial au Sport Africain dans les Anciens Territoires Français d'Afrique Occidentale (1920–1965)* (Paris: L'Harmattan, 1997). New works from young scholars are also emerging, for example, P. Massao, 'Sport in Africa – Do Women Have a Chance?' *Play the Game: Third International Conference, 10–14 Nov. 2002*, Copenhagen; P. Massao and K. Fasting, 'Women and Sport in Tanzania', in I. Hartmann and G. Pfister (eds), *Sport and Women: Social Issues in International Perspective* (London: Routledge, 2002).

2. Among studies available, some of which are more polemical than others are, S. E. Akpabot, *Football in Nigeria* (London: Macmillan Publishers, 1985); P. Alegi, 'Keep Your Eye on the Ball: A Social History of Soccer in South Africa, 1910–1976' (Unpublished Ph.D. Thesis, Boston University, 2000); P.C. Alegi, *Moving the Goalposts: Playing Styles, Sociability and Politics in South African Soccer in the 1960s* (Boston MA: African Studies Center Boston University, 2000); O. Amadasun, *History of Football in Africa* (Lagos Nigeria: Times Books Limited, 1994); S. Baller, 'Playing Football in a Postcolonial City: The Nawetaan Championship in Pikine (Senegal)', www.vad-ev.de/papers/baller.pdf (2002); S.A. Cisse, *Sénégal, Carton Rouge* (Dakar Sénégal: Niamagne, 1995); P. Darby, *Africa, Football and FIFA: Politics, Colonialism and Resistance* (London, Portland OR: Frank Cass, 2002); D. Gaye, *Crises et Perspectives du Football Sénégalais* (Saint-Louis Senegal: Xamal éditions, 1999); J. Nauright, *Sport, Cultures and Identities in South Africa* (Cape Town: David Philip, 1998); S. Odegbami, *Issues in Nigerian Football* (Lagos: Save Nigerian Football Campaign, 1999).

3. A. White and D. Scoretz, *From Windhoek to Montreal: Women and Sport Progress Report 1998–2002* (Montreal: International Working Group on Women and Sport, 2002).

4. Personal electronic communication with Dr Viken Djizmedjian, 28 Oct. 2002. An article about the competition is listed in the table of contents of September 2002 issue of CAF News. However, the online PDF version is missing the last seven pages. See http://www.cafonline.com/Pub/CAF%20NEWS%2076.pdf.

5. http://www.safa.net. The President's welcome message on the site as of 2 March 2003 focuses on their 'newly-structured dynamic site that will encompass a wealth of information'. See http://www.safa.net/welcome.asp.

6. This is true of major international organizations as well. In 1997 I found interesting reports on the IOC Website on women and the Olympic movement that no longer exist on their site. International Olympic Committee, 'Women and the Olympic Movement with an Appendix', see http://www.olympic.org/efwom.html and http://www.olympic.org/efwoma1.html, 1997.

7. The Stanford and Berkeley libraries combined have the largest collection West of the Mississippi in the United States.

8. The West African Research Association funded my trip. During my stay, I was affiliated to the West African Research Center. Abdou Karim Sylla ably assisted me in my research.

9. For a summary of this see M. Saavedra, 'Gender and Sport', in P. Essed, A. Kobayashi and D. T. Goldberg (eds), *A Companion to Gender Studies* (London: Blackwell Publishing, forthcoming in 2003).

10. Darby, *Africa, Football and FIFA*.

11. In the aftermath of the 2002 FIFA presidential elections, relations between CAF, FIFA and individual national associations have been strained. With some NAs having supported Sepp Blatter and others, the CAF president, Issa Hayatou, there has been purging at both organizations of those who took the 'wrong' side. Whether in the long run this will affect support for specific projects in the specific countries remains to be seen.

12. J. Phillips Rogers, 'The Future of Women in Football', *Women's Soccer World Magazine*, Special Edition WW Cup, (1999).

13. M.M. Dhakaba, 'Women's Soccer Hanging by a Thread', *The Monitor*, 4 January 2003 (Kampala, Uganda, 2003).

14. FIFA Communications Division, 'FIFA Executive Resolves to Boost Women's Football', *Media Information online* (Zurich, 2002).

15. http://apps.fifa.com/scripts/runisa.dll?M2:gp::67173+futuro/eduprog/9700/index+E.

16. FIFA, 'Progress Report 1999–2000, the House of FIFA: Goal and Financial Assistance Program' (Zurich, 2002). http://www.fifa.com/goal/2002/TheHouseof Fifa_2002_08.pdf.

17. PANA, 'FIFA to Promote Women's Soccer', *Panafrican News Agency (Dakar)* (Dar Es Salaam0:

Tanzania, 2001). http://allafrica.com/stories/200104210005.html.

18. F. Hilton-Smith, 'Women's Soccer in Africa: Against All Odds', May 1999, *Network* (A Publication of the Women's Soccer Foundation, 1999).

19. S. Ateka, 'CECAFA to Start Women's Cup', *The East African Standard* (Nairobi, 2002). http://allafrica.com/stories/20020128069l.html.

20. A. Olajire, 'Football with a Woman's Face', *Africa Today* (July 2001), see http://www.africatoday. com/jul01football.htm.

21. A sophomore at Robert Morris College in the US, she was the top scorer at the December 2002 Nations Cup Tournament.

22. The Senegalese Men's National Team won the award.

23. CONFEJES, 'Programmation 2002, Programme I: Programme de Promotion de la Participation des Jeunes Filles et des Femmes aux Activités Sportives – Fiche Projet', (Dakar: CONFEJES, 2002).

24. T. Ndemera, 'Marimo Threatens to Resign', *The Herald*, 28 November 2002 (Harare, 2002). http://allafrica.com/stories/printable/200211300222.htm.

25. Hilton-Smith, 'Women's Soccer in Africa: Against All Odds', 3.

26. Just a few examples follow: On 28 April 1993, a plane crash in Libreville, Gabon killed 18 players and five officials of the Zambian men's national team. In 1996 a bus carrying all the members and coaches of a Nigerian women's football team ran off a bridge during a storm while returning from a match. In September 2002, several young players from two football academies were among the 1,863 who died when the Joola ferry sank off the coast of Senegal in the second worst maritime disaster ever.

27. For instance, see the CONFEJES submission to CAF's 2002 Football Forum. CONFEJES, *Forum sur le Football en Afrique: Contribution du Secrétaire Général de la Confejes (Le Caire Les 21 Et 22 Octobre 2002)* (Dakar: CONFEJES, 2002).

28. I am aware of a number of projects connecting soccer teams in North America with teams or leagues in various African countries. Inevitably, the glowing stories and pictures of those who have received assistance indicate that only male teams have benefited.

29. M. Brady and A. Banu Khan, *Letting Girls Play: The Mathare Youth Sports Association's Football Program for Girls* (New York: Population Council, 2002).

30. See Cisse, *Sénégal, Carton Rouge;* and Gaye, *Crises et Perspectives du Football Sénégalais.*

31. Interview with Eliot Khouma, Jan. 1999, Dakar, and A.B. Thiam, 'Evaluation de certaines qualités physiques chez les footballeuses sénégalaises' (Unpublished Mémoire de Maîtrise de Science et Technique de l'Activité Physique et du Sport [STAPS]: Institut National Supérieur de l'Education Populaire et du Sport, 1996), p.7.

32. This is not at all unlike the history of women's football in Britain. In fact the situation there was probably worse. See S. Lopez, *Women on the Ball: A Guide to Women's Football* (London: Scarlet Press, 1997).

33. Ligue de Football de Dakar, *Rapport D'activitiés Saison 1997–1998* (Dakar: Assemblee Generale Ordinaire 5 Decembre 1998 a l'INSEPS, 1998).

34. N. Portley, 'Kicking Off a Girls' Soccer Team in Yoff', *Yégóo: Magazine of Intercultural Exchange*, 2, June 2001, 15–22.

35. A. Thiam, 'Preliminatoires Nigeria 2002: Sénégal-Guinée Bissau', *Sud Quotidien* (2002). http://fr. allafrica.com/stories/200207260358.html.

36. S. Burkert, 'Africa – Women's Championship 2002', *Rec.Sport.Soccer Statistics Foundation* (2003). http://www.rsssf.com/tablesa/afr-women02.html.

37. Baller, 'Playing Football in a Postcolonial City: The Nawetaan Championship in Pikine (Senegal)'; J.-P. Tine, 'Evolution de la Violence dans le Footbal "Navetanes" de 1991 à 1995: Cas de L'ODCA, Ville de Dakar' (Unpublished Mémoire de Maîtrise de Science et Technique dè l'Activites Physique et du Sport [STAPS]: Institut National Supérieur de l'Education Populaire et du Sport, 1996).

38. T.K. Biaya, '"Crushing the Pistachio": Eroticism in Senegal and the Art of Ousmane Dago', *Public Culture*, 12, 3 (2000); M. Saavedra, 'Muscular Femininity: Women, Sports and Development in Dakar, Senegal', *African Studies Association Annual Meeting* (Columbus, Ohio, 1999).

39. J.-J. Manga, 'La Pratique Feminine des Sports de Combat Vue par les Elèves de Quartre Lycées de Dakar: l'Example du Judo et de la Lutte' (Unpublished Mémoire de Maîtrise de Science et Technique de l'Activité Physique et du Sport [STAPS]: Institut National Supérieur de l'Education Populaire et du Sport, 1994).

40. See C.S.D. Sissoko, 'La Femme, les Activités Physiques et Sportives et L'Islam' (Unpublished Mémoire de Maîtrise de Science et Technique de l'Activité Physique et du Sport [STAPS]: Institut

National Supérieur de l'Education Populaire et du Sport, 1990).

41. Anon., 'Comparative Report of the 3rd Moslem Women Games', *Solidarity: Journal of the Islamic Federation of Women's Sports*, 1 (2003).

42. From the FIFA Website, http://apps.fifa.com/scripts/runisa.dll?S7:gp::67173+women/refs/list+E.

43. M. Wole Mosadomi, 'Niger State Gov Bans Female Soccer', *Vanguard* (Lagos, Nigeria, 2003). http://allafrica.com/stories/200303030159.html.

44. Middle East Times, 'Muslim State Bans Women's Soccer', *Middle East Times, International Edition* (Cairo, 2000). http://metimes.com/2K/issue2000-2/sport/muslim_state_bans.htm.

45. Olajire, 'Football with a Woman's Face'.

46. B. Callaway and L.E. Creevey, *The Heritage of Islam: Women, Religion, and Politics in West Africa* (Boulder, Colorado: Lynne Rienner, 1994).

47. Albeit, incidents of adultery are receiving even more attention with the international campaign to oppose the death sentence by stoning given by the Zamfara justice system to Amina Lawal, a young unwed mother.

48. C.A. Abisuga and H.A.C. Awurumibe, 'Genesis of Female Soccer in Nigeria', *Networks, A Publication of the Women's Soccer Foundation*, 4, 1 (1993). This version was excerpted from Abisuga and Awurumibe, *Genesis*.

49. Abisuga and Awurumibe, 'Genesis'.

50. http://www.cris.com/~jg189/wsf/networks/vol4num1.html#nigeria.

51. O. Obayiuwana, 'The Confident Falcon', *BBC Sport Online*, (2002). http://news.bbc.co.uk/football/africa/2153839.stm.

52. Olajire, 'Football with a Woman's Face'.

53. R. Amoh, 'Goal Queen: Exclusive Interview with Mercy Akide', *African Soccer Magazine* (Jan./Feb. 2001).

54. Olajire, 'Football with a Woman's Face'.

55. Abisuga and Awurumibe, 'Genesis'.

56. Ibid.

57. Ibid.

58. Olajire, 'Football with a Woman's Face'. The women's international appearances began just when there was uncertainty about Nigeria's international sporting status. From 1995 through 1997, Nigeria faced the uneven implementation of international sanctions in sport, much the way that South Africa did under the apartheid regime. The sanctions were implemented after the execution of Ken Sara Wiwa by the Abacha regime. Several European countries denied visas to Nigerian athletes in the wake of the hanging of environmental activist Sara Wiwa. D. Ikhazuagbe, 'Sanctions Are Snuffing the Throb from Nigerian Sports', *The Post Express*, 19 May 1997 (1997). However, the sanctions did not apparently affect the women's side.

59. Olajire, 'Football with a Woman's Face'. Sam Okpodu replaced Mabo as head coach a few months before the 2002 Championships.

60. And apparently male players too. There have been charges that Nigeria has fielded male players in the past and some have called for sex-testing, a controversial position given that the IOC has finally dropped its sex-testing programme after years of protest. See Hilton-Smith, 'Women's Soccer in Africa: Against All Odds'. Iyabo Abade, the top scorer in Nigeria's women's league and selected for the national team, was thrown out of women's football in 1998 for being transgendered. She is a fully formed female and was raised as a female, but has small male genitalia. She is currently coaching a women's team. S. Audu, 'Nigerian Plans Return to Women's Team after Sex Change Operation', *Agence France Presse* (2001). http://www.transgender.freeserve.co.uk/tg/archive/2001-01-03/archive066.html.

61. Olajire, 'Football with a Woman's Face'.

62. According to Nauright, the first games were played in 1866. Nauright, *Sport, Cultures and Identities in South Africa*, p.103. The SAFA Website puts the date at 1862 (www.safa.net).

63. Nauright, *Sport, Cultures and Identities in South Africa*, p.104. For rugby, 'preferred' is too neutral a word. Rugby was a 'central defining cultural symbol for white South Africans', and reinforced 'notions of dominant white masculine power'. Ibid., p.99.

64. Alegi, *Moving the Goalposts*; Nauright, *Sport, Cultures and Identities in South Africa*.

65. Mamdani would argue that colonialism and apartheid are different variants of the same thing. M. Mamdani, *Citizen and Subject: Contemporary Africa and the Legacy of Late Colonialism* (Princeton N.J.: Princeton University Press, 1996).

66. Darby, *Africa, Football and FIFA*, p.71.
67. In 1968, facing a threatened boycott by some 50 nations, the International Olympic Committee uninvited South Africa to the Mexico City games, and in 1970 expelled them from the Olympic movement. By 1970, many international sporting bodies followed suit. D. Booth, *The Race Game: Sport and Politics in South Africa* (London; Portland OR: Frank Cass, 1998), pp.96–9.
68. Darby, *Africa, Football and FIFA*, pp.71–82.
69. Alegi, *Moving the Goalposts*; Nauright, *Sport, Cultures and Identities in South Africa*, pp.78 and 107.
70. Alegi, *Moving the Goalposts*.
71. Personal communication with K. Mathers, March 2003. Note that access to an adequate education was denied to the vast majority of the population.
72. Hargreaves, 'Women's Sport, Development and Cultural Diversity: The South African Experience'; Nauright, *Sport, Cultures and Identities in South Africa*, p.69; Roberts, *Against the Grain: Women and Sport in South Africa*. Rugby was also generally disallowed for girls. See Nauright, *Sport, Cultures and Identities in South Africa*, p.54.
73. *Drum*, 473 (Sept. 2001).
74. S. O'Connor, 'In a League of Their Own', *The Teacher*, www.teacher.co.za/200105/01-soccer.html, (2001).
75. Molefi Oliphant, Foreword to SAFA/Sanlam Women's League Handbook 2001/02. http://www.safa.net/safa_general/index.asp?sectionid=59.
76. Alegi, *Moving the Goalposts*, p.14. He also notes the paradox that even as the crowds attending the matches became more politically mobilized and violent, there was also a rise in attendance by women, children and families (pp.18–19).
77. 'Soccer goes Sexy', *Drum*, 139 (Oct. 1962), p.18. Reference in this study is made to a women's team that had just won the Tanganyika national union youth league cup in Dar es Salaam the previous month. This DSM team and the team they beat, the Tabora women's team, were mentioned in an article, 'The Girls are Going Places' in the August 1962 issue of *Drum*, 137, pp.11 and 13.
78. Nauright notes that there is little yet written on the history and sociology of South African women's sport. See Nauright, *Sport, Cultures and Identities in South Africa*, p.20. The main works available are by Cheryl Roberts and Jennifer Hargreaves. See Hargreaves, 'Women's Sport, Development and Cultural Diversity: The South African Experience'; Roberts, *Against the Grain: Women and Sport in South Africa*.
79. G. Brown, 'An Overview of Women's Football in South Africa', *1997 Soccer Indaba: Walls to Bridges* (South Africa: South African Football Association, www.safa.net, 1997). On the web at http://www.safa.net/publications/index.asp?ownerid=5&sectionid=59.
80. See O'Connor, 'In a League of Their Own'. Also, personal communication with K. Mathers, whose grandfather was active in organizing women's football in Wynberg, Cape Town.
81. M. Merton, 'Cinderellas Want to Get to the Ball', *Mail and Guardian* (South Africa, 2001). http://www.warmafrica.com/index/geo/5/cat/3/a/a/artid/print/?cat/3/geo/artid/2.
82. Brown, 'An Overview of Women's Football in South Africa'.
83. Among other features, they plan to offer the history of football in South Africa from the first ever match played in 1862 up until the present. From a message from the president on their home page, www.safa.net, 7 March 2003.
84. http://www.safa.net/history/index.asp?histid=7&sectid=12.
85. Since 1993, 20 new teams have emerged from Gauteng and neighbouring areas. http://www.safa.net/teams/team_details.asp?team=2.
86. http://www.safa.net/history/index.asp?histid=18&sectid=22.
87. http://www.safa.net/history/index.asp?histid=10&sectid=14.
88. http://www.safa.net/history/index.asp?histid=19&sectid=23 and http://www.safa.net/history/index.asp?histid=20&sectid=24.
89. Brown, 'An Overview of Women's Football in South Africa' and http://www.safa.net/history/index.asp?histid=6&sectid=11.
90. http://www.safa.net/history/index.asp?histid=16&sectid=20.
91. http://www.safa.net/teams/team_details.asp?team=2 Banyana Banyana, http://www.safa.net/history/index.asp?histid=22&sectid=26 and http://www.safa.net/results/match_details.asp?comp=580&v=rep. Note that in a January 2002 qualifying match for the U-19 World Cup, Basetana won a match against the Central African Republic in Bangui in front of a crowd of 10,000. In the Championship Final in April 2002, they were beaten by Nigeria, 3-2, back in Sebokeng, South Africa

where only 3,000 attended. Nigeria's U-19 squad went on to the World Cup in Canada in August 2002 as the sole representative from Africa. They lost to Denmark (2-1) and Canada (2-0) and drew with Japan (1-1), failing to go forward from their group.

92. http://www.safa.net/history/index.asp?histid=14&sectid=18.
93. http://www.safa.net/history/index.asp?histid=23&sectid=27.
94. http://www.safa.net/teams/team_details.asp?team=2. Note that unlike the 1997 Indaba which addressed all aspects of South African football and which is exhaustively documented, other than this one mention, a record of the Women's 1999 Indaba cannot be found on the SAFA Website.
95. BBC, 'Riot Ends African Women's Final', *BBC Sport online* (2000) http://news.bbc.co.uk/sport/hi/english/football/newsid_1040000/1040568.stm, and D. Kekana and M. wa Afrika, 'Brick-Hurling Fans Halt Banyana Final', *Sunday Times* (South Africa, 2000). http://www.suntimes.co.za/2000/11/26/news/news02.htm
96. http://www.safa.net/teams/team_details.asp?team=2.
97. http://www.safa.net/competitions/competition_details.asp?comp=101. The word 'Halala' expresses joy similar to 'Hooray' or 'Well done' in Zulu.
98. http://www.safa.net/safa_general/index.asp?sectionid=59.
99. Merton, 'Cinderellas Want to Get to the Ball'.
100. K. Martheze, 'FAB Strive to Improve Fate of Footballers', *Dispatch Online* (East London, South Africa, 2000). http://www.dispatch.co.za/2000/02/11/sport/SOCCER.HTM.
101. M. Allie, 'Desiree Ellis', *Players: Living for the Game* (2002); Merton, 'Cinderellas Want to Get to the Ball'. http://www.footballculture.net/players/int_ellis.html.
102. Team Chicago Athletics, 'Inter-Africa Women's Soccer Tournament', *Kick International*, X, 2 (2002).
103. Merton, 'Cinderellas Want to Get to the Ball'.
104. Darby, *Africa, Football and FIFA*.
105. Culled from various online newspaper reports and the RSSSF site http://www.rsssf.com/results-afr.html.
106. A more detailed study would be required to adequately compare sponsorship levels.
107. Olajire argues that this is the case. See Olajire, 'Football with a Woman's Face'.

14

Women's Football in Brazil: Progress and Problems

SEBASTIÃO VOTRE and LUDMILA MOURÃO

In *Women's Football in Brazil*[1] we analyse the progress and problems women footballers have had, and have to deal with, in the face of resistance, misunderstanding, covert and overt rejection and prejudice from their families and relatives, from the media and from educational authorities. The data come from women players who played football before 1980, as well as those who are presently active and visible as top athletes. Reports from newspapers and magazines, and web registers are also utilized. As the archetypal male sport in Brazil, men have played football since the end of the nineteenth century. In spite of various obstacles, women have played football, at least since 1975. But the boom of women's football happened after football ceased to be forbidden to women by law in 1979. The first Women's Football Championship took place in 1981. Media and companies offered reasonable support. However, women's football could not survive as an amateur activity, and women still had to face prejudice, resistance and rejection, and struggled to continue playing without support for either national or international participation. Nevertheless, in 1988, in the International Championship of Women's Football, in China, Brazil took third place and in the Atlanta Olympics of 1996 they managed to obtain the fourth place.

PROGRESS

Only in 1979 did football stop being a forbidden sport to Brazilian women. Emancipation came with the women's liberation movement that spread in the 1970s. Football quickly made its way among women throughout the country, and four years after its liberation, women's teams were organized, mainly in the Brazilian States' capitals and in large and middle-sized cities where there were clubs available with opportunities for the development of women's football.[2]

In Rio de Janeiro, the reference point taken in this paper, the huge sand strip of Copacabana Beach was the first place where women's football teams played. Several other teams were organized in other districts in town, far from Copacabana. In other Brazilian cities girls and women began to play football.

The famous beaches in Rio de Janeiro's 'fancy' south zone (Copacabana, Leblon and Ipanema) hosted women's teams with different characteristics. Those

254

teams played on the sand, mostly after office hours. Some came to the sand pitches to play football after their jobs as maids in the city's south zone homes located in the beach-adjoining neighbourhoods.

In the mid-1980s according to newspapers in Rio de Janeiro, including the *Jornal dos Sports* and the *O Dia*, and in São Paulo, including the *A Gazeta Esportiva*, the number of teams exceeded 3,000. There were first and second divisions. There were also official championships in the following Brazilian States: São Paulo, Paraná, Rio de Janeiro, Minas Gerais, Paraíba, Pernambuco, Pará, Goiás, Rio Grande do Sul, Bahia and Santa Catarina.

Paradoxically, despite these developments, the perspective for sport was gloomy and the future pointed to an increasing national impoverishment. On the one hand, the organization and the number of women's teams advanced; on the other hand, the pressure for resources needed to support training also grew. The clubs and associations responsible for the creation of those women's football teams had no resources for them. The more competitive women's football became and the better the performance of the teams, the more the sport required investment in the skills of its players, in its organizational structure, in its local, state, national and international tournaments. One anecdote nicely illustrates the lack of investment in women's football: on Saturday, 25 August 1984, the São Cristóvão team and the Tomazinho de São João de Meriti team, both from the metropolitan area of Rio de Janeiro City, were unable to play a match because their jerseys were white and neither one of them had a set of alternative strips.

Let us take the women's football team of the Esporte Clube Radar as a point of departure for the women's football in Rio de Janeiro – and, to a certain extent, in Brazil as a whole, although it should not be forgotten that there were many other women's teams in the city and in the state, to be mentioned later. This team created, and encouraged, the development of women's football in Rio de Janeiro and in Brazil, with its efficient leadership and effective performances.

The first women's football championship took place in Rio de Janeiro in 1981. Several teams made up of beach football players were involved, and Radar was the champion. In 1982, Radar beat all its opponents. Then representing Brazil, it played in the final against Jalisco at the Brazil-Mexico Cup of Friendship. In 1983, with the sponsorship of Banco Econômico, the same team, now named Women's Football Radar Mondaine participated in the United States Women's Football National Championship. The journey to the United States took 20 days, and they played in Miami, New Jersey and New York. They beat the Florida women's state team, 1-0; against Tampa Bay women's team, the score was 4-1, and they drew with the Florida Champions, 1-1. On the same trip, the Brazilian team made a stop over in Chile and played against the Província de Cordilheiras. They won 16-0. In 1983, Radar had been invincible for 76 matches.[3]

Due to its outstanding performance and to its national and international prestige, Radar ended up taking on the mantle of Brazilian women's football representative in the period before the national team was set up. The comments of the President of Radar, published in a sports periodical at the time, provide the reason: 'Radar represents women's Brazilian football because it is the Brazilian bi-champion and holder of many other titles.'[4]

It is ironic that Radar established its team and became famous without ever having its own ground: it always played on Copacabana Beach sands. So, for a long time, the Casa do Marinheiro hosted Radar's women's football team training sessions. A Brazilian Navy Sports Centre, Casa do Marinheiro, located on the Avenida Brasil, in the district of Bom Sucesso, in the city's north zone, offered a very atypical hospitality. At the time, the Navy admitted only male military individuals at senior levels. Women were hired exclusively for clerical work. Even so, the Brazilian Navy opened its premises for five hours a day to the Radar women's football team. In 1984, the Casa do Marinheiro invited the Radar team to a barbecue dinner party to celebrate the bi-champion title it had won in 1983–84. The Casa officers took their wives and families to the party, a fact that indicates that football had been fully accepted, at least by the military. The officers and their families pushed aside the taboo against women's football in Rio de Janeiro social life.[5]

A referee earned about 10,000 cruzeiros per match in the 1980s. Professional women players (there were some) earned as much as 300,000 cruzeiros per month, training four or five hours a day. However, the Globettes, a team of television celebrities – not players – created by the Globo Television Network, made as much as 300,000 cruzeiros per match.[6]

The expense of the transportation of players from Copacabana to Avenida Brasil (about 30km away), in addition to the cost of clothing, shoes and other items, came to a sum that Esporte Clube Radar could not afford. In a climate of strong pressure for professional qualification, they searched for a partnership with sponsoring institutions, such as companies and banks. In Rio de Janeiro, the eventual support of Banco do Rio de Janeiro, BRJ, was so significant that the club was renamed Radar-BRJ in November 1983.

The President of Radar, Eurico Lyra, made the following statement about the sponsorship of the Banco BRJ:

> We must highlight the essential relevance of the sponsorship given by Banco BRJ, which helps us financially, covering over 50 per cent of our expenses, making it possible for us to have a team with a high-level structure only comparable to the standards of Brazilian major clubs. The Directors of BRJ, Wellman de Queiroz and Júlio Singer, have always believed in Radar and have given us much support, mainly when the team was taking its first steps. And now we are proud to state that BRJ's investment return is large both in publicity and community terms.[7]

Although there have never been sufficient resources, the number of sponsors has been relatively large at various moments in the history of amateur women's football in Rio de Janeiro: Mondaine, Casas Pernambucanas, Coppertone, Banco

Econômico, BRJ and Goldencross, among other companies, have all acted as sponsors at one time or another.

The São Paulo Championship in 1984 demonstrated that women's football had reached a mature stage. There were representatives from several Brazilian States: Bahia, Minas Gerais, Pernambuco, Paraíba, Paraná, Rio Grande do Sul, Rio de Janeiro and São Paulo, and a representative from Venezuela.[8] The São Paulo City Sports Department offered accommodation and subsistence for all the visiting teams.

Other indications of maturity were the statements made by the players, provided below, redolent with typical football metaphors and similes of war, confrontation, luck, determination and *esprit de corps*. They reveal a similarity of maxim, whether the game involves men or women.[9] Take the words of Kátia,[10] Cruzeiro's player: 'if the players from Bahia are prepared, we are also all set to fight for victory. So the Bahia girls can start getting ready right now, because this match won't be an easy task.'[11] Jânia, on the Bahia team, proposes the team fights with total and optimistic determination, without any constraints: 'Optimism must always be there, and our team is an optimistic group. We will walk to the field to win and to contest the great final match.'[12] Jânia is one of the greatest scorers on her team. She scored two goals against Sport, but she attributes them to her team, and places the team above her own performance: 'Of course we like to score goals and to celebrate them enthusiastically. But I understand that the victory of the team comes first. It does not matter which player scored the goal.'[13] And Vera, from the Centro Educacional Vila Maria de São Paulo, affirmed the relevance of team spirit, courage and determination: 'When we registered our team, lots of people underestimated our courage and said our team was too weak and for us to be there would simply make up numbers in the tournament ... Our team joined the competition with great determination and courage ...' – 'Football is decided on the field limits and we can surprise Radar as we have surprised Pinheiros.'[14] However, not all women players talk and act in the same way.

Female aggression is denounced by the top model and player Isabel, from Internacional, a team from the city of Porto Alegre in the south of Brazil. Easy-going and quite determined, she faces a lot of prejudice in her daily life, mainly from the macho–biased, who cannot understand why such an attractive girl has decided to play football. Bel, however, acknowledges that the prejudice is also rampant among her companions: 'many of them want to equal men but this is a silly attitude. Femininity cannot be breached or you will lose your identity. I am the same person in a fashion show and on a football field.'[15] By and large, the above statements suggest that women's football is above the constraints of gender. It is gender-free football, fed by the metaphors of war: the game is a war and the war is a game.

In 1984 a team made up of players from the northern state of Pará beat the strong Radar. This indicates that women's football was becoming consolidated in several regions in the country. The victory of Pará over Radar, considered the best

Brazilian team on that occasion, and one of the best in the world, firmly demonstrates the strength of football played in the extreme north of Brazil. Furthermore, consolidation is underlined by the fact that, during the São Paulo Cup (1984), the media revealed that there were over 3,000 women's football teams in Brazil, scattered over more than ten Brazilian States.

In 1985 there were signs of the increasing strength of women's football in the draw between Bangu and Radar, teams that were favourites in the first round of the Carioca (Rio de Janeiro) Cup. The *Jornal dos Sports* ended its report with the following comment: 'With this result, Madureira remains well ahead, at the top of the list, seconded by the Canto do Rio.'[16] This remark demonstrated the strength of women's football, since Madureira and Canto do Rio were strong teams, and could hold their own with Radar and Bangu, the centres of attention.

Additional evidence of consolidation was the proposal that the First World Championship of Women's Football Clubs in February 1985 should be held in Brazil. The event was to take place one week before Carnival. The idea was to bring together club teams from different parts of the world in São Paulo and Rio de Janeiro. Teams from Italy, Sweden, Chile, Japan and Korea would play in São Paulo, and teams from England, Portugal, Argentina, Suriname and the team of Radar would play in Rio de Janeiro.

However, despite all these clear indications of the consolidation of women's football in Brazil in the mid-1980s, there was still no Brazilian women's national team! Thus the reasons offered earlier by Lyra for Radar to represent Brazil in the international competition were sensible. At the same time, they demonstrated the lack of both a political and administrative structure of Brazilian women's football, and the lack of interest of sports authorities at various levels to address the problem. They were simply too involved with the significant problems of men's football.

In the 1980s women's football had a first division (large clubs) and a second division (small clubs), which suggested a healthy growth of the sport. Nevertheless, due to large clubs' opposition to professional preparation in women's football, the second division – which was amateur – progressed more rapidly than the first division, which was kept as amateur.

How visible was Brazilian women's football in South America, in the 1970s and 1980s? The evidence suggests its visibility was low, due to the crushing power of men's football in those countries and the massive investment made by state governments to gain popularity by supporting men's football. Despite its growth, women's football was an activity with low social visibility. In a gesture that could be considered at once co-operative and paternalist, the media gave their support and provided visibility, but it cannot be compared to the visibility given to men's football. What is clear from media reports from those days was that the media's support was ambiguous, highlighting the erotic, exotic and sensual aspects, or exploring the polemical sexual issue that associated women's football with women 'masculinization'. But what was the price for that support and what did it bring in return? The impression to be gained from reading the printed media material was that it possessed a certain anecdotal, humorous, satirical tone that at times described women's football as a ridiculous practice and often as a laughable activity.

A Gazeta Esportiva, in its 15 October 1984 issue, refers to the five-year invincibility of Sport Clube de Recife, from the date it had been founded.[17] The fact that the team remained unbeaten for 79 matches could mean that it was a powerful team among other powerful teams in Brazil. Nevertheless, the team played only 79 times in five years. Clearly there were not many opponents. In short, the number of strong teams in Brazilian cities and states was not large, and the lack of strong teams produced the invincibility of SCR.

The growing interest in women's football throughout Brazil cannot be denied. It resulted in the creation of a Women's Clubs Brazilian Association (FCBA), pioneered by the São Paulo City Sports Department. The president of FCBA was Fábio Lazzari, who was the sports' promotion director at that Sports Department. He worked hard for men's football at all levels, and encouraged women's football. The honorary president of FCBA was the Sports Secretary, Andrade Figueira. The Association was responsible for creating the environment and the structure that eventually ensured the creation of a Brazilian team to participate in the 1988 World Championship in China.

There are indications that there was institutional support for women's football, to ensure the establishment of a Brazilian women's team, both for Brazil's participation in domestic and international events, such as the international championship held in São Paulo and Rio de Janeiro, and foreign events such as the World Championship in China in 1988. Support came from FIFA, CBF (Brazilian Football Confederation), and FCF (Rio de Janeiro City Football Federation). In other words, there was a consensus about the need for a national women's team. This was reinforced by the best Brazilian players. They felt isolated, and obviously wished to play for their country against other countries. The newspapers also played their part in exerting pressure for a Brazilian women's team. *A Gazeta Esportiva*, in October 1984, stated: 'if players were recruited to make up a Brazilian women's football team, Márcia Honório, from Juventus, would certainly be one of them. At the age of 22, born in Caireiras, she travels every day to work out and train. She has been playing football for 11 years.'[18] These are her own words: 'I started playing with the Expedicionário de Franco da Rocha. At the beginning my mother was against the idea and only my father gave me support. But now all the folks at home really back me up.'[19] She herself openly stated that she was working to be selected for the Brazilian women's team. Márcia saw her efforts as a symbol of liberation from the taboo against women's participation in football: 'there was a taboo in the past. But now football is proudly played by women, just like any other sport.'[20]

Cenira was also very confident that she would be selected for the national team to compete in China in 1988. However, it was clear that improvements in women's football were essential in the future: 'we need competent managers, not the ones who just want to become famous. Women's football has already become a fact.

The critiques must come from the people who really do something and not from those[21] who do nothing but make trouble.'[22]

Evidence of the less than satisfactory attitude taken by sports authorities, in relation to women's football, comes in the references made by a leading football manager, Eurico Lyra, and Fábio Lazzari, the sports promotion director of the São Paulo City Sports Department, and president of the Brazilian Association of Women's Football Clubs. They referred, enthusiastically, to what should be considered as normal: the support by FIFA, FCF and CBF. Lyra wrote that João Havelange, the FIFA's president, had become excited about the idea of a Brazilian women's team: 'Havelange wants the Brazilian team to have a basis for the next world competition, and this will come out from the very tournament (international, planned for 1985) that we are going to promote.'[23] It is regrettable that a single event such as a tournament was used as an opportunity to create the Brazilian national team. The conventional procedure is, of course, that players are chosen by CBF according to their performance in their clubs in regional and national tournaments.

In 1984, in a historical match against Atlético Mineiro (7-0), Radar's most spectacular goal was scored in the twentieth minute. Cenira placed the ball high in the corner of the net. The goals ended in the twenty-fourth minute, when Cenira scored another beautiful goal, regrettably not witnessed by Atlético Mineiro fans, who had already left during the first half of the game, when the third goal had been scored. Here are the words of the scorer: 'I always try to improve my skills by going to Maracanã and observing the way great stars play.'[24] Cenira scored ten goals at the III Taça Brasil (III Brazil Tournament). She says that becoming three-time champion silenced the people who did not believe in the team: 'No one is better than we are. We are the best in the country and we have proved it by winning the championship for the third time.'[25] Cenira explained that she is used to being the scorer in competitions: 'in the state championship in 1983, I was the best, with 32 goals. I am now at a good stage in my career and whenever there is an opportunity, I do not waste it. I will put the ball into the net any way I can. I won't miss it.'[26] In a sentence, Cenira is an icon of footballing skill, instinct and glamour. Her beauty lies in her technical ability.

From the southern state of Rio Grande do Sul, Isabel Cristina, Bel, represents the answer to machismo and harassment. She was chosen as the most beautiful player in the 1985 Brazilian Cup. Her beauty and her sexual appeal to press, photographers and fans ensure an ambiguous title: 'Bel, the professional model without prejudices.' Bel became involved in football after her father gave her a ball as her first gift: 'We are three sisters at home. I am the youngest. It just happened that my father wanted to have a son when I was born. To make up for his frustration, the gifts he started giving me were balls. That is how I developed my passion for football.'[27] Bel is an icon of sensual femininity in football. Her glamour is not technical but sexual. Cenira and Bel represent two faces of women's football: skill and sensuality. As yet these are not combined in one female footballer.

PROBLEMS

The Brazilian international tournament was to take place in February 1985 in São Paulo and Rio de Janeiro, a few days before Carnival. The date was close. However, the press did nothing. The media acted as if nothing was happening or about to happen. Promotion clearly was not satisfactory. Visibility was non-existent. Recognition was minimal. In the words of Eurico Lyra: 'We will be holding the Women's Football Clubs World Championship in Brazil in February 1985 and nobody knows about it.'[28]

Due to the lack of visibility and legitimacy of women's football in a society that traditionally values men's football, the situation was critical. According to Lyra, women's football was still an amateur sport going through unhappy circumstances: '... it is a vicious circle: the sport does not develop because it is not appropriately promoted;[29] and it does not deserve appropriate promotion because the great clubs in Rio de Janeiro do not play it; there is no solution'.[30]

As a result, women's football has ended up adopting the standards of a second division team. In fact, the growing trend has been that in the Brazilian States no first-division club has participated in the women's football championship. But the second-division clubs, with fewer resources and poorer infrastructure, have had their women's teams sponsored by members who have invested money from their own pockets.

What has produced the problems in women's football, in the country of football (albeit men's football)? Paradoxically, the main obstacles, it would appear, were the struggle for the right to achieve professional status, and to attain the same status as men's football. These efforts ended up by undermining and devitalizing women's football development. This fact, added to the conservative reaction of the machismo sectors in Brazilian society, which did not approve of women's presence in an arena typically reserved for men, and the fact that football was considered too rough a sport for women, which brought about a ban until 1979, has resulted in progress backwards as well as forwards.

The truth is that there was not the will, space or structure in large clubs for women's football, so it was either set aside in the clubs' organization or was left to the clubs' women's departments. These departments were traditionally in charge of social events. They were simply not ready to deal with the commitments and tasks related to the maintenance of a complete team with 22 players, coaches, trainers, massagers, doctors, equipment staff and fitness coaches. Furthermore, even if they wished, clubs were not able to raise the necessary resources to launch sponsorship funds to pay the players who had to dedicate at least four hours a day to their training. In addition, society's support as a whole was weak and inconsistent. In particular, the women's football fans were not visible, in living history or memory. There were far too few groups of organized fans; nothing comparable to the number of organized fans' groups for men's football, which represent a vital source of financial support.

An important obstacle was that the media has been ambiguous, sometimes highlighting the players' beauty, sometimes focusing on their 'peculiar' habits, and at other times emphasizing the anecdotal and esoteric features of the 'fragile' women's football. This is clear from the titles of newspaper reports such as: 'They are also good at playing football', 'Drops to refresh your eyes', 'Pussy-cat', and the like.

However, all has not been totally black. Some top managers' 'passionate' support prevailed, such as, for example, Eurico Lyra, who paid from his own pocket for a large part of the expenses associated with the maintenance of the women's football teams, including the players' transportation and accommodation fees when they travelled, as well as their salaries. In the 1980s, the most viable solution for the cost of women football players' professional preparation was similar – in smaller proportion – to what happens nowadays in several other Brazilian sports. Companies sponsored their activities and thus they managed to survive. The sponsorship offered by Banco BRJ, to Radar team, mentioned earlier, was a sign that the strategy was feasible. Banco BRJ covered more than 50 per cent of the team's expenses.[31]

However, Radar was the exception, not the rule. As stated already, since the clubs had their budgets committed mostly to the men's football teams, sponsorship for the women's football had to come mostly from top managers' pockets and from anonymous sponsors, individuals who were interested in women's football. This was not a self-sustainable plan. Consequently, the lack of funds to pay the players was the effective reason for the eradication of professional women's football in Brazil. Given that women did not want to become amateur players, women's football experienced a rapid decline, which lasted for the whole of the 1990s.

For the most part, throughout the country, there were women players on the field, but directors, managers, coaches, supervisors, fitness coaches and massagers, as well as the linesmen and most referees, were men. Today as yet there are no registers of women in football management positions and no record of women's attempts to change the situation. There have been some women referees in Rio de Janeiro City, but they have never refereed major matches. *A Gazeta Esportiva* stated, in 1983: 'The São Paulo City Administration has invited the referees Vanda Virla, Cláudia Guedes and Elizabeth Falcão from Rio de Janeiro, to go to São Paulo. They are refereeing the friendly matches played near the São Paulo Capital, organized by the teams that were eliminated at the early stages of the Cup.'[32] This situation remains more or less the same, today, at the beginning of the twenty-first century. Women on and off the field have a long way to go in Brazilian football.

Women players have frequently complained that, to quote a newspaper, 'the audience had a rather macho-oriented behaviour, but that behaviour usually lessened when the result was positive, that is, when the team won a difficult and exciting game'.[33]

There have been too few women doctors involved in the production of information related to risks inherent in the playing of football by women. Dr Pricela Celano is the only one referred to in the media. She has specialized in issues and problems related to women's sports, and has recommended that players avoid the ball's impact on their breasts in order to prevent mastitis. References to the health risks associated with the practice of women's football were persistent.[34] Nevertheless, the women players performed well and there is no record of any health problems caused by their four or five-hour daily training or by their competing in conditions comparable to men's football. Greater scrutiny of the health advantages of football to women, done by experts, is a pressing need to overcome misconceptions and mythologies.

The media presented the Third Brazil Cup as if it were a parade of Carnival Samba Schools with characteristics of a fashion show. The tournament included 102 players from several Brazilian States such as São Paulo, Minas Gerais, Rio Grande do Sul, Pará, Goiás and Rio de Janeiro. As stated earlier, the idea was to select a national team to represent Brazil in the World Cup, officially organized by FIFA, in January 1988, in China. Mariucha Moneró's report in *A Gazeta Esportiva* was typically provocative, by associating women's football with samba, which enhances Brazilian women's sensuality. She even made references to and highlighted the famous Samba 'School' Mocidade Independente, to describe the Radar's back:

> Fingernails red polish, shiny lipstick, hairdo, black shorts and yellow jersey: that is Neusa Cavalheiros' look. Braids decorated with colourful beads, the hairdo launched by Stevie Wonder enhanced the beauty of Mocidade Independente's charming samba dancer, Cilda, who was also wearing shorts and a jersey in the blue and yellow colours. But the two of them were not part of a Samba School rehearsal show. They were in a football field. The former was a lineswoman in yellow and the latter was the back on Radar's football team, at the opening of the Women's Football Brazil cup, at the Portuguesa Stadium, in the Rio de Janeiro city district of Ilha do Governador.[35]

Moneró compared football to 'feminine' frivolous activities and habits in the Brazilian culture and her comments were labelled 'women's talk': 'besides football, there are lots of other things happening in a game between women, starting with the public, which cheers enthusiastically for their favourite players, going on to men's insulting comments and moving on to "women's talk" during the game, on the reserve players' bench and in the dressing rooms, where football is a practically forgotten topic.'[36]

Reference has already been made earlier to the 'insulting comments' by men. They were offensive and degrading censoring women because they were at a place, where, according to Moneró, men were entitled to be, not women. 'You should be in the kitchen', 'move to the laundry sink, do the clothes washing'.[37] According to Moneró, 'what they want to prove is that, just like men, they can play football with the same skills and techniques as men, without minding the insulting comments',[38] or, at least, without reacting explicitly to those comments, as can be attested to in the following passage, reported by Radar's Cenira: 'Today, when I came into the field, I heard a guy say that I should be at a laundry sink, washing clothes. But I did not bother to reply to him, although I was angry. My reaction came later, with the ball at my feet' – said Cenira, who had scored three goals in the match that day.[39]

Cenira's comments reveal how deep the machismo prejudice goes against the women's presence in the arena reserved in Brazil for men's football. Both men and the *woman* journalist were prejudiced. The worldwide masculine tolerance of women's presence in the men's football niche is clearly revealed here: when women produced good results, the prejudice was stilled, but when performance was poor it was very aggressive. Reference to Cenira's boyfriend in Moneró's report was evidence that she did not have a homosexual orientation – a positive aspect of the report, because there is a strong relation between women's playing football and women's 'masculinization'.

It must be recognized that both violence and cheating rampant in women's football contributed to its failure to prosper. In 1983, the Rio de Janeiro City Football Federation received 42 lawsuits dealing only with women's football, 90 per cent of which related to players sent off from the field for 'unsportsmanlike' behaviour. The games' reports include outrageous four-letter words and physical and verbal aggression to referees, linesmen and other players.

The level of aggression among Brazilian players in the 1980s is extraordinary. The number of women players sent off for 'unsportsmanlike' behaviour was proportionally higher than the corresponding number in men's football. Actions like the following happened all the time: the referee Sônia Rezende whistled for a foul in favour of Tuna Luso team and a player from the Atlético team hit her in her face.

The most frequently reported incident involving violence in women's football is reported below. The women's team of Bangu Atlético Clube, also from Rio de Janeiro, had the famous manager Castor de Andrade as its patron and honorary president. The team was unbeaten for 125 matches, and it finally lost to Radar, in the first stage of the state tournament in 1983. The match became notorious because of violence by Castor de Andrade, his bodyguards and the Bangu players against the referee and the linesmen in the match.

The incident[40] unfortunately became infamous for the level of violence that women's football had reached. The report stated:

> Beating up at the women's' football match.
> The match between Radar and Bangu in the town of Moça Bonita, yesterday, ended with violence and aggression against the referee and the press members. Reacting badly to the Bangu team's defeat, the bodyguards, the honorary president, Castor de Andrade, fans and players punched and kicked the referee Ricardo Ferreira.[41]

The outcome was a shocked and frightened Radar:

> Whoever went into Radar's dressing room after the match against Bangu would never imagine that the team had won. Some of the players were crying, others hugging one another, others simply looked astonished at the equally shocked coach Fred. None of them hid their worry and fear of being threatened by the opponent's fans as they left the stadium.[42]

What was the reason for such an outburst in women's football, far more serious than anything in men's football? One explanation arguably, is over-compensation. Women, so used to being 'mistreated', used the same weapons in response. For the men involved too, violence against women was a cultural commonplace.

The press recorded the incident but did not place much importance on it, neither did the president of the Rio de Janeiro City Football Federation, who explained away the incident with the following words: 'Football is passion. Passion will lead people to that.'[43]

In the 1990s women's football decayed year by year. Beyond first division clubs, second division ones closed the doors to women's football. Paradoxically, Brazilian players were recognized abroad, but there was no more room for them in Brazil. The twentieth century ended with no women's football team in Rio de Janeiro. The official national team has never been well organized. Individuals or private companies recruited Brazilian players who took part in foreign tournaments on an informal basis.

CONCLUSION

The conclusion from an analysis of the recent situation in Brazilian women's football is not complicated. Minimal conditions for a national team are non-existent. There is no private or institutional support for the professional players who play football either in club teams or in the national team. There is no movement in favour of professional preparation for women's football, which struggles to survive even as an amateur sport. The political and administrative structure required to support women's football is unavailable from the government – local or national. Whenever there is talk of women's football, the erotic dimension again takes precedence over the technical. This was the situation as recently as 2001, in the Women's Football State Championship promoted by the São Paulo Football Federation.[44] The tournament brought together 600 players with a maximum age of 23. The emphasis was on their beauty. Failure to be sufficiently beautiful ensured non-involvement, no matter how good their footballing skills might be. The state of women's football today suggests that Brazil has little to be proud of and much to be ashamed of.

NOTES

1. The authors wish to express their grateful appreciation of Professor J.A. Mangan's invaluable assistance with the presentation of this essay.
2. M. Silva, M. Costa and J.G. Salles, 'Representação social do futebol feminino na imprensa brasileira', in S. Votre (ed), *Representação social do esporte e da atividade física – ensaios etnográficos* (Brasília: DF, Ministry of Sports, 1998), pp.103–18.
3. The Radar figures in 1984 were: general number: 179 victories, 560 goals scored against opponents and 51 against its own team, 14 tied scores and only two defeats. President: Eurico Lyra; Director: Álvaro Brittes; Coach: Professor Varella; Supervisor: Aníbal Pimpão; Fitness Coach: Pedro Paulo; Massage Therapist: Sérgio Prado. Players: Margaret, Rosa, Mary, Jurema, Danda, Sally, Pelé, Cenira, Lúcia, Ana Elzinha, Lica, Marisa, Clida, Fia, Catarina, Rata, Dicró, Russa and Eliane.
4. *Jornal dos Sports*, 1983.
5. That attitude was by no means shared by the average population, with a patriarchal and male-oriented tradition. This fact will be presented later in this essay.
6. There is a tendency, in Brazil, to associate models of femininity with women's sport. That trend has always been the case for football. The teams that presented excellent sports ability in their football practice were challenged by teams made up of TV artists and models that featured Brazilian women's beauty, grace and femininity. In this case, the team was made up of actresses from Globo Television Network, that is, the Globettes. The Globettes' participation in women's football reveals the difficulties the Brazilian people have in justifying that sport as a possibility for the female public, because Brazilian society associates male football with its male identity.
7. *Jornal dos Sports*, 1983.
8. Suriname was also expected to participate, but did not.
9. This was also the tone of women who played football in the latter part of the 1990s. See L. Reis, 'Representações da mulher que joga futebol' (Rio de Janeiro: RJ, Master's Thesis, Universidade Gama Filho, 1997).
10. Players are identified by their nicknames or Christian names, when it is not possible to find out their full names.
11. *Jornal dos Sports*, 1983.
12. Ibid.
13. Ibid.
14. Ibid.
15. Ibid.
16. *Jornal dos Sports*, 1985.
17. It had been founded before Radar, which was created in 1981.
18. *A Gazeta Esportiva*, Oct. 1984.
19. Ibid.
20. Ibid.
21. It is worth remarking that Cenira is referring to managers, and she does not specify if they are men or women, but the fact is that the managers and coaches were always male, never female. This is still true in Brazilian women's sports, in which the number of female coaches is irrelevant when compared to the number of male coaches. G. Aragão, *Social Representations of Women in Decision Making Positions in Sporting Teams of Rio de Janeiro* (Rio de Janeiro, RJ: Universidade Gama Filho, 2002). There has never been any movement in favour of female managers' appearance or hiring. The fact that men manage and command women's football at all levels seems to be normal.
22. Ibid.
23. *A Gazeta Esportiva*, Oct, 1984.
24. Ibid.
25. Ibid.
26. Ibid.
27. *Jornal dos Sports*, 1985.
28. *Jornal dos Sports*, Jan. 1985.
29. Eurico Lyra's words referred to one of the problems women's football had in relation to sponsors' interest, namely, the fact that it was played by small clubs that had no tradition in male football. Research is necessary to discover whether that was a true constraint.
30. *Jornal dos Sports*, Jan. 1985.

31. Until today, in 2003, two streamers strategically placed at the Main Entrance to Esporte Clube Radar on Rua Mascarenhas de Morais, 691, in Copacabana display the inscription RADAR–BRJ, Campeão de 1983–1984 (RADAR–BRJ, 1983–1984 Champion).
32. São Paulo City Cup, from the 1983 championship.
33. These words, published in *O Dia*, Oct. 1984, come from Cenira, the best player in the 1983 and 1984 Championships.
34. *A Gazeta Esportiva*, Jan. 1985.
35. *A Gazeta Esportiva*, Feb. 1985.
36. Ibid.
37. We have already referred to the meaning of those 'slandering comments' made by men. They were in fact offensive and degrading, censoring women because they were at a place, where, according to the commentator, men were entitled to be not women. 'You should be in the kitchen', 'move to the laundry sink, do the clothes washing', etcetera.
38. *A Gazeta Esportiva*, Feb. 1985.
39. *A Gazeta Esportiva*, Oct. 1984.
40. *Jornal dos Sports*, Oct. 1983.
41. Ibid.
42. Ibid.
43. However, the effect of the turmoil was not as great as is usually reported. See the note published by *Jornal dos Sports*, commenting on the second round:
    Radar and Bangu: a peaceful 0 x 0.
    There was no violence, neither in nor out of the field. Nothing that could remind us of the bellicose game between Bangu and Radar in the First round in the dispute for the women's football championship title. A few policemen showed up in the field on Avenida Teixeira de Castro, but they had nothing to do to hold back players or fans. And to complete the picture, no one made any goal and the final score 0 x 0 was fair to the football performance presented by both teams.
44. J. Knijnik and E. Vasconcelos, 'Mulheres na área no país do futebol: perigo de gol', in A. Simões (org), *Mulher e esporte – mitos e verdades* (São Paulo; SP: Manole, 2003), pp.165–76.

Soccer: A World Sport for Women

FAN HONG

It is not exactly the kind of context you would expect for a movement for gender equality, but by a strange turn of events, soccer (association football), the traditional bastion of masculinity and the symbol of men's prestige and privilege, has become something of a significant talisman for women's egalitarian progress in sport.[1] Women breached this traditional bastion of masculinity in the late twentieth century.

In Canada, a country known as a hockey nation, far more Canadian girls now play soccer (28 per cent) than ice-hockey (six per cent). In Norway, soccer is the most popular sport for women, and men's soccer now plays second fiddle at best. In Britain, in 2002, soccer overtook netball, which was traditionally the most popular women's game, for the first time with 61,000 British women bending it like Beckham in clubs affiliated to the Football Association. In China, women's soccer is one of the fastest growing female sports and the women's national team has achieved outstanding results on the international stage. Nationally, female soccer players were used as models of resolution to inspire Chinese male soccer players to qualify for the 2002 World Cup. In the United States, there are over eight and a half million known female soccer participants. The new eight-team Women's United Soccer Association (WUSA) was established in 2001. It has top players from the United States as well as the best internationals from 20 different countries. In Africa, the current African Women's Championship in Nigeria attests to the gradual growth of women's soccer across the continent.[2] Feminist activism, fervent nationalism, political ambitions, corporate funding, governmental sports policies and cultural change have created a 'women's soccer revolution' in North and South America, Asian, Africa and Australasia. Women's soccer, a game that now embraces nations, cultures, ethnicities and classes, has become a world sport for women. It represents modern feminism: unapologetic, individualistic, empowered and assertive.

Soccer, Women, Sexual Liberation provides a variety of insights into the cultural, political and economic forces that have contributed to women's increased opportunities in sport, but also reminds us of the fragility of those opportunities. In this regard, it is a critique of patriarchy, masculinity and the male-dominated institutionalized world of soccer. In Europe, many clubs still only pay their female players' expenses. In China, while professional soccer is progressing, no amateur games exist due to political favouritism, economic denial and cultural bias. Many girls and women, therefore, are excluded from the sport, and Chinese women's soccer faces a serious problem of lack of recruitment.

Perhaps the greatest comparison between men's and women's soccer is the remuneration. Sun Wen, the Chinese captain, 'Golden Boots' of the Third Women's World Cup, one of the best female players in the world, earns about £2,000 a year when she plays in China, but an average Chinese first division male player earns £18,000 a year. Kelly Smith, arguably Britain's best-known female soccer player, who plays in the US for the Philadelphia Charge, earns only about £35,000 a year, less than many male Premiership players get each week. One of the best-paid men in soccer in the world is David Beckham, who earns over £1,000,000 a year. In contrast, the best paid woman in soccer is Mia Hamm, who earns about £75,000 a year and who is promoting the film *Bend it Like Beckham* in America, where she is more famous than he is.[3] Not only this, but women players get far less and poorer quality media exposure and far less sponsorship. The plain fact is that the institutionalized game represents male superiority and female inferiority. Indeed, sport in general and soccer in particular, to some extent, is 'an anchor to neoliberal economics and neoconservative policies through its strong beliefs in inequality and the ideal that heroic masculinity is based on inequality.'[4]

Thus, perhaps the most provocative question arising from *Soccer, Women, Sexual Liberation* is what is the future of women's soccer? FIFA itself has stated that women's soccer should be 'feminized'.[5] In other words, it seems, not only more female spectators, but also more 'feminine' players are required. A straw in the wind is provided by Sky digital, which launched Sasi in Britain in 2003, a glamorous international seven-side soccer league for women. Spyros Melaris of Waterfall Production, the company behind the new league, claimed excitedly: 'It is a television show; like *Gladiators* but soccer.'[6] Fortunately, the Football Association considers that this 'show' with women in figure-hugging outfits spurred on by cheerleaders, will do more harm than good: 'It gives the impression that only beautiful, glamorous women can play soccer. That is not sport – just something for men to ogle at.'[7] The dangerous prospect of women as 'soccer sex objects' was raised in the Prologue. It deserves emphasis here in the Epilogue.

Feminists offer one solution – part possible and part impossible. They have argued that historical efforts to end restrictions on women's sport participation through accommodation and apology have not worked. These efforts 'distanced females from "normal" (that is, male) athletes' and 'lent further credibility to the notion that women were different, inferior athletes, and that sport was not a "natural" arena for women'.[8] Joan Festle, an American historian, has stated further that this assessment does not mean 'that women should have or should in the future adopt the male model of sport. There has been much to criticize in [this] dominant model.'[9] Nancy Theberge, a feminist sports sociologist, has asserted: 'the challenge lies in defining and implementing models that resist the problems of the dominant model while maintaining features that enable pleasure, satisfaction and the sense of empowerment'.[10] Varda Burstyn, a sociologist in gender relations, has gone further and argued rather unrealistically that the focus should not be on finding suitable models for women, but on change in the gender arrangements and masculine ideals of the culture of sport itself. A new sports culture should be created. The new culture should 'shift the emphasis from aggressive and competitive to cooperative and expressive games', and through this new cooperative sports culture men and women will find ways to reject the ethic of competition and domination, and balance 'masculine' with 'feminine' in sport in particular and in society in general.[11] She overlooks the plain fact that in sport both men *and* women like competition as spectators and participators. Hers is a Utopian feminism.

A final comment – whatever the problems ahead, and there are many as *Soccer, Women, Sexual Liberation* makes clear, women's soccer is here to stay. It conforms to a world trend in sport: feminism, commercialism and globalism. Change in the world of soccer is certain. As Andrei Markovits and Steven Hellerman claim: 'Why should a world that was created by very particular social forces and their interaction ... define hegemonic sports culture for ever? Change has already arrived and will certainly increase with the passage of time.'[12] A new era for women's soccer has begun.

NOTES

1. Paraphrase of Andrew Sullivan's article on women's golf, 'With a Single Swing, She Liberates Feminism', *The Sunday Times*, News Review, 25 May 2003, 5.
2. Please see M. Ann Hall's essay on Canada, Kari Fasting's piece on Norway, Fan Hong and J.A. Mangan's contribution on China, Andrei Markovits and Steven Hellerman's essay on the United States, Jean Williams' piece on Britain and Martha Saavedra's study on Africa in this book. See also Jane Mulkerrins, 'Women Drop Netball to Bend it Like Beckham', *Sunday Times*, 16 March 2003, 23.
3. See Mulkerrins, ibid.
4. Michael Kaufman and Michael Messner, 'Foreword', in Varda Burstyn, *Manhood, Politics and the Culture of Sport* (Toronto: University of Toronto Press, 1999), p.xii.
5. See 'The Future is Feminine' dated 1995 and posted on FIFA website: www.fifa.com. See also Eunha Koh's essay on Korea in this book, pp.67–79.
6. Cited in Mulkerrins, 'Women Drop Netball to Bend it Like Beckham'.
7. Ibid.
8. Joan Festle, *Playing Nice: Politics and Apologies in Women's Sports* (New York: Columbia University Press, 1996), p.289. See also Nancy Theberge, 'It is Part of the Game: Physicality and Production of Gender in Women's Ice Hockey', paper presented at De Montfort University Bedford Faculty research seminar in May 2003. Theberge also suggested that among the many discussions of the adapted model are Nancy Theberge, 'Women's Athletics and the Myth of Female Frailty', in Jo Freeman (ed.), *Women: A Feminist Perspective*, 4th edn (Mountain View, CA: Mayfield, 1989), pp.507–22; Susan Cahn, *Coming on Strong: Gender and Sexuality in Twentieth Century Women's Sport* (Cambridge: Harvard University Press, 1994), pp.55–82; Helen Lenskyj, *Out of Bounds: Women, Sport and Sexuality* (Toronto: Women's Press, 1986); Bruce Kidd, *The Struggle for Canadian Sport* (Toronto: University of Toronto Press, 1996), pp.94–145.
9. Festle, *Playing Nice*, p.289.
10. Theberge, 'It is Part of the Game', p.23.
11. Burstyn, *Manhood, Politics and the Culture of Sport*, pp.275–6.
12. See Andrei Markovits and Steven Hellerman's essay in this book: 'Women's Soccer in the United States: Yet Another American "Exception"', p.27.

Select Bibliography

Women's Soccer in the United States: Yet Another American 'Exceptionalism'
ANDREI S. MARKOVITS and STEVEN L. HELLERMAN

Guttmann, Allen, *From Ritual to Record: The Nature of Modern Sports* (New York: Columbia University Press, 1978).
Longman, Jere, *The Girls of Summer: The US Women's Soccer Team and How it Changed the World* (New York: HarperCollins, 2000).
Markovits, Andrei S. and Steven L. Hellerman, *Offside: Soccer and American Exceptionalism* (Princeton, NJ: Princeton University Press, 2001).

The Game of Choice: Girls' and Women's Soccer in Canada
M. ANN HALL

Hall, M. Ann, *The Girl and the Game: A History of Women's Sport in Canada* (Peterborough, ON: Broadview Press, 2002).
Newsham, Gail J., *In a League of Their Own: Dick, Kerr Ladies* (London: Scarlet Press, 1998).

Chains, Challenges and Changes: The Making of Women's Football in Korea
EUNHA KOH

Giulianotti, Richard, *Football: A Sociology of Global Game* (Cambridge: Polity Press, 1999).
Korea Football Association, *100 Years History of Korean Football* (Seoul, Korea: Rasara, 1986).
Korea Sports Council, *70 Years of Korea Sports Council* (Seoul, Korea: Korea Sports Council, 1990).
Kwak, Hyung-Ki, Jin-Soo Lee, Hak-Rae Lee and Young-Moo Lim, *Korean Sport History* (Seoul, Korea: Gisik Sanupsa, 1994).
Larson, James F. and Heung-Soo Park, *Global Television and the Politics of Seoul Olympics* (Boulder, CO: Westview Press, 1993).
Lim, Burn-Jang, *Sport and the Modernisation of the Korean Society*, Paper presented to the 6th Annual Conference of Japanese Society of Sport Sociology (Kyoto, Japan, 26–28 March 1997).
Rowe, David, Jim McKay and Toby Miller, 'Come Together: Sport, Nationalism and the Media Image', in L.A. Wenner (ed.), *Mediasport: Cultural Sensibilities and Sport in the Media Age* (New York: Routledge, 1998).

Na, Young-Il, 'The Development of Sport in Modern Korea', *Proceedings of the 2001 International Conference on Sport Management and Sport History: Humanities and Social Sciences of Sport in the Twenty-first Century* (Taiwan, 13–14 July 2001).

Asserting the Right to Play – Women's Football in Denmark
ANNE BRUS and ELSE TRANGBÆK

Brus, Anne, 'Desserten kom først— om kvindefodboldens udvikling i Danmark frem til optagelsen af kvindefodbolden i DBU i 1972' ['Sweeties Before Dinner – Women's Football in Denmark Before the Admission to DBU in 1972'] (Unpublished Masters Thesis, Institute of Exercise and Sport Sciences, University of Copenhagen, 2002).

Hargreaves, Jennifer, *Sporting Females* (London: Routledge, 1994).

von der Lippe, Gerd, *Endring og motstand mot endring av femininiteter og maskuliniteter i idrett og kroppskultur i Norge: 1890-1950 – med et sideblikk på Tyskland, Sverige og Danmark* [*Changes and Resistance to Changes of Femininities and Masculinities in Sport and Bodyculture in Norway: 1890-1950 – Including an Analysis of Germany, Sweden and Denmark*] (Oslo: Norges Idrettshøgskole, 1997)

Lopez, Sue, *Women on the Ball: A Guide to Women's Football* (London: Scarlet Press, 1997).

Possing, Birgitte, 'Køn og kvindelighed – hvilke historiske kategorier?' ['Gender and Femininity – in a Historical Perspective'], *Den jyske Historiker*, 58–9 (1992) (Aarhus Universitetsforlag).

Scraton, Sheila, Kari Fasting, Gertrud Pfister and Anna Bunuel, 'It's Still a Man's Game? – The Experiences of Top-Level European Women Footballers', *International Review for the Sociology of Sport*, 34, 2 (1999).

Skjerk, Ole, 'Team Handball in Denmark 1898–1948: Civilisation or Sportification', in Else Trangbæk and Arnd Krüger (eds), *History of Phycical Education and Sport from a European Perspective* (Copenhagen: Institute of Exercise and Sport Sciences, 1999).

Torkildsen, Roy Kenneth, 'Norsk kvinnefotball – en historisk undersøkelse om norsk kvinnefotballs utvikling' ['Women's Football in Norway – the Development of Norwegian Football in a Historical Perspective'] (Unpublished Masters Thesis, University of Levanger, Norway, 1993).

Trangbæk, Else, 'Gender in Modern Society: Femininity, Gymnastics and Sport', *The International Journal of the History of Sport, The Nordic World*, 14 (1997).

Trangbæk, Else, 'I medvind og modvind' ['With Success and Opposition'], in A. Lykke Poulsen (ed.), *Kvindeliv – Idrætsliv – Om kvindeidræt i Danmark 1850 til 2000* (Copenhagen: Kvindehistorisk Museum og Institut for idræt, 1998).

Williams, John and Jackie Woodhouse, 'Can Play, Will Play? Women and Football in Britain', in John Williams and Simon Wagg (eds), *British Football and Social Change: Getting into Europe* (Leicester: Sir Norman Chester Centre for Football Research, 1991).

The Fastest Growing Sport? Women's Football in England
JEAN WILLIAMS

Bale, John, *Sport and Place* (London: Hurst, 1982).
Lopez, Sue, *Women on the Ball: A Guide to Women's Football* (London: Scarlet Press, 1997).
Melling, Ali, '"Ray of the Rovers:" The Working Class Heroine in Popular Football Fiction 1915–25', *The International Journal of The History of Sport*, 16,1 (April 1998).
Newsham, Gail, *In a League of their Own: Dick, Kerr Ladies* (London: Scarlet Press, 1998).
Russell, Dave, *Football and the English: A Social History of Association Football in England, 1863–1995* (Carnegie: Preston, 1997).
Williams, Jean, *A Game for Rough Girls? A History of Women's Football in England* (London: Routledge, 2003).

The Challenges of Women's Football in East and West Germany:
A Comparative Study
GERTRUD PFISTER

Baur, J., G. Spitzer and S. Telschow, 'Der DDR-Sport als gesellschaftliches Teilsystem', *Sportwissenschaft* 27, 4 (1997), 371.
Brändle, F. and C. Koller, *Goooal!!! Kultur- und Sozialgeschichte des modernen Fußballs* (Zürich: Orell Füssli Verlag, 2002).
Brüggemeier, F.J. (ed.), *Der Ball ist rund* (Essen: Klartext, 2000).
Diemer, S., *Patriarchalismus in der DDR* (Opladen: Leske und Budrich, 1994).
Fechtig, B., *Frauen und Fußball* (Dortmund: sFeF, 1995), p.25.
Helwig, G. and H.-M. Nickel (eds), *Frauen in Deutschland 1945–1992* (Bonn: Akademie Verlag, 1993).
Pfister, G., *Frau und Sport: Frühe Texte* (Frankfurt: Fischer, 1980).
Pfister, G., *Sport im Lebenszusammenhang von Frauen* (Schorndorf: Hofmann, 1999).
Pfister, G., K. Fasting, S. Scraton and B. Vasquez, 'Women and Football – A Contradiction? The Beginnings of Women's Football in Four European Countries', *The European Sports History Review* 1 (1998), 1–26.
Ratzeburg, H. and H. Biese, *Frauen Fußball Meisterschaften* (Kassel: Agon, 1995).

Women's Football in the Republic of Ireland: Past Events and Future Prospects
ANN BOURKE

Cashmore, E., *Making Sense of Sports* (London: Routledge, 2000).
Dunning, E., *Sport Matters* (London: Routledge, 1999).
Hannigan, D., *The Garrison Game* (Edinburgh: Mainstream Publishing, 1998).
Jarvie, G. and J. Maguire, *Sport and Leisure in Social Thought* (London: Routledge, 1994).
Laker, A. (ed.), *The Sociology of Sport and Physical Education* (London: Routledge, 2002).
Lopez, S., *Women on the Ball: A Guide to Women's Football* (London: Scarlet Press, 1997).
Slack, T., *Understanding Sport Organisations* (Champaign, IL: Human Kinetics, 1997).
Wagg, S. (ed.), *Giving the Game Away* (London: Leicester University Press, 1995).
Watt, D., *Sports Management and Administration* (London: E & F Spon, 1998).

Football Feminine – Development of the African Game:
Senegal, Nigeria and South Africa
MARTHA SAAVEDRA

Abisuga, C.A. and H. Awurumibe, *Genesis of Female Soccer in Nigeria* (Lagos Nigeria: Starmark Consultants, 1991).
Amadasun, O., *History of Football in Africa* (Lagos Nigeria: Times Books Limited, 1994).
Baker, W.J. and J.A. Mangan (eds), *Sport in Africa: Essays in Social History* (New York, London: Africana Publishing Company, 1987).
Cisse, S.A., *Sénégal, Carton Rouge* (Dakar Sénégal: Niamagne, 1995).
Darby, P., *Africa, Football, and FIFA: Politics, Colonialism, and Resistance* (London; Portland OR: Frank Cass, 2002).
Deville-Danthu,
Gaye, D., *Crises et Perspectives du Football Sénégalais* (Saint-Louis Senegal: Xamal éditions, 1999).
Nauright, J., *Sport, Cultures, and Identities in South Africa* (Cape Town: David Philip, 1998).
Wagner, E.A. (ed.), *Sport in Asia and Africa: A Comparative Handbook* (New York, Westport and London: Greenwood Press, 1989).

Notes on the Contributors

Ann Bourke is currently a lecturer in International Business and the Academic Director of the CEMS (Community of European Management Schools) Programme at the Smurfit Business School in University College Dublin.

Anne Brus is a master of science from the Institute of Exercise and Sport Sciences, University of Copenhagen, Denmark.

Kari Fasting is a professor at the Department of Social Science at the Norwegian University of Sport and Physical Education in Oslo, Norway. She became the first elected chair of this institution and served as the rector from 1989 to 1994. She is the Vice-President of the executive board of Women's Sport International.

M. Ann Hall is Professor Emeritus in the Faculty of Physical Education and Recreation at the University of Alberta, Edmonton, Canada where she has taught for over 30 years.

Steven L. Hellerman is a doctoral candidate in political science at Claremont Graduate University in California.

Jonny Hjelm is an associate professor at the Department of Historical Studies, Umeå University, Sweden.

Fan Hong is reader in Department of Sports Sciences at De Montfort University in England.

Eunha Koh is at the Department of Kinesiology, University of Maryland.

Boria Majumdar is at St John's College, University of Oxford.

J.A. Mangan is Director of the International Research Centre for Sport, Socialization and Society at De Montfort University, Bedford.

Andrei S. Markovits is Karl W. Deutsch Collegiate Professor of Comparative Politics and German Studies at the University of Michigan, Ann Arbor.

Ludmila Mourão teaches at the Universidade Gama Filho, Rio de Janeiro. She is researching the history of the physical-sporting activities of Brazilian women.

Eva Olofsson teaches within the study programme for sport and fitness management and the PE teacher education programme at the Department of Education at Umeå University, Sweden.

Gertrud Pfister is a professor at the Institute of Exercise and Sport Sciences, University of Copenhagen. She is the Vice-President of the German Gymnastic Federation, and Head of the Scientific Committee of the International Association for Physical Education and Sport for Girls and Women.

Martha Saavedra is the Associate Director of the Center for African Studies at the University of California at Berkeley. A veteran of Title IX battles, she has played soccer for 30 years and now coaches her son's team.

Else Trangbæk is Associate Professor at the Institute of Exercise and Sport Science, Department of History and Social Sciences, Copenhagen University. She is the founder of the Danish Society for Sport History and chairwoman from 1984–96.

Donna de Varona is a two-time Olympic swimmer. She won gold medals in the 400-metre individual medley and the 4x400-metre medley relay at the 1964 Olympic Games. She served as Chairwoman of the 1999 Women's World Cup Organizing Committee. Ms de Varona is a national radio and ABC Sports television commentator.

Jean Williams is Senior Lecturer at De Montfort University, Leicester, in the School of Historical and International Studies. She is currently leading an international research project: Women's Football on Five Continents: A Case Study Approach, funded by Fédération Internationale de Football Association (FIFA).

Sebastião Votre is Professor of the Semiotics of Sport and Physical Activities at Universidade Gama Filho, Rio de Janeiro.

Abstracts

Women's Soccer in the United States: Yet Another American 'Exceptionalism'
Andrei S. Markovits and Steven L. Hellerman

Arguably, women's soccer in the United States has been among the best played and extensively watched in the world. Not only has the American national team won more international championships than any other national team, but the WUSA (Women's United States Soccer Association), a professional league, has become the top women's professional league in the world, attracting the best women soccer players from countries such as Germany, Norway, Brazil and China. Furthermore, in terms of female soccer players, the United States – with nearly 10 million registered participants – leads the world by a wide margin. Yet, unlike in many countries of the world, soccer remains a minute feature on the topographical map of American sports space. Why is this the case? This study will consider this fascinating dilemma.

The Game of Choice: Girls' and Women's Soccer in Canada
M. Ann Hall

While Canada is known as a hockey nation, it is not particularly noted for soccer. Far more Canadian girls play soccer than ice hockey, and the growth during the 1990s and into the new millennium has been spectacular. For the past several years, females have accounted for over one-third of the new registrations each year. Soccer did not always welcome females, especially if they wanted to play on boys' teams, which many had to do before clubs, leagues, schools and universities began to initiate programmes for girls and women. The remarkable growth of grassroots soccer among female youth in the 1980s and 1990s has paid off in the development of a women's national team programme, first initiated in 1986. Professionally, several Canadians now play in the eight-team Women's United Soccer Association. This chapter traces the development of women's soccer in Canada from its beginnings in the 1920s to its present day popularity, pointing out some of the issues, problems and struggles still remaining.

Will the 'Iron Roses' Bloom Forever? Women's Football in China: Progress and Problems
Fan Hong and J.A. Mangan

Since the 1980s football has become one of the fastest-growing female sports in China. Female players have forced their way into this traditional bastion of male identity and prestige with confidence, and in doing so, have projected radical and successful images of femininity. The national team obtained second place at the Third World Cup and won the Asian Cup and the Asian Games ten times. (Note: They are different competitions.) The Chinese proudly call them 'Iron Roses'. With these successes behind them they were used recently as models to inspire Chinese male footballers to qualify for the World Cup in 2002. Women football players strongly challenge traditional Chinese culture and symbolize the ideal gender relations of post-1949.

Chains, Challenges and Changes: The Making of Women's Football in Korea
Eunha Koh

Gender discrimination and inequality in sport have always been witnessed in the East and the West alike. However, it is different in Korea from Western countries due to the fact that female bodies had been hidden from public view until recently. Confucian tradition had held to the opinion that sport, especially active contact sport, was not proper for girls and women in Korea and excluded women from sports fields since the introduction of modern sport at the beginning of the twentieth century. As a result, women's football has gained little support from the government and the public, while men's football has enjoyed respect as one of the most popular national games. Recent victories of the women's national football team in international events have offered the opportunity for women's football to attract public attention after 50 years of struggle against prejudice and indifference. However, it is argued that recent attention to women's football was the result more of the strong nationalism in Korean sport culture than the rise of women's status in sport or the changes in gender relations in society. In the age of women's struggle for recognition, women's football is expected to play a significant role in establishing a new era for female athletes in particular, and Korean women in general.

Forwards and Backwards: Women's Soccer in Twentieth-Century India
Boria Majumdar

Women's soccer has hardly been given due attention in existing studies on Indian sport. This essay traces the evolution of the women's game in India, locating it in the politico-economic context of the 1930s. With the establishment of the All India Women's Congress in 1918, attempts were made to give women a voice absent through the nineteenth century. As part of this broader movement for emancipation, sport, especially cricket and football, gained currency among Indian women. Period vernacular tracts commented on the virtues of these sports, claiming that sporting prowess would stimulate the movement for women's emancipation. Using the film *Bend it Like Beckham* as an entry point, which portrays the story of a modern young British Sikh girl who aspires to be a professional footballer, this essay attempts to retrieve the lost history of Indian women's football. It also deals with the sad plight of women footballers in modern-day India, the reasons behind the dismal state of the game, and offers comments on the challenges that confront women footballers in contemporary India.

Asserting the Right to Play – Women's Football in Denmark
Anne Brus and Else Trangbæk

In 1970 the Danish Football club Boldklubben Femina (BK Femina) became unofficial world champions. The success of BK Femina women's football team was not a coincidence and should be placed in the context of a ten-year struggle to have football accepted as a sport for women in Denmark. This essay examines three consecutive periods in Danish women's football: the establishment of women's football in Denmark before 1970; the time of women's admission to the Danish Football Association (DBU) in 1970–72; and finally, the development of women's football in the DBU from 1972 to 2002.

The Fastest Growing Sport? Women's Football in England
Jean Williams

Britain pioneered the first phase of football's popularity among women during, and shortly after, the First World War. The English Football Association found this threat to the idea of football as a game for men sufficiently serious to ban women's football in 1921. Shortly after the ban was lifted, over five decades later, the Sex Discrimination Act of 1975 was drafted with the intention of exempting professional football from advances in female equality. The relevant clause that limits women's access to competitive football continues to survive and equality of opportunity continues to be contested at all levels of the game. Nevertheless, women express several kinds of freedom when they participate in football, in spite of the traditional stereotypical media slur of women players as either 'butch' or 'girly'. This contentious connection means that in the foreseeable future women's football in England will continue to be about much more than the game itself.

The Challenges of Women's Football in East and West Germany: A Comparative Study
Gertrud Pfister

In the world of football women have always played a marginal role and this is still true today. Why have women had to overcome so many obstacles just because they wished to play football? Were women football players living in socialist systems confronted with the same problems as like-minded women in capitalist systems? These are the questions that will be answered here, using the development of women's football in the Federal Republic of Germany and the German Democratic Republic as an example.

Small Country – Big Results: Women's Football in Norway
Kari Fasting

The study opens with a description of the development of women's football in Norway. It can be traced back to the beginning of the twentieth century, but it was only in 1975 when the Norwegian Football Association formally recognized it. Prior to 1975, the pioneers of women's football struggled hard to get women's football accepted. Today, women's football is the most popular sport for girls and women in Norway, in spite of the fact that it is still regarded as a masculine sport. The reasons for the enormous increase in female football players are discussed. One major factor seems to be the work of a women's committee appointed by the Football Association when women's football was first accepted in the middle of the 1970s. For the Committee, the education and promotion of female leaders, coaches and referees, as well as the need to increase the number of players, were important. The essay concludes with results from a study about the experiences and the meaning of football in the lives of Norwegian female football players of today.

Women's Football in the Republic of Ireland: Past Events and Future Prospects
Ann Bourke

This study provides a brief outline of the history of women's football in Ireland, the pivotal event being the formation of the Ladies Football Association of

Ireland (LFAI) in 1973. In the United States, association football has been promoted mainly via the national teams (men's and women's), instead of having the domestic game produce the national team as happens in virtually every other country. This situation is somewhat similar to that pertaining to women's football in Ireland. While there are 16 Senior and Schoolgirls Leagues affiliated to the LFAI, the greater proportion of resources is devoted to improving the fortunes of the national team. The interdependent ties between the interlocked groups of coaches, players, trainers, managers, medical teams, parents and various organizations including FAI, UEFA, LFAI, FIFA, Provincial Councils, media, and schools that influence women's football are discussed and illustrated using Clark's football figuration. The study concludes by identifying the key factors that have both advanced and constrained the development of women's football in Ireland and includes recommendations for the future development of the game.

A Breakthrough: Women's Football in Sweden
Jonny Hjelm and Eva Olofsson

This essay focuses on the development of women's football in Sweden between 1965 and 1980. The growth of modern women's football in Sweden was dependent on factors that were essentially extended to the football movement. However, the formation of teams, the establishment of leagues and so forth, were the results of formidable efforts by 'pioneers' within women's football. Leaders within men's football initially assumed a passive 'wait-and-see' attitude. Women's football challenged the masculine traditions of football in a manner that took the Swedish Football Association by surprise. When for various reasons the 'wait-and-see' attitude became impossible to sustain, **the Football Association decided** to integrate women's football **into the football movement**. The purpose of this integration was to control the development of women's football and ensure that women's football would not have a detrimental effect on men's football with regard to material and nonmaterial resources.

From Heydays to Struggles: Women's Soccer in New Zealand
Barbara Cox and Shona Thompson

The establishment of women's soccer in Auckland, New Zealand in 1973 reflected a growing world-wide trend: women's increasing involvement in sport, especially sports traditionally associated with men. This chapter explores the changing face of women's soccer in New Zealand during the past 30 years, using interviews with elite soccer players and analyses of newspapers. This exploration suggests that there has been a marked shift in the way the media perceives and reviews women's soccer, and in the players' understanding of what it means to be women soccer players. It further suggests that women's football has been emancipatory, demonstrating that femininity is an evolving process.

Football Feminine – Development of the African Game: Senegal, Nigeria and South Africa
Martha Saavedra

Football is by far the most popular sport throughout Africa. More than a sport, football in most African countries has deep political, social and economic ramifications. Yet, the game that garners this position is explicitly the men's game. What of the women's game? African women are playing football. In some nations, officials, both in sport and political realms, have actually prioritized the development of the women's game. Yet, women footballers are often greeted with scepticism, neglect, and sometimes outright hostility. This study explores the major issues facing the development of African women's football and suggests many avenues for research, policy and advocacy.

Women's Football in Brazil: Progress and Problems
Sebastião Votre and Ludmila Mourão

Football is a male sport in Brazil. Small wonder as women were forbidden to play football by law until 1975. Federal Club, the first official women's team was established only in 1977. Women's football progressed rapidly in the early 1980s due to support from big companies, such as Coppertone, Pernambucanas, Cinzano and Unibanco. Radar Club, the most famous women's soccer club, was created in 1982. Unfortunately, during the championships of 1984, fighting broke out between Radar and Bangu. The media and educational authorities used this to attack women's participation in football and financial support from big companies was withdrawn. However, Brazilian women continued to play football and not without international success. The Brazilian women's team obtained third place at the International Women's Football Championships in 1988, first place at the First Women's Football World Championships in 1991 and fourth place at the Atlanta Olympics in 1996. This study will consider the progress of Brazilian women's football against a background of national discouragement, covert and overt resistance and gender prejudice.

Index

Women, Sport and Society in Modern China

Holding Up More than Half the Sky

Dong Jinxia, University of Beijing

'Women hold up half the sky' and 'Women can do what men can do' are not just popular slogans peddled by Chairman Mao, but recent actualities of China's elite sport. In every Olympics since 1988 women have increased their representation over men. Their extraordinary performances have thrust Chinese women into the global limelight and sparked considerable interest, not to mention controversy with accusations of drug violations, and yet there remains a paucity of analytical literature on Chinese elite women's sport not only in China but throughout the world.

Drawing on Chinese sources hitherto unavailable in the West, official documents and interviews with top athletes, Dong Jinxia explores the rise of the Chinese super-sportswomen and their relationship with politics, culture and society before and during the Cultural Revolution and through China's transition to a market economy. This evenhanded and readable work will appeal to students of sports studies, journalists and general readers fascinated by the rise of the Chinese women superathletes.

304 pages 18 illus 2002
0 7146 5235 0 cloth £42.50/$59.50
0 7146 8214 4 paper £17.50/$24.50
Sport in the Global Society No 35

UK: Crown House, 47 Chase Side, Southgate, London N14 5BP
Tel: +44 (0)20 8920 2100 Fax: +44 (0)20 8447 8548

North America: 920 NE 58th Avenue Suite 300, Portland, OR 97213-3786 USA
Tel: 800 944 6190 Fax: 503 280 8832

Website: www.frankcass.com E-mail: sales@frankcass.com

Frank Cass publishers

Cricket and England

A Cultural and Social History of the Inter-war Years

Jack Williams, John Moores University, Liverpool

'Jack Williams's excellent book ... tightly focused, well-written and adept at putting cricket into a broader cultural framework.'
The Guardian

'Thorough and searching, this is a valuable book.'
The Journal of the Cricket Society

'Exhaustively researched and exhaustingly detailed.'
Choice

In the 1920s and 1930s, cricket had a vital role in how the English imagined themselves and their social world. Assumptions attached to the high level of sportsmanship within cricket and the associations of cricket with the Church, respect for tradition, the Empire, the public schools and reverence for pastoralism meant that cricket was represented as expressing a distinctively English form of moral worth. This study by Jack Williams shows that the images of cricket, and how far the world of cricket conformed to them are essential for understanding English culture and society between the wars.

224 pages illus 1999
0 7146 4861 2 cloth £39.50/$54.50
0 7146 4418 8 paper £17.50/$26.50
Sport in the Global Society No 8

UK: Crown House, 47 Chase Side, Southgate, London N14 5BP
Tel: +44 (0)20 8920 2100 Fax: +44 (0)20 8447 8548

North America: 920 NE 58th Avenue Suite 300, Portland, OR 97213-3786 USA
Tel: 800 944 6190 Fax: 503 280 8832

Website: www.frankcass.com E-mail: sales@frankcass.com

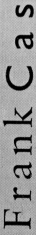

Frank Cass publishers

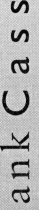

Sport in Latin American Society

Past and Present

Past and Present

J A Mangan, University of Strathclyde and Lamartine P DaCosta, Gama Filho University (Eds)

Modern sport is important to the lives of countless millions in Latin America as it is the world over. It offers an ecstasy as potent as any religion, an escapism as real as any cinema, an enjoyment as intense as any carnival. It is the tool of governments, the toy of oligarchs and the passion of peoples. Sport in Latin American Society celebrates the infancy, adolescence and maturity of modern sport on thesub-continent. It explains the ways in which sport illuminates cultural migration and emigration, indigenous assimilation and adaptation, and shows how sport indicates and reflects social, political and economic change.

Contributors: J A Mangan, J Arbena, Cesar R Torres, Vic Duke, Liz Crolley, Thomas Carter, Cesar Gordon, Ronaldo Helal, Robert Chappell and Lamartine P DaCosta.

224 pages 2002 0 7146 5126 5 cloth £42.50/$59.50
0 7146 8152 0 paper £17.50/$24.50
Sport in the Global Society No 33
A special issue of the International Journal of the History of Sport

UK: Crown House, 47 Chase Side, Southgate, London N14 5BP
Tel: +44 (0)20 8920 2100 Fax: +44 (0)20 8447 8548

North America: 920 NE 58th Avenue Suite 300, Portland, OR 97213-3786 USA
Tel: 800 944 6190 Fax: 503 280 8832

Website: www.frankcass.com E-mail: sales@frankcass.com

FrankCass publishers

Football, Europe and the Press

Liz Crolley and **David Hand,** both at Manchester Metropolitan University

Is the stereotype of the French as a nation producing stylish, elegant football reflected in all European countries? Are there differences in the reconstruction of the traditional image of the Germans being efficient and technically competent? How and why are such stereotypes constructed? Can football journalism be seen as a last bastion where simplistic views on a nation's identity can be aired, or does it reflect the same sort of complexity as other sections of the media when it comes to a nation's identity? This lively, cross-cultural examination of image and identity attempts to answer all these questions by comparing the football journalism of five European countries: France, England, Germany, Italy and Spain. It shows what the language of football writing says about perceptions of identity in Europe.

The book is based on detailed studies of the language used in football match reports and related articles appearing in a representative sample of quality daily newspapers including The Times, Le Monde, Süddeutsche Zeitung and El País. The result is a unique, lively and timely analysis of image and identity in European football writing which will appeal to a wide audience.

200 pages 2002
0 7146 4957 0 cloth £42.50/$59.50
0 7146 8017 6 paper £17.50/$26.50
Sport in the Global Society No 24

UK: Crown House, 47 Chase Side, Southgate, London N14 5BP
Tel: +44 (0)20 8920 2100 Fax: +44 (0)20 8447 8548

North America: 920 NE 58th Avenue Suite 300, Portland, OR 97213-3786 USA
Tel: 800 944 6190 Fax: 503 280 8832

Website: www.frankcass.com E-mail: sales@frankcass.com

FrankCass publishers